THE sailing BIBLE

THE sailingBIBLE

THE COMPLETE GUIDE FOR ALL SAILORS
FROM NOVICE TO EXPERT

Jeremy Evans • Pat Manley • Barrie Smith

FIREFLY BOOKS

A FIREFLY BOOK

Published by Firefly Books Ltd. 2009

Copyright © 2009 Adlard Coles Nautical

First printing

Publisher Cataloging-in-Publication Data (U.S.)
Evans, Jeremy.
    The sailing bible / Jeremy Evans, Pat Manley, Barrie Smith.
[400] p. : col. ill., col. photos. ;   cm.
Includes index.
ISBN-13: 978-1-55407-429-7
ISBN-10: 1-55407-429-0
1. Sailing – Handbooks, manuals, etc. I. Manley, Pat. II. Smith, Barrie. III. Title.
797.124   dc22   GV811.E93 2009

Library and Archives Canada Cataloguing in Publication
Evans, Jeremy
    The sailing bible / Jeremy Evans, Pat Manley, Barrie Smith.

Includes index.
ISBN-13: 978-1-55407-429-7
ISBN-10: 1-55407-429-0
    1. Sailing--Handbooks, manuals, etc.
I. Manley, Pat II. Smith, Barrie III. Title.

GV811.E83 2009   797.124   C2008-904937-3

Published in the United States by
Firefly Books (U.S.) Inc.
P.O. Box 1338, Ellicott Station
Buffalo, New York 14205

Published in Canada by
Firefly Books Ltd.
66 Leek Crescent
Richmond Hill, Ontario L4B 1H1

Printed in China

The publisher gratefully acknowledges the financial support for our publishing program by the Government of Canada through the Book Publishing Industry Development Program.

3 4015 06984 4569

Contents

Weather 310

Maintenance 338

Safety at Sea 364

Welcome to sailing

Sailing is a fantastic sport that relies on two great elements — wind and water — both of which are natural and free! It offers great value for all those who want to enjoy the wonderfully simple sensations of being blown along by a breeze in your sails. This book — arranged in the following sections — aims to tell you everything you need to know about this great sport.

Starting out

How did sailing evolve from tough working boats and millionaires' yachts to a sport enjoyed by millions of sailors today? Democracy and technology have taken over, providing an activity that can be enjoyed by all ages at all levels, ranging from recreational to professional. The first section of this book explains how you can learn to sail and get into the sport, and provides a guide to the similarities and differences between sailing small dinghies, larger keelboats, multihulls or larger cruising yachts.

Learning to sail

How does the wind actually drive a boat? In the old days, it was simple: the crew of a Viking long ship or square-rigger merely sailed with the wind behind them, but now we can sail in any direction except directly toward the wind. This section explains the difference between "points" of sailing known as beating, reaching and running, and the changes in direction known as tacks and jibes. It goes on to cover how sail power provides forward drive and how sail trim and the rudder are used to steer the boat.

Sailing maneuvers involve changing direction, not least when you meet another boat, so a vital question is "Who has right of way?" Knots and ropework are also basic elements of learning to sail, as are staying warm and choosing the right gear.

Dinghy sailing

Dinghies and beach cats are the smallest sailing craft. They also provide the cheapest introduction to the sport and get you physically closer to wind and water. The choice of different boats is huge, so in this section we have made a selection of popular classes, explaining how they are designed and built, and how to rig them. Choosing where to sail is important, too, as is how you launch and sail away from the shore. You'll find details here about all of these, plus information on racing around a course, dinghy maintenance, and trapeze and spinnaker technique for high-performance sailing.

Cruiser sailing

A cruiser or yacht provides the opportunity to live afloat. It's a wonderful lifestyle, whether you're sailing in sunshine or snuggled up somewhere in the comfort of the cabin down below. This section explains the principal elements of a cruiser, how to rig and reef the sails, how to sail in all directions, how to use the engine should the wind fail, how to leave or enter a dock or marina, how to deal with wind and tide, and how to choose an anchorage or pick up a mooring. It also explains what to do in rough weather or fog.

Remember that you'll want to go ashore, so you'll need a tender – also covered in this section.

Below: **Sailing is for all ages and all types of boats. Dinghies can provide a great low-cost entry to discovering all the fun of harnessing the wind.**

Navigation and weather

You need to know where you're going and how to get there. Navigation was once a difficult subject, but has become much more accessible due to the availability of GPS. The classic style of navigation, however, is still important — everyone who sails a yacht should know how to read a chart, plot a course and calculate the movement of tides. Weather plays a major role in sailing, and though we have never been more blessed by reliable forecasts, understanding weather systems and their effect on your sailing will be an invaluable help.

Boat maintenance

Many dinghies are virtually maintenance free: just hose off any salt and put them away. By contrast, yachts require annual maintenance to ensure that everything works perfectly the following season. This section explains how to look after every element of the yacht including the hull and deck, sails, engine, electrical, plumbing and safety equipment.

Safety

Finally, you need to sail safely. To do this, you must plan ahead, use the right equipment, avoid collisions, learn how to read signals and acquire a basic knowledge of first aid and emergency repairs.

We hope you enjoy this book and that it leads to many years of sailing pleasure. It truly is a fabulous sport.

Above: **Where do we go next? Navigation is all part of the fun and challenge of sailing, and it has been made simpler and more effective thanks to modern technology.**

Below: **Yacht racing is fantastic for team building. This Finnish-built Swan is recognized as one of the great models.**

Starting Out

Sailing for everyone

Sailing has never been so much fun or so accessible. Today there are many ways to enjoy the sport, with different types of sailing available to all. Whether for pleasure or sport, sailing is about choice and enjoying the freedom of the seas.

Gone are the days when sailing was an elite sport. Today, beginners can start to sail wherever there is water and a fair wind. Central to the pleasure of sailing is being able to test your skills against the elements and having control over where you are going on the water, free to sail where you like with minimal restrictions.

Sailing evolved though trade and exploration. Our ancestors would be astonished at the idea of sailing for pleasure, when in the past the only alternative to rowing or paddling was to sail. The main source of power for the Vikings, for example, was a battery of sails set square to the wind to drive the ship downwind.

Throughout history, people around the world have found new and unique ways in which to sail a functional vessel. In the Netherlands, a small ship known as a *jaghen* was occasionally used for pleasure and from this the word "yacht" entered the English language in the 17th century.

It was only during the 19th century that yachting for pleasure and competition became established. A few sailors became the pioneers of cruising offshore and making a passage. The early part of the 20th century was a golden era for

Above: **The modern skiff style of dinghy provides maximum power-to-weight ratio for a full-bore sailing experience.**

Left: **Take it easy! The crew of this Hobie 16 are due for a spectacular capsize — all part of the fun of catsailing.**

yachting. Large racing yachts known as the J-class were mostly sailed by professional crews but were prohibitively expensive. It wasn't until shortly after World War II that sailing as we know it today really began.

The dinghy

The development of plywood opened up sailing after the war and dinghies started to become popular. Plywood was seen as the ideal material for building strong, lightweight boats that were fast and easy to construct. Plywood particularly appealed to those who could build their own. Then in the 1960s many new designs began to appear on the market. Many small boat-building companies were set up to cater for increasing demand for the sport. It was a cheap and accessible way to sail, for fun or

competitive sailing from club racing to Olympic championship.

Glass-reinforced plastic (GRP), or fiberglass, was introduced in the 1960s as a flexible alternative, and today building materials continue to evolve, leading to the creation of even lighter, stronger boats.

Cruising

In the early 20th century, racing was too expensive for many to take part. But cruising developed from amateur yacht racing and became more accessible. Cruising yachts were smaller and purpose built.

Increasing affluence and a growing availability of mooring facilities have allowed many more people to keep their own boats. Even if you don't have a boat, cruising has been opened up to a wider number of people through charters, flotillas, sailing schools and sail training vessels.

Above: **You can sail anywhere where there is wind, but a warm air temperature makes it feel great!**

Below: **Yacht racing provides a lot of fun for the whole crew — each boat may need a dozen or more to handle the sails.**

How can I learn to sail?

There are so many ways to go sailing that it can be hard to know where to start. If you live in a sailing area, or if you have friends or family who already sail, the sport is very accessible. If you have no personal experience or contacts, it can seem more difficult to get involved. Here are some of the ways you can learn to sail.

The first question to ask is what sort of sailing you see yourself taking part in. Perhaps you're attracted to racing around a local bay or lake in a small dinghy, or you may like the thought of a larger boat suitable for day sailing or cruising, perhaps in larger waters. Whatever your preference, a dinghy is always a good way to learn and you can move on to a bigger boat later.

Learn in a dinghy

Small dinghies are for single-handed (one person) handling, while larger dinghies can have room for several people. Most dinghies used for instruction are stable in the water and excellent to learn in. You learn to steer on your own and are in control of the sails yourself. The dinghy is light and responds quickly so you feel the effect of your actions almost immediately. It also means that you have to react and move quickly so that weight is distributed correctly in the dinghy. Because you are close to the water, you are likely to get wet in a dinghy. It also tips over easily, so you will have to learn how to respond to a capsize.

Dinghies are often owned by sailing schools and clubs, which are good places to start. When you learn

Right: **Youngsters get their first sailing lesson, ready to go afloat. Buoyancy aids are mandatory for all dinghy sailing; helmets protect young heads from the boom, but are not necessary when basic techniques are mastered.**

TIP

Try out a range of boats to find out which you enjoy the most and the differences in how they sail. Look for good performance, safe sailing and general enjoyment. Learning in a dinghy gets you closest to the effects of wind and water. It's the best possible way to start.

Right: **Learn to sail a yacht with a sailing school. Courses may last as long as five days, during which you will live on board.**

Above: **A small, self-righting dayboat such as the Hawk 20 provides a great compromise between dinghy and cruiser sailing.**

you may have an instructor on board at first but you should be prepared to learn on your own.

Learn in a keelboat

Some sailing schools teach beginners in a keelboat designed for day sailing. A keelboat has a weighted keel underneath its hull instead of a centerboard or daggerboard. This makes it more stable than a dinghy, but it is also less responsive, heavier and can be harder to control. It is less important for your weight to be distributed correctly in a keelboat and you will not normally capsize in the way you might in a dinghy.

Learn in a cruiser

Another option is to learn in a cruiser, which is larger than a dinghy or keelboat and has the facilities to let you stay on board for longer passages. They are excellent for teaching the many skills required, although the beginner may not find the cruiser as responsive as a dinghy. Sailing schools offer excellent courses aboard cruisers. They are administered by governing bodies of the sport and provide qualified instructors with structured courses. There are courses suitable for all levels of ability, from complete beginners through to experienced skippers.

SUMMARY

Where can you learn to sail?

✪ Local sailing clubs
✪ Organized sailing vacations
✪ Sailing schools
✪ Trips with an experienced skipper

There are numerous books, magazines and websites aimed at beginners. It is generally better to choose somewhere endorsed by a sailing organization.

What is a dinghy?

A dinghy is a small sailing boat that can range in length from 7–16 feet (2–5 m). Dinghies are designed to be sailed single-handedly or double-handedly, but some larger cruising dinghies may have room for four or more people on board.

Most single-handed dinghies have just a mainsail, while double-handed dinghies have a mainsail controlled by the helmsman to manage, and a smaller sail known as a jib controlled by the crew. There may also be a third sail, or spinnaker, flown at the front of the boat when the wind is blowing from behind.

Staying upright

Unlike yachts, dinghies do not have a heavy keel underneath the hull to prevent the wind from blowing them over. The crew of a dinghy use their body weight and trim the sails to ensure the dinghy stays upright. Some dinghies are very stable and require only a modest amount of sailing ability and physical input from the crew; others are extremely unstable with very powerful rigs that require a great deal of skill. It's important to choose the right kind of boat for your agility and ability!

Above: **Two of the most popular dinghies come ashore at a sailing club — a single-handed Laser and double-handed Mirror (red sails).**

Underneath the hull

All dinghies have a retractable foil under the hull to prevent the boat from being blown sideways. This foil is either a centerboard that swivels through 90 degrees into a centerboard case in the middle of the cockpit, or a daggerboard that lifts vertically in a daggerboard case, or trunk, and should be totally removed when the boat comes ashore. A rudder at the back of the boat is used to steer, using a tiller. Most dinghy rudders swivel upward for coming ashore.

Skimming across water

With no heavy keel dragging underwater, dinghy hulls are designed to plane. This is a wonderful sensation that feels like taking off. When the wind is strong enough (for most dinghies, planing requires at least a force 3 to 4 breeze) the front of the hull will lift out of the water and the boat will skim on its stern at a much increased speed, leaving a flat wake behind.

> **TIP**
>
> A single-handed dinghy is probably the best way to learn as you are solely responsible for how the boat sails and you will quickly pick up skills.

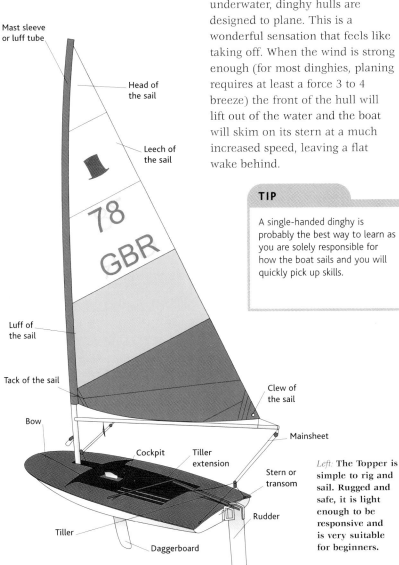

Mast sleeve or luff tube

Head of the sail

Leech of the sail

Luff of the sail

Tack of the sail

Bow

Cockpit

Tiller extension

Clew of the sail

Mainsheet

Stern or transom

Rudder

Tiller

Daggerboard

Left: **The Topper is simple to rig and sail. Rugged and safe, it is light enough to be responsive and is very suitable for beginners.**

Lightweight hulls

In order to plane, a dinghy hull needs to be reasonably light. Early dinghy designs were often built in marine plywood. This is still popular, but it has largely been superseded by hulls molded in plastic such as fiberglass, FRP (foam reinforced plastic) or polyethylene.

Masts and sails

The simplest single-handed dinghies have an unstayed mast, which fits into a hole in the deck and does not need further support. Most double-handed dinghies, by contrast, require wires to provide extra support for the rig: a single forestay at the front and two shrouds at the side. Masts and booms are mainly straight or tapered aluminum tubes, with carbon fiber used on some high-performance dinghies. Traditional material for mainsails and jibs is a white woven polyester cloth known as Dacron. Laminate plastic materials such as Mylar are popular for high-performance sailing.

Transport on land

Dinghies are designed to be kept onshore. A two-wheeled dolly is used to push the dinghy to and from the water. A separate road trailer can be pulled by a car.

Right: **The Wayfarer is both tough and seaworthy and simple to sail. It is also stable and difficult to capsize. It can hold a crew of up to six people.**

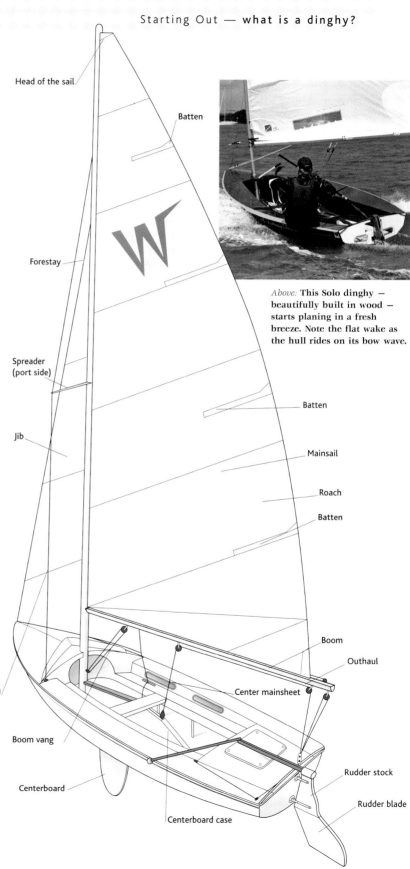

Above: **This Solo dinghy — beautifully built in wood — starts planing in a fresh breeze. Note the flat wake as the hull rides on its bow wave.**

Head of the sail

Batten

Forestay

Spreader (port side)

Jib

Batten

Mainsail

Roach

Batten

Boom

Outhaul

Center mainsheet

Shroud (port side)

Boom vang

Centerboard

Centerboard case

Rudder stock

Rudder blade

What is a keelboat?

A keelboat has a heavily weighted keel underneath the water, which in normal conditions prevents the boat from capsizing like a dinghy. The boat may heel over on its side, but the pendulum effect of the keel will normally swing it back upright. Like a yacht, the depth of the keel limits where keelboats can safely sail.

A keelboat normally has a length of about 20–30 feet (6–9 m). Keelboat sailing is a good alternative to learning to sail in a dinghy, although maneuvers take longer because the boat is larger and heavier, with greater loads on the sails and sheets (the ropes used to manage the sails) so the boat will probably have winches. Keelboats can provide some exciting sailing due to their large sail area.

How a keelboat performs depends on its design. Some heel at an angle when sailing upwind while newer, lighter types are classified as high-performance sports boats, which need to be sailed as upright as possible. They rise up on a plane going downwind (when the wind is behind), providing exciting sailing for a crew of normally four to six people.

Aboard the keelboat

The majority have open cockpits designed for a crew of two or three, which makes them more suited for racing or daysailing than as family boats. However, some keelboats do have basic accommodation, which can be used as shelter from the wind or wet or even to provide basic overnight accommodation.

> **TIP**
>
> Learning to sail in a keelboat is more comfortable and less wet than sailing in a dinghy. They can also provide a perfect compromise between dinghy performance and the stability of a yacht.

Right: **Despite the design being more than a hundred years old, the Star has kept going as an Olympic keelboat which is raced by a two-person crew.**

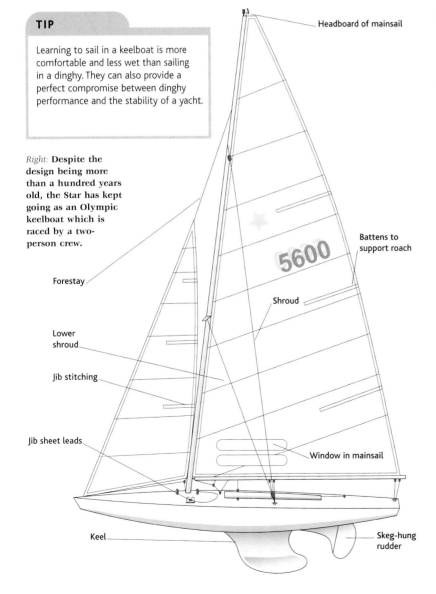

Headboard of mainsail

Battens to support roach

5600

Forestay

Shroud

Lower shroud

Jib stitching

Jib sheet leads

Window in mainsail

Keel

Skeg-hung rudder

Above: **Keelboats may heel (tip over) but rarely capsize.**

Wet or dry sailing

Unlike a dinghy, most keelboats are left in the water during the sailing season. At the end of the season they normally come out for a hull cleaning and antifouling to prevent the buildup of weeds, barnacles and deposits.

Retracting keel

If a keelboat has a lifting keel it is quite easy to launch or retrieve the boat on a trailer, thus turning it into a "trailer sailer" that can be parked at home. The lifting keel is not designed to be lifted while sailing, so you will need to be aware of the depth of water you are sailing in. A small keelboat with a fixed keel can also be trailed, but may need a crane to help lift it out of the water.

Above: **Some keelboats are as small as a dinghy. This SRD has a lifting keel that combines keelboat stability with dinghy performance.**

Below: **Many small keelboats have a lifting keel that makes them easy to launch and trailer.**

Below: **The Yngling is the women's keelboat class in the Olympics.**

What is a multihull?

Multihulls such as a catamaran or trimaran have more than one hull. Catamarans have two hulls joined by crossbeams or a deck. Trimarans have a main central hull joined to two smaller hulls on each side known as "floats." Both catamarans and trimarans have evolved from proas, traditional native crafts with a slim single hull supported by an outrigger, intended to prevent the boats from turning over.

Advantages of multihulls

A multihull is more stable than a monohull. It has a wide base supporting the rig, with two hulls or two floats helping to prevent the boat from heeling over when the wind drives the sails.

A small multihull such as a beach cat can use bigger sails than a similar size monohull, since the crew have greater leverage to hold the boat upright. The hulls can also be considerably slimmer than a similar size dinghy. With more sail area powering the boat and less wetted surface area creating less drag through the water, the multihull can sail faster.

Unlike yachts, larger multihulls require no ballasted keel to keep them upright. They can sail in shallow water, dry out on the beach and do not have a keel dragging though the water under the boat slowing it down.

Types of hull

The monohull takes up least space in a marina, while the trimaran is the widest of all. However, many smaller trimarans are designed with floats that fold inward, so they become no wider than a monohull yacht.

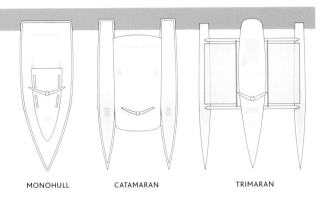

MONOHULL   CATAMARAN   TRIMARAN

Below: **This 60-foot (18 m) racing trimaran is a superb high-performance machine, raced with a full crew inshore and single-handed in competition.**

Cruising catamarans are not only long but also very wide. They have far more accommodation space than a yacht of equivalent size, and they don't heel over. Small daysailing catamarans and trimarans are specially designed to make fast, exciting sailing accessible to disabled sailors, without danger of capsize.

Disadvantages of multihulls

Multiple hulls make multihull construction more expensive than similar size monohulls. Larger multihulls also rely on their light weight in order to achieve best performance, or they will tend to drag in the water. Complex lightweight construction may boost the cost considerably.

Some cats do capsize. They are no more difficult to pull upright than a similar size dinghy, but the righting process takes longer. Offshore racing catamarans and trimarans occasionally get blown over and turn upside-down if they are being sailed too hard. Larger multihulls are carefully designed not to capsize.

Below: **Flying the hull provides a delightful sailing experience and is a lot easier than it looks. When sailing the Hobie 15, balance your weight further outboard as the boat begins to heel over. Tuck one foot under the hiking strap for balance. Use the hand that is forward to hold and control the mainsheet and the other to steer.**

Above: **The Hobie 16 is the most popular cat of all time, designed to slide on and off the beach on its characteristic banana-shaped hulls.**

Beach cats

A beach cat is the multihull equivalent of a dinghy, ranging from 13–20 feet (4–6 m) in length, with a mesh trampoline forming a semi-rigid platform between the beams and hulls. As the name implies, "beach cats" can be launched or landed on a beach, but are just as likely to be based in a dinghy park. Like a dinghy, all beach cats are primarily designed for single-handed or double-handed use.

Recreational beach cats tend to have a fixed skeg (fin) under each hull, which acts like a keel to prevent the boat from being blown sideways. Cats designed for racing tend to have a daggerboard in each hull; the Olympic Tornado is the only international cat class fitted with a swiveling centerboard.

What is a cruiser?

Many of the features you have discovered on small boats can be found on a cruiser, which is a yacht with living accommodation down below. Because of the multitude of cruisers available, there are many variations on all its key features and a different set of equipment on every boat.

The rig

Most cruisers are rigged as a Bermudan sloop, the simplest type of rig. Typically a cruiser has a mast supported by standing rigging, with a forestay (a wire to support the mast) from the top of the mast to the bow. A backstay runs from the top of the mast to the stern and balances the forestay. The mast is also supported by a number of shrouds, which run from the deck up to one or two sets of horizontal spreaders that are attached to the mast.

The sails

A Bermudan sloop has a mainsail and one or more headsails. The mainsail is normally stowed on the boom when not in use, protected by a sail cover. A selection of headsails is used, depending on the strength of the wind. They are attached to the forestay on the bow of the boat, and normally stowed down below when not in use. Typically these sails would include a genoa for light winds, a working jib for stronger winds and a storm jib for very windy

conditions. Many modern cruisers now have roller reefing of the headsail so that, when not in use, the sail is stored around the forestay.

Below: **Modern cruising yachts combine an easily handled rig, reliable performance and plenty of live-aboard comfort for the crew.**

TIP

You can learn a lot about sailing by crewing for others on a cruiser. Most modern medium-sized yachts are designed to be managed by a crew of about four. Longer trips and overnight passages will require experienced crew.

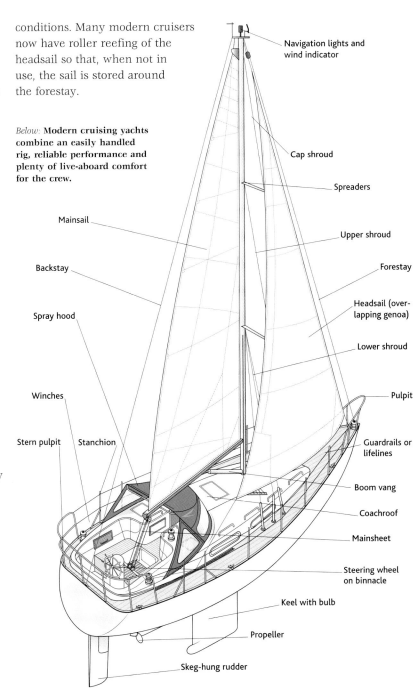

Navigation lights and wind indicator

Cap shroud

Spreaders

Upper shroud

Forestay

Headsail (over-lapping genoa)

Lower shroud

Pulpit

Guardrails or lifelines

Boom vang

Coachroof

Mainsheet

Steering wheel on binnacle

Keel with bulb

Propeller

Skeg-hung rudder

Mainsail

Backstay

Spray hood

Winches

Stern pulpit

Stanchion

Different keels

The hull of a traditional yacht has a long integral keel with ballast placed inside. Fin (single) keels come in many different shapes. A yacht designed for racing will have a slim, deep keel with ballast concentrated in a bulb at the end, providing maximum leverage with minimum drag through the water. The yacht will only be able to sail in water deep enough for its keel.

Types of keels

The traditional full-length keel was originally built as part of the hull. Modern yachts have a fin keel that is bolted to the base of the hull. Variations such as bilge keels (facilitating sailing in shallower water) are bolted to either side of the hull and are shorter.

LONG KEEL

FIN KEEL

BILGE KEEL

Left: **A group of yachts cruising in light winds and calm waters.**

Above: **When on deck, the crew spends most of its time in the safety of the cockpit.**

A cruising yacht will compromise on sailing performance with a keel that is fairly long and not too deep. This provides structural integrity with the hull and allows the yacht to sail or moor in quite shallow water. It will also hold the yacht reasonably upright, preventing it from being blown sideways and enabling it to sail at an angle toward the wind. Some cruising yachts have twin keels on either side of the hull, called bilge keels. As well as providing very shallow draft, bilge keels allow a yacht to dry out on an ebb tide, sitting upright on its two keels. However, bilge keels generate greater drag and less lift than a single keel so may not perform as well.

The deck

The cockpit is the working area of the cruiser, where the helm steers the boat and adjusts the sheets (ropes that adjust the sails). Sidedecks run around the edge of the boat and stanchions support the guardrail around the deck. Fair-leads and cleats to guide and tie mooring lines will be found at the back and front of the boat. Other equipment on the deck includes winches for hauling sheets, tracks for carrying jib sheets and standard safety equipment.

Different types of boats

There are a number of different types of sailing boats available. These are the ones you are most likely to come across on the beach or in an anchorage. They are also the ones on which you are most likely to sail.

Dinghy

A small, lightweight dayboat that is sailed by one or more people. The crew use a combination of sailing skills and body weight to hold the boat upright. A retractable centeroard prevents the dinghy being blown sideways.

Beach cat

A twin-hulled variation on a dinghy, with a mesh trampoline suspended between the hulls.

Keelboat

A small dayboat fitted with a keel is more stable than a dinghy and will rarely capsize. It combines the sailing style of a dinghy with the handling of a yacht and can carry up to five people. Generally kept on a mooring.

	Dinghy	Beach cat	Keelboat
Brief description	Most dinghies are designed specifically for single-handed or double-handed use. Power is provided by a mainsail, mainsail and jib, or mainsail, jib and spinnaker. The crew may hike over the side or use trapeze wires to stand on the side of the boat.	Catamarans provide high speed with stability, due to being able to carry a lot of sail power on a wide platform with very narrow hulls.	Keelboats range from dinghy-style boats with an open cockpit, sailed and raced by two people, to larger dayboats with an enclosed deck and small cabin providing some protected space for the crew. Some have a lifting keel for trailer sailing.
Key strengths (pros)	Dinghies provide low-cost sailing. They are easy to handle and store. They react instantly to the wind. Little maintenance is required. They are fitted with buoyancy so cannot sink.	Most are designed for single- and double-handed use, but often have enough space to take extra people for joy rides! Many are fitted with trapezes for both helm and crew, adding to the thrill of sailing. Stable at rest. Very fast and a lot of fun.	Keelboats are stable and secure. They have reliable sailing performance and do not capsize in normal conditions.
Key shortcomings (cons)	With little protection from the elements, the crew may get wet and cold. Most dinghies will capsize.	They are more cumbersome to launch and handle than a dinghy and slower to tack. The beach cat is less responsive than a dinghy.	More expensive to own and more difficult to launch than a dinghy. Less responsive than a dinghy. Should they capsize, they may sink.
Suitable for	Anyone who feels fit, wants to get close to the elements and enjoy "seat of the pants" sailing, from family fun to high performance.	Blasting on a stable platform and learning to trapeze.	Responsive sailing close to the elements, without serious risk of a capsize, plus the added bonus of being able to sail with more people.

Cruising yacht

A larger boat that provides liveaboard accommodation. Fitted with a keel or a lifting keel for shallow water. Cruising yachts in the size range of 26–32 feet (8–10 m) allow up to six people to live on board.

Cruising multihull

A catamaran (two hulls) or trimaran (three hulls) with a cabin. A cruising multihull has no keel and relies on its width for stability. It can sail in shallower water and has less drag under the hull, which may let it sail faster.

Ocean racer

A yacht designed specifically for racing, providing maximum power-to-weight ratio and minimum acceptable comfort for its crew. This style of yacht is powerful, very sophisticated and extremely expensive.

Traditional yacht

A traditional yacht may be an original wooden boat that has been restored, or a modern fiberglass replica. Enjoy a delightful retro sailing experience, combined with modern construction and comforts.

Most have a single mast and roller furling headsail, making it as easy as possible for the crew to manage the boat. Auxiliary power is provided by a diesel engine. Cruising speed for an average-size yacht is 5 knots.

Cruising catamarans have a lot of space with cabins in each hull and a main cabin stretched between the hulls. Cruising trimarans have less space, with all the accommodation in the main hull and limited storage space in the two outer hulls that act as floats.

Cruising yachts that race are known as "cruiser-racers," providing a good compromise between cruising comfort and racing performance. Most racing yachts fall into this category, but the elite tend to opt for dedicated racing machines that are of little use for cruising.

Many traditional yachts are recognizable by a gaff mainsail, often with characteristic tan sails. Some may be ketch- or yawl-rigged with a second, shorter mast near the stern, or schooner-rigged with an additional – often slightly shorter – mast ahead of the main mast.

Liveaboard sailing lets you cruise where you want. Comfortable for a family or friends. Easily handled under sail or power.

No keel means less drag, less weight and less depth required under the boat. Some cruising multihulls are a lot faster than equivalent size yachts. Cruising catamarans can have super accommodation.

Superb racing is available around the world. A racing yacht gets close to the dinghy style of "seat of the pants" sailing. Great for sailing as a team.

The pride of owning and sailing a classic. Admiring looks from other yachtsmen. Sturdy and dependable sailing qualities.

More expensive to buy and own, with high mooring and maintenance costs. Nothing like as responsive or instinctive as sailing a dinghy.

Very wide to berth in a marina. Cruising catamarans can have poor sailing performance upwind. Higher cost than a monohull yacht.

Yacht racing ranges from expensive to incredibly expensive. Racing offshore can be cold, wet and uncomfortable.

Slower under sail than conventional yachts. More cramped down below. A wooden traditional yacht is time consuming and expensive to maintain.

People who want to sail to different places. Cruising with family or friends can be a wonderful experience in good weather.

Good combination of stability and speed, plus the ability to motor or anchor in very shallow water.

Competitive people who enjoy the cut and thrust of high-performance sailing at close quarters.

People who really take pride in what they sail and are content to sail slowly and peacefully. After all, what's the hurry?

Learning to Sail

The 360-degree sailing circle

Sailing allows you to harness the free power of the wind to sail in any direction. A dinghy or yacht can even sail close to the direction the wind is blowing from, unlike the old square-riggers, which could only sail where the wind would take them.

Sailing toward the wind

Sailing as close as possible toward the wind is known as "beating to windward." Despite centuries of development, a sailboat cannot and never will be able to sail directly into the wind, which is the "no-sail zone." The only way you can sail through the no-sail zone is to "tack": changing direction by going through the wind so that the wind blows on the other side of the sails. A series of tacks will eventually lead you to a point that is directly upwind.

The type of boat and its rig will determine how close it can really sail toward the wind. Beating to windward at an angle of about 30 degrees to the wind direction is optimum for a racing boat, but the angle may be greater than 45 degrees for a less efficient cruising boat.

Sailing across the wind

When you move the bow further away from the wind, so that it is blowing more onto the side of the boat, this is called "bearing away." When the wind is coming from the side of the boat, this is called "reaching." This may be a "close reach" with the wind blowing partly from in front, a "beam reach" with the wind blowing directly from the side, or a "broad reach" with the wind blowing partly from behind.

Reaching is generally the fastest and most enjoyable point of sailing for all boats, with the wind direction allowing the boat to be driven forward at maximum speed and comfort.

Sailing with the wind

If you move the bow further away from the wind (bear away) so that the wind is blowing from behind the boat, you are "running." If the wind is blowing from directly behind, you are "running dead downwind."

Contrary to what you might expect, this is not a particularly enjoyable way to sail. The wind is only blowing onto the "windward" (closest to the wind) side of the sail, pushing it along like an old square-rigged sailing ship. Without an extra downwind sail, known as a "spinnaker" (a large lightweight sail), the boat will feel quite slow as it is not well powered by the wind. It may also feel unstable, because it is a lot more difficult to maintain balance and prevent rolling with the wind blowing from behind, particularly if there are waves.

Beware jibes

If you bear away further from the wind, so that it is blowing from behind on the other side, the boat will be "running by the lee." You need to be careful. The wind may suddenly get behind the mainsail and slam the boom over ("jibe"). You must always ensure that when you jibe it is intentional, and everyone is aware. In a safe jibe, the mainsail swings in a controlled way across the boat.

Below: **Changing direction. These yachts are approaching on a run, jibing from starboard to port tack, and then heading up onto a beat.**

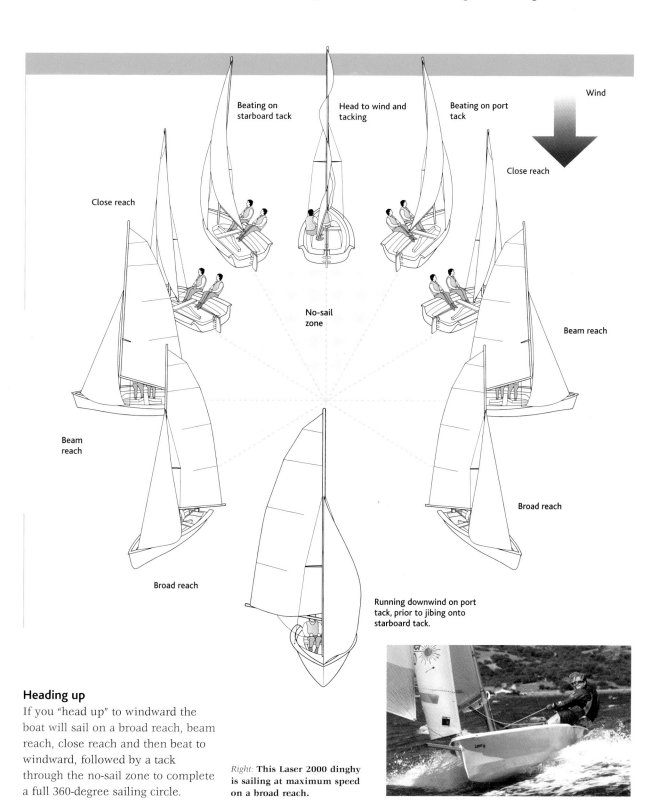

Wind

Beating on starboard tack

Head to wind and tacking

Beating on port tack

Close reach

Close reach

Close reach

No-sail zone

Beam reach

Beam reach

Broad reach

Broad reach

Running downwind on port tack, prior to jibing onto starboard tack.

Heading up

If you "head up" to windward the boat will sail on a broad reach, beam reach, close reach and then beat to windward, followed by a tack through the no-sail zone to complete a full 360-degree sailing circle.

Right: **This Laser 2000 dinghy is sailing at maximum speed on a broad reach.**

Sail power provides forward drive

The wind in the sails drives the boat forward. But the sails need to be at the correct angle to provide airflow over both sides of the sail. An underwater foil such as a centerboard or daggerboard helps push the boat forward and prevents it from being blown sideways.

Pressure drives the sails

Unless you are sailing directly downwind (away from the wind), modern rigs are designed so that wind flows over both sides of the sails. The wind separates when it hits the leading edge of the headsail (front sail) or mainsail and accelerates around its two curved sides. This creates positive high pressure on the windward (facing toward the wind) side of the sail and negative low pressure on the leeward (facing away from the wind)

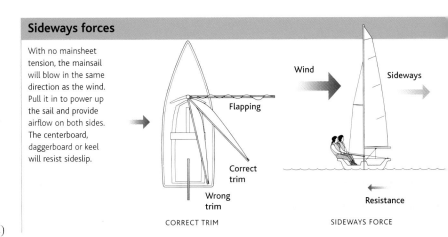

Sideways forces

With no mainsheet tension, the mainsail will blow in the same direction as the wind. Pull it in to power up the sail and provide airflow on both sides. The centerboard, daggerboard or keel will resist sideslip.

Flapping

Correct trim

Wrong trim

CORRECT TRIM

Wind

Sideways

Resistance

SIDEWAYS FORCE

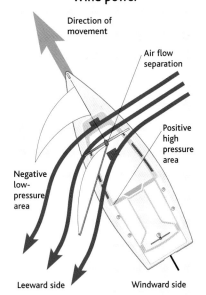

Wind power

Direction of movement

Air flow separation

Positive high pressure area

Negative low-pressure area

Leeward side

Windward side

Above: **Wind separates and flows over both sides of the sails. The difference in pressure helps to increase forward drive. The slot between headsail and mainsail increases wind flow across the leeward side of the mainsail.**

side of the sail. The difference between these pressures creates a powerful force that sucks the sail to leeward, pushing the boat forward.

Sheeting the sails

The crew set the angle of each sail by adjusting the "sheet" — the rope used to let the sail out or pull the sail in. On a boat with two sails, the "slot" is the narrow passage between the headsail and mainsail. Adjusting the width of the slot plays an important role in how effectively air flows over the leeward side of the mainsail.

Forward not sideways

The curved shape of the sail (known as "camber") will affect windward and leeward airflow. Unless the wind is blowing directly from behind, there will always be a force on the sail, which pushes the boat sideways (known as "leeway"). This becomes strongest when a boat is sailing at slow speed toward the wind. On

modern boats leeway is reduced by the underwater foil of a dinghy or catamaran. This foil not only provides natural resistance to being pushed sideways due to its underwater area, but its shape also provides a lifting force (called hydrodynamic lift) toward the wind when required.

Heeling over

The underwater foil of a dinghy is most effective at preventing leeway when it points almost straight down underwater. It also generates most lift to windward when the boat is sailing fast. Sailing techniques allow the crew of a dinghy to keep the rig upright and the boat flat on the water, even when the wind is blowing hard.

It is not possible to hold a yacht upright just by using crew weight: if there is a breeze the yacht will always heel over to leeward. The maximum desirable angle is about

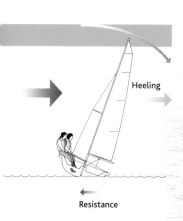

Heeling

Resistance

HEELING FORCE

Below: **The keel of this Maxi yacht helps transform the wind blowing across the sails into forward drive. If the yacht heels too far, it will slip sideways.**

30 degrees. If the yacht heels over further, it will increasingly be blown sideways. It will sail more slowly as the side of the hull sinks into the water, and become more difficult to steer as the rudder loses its effect.

Left: **A dinghy such as this Xenon is designed to be sailed flat, not heeled, for maximum efficiency.**

TIP

The more you move closer to the wind and pull in the sails the more you will slide sideways. If you can put down the centerboard this will help counteract the sideways push. As you turn away from the wind you can pull up the centerboard and let the sails out.

Experiencing the wind

Neither the wind's direction nor its speed remains static when you go sailing. To understand the effect of wind on a boat you need to learn the difference between true and apparent wind.

Experiencing the wind

✪ True wind is the wind direction and speed encountered when you stand still.

✪ Apparent wind is the wind direction and speed encountered when you are moving.

If the true wind is blowing at a speed of 10 knots and you could head directly into the wind at a speed of 5 knots, the apparent wind speed would be 15 knots. If the true wind was blowing at 10 knots and you were sailing directly away from the wind at a speed of 5 knots, the apparent wind would be 5 knots.

The apparent wind is a combination of the true wind and the wind created by the boat's movement. If you could sail directly into the wind it would feel stronger than it really is. When sailing away from the wind it feels lighter.

True and apparent wind (1)

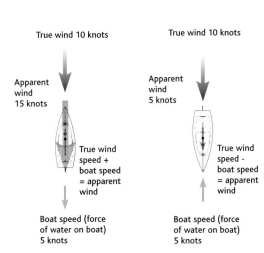

True wind 10 knots

Apparent wind 15 knots

True wind speed + boat speed = apparent wind

Boat speed (force of water on boat) 5 knots

True wind 10 knots

Apparent wind 5 knots

True wind speed - boat speed = apparent wind

Boat speed (force of water on boat) 5 knots

Apparent wind is always strongest when beating toward the wind and weakest when running away from the wind. Wind conditions tend to feel warmer and more benign sailing downwind and more challenging sailing upwind, which can provide a very different experience!

Induced wind

True and apparent wind will only blow in the same direction when the boat is sailing directly downwind, with the wind behind. Sailing in any other direction, the wind induced by the forward motion of the boat will change the angle of the apparent

Left: **Sailing with the wind directly behind, apparent wind is reduced. This Enterprise is goosewinging with the jib held out to windward.**

wind. The faster a boat is sailing, the more the angle of the apparent wind will move ahead of the boat. This helps explain why any sailing craft that is sailing spectacularly fast (such as a windsurfer, catamaran or racing dinghy) appears to have its sails pulled in at a tight angle to the wind, even when sailing on a broad-reaching course with the true wind direction blowing from behind the boat. The faster the boat goes, the more it will need to bear away downwind.

Driving the hull

Sail power has to overcome resistance to drive a boat through the water. Wind resistance is caused by the rig, the hull, the crew and anything else that obstructs the flow of the wind. It is also caused when the underwater foils or keel push and drag through the water.

A dinghy is designed to have the least amount of resistance when sailed upright. The more a dinghy heels over, the more the resistance will increase, slowing the boat down and making it difficult to handle.

Water dragging on the hull as it flows under the boat slows the boat down. If the amount of boat in contact with the water is reduced, there is less friction. This makes correct sail trim vital. For instance, in light winds the crew should sit forward in the cockpit to lift the stern and prevent it from dragging through the water.

True and apparent wind (2)

Apparent wind makes little difference if you are sailing slowly, but has a major impact at high speed. All skiff-style boats, such as the 49er and 29er, are designed to provide maximum performance when sailing on apparent wind. They need a good breeze to perform effectively.

The effect of the apparent wind feels strongest when the boat is close-hauled. When a boat is sailing at 45 degrees to the wind, the wind instrument reading will show 30 degrees of apparent wind (i.e., induced wind) and the apparent wind increases to 14 knots.

If the boat moves round to a beam reach the apparent wind moves ahead as the boat accelerates on a beam reach.

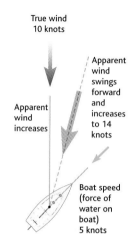

True wind
10 knots

Apparent wind swings forward and increases to 14 knots

Apparent wind increases

Boat speed (force of water on boat)
5 knots

Close-hauled: apparent wind increases and the wind angle becomes tighter as boat speed increases.

Right: **The speed of this RS500 through the water changes the angle of the apparent wind, so the sails are sheeted in on a reaching course.**

Wind in your sails

Your enjoyment of sailing will be governed by a number of factors. These include the strength of the wind, the state of the water and the direction in which you are sailing.

How much wind do you need?

You need the right amount of wind to go sailing: not too little, not too much, just perfect! Wind speed for sailors is generally measured in knots (nautical miles per hour) with the power of the wind expressed in "forces" on the Beaufort Scale (see also page 336).

- ❂ Force 0 which means *no wind*, or force 1, which means a *very light wind*, are not enough to go sailing.
- ❂ Force 2 means a *light breeze*, which is the minimum required wind speed to enjoy sailing and is ideal for learning. It's sufficient to drive the boat, but everything will happen slowly, which makes it easier for an inexperienced crew.
- ❂ Force 3 is a *gentle breeze*, when sailing starts to be fun. The boat will heel over and move faster through the water, but should still be easy to control. A good wind for novice sailors, but more care is required or, in a dinghy, you may get caught out and capsize.
- ❂ Force 4 is a *moderate breeze* with wave tops starting to break. This is a good wind for intermediate and advanced sailors, but very difficult for novices without expert help on hand. Dinghies start to sail fast and capsize; yachts heel over and the sails may need reefing (reducing in size) to stay more upright.
- ❂ Force 5 is a *fresh breeze* with a lot of white horses (breaking wave tops). This is getting windy! Experts will love it, intermediates may struggle. Novices must have expert help.
- ❂ Force 6 is a *strong breeze* and very windy for sailing. It is not suitable for novices, though they may enjoy the experience of sailing both dinghies and yachts with an expert in tough conditions.
- ❂ Force 7 is a *near gale*, no longer sailable by dinghies. Any yachts that are sailing should be well reefed down and heading for shelter.

Above: **Force 3–4 is perfect for cruising. If the boat heels any more, it's time to put one reef in the mainsail.**

Right: **Full-bore at force 5. Perfect conditions for an experienced crew on a Hobie 16.**

Left: **Gusty conditions require easily handled sails. This Parker 275 has a short-footed jib that is very quick to trim.**

Right: **This yacht is well reefed with a tiny mainsail and rolled headsail in force 7. In even stronger winds, it would require a storm jib.**

What about water conditions?

The state of the water plays a big role in how you experience sailing. If the water stays flat, there is nothing to stop the boat or throw it off course. If there are waves, the boat may roll, pitch or wallow, which is uncomfortable for the crew and makes it difficult to keep things under control. Different waves have different effects. Short, steep waves can be more dangerous than long, rolling waves, particularly when sailing in shallow water. Tidal flow plays a major effect on waves, pushing them up in one direction, smoothing them out in the other.

www.wildwind.co.uk

Which direction is best?

There can be a huge difference between sailing toward the wind (upwind) and sailing with the wind (downwind). Sailing downwind reduces the apparent wind (see page 33) so the crew will feel warmer and the boat feels easier to control, although it may start to roll. This is due to lack of stability with the wind blowing from behind. "Heading up" so that the wind is partly blowing over the side onto a broad reach can cure this.

Sailing upwind increases the apparent wind. The crew will feel colder, waves may splash them, and the boat will heel over and may feel more difficult to control. Reefing the sails, thus reducing the effect of the wind blowing the boat over, can rectify this.

Steering with a rudder

The rudder is the main control used to change direction. The tiller is attached to the rudder or wheel, enabling you to turn the rudder from side to side. A tiller extension allows you to steer more comfortably while sitting on the side of a boat.

Steering a dinghy

Dinghies have a removable rudder, which is hung on pintles attached to the transom (back of the boat). Most dinghy rudder blades can swivel vertically through an arc of about 120 degrees, allowing them to be lifted for coming ashore and lowered for sailing, using a control line or shock cord to hold the rudder blade down.

The helmsman steers by pushing or pulling the tiller and tiller extension to change the angle of the rudder blade as it moves through the water. The tiller extension allows the helmsman to steer when sitting on the sidedecks or hiking out to keep the boat upright.

Steering a catamaran

A catamaran has two rudders, one for each hull. Each rudder has a tiller connected by a tiller bar across the back of the boat. A tiller extension is attached to the middle of the tiller bar, allowing the helmsman to steer from the side of the boat. A telescopic tiller extension with adjustable length is useful for steering from the trapeze (a belt and line used to help a crew hike out beyond the edge of a boat to counteract the boat's heel) on high-performance dinghies and catamarans.

Below: **Balancing the boat and its sails is important for steering a high-performance dinghy such as the National 12.**

Left: **The rudder must be pushed down vertically for sailing. If it is not right down, you will get weather helm with a heavy pull on the tiller.**

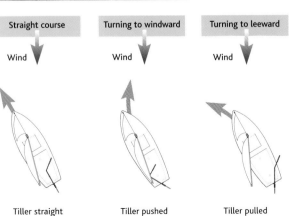

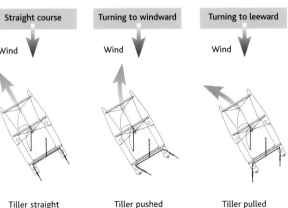

Straight course	Turning to windward	Turning to leeward	Straight course	Turning to windward	Turning to leeward
Wind	Wind	Wind	Wind	Wind	Wind
Tiller straight	Tiller pushed	Tiller pulled	Tiller straight	Tiller pushed	Tiller pulled

Left: **A catamaran is less sensitive than a dinghy. The sails must be trimmed correctly to help steer the boat with its double rudders.**

Steering a cruiser

Most modern yachts have a rudder positioned behind the keel underneath the boat. A rudderpost connects the tiller or wheel to the forward part of the rudder, which ensures that it feels balanced and the boat is light to steer.

Smaller yachts are steered by a tiller, which may have a tiller extension to allow the helmsman to sit on the side of the cockpit. One disadvantage of a tiller is that it will sweep across the cockpit when the helmsman tacks or jibes, so the crew must stay clear. However, when the yacht is moored, the tiller can be left in a vertical position, which provides maximum cockpit space for those on board.

Steering with a tiller

Some newcomers to sailing find steering with a tiller confusing the first time. Push the tiller away to head up toward the wind; pull the tiller toward you to head away from the wind. After a few attempts, it will become second nature!

Steering with a wheel

Larger yachts from about 26 feet (8 m) in length overall are sometimes steered by a wheel mounted on a pedestal known as a binnacle and connected to the rudder by cables. The wheel provides a lighter touch and makes steering easier to control, but is less responsive than a tiller, more complex to engineer and takes up more space in the cockpit. The larger the wheel, the more precise the steering will be. Some yachts have two wheels, allowing the helmsman to steer from either side and allowing more space in the cockpit.

The method is similar to steering a car, but imagine the car is a four-wheel drive making its way across a bumpy field, over snow or among sand dunes! Gusts of wind, waves and the boat heeling over require constant adjustments to the wheel; you may need to make slight changes in direction every few seconds.

Steering with the sails and boat

Steering a dinghy or yacht is not quite as simple as just changing the angle of the rudder. That may work in light winds, but in stronger winds pressure in the sails will also tend to steer the boat. To bear away from the wind, you must let out the mainsail and reduce pressure. To head up toward the wind, pulling in the mainsail will increase pressure and help the boat to turn. Keep the boat as upright as possible when you turn so that the rudder has maximum effect. If you let the boat heel right over, the rudder's efficiency will decrease with part of its blade lifted out of the water.

Below: **This cruiser-racer has twin wheels, allowing the helmsman to steer from either side.**

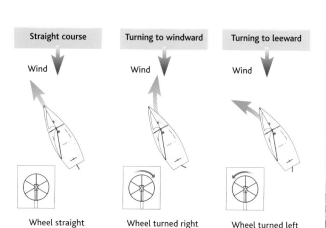

Straight course

Wind

Wheel straight

Turning to windward

Wind

Wheel turned right

Turning to leeward

Wind

Wheel turned left

Sail trim

Trimming the sails to the correct angle to the wind is an essential skill, which comes with practice. With a little experience you begin to get the feel of the boat in different types of weather conditions.

Above: **An asymmetric spinnaker provides a big power increase on this Omega. Mainsail, jib and spinnaker are sheeted in until they don't flap.**

The sheet is your accelerator

The sheets (lines), which are used to pull in the sails, act like an accelerator. Pull the sheets in to power up the sails and drive the boat forward; let the sheets out to depower the sails and slow the boat down.

Both mainsail and jib should be sheeted in at the correct angle to the wind. If a sail is not sheeted in far enough, it will flap and produce limited power. If a sail is sheeted in too far it will create turbulence, which reduces power. Either way, it does not allow the full power of the sail to drive you forward. So you've got to get the sheeting angle just right.

The perfect sheeting angle

Sails are not flat. Looking from the front (luff) to the back (leech), they have a curved shape (camber), which helps provide the power in the sail. What's more, the back edge (leech) of the sail also has a curve, which tends to lessen toward the top of the mast, producing a slightly twisted shape when seen from behind.

The result is that you cannot get a perfect sheeting angle for every part of the sail, but you can come close with a compromise. Telltales (short strips of cloth or plastic attached near the leading edge on both sides of the sail) help you achieve this compromise. When the sail is correctly sheeted, telltales on

Using telltales

Sail setting	Comment
Correct trim	Telltales are parallel on both windward and leeward sides
Undertrimming	The windward telltale is higher than it should be: pull in the sheet
Overtrimming	Leeward telltale is higher than it should be: let out the sheet

Above: **You can see the lowest telltales streaming perfectly on the jib.**

both the windward and leeward side of the sail should stream back horizontally. When the windward telltales stream upward you need to pull in the sheet. When the leeward telltales stream upward you need to let out the sheet.

Taking off

If you sit in a dinghy and let all the sheets go, the boat will naturally lie side-on to the wind, which will blow slightly from ahead. In this position, the boat will be gently blown sideways by the wind, with the resistance of the daggerboard also driving it slightly ahead.

To take off, sit on the side of the boat, which should be balanced so it is virtually level, hold the tiller extension firmly in your back hand and move the rudder blade to its central "straight ahead" position. Take the mainsheet in your front hand and pull it in slowly until the sail stops flapping. Keep sheeting in until the telltales are streaming horizontally on both sides. The boat will start sailing forward.

Start sailing on a beam reach, with the wind blowing from the side. Experiment with pulling in the mainsail to speed up and letting out the mainsail to slow down.

Windward helm

Under sail power, many boats have a slight tendency to "windward helm" or "weather helm." This means that if you let the tiller go, the boat will automatically turn up toward the wind. "Windward helm" is indicated by a slight pull on the tiller extension. This is perfectly normal and has the benefit of providing a more precise feel to steering the boat.

The opposite of windward helm is leeward helm, meaning that the boat has a natural tendency to sail away from the wind, which can make the boat difficult to control. Leeward helm is not desirable and should never be experienced on a correctly set up boat.

Keep it flat

All modern dinghies are designed to be sailed flat on the water with a minimal angle of heel. If you let the boat heel too far, it will start to slide sideways (making leeway) as the daggerboard fails to grip and windward helm will increase as the rudder blade lifts out of the water. If you cannot hold the boat upright, let out the sheet a little.

Left: **The crew of this National 12 demonstrate perfect trim, with the wind blowing across the boat. Note how they hold the boat completely flat, with the stern lifted.**

Right: **Sailing to windward in a Laser, the mainsheet is pulled right in so it does not flap.**

Sailing maneuvers

Learning the basic maneuvers for stopping, turning the boat and changing direction is based on good wind awareness. Practice the maneuvers in fine conditions, to get to know the feel of the boat and to be in control.

Heading up

Heading up is steering toward the wind. If sailing on a beam reach, with the wind blowing from the side, push the tiller away. The boat will start to turn toward the wind. You will find yourself at a different angle to the wind, so pull in the mainsheet to keep power in the sail. Let the boat head up slowly until it is pointing at about 45 degrees to the wind. Straighten out your course by centralizing the rudder. Make a final adjustment of sail trim to ensure telltales are horizontal on both sides.

If you want to sail closer to the wind, head up until the windward telltales begin lifting with the mainsheet pulled tight in. That is as close as you can sail to the wind — any closer, and the boat will stall.

Below: **Perfect balance, sailing upwind. This is as close as you can go without tacking.**

To keep sailing properly, pull the tiller toward you until the windward telltales are horizontal once again.

Tacking

Tacking is steering the bows of the boat through the wind blowing directly from ahead. The boat must be powered up and moving as you

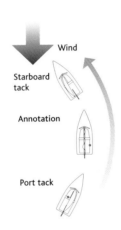

Wind

Starboard tack

Annotation

Port tack

Left: **When tacking, the boat turns head to wind, then bears away to start sailing in the new direction. Here the boat has changed from port to starboard tack.**

Above: **When tacking, the helm steers into the wind by pushing the tiller away.**

Above: **When jibing, the helm bears away by pulling the tiller. To maintain control, it is important to keep the boat flat.**

steer into the tack. If not, it may get stuck head to wind "in irons" and begin drifting backward.

Jibing

Jibing is steering the stern of the boat through a wind blowing directly from behind. Unlike a tack, the sails will be powered up throughout the turn, which can make jibing quite tricky in stronger winds.

Bearing away

Bearing away means sailing away from the wind. Sailing on a beam reach, with the wind blowing from the side, pull the tiller toward your body. The boat will start to turn away from the wind. You will need to let out the mainsheet to allow the boat to turn: if the mainsheet remains sheeted in, wind pressure will tend to tip the boat over instead of allowing it to bear away. Let the boat bear away slowly until it is pointing at about 135 degrees to the wind, on a broad-reaching course. Straighten out by centralizing the rudder.

You can bear away until the wind is blowing directly from behind the boat, which is now on a dead run. The sails should be let out to the maximum. Telltales will have no effect since there is little or no windflow over the leeward side of the sail.

To avoid the possibility of an inadvertent jibe, head up a little so that the wind is blowing over the stern from the windward side.

Below: **The helmsman steers with the tiller and handles the mainsheet, while the crew controls the jib.**

Should I learn in a dinghy or yacht?

Learning to sail in a dinghy gets you as close as possible to the effects of wind and water. It provides immediate feedback on your progress, rewarding success and helping you learn from your mistakes. Beginning to sail always involves a certain amount of trial and error, and the downside should be no more than an occasional capsize!

Learning to sail in a yacht provides a different kind of experience. The yacht is likely to feel considerably more solid and stable, with the added advantage of your being able to resort to the

Right: **Bearing away down-wind. The boom will swing across (jibe) as the stern changes its angle to the wind.**

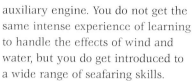

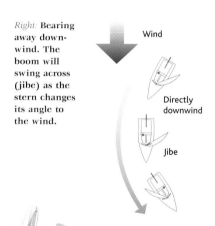

Wind

Directly downwind

Jibe

auxiliary engine. You do not get the same intense experience of learning to handle the effects of wind and water, but you do get introduced to a wide range of seafaring skills.

Learn to sail in a dinghy first if possible. You can then transfer those skills to yacht sailing, with better appreciation of wind and water.

Perfect balance

With perfectly balanced sails the boat will move ahead with balanced helm. If there is too much drive from the mainsail the boat will turn towards the wind. This is known as weather helm. If there is too much drive from the jib, the boat will turn away from the wind. This is known as lee helm.

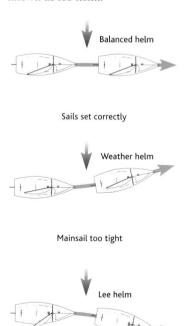

Balanced helm

Sails set correctly

Weather helm

Mainsail too tight

Lee helm

Mainsail out too far

Who has the right of way?

It is vital to understand the sailing rules of the road, which determine who has right of way. It is even more important to abide by those rules and avoid a collision at all costs.

All craft must keep a proper lookout

❂ Watch where you are heading and be ready to change course to avoid other boats.

❂ Beware of having your view to leeward obscured by the sails. This can be a problem with the jib on a dinghy or the genoa (large overlapping headsail) on a yacht.

❂ If you need to change course urgently to avoid a right-of-way boat, make your intentions clear with an exaggerated turn to port or starboard so that the other skipper realizes you are taking action.

Different tacks under sail

Boats sailing on starboard tack (with the wind blowing over the starboard side) have right of way over boats sailing on port tack. If you can't remember, think green and red. Green (starboard) is for go. Red (port) is for stop.

To avoid a starboard-tack boat, the port-tack boat can slow down, tack or bear away behind its stern. But if the port-tack boat fails to take any action, the starboard-tack boat must try to avoid a collision. Don't assume a skipper on collision course will have seen your boat or know what to do.

Above: **The dinghy in the foreground is on a port tack and must give way to the dinghy on starboard tack.**

Right of way

A: Windward boat keeps clear. The boat that is sailing closer toward the wind has the right of way.

B: Port tack keeps clear. The port-tack boat must tack, slow down or pass behind the starboard-tack boat.

C: Overtaking boat keeps clear. This also applies when a sailboat overtakes a powerboat.

D: Turn to starboard under power or sail. Approaching head on, make your intentions clear.

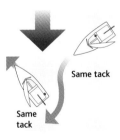

Same tack

Same tack

A. Windward boat keeps clear

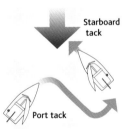

Starboard tack

Port tack

B. Port tack gives way

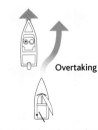

Overtaking

C. Overtaking boat keeps clear

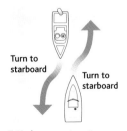

Turn to starboard

Turn to starboard

D. Under power, turn to starboard

Same tack

When two boats are on the same tack (either port or starboard tack), the overtaking boat must keep clear.

When two boats are converging on the same tack the yacht that is to windward (closest to the wind) must keep clear.

When sail meets power

Sail has right of way over power. However, do not assume that a boat that is sailing always has right of way. Sail must frequently give way to commercial shipping. Any large powercraft, which is "hampered" by

Below: **The overtaking boat must keep clear of the boat in front. The sailor turns to port to avoid hitting the other boat's transom.**

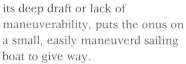

its deep draft or lack of maneuverability, puts the onus on a small, easily maneuverd sailing boat to give way.

The driver of a small powercraft such as a jet ski or speedboat may not understand the rules of the road or be willing to give way. The skipper of a sailing boat has a duty to avoid collision. And if a boat that is sailing overtakes a powercraft, the overtaking sailboat must keep clear.

Under power

If a yacht is under power or a dinghy is using an outboard engine, they should abide by the same rules of the road as a powercraft.

If two powercraft are on a head-on course, they should both turn to starboard. If two powercraft are on a converging course, the boat to starboard has right of way. The easiest way to work this out is to imagine the navigation lights on the other boat. If you can see green (starboard) you can go, because the other boat is on your port side. If you can see red (starboard) you must take avoiding action, because the other boat is on your starboard side.

Above: **This yacht is on starboard tack and has right of way over any sailboat on port tack. However, it may have to give way to a larger vessel (sail or power) that needs to stay in the deep channel.**

Racing rules

The rules for racing give exactly the same priority: avoid a collision at all costs. However, due to the close proximity of a lot of boats all intent on winning — particularly at the starting line or turning round marks of the course — the rules are considerably more complex. They are summarized on pages 162–63.

Left: **Racing rules are designed to avoid collisions. In this situation, the blue Lark must keep clear of the gray Lark and cannot force a passage.**

Basic knots

You only need a few knots for sailing — but you should be able to tie and untie them easily. Practice so that you know you can tie the basic knots in any conditions, whether quickly or in the dark.

Why do you need knots?

Sailing boats have a lot of lines, used for sheets, halyards, control lines and mooring. In order to sail safely you need to be proficient in a basic repertoire of knots. You must be able to tie these quickly, virtually without thinking, yet be confident that the knot will hold. Practice each knot with both thick and thin diameter lines. Keep practicing until each knot turns out perfect every time. It is a great idea to practice a few knots every time you go sailing — just to make sure you haven't forgotten how to get them right.

Below: **Practice makes perfect. It's never too early to start tying knots, and the knowlege will last a lifetime.**

Figure-eight

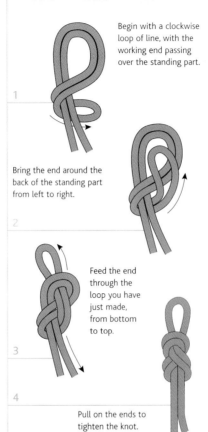

Begin with a clockwise loop of line, with the working end passing over the standing part.

Bring the end around the back of the standing part from left to right.

Feed the end through the loop you have just made, from bottom to top.

Pull on the ends to tighten the knot.

This is an easy and useful stopper knot (tied with a single or double line) so the line or the end of a sheet doesn't escape through a fitting. It doesn't jam and can be undone easily.

Bowline

Form a bight of line with the working end on the right. In the standing end form a small loop.

Insert the working end through the loop.

Bring the working end around the back of the standing line and through the loop.

Tighten by pulling down on the large loop created by the knot.

This is possibly the most useful knot of them all. It makes a fixed loop at the end of the line, which will not slip but is always easy to untie when the load is removed.

Clove hitch

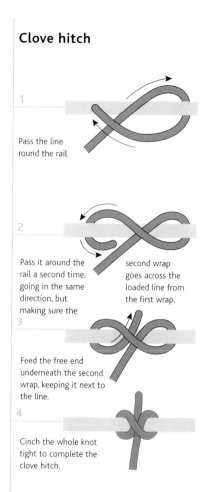

1
Pass the line round the rail.

2
Pass it around the rail a second time, going in the same direction, but making sure the

second wrap goes across the loaded line from the first wrap.

3
Feed the free end underneath the second wrap, keeping it next to the line.

4
Cinch the whole knot tight to complete the clove hitch.

This knot offers a fast, easy way to secure a line to a rail, post or spar. It will not bind under load, and is therefore very easy to untie. However, it can be insecure, and can slip under heavy load.

Round turn and two half-hitches

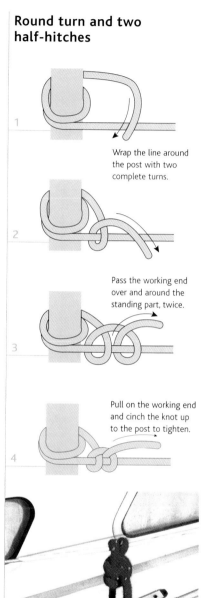

1
Wrap the line around the post with two complete turns.

2
Pass the working end over and around the standing part, twice.

3

4
Pull on the working end and cinch the knot up to the post to tighten.

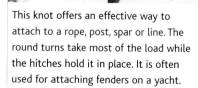

This knot offers an effective way to attach to a rope, post, spar or line. The round turns take most of the load while the hitches hold it in place. It is often used for attaching fenders on a yacht.

Single sheet bend

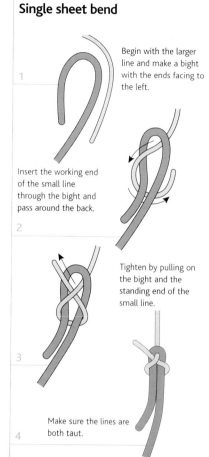

1
Begin with the larger line and make a bight with the ends facing to the left.

Insert the working end of the small line through the bight and pass around the back.

2
Tighten by pulling on the bight and the standing end of the small line.

3

4
Make sure the lines are both taut.

This knot is used to join two lines of different thicknesses and is quick to tie. However, it can easily slip if the lines are very different or slippery. "Double" it by passing twice around the bight.

Ropework

Lines are used for different purposes on a boat and have different dimensions and qualities. The strength of line depends on how it is made, its diameter and the material it is made from.

Different types of lines

All lines, whether made from natu or synthetic materials, are made from strands of yarn, twisted or braided into finished line.

1. Braided lines have a central cor of strands protected by an outer casing. This creates a line that off the best compromise between strength, stretch resistance and lightness of weight. Braided line is widely used for control lines, halyards and sheets.
2. Stranded or "laid" line is made with three or more polyester strar wound in a spiral. Prestretched stranded line provides a cheaper alternative to braided line for sheets and halyards, and is widely used for mooring lines.

Securing lines

The butterfly cleat provides the simplest solution to holding a line under load. To secure the line, take

Above: **Braided line is secured around a horn cleat on a pontoon. Note how the line is wrapped around the base of the cleat and then over the horns.**

a turn around the base of the cleat. After the first full turn, continue with one or more figures-eights. Finish off with a "twisted" locking turn for extra security (but never use on sheets, which may have to be released quickly).

Left: **Clutches mounted on the top of the coachroof are used to hold lines such as halyards and reefing lines, which are led back from the base of the mast.**

Coiling line

1. Pull out an equal length of line for each coil. Use your thumb and forefinger to twist the top to ensure each coil hangs straight. 2. Leave enough line to take several turns around the main body of coils. 3. Pull a loop through the top hole in the coils. 4. Pull the loop down over the coils. 5. Tighten the free end. The coiled line is secure and ready for storage or use.

Jamming cleats

Pull the line downward through the jaws to cleat the line. Pull the line upward to uncleat it.

Jammers

Most yachts have jammers for controlling lines. Pull the line through the jammer with the lever in the "down" position to keep the line locked. To release a line under load, first ensure that the slack is taken up on a winch, which will take over the load. Push the jammer lever "up" to unlock the line, keeping tension on the winch.

Winches

Always wind a line clockwise around the drum of a winch. Add more turns to increase friction. Never place fingers and thumbs between the line and the drum. Pull the line straight from the drum, not upward, which may create a "riding turn" with one loop of the line riding up and jamming.

Above: **Unused line is best stored in a neat coil that can be stowed away in a locker or hung up. The coil should be well secured so that it will remain coiled tidily and can be used quickly and easily without getting into a tangle or twisting up.**

Coiling line

Always keep things tidy. Line should be coiled to form a neat bundle of loops, which can be uncoiled and used in seconds. If you leave loose line in an untidy bundle, it will almost certainly tangle and snag.

To coil a line, make clockwise loops with one hand and hold the coils with the other hand. Make sure each loop is the same size by paying out an even length of line for each coil. Due to its construction, line tends to twist when coiled. You can overcome this by twisting the line between thumb and forefinger as you make the loop. Some line is most easily coiled in figure-eight loops.

When coiling a large amount of line, it may not be possible to hold the coils with one hand. You can make the coils on the deck instead,

or get someone to hold out their arm. Secure the bundle of coils by taking three turns around the top part with the end of the line. Push a loop through the middle of the coils and turn it over the top of the coil before tightening the free end.

Line sense

If a line is under load, make sure it is secure. Beware of grabbing a line that is running free; for instance, if a sheet slips off a winch. A line under load creates friction that can "burn" the unprotected palm of your hand.

Line will fray due to being constantly pulled through a fairlead, block or bow roller. The outer casing will become damaged or a strand may start to fail. Lines should be regularly checked for wear and chafe and replaced if damaged.

Synthetic line should be cut with a "hot knife" available from chandlers, to ensure that the end of the line cannot unravel or separate from its casing.

Below: **Line used for a genoa or jib sheet is led around the drum of a winch, and then secured by being jammed into the self-tailing jaws.**

Uses of lines

✪ Nylon (polyamide)

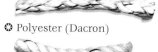

Anchoring, mooring, permanent moorings and towing

✪ Polyester (Dacron)

Kedge and/or anchor warps and dayboat anchoring

✪ Polypropylene

Mooring alongside, floating safety lines and general purpose

✪ Spectra, Dyneema, Kevlar

Halyards, sheets, guys and control lines on racing yachts and dinghies

Staying warm

Sailing is a sport that requires good-quality equipment and specialized clothing for comfort and safety. Your head, feet, hands and eyes all need protection from both the elements and from potential hazards around the boat.

Wind, water and sun

The perfect sailing day provides a fair breeze with air temperature pleasantly warmed by the sun. You may be lucky enough to enjoy a fine-weather sailing location when little more than a T-shirt and shorts will be required on board a dinghy or a yacht. But that is the exception rather than the rule — sailing has a tendency to be a chilly sport in which you need to dress for the weather.

The good news is that sailing clothing has become so sophisticated that sailors in most countries can enjoy their sport all year round.

Wind chill

It may be a fine, sunny day on dry land, but "wind chill" will be more noticeable on the water. The effects of wind chill are greatest when sailing into the wind, and least when sailing away from the wind. If you are being splashed by waves, wind chill will make you cooler still, and if you have capsized and fallen into the water, it will make you a lot colder when you start to sail again.

The comfort zone

Modern sailing clothes are designed to keep you warm, keep you dry and allow you to move around the boat with minimal restriction. Specialized clothing manufacturers estimate that water transmits heat 30 times faster than air, so wet skin gets cold 30 times faster than dry skin. To keep warm in the worst conditions, you need to stay dry. Your clothing needs to transport body moisture away from your skin, hold dry, warm air close to your body, and keep out water.

Yacht sailing

A three-layer system is optimal for yacht sailing.

❂ The base layer next to your skin wicks the sweat away from your body to ensure you don't get cold. Synthetic fabrics like polypropylene and polyester are best. Natural fabrics such as cotton soak up moisture instead of expelling it.

❂ The middle layer provides insulation, which holds warm air

Below: **Wind and water will cool you down, so always dress to stay warm!**

THERMAL
TURTLE
NECK AND
PANTS

BASE LAYER

A range of clothing

close to your body while helping to transmit sweat to the outer layer. Special materials such as Gore-Tex are purposly designed for this.

✪ The outer layer needs to be totally water- and windproof, but must continue the process of transmitting sweat away from your body by using a breathable, waterproof fabric.

Rollaway hood

Prismatic reflector

COASTAL JACKET

Dinghy sailing

Dinghy sailors get closer to the water than yacht sailors; what's more, if they capsize it becomes a full immersion sport. The main priority is to stay warm inside clothing that allows you to move around the boat.

✪ Neoprene wetsuits (steamers) are best for most conditions, providing a snug fit. They keep most of the water out and the warmth in.

A loose-fitting, breathable waterproof smock provides an extra layer of protection for colder weather.

✪ Drysuits are totally waterproof for sailing in very cold weather.

✪ A waterproof smock and pants provides a comfortable alternative for dinghy sailing, but the base layer or mid-layer worn below will get soaked if you capsize.

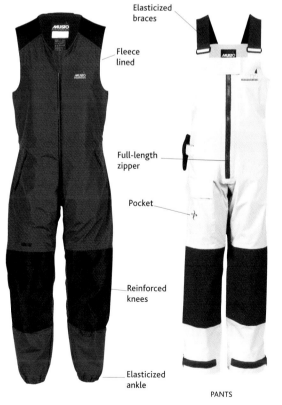

Elasticized braces

Fleece lined

Full-length zipper

Pocket

Reinforced knees

Elasticized ankle

MIDDLE LAYER

PANTS

OUTER LAYER

Thigh pocket

Articulated knees

Single lined neoprene wetsuit

WETSUIT

DINGHY DRYSUIT

Full protection

It is important to protect your extremities from the cold when sailing, so choose good footwear, hat and gloves. You also need to protect your skin and eyes from the damaging effects of the sun.

Head protection

WARM HAT

Your head can be a major area of heat loss in cold weather. A synthetic fleece beanie will keep the heat in, but also dry quickly if it gets wet. And it doesn't restrict hearing when pulled down over your ears.

Some sailing schools require novice sailors (particularly young children) to wear helmets. Their main role is to protect you from being unexpectedly hit on the head by the boom. Once past the novice stage, very few sailors wear helmets; they make it difficult to sense what the wind is doing. A sun hat is a wise addition if cruiser sailing in a warm climate.

DECK SHOES

Foot protection

Sailing barefoot seems like a nice idea, but in most circumstances it is not advisable. Moving around a dinghy or yacht, your foot may connect with something hard or sharp, resulting in injury. Launching or landing a dinghy or yacht may involve walking on stones, with the possibility of broken glass, rusty cans and other unpleasant things.

You need the best possible grip when sailing, particularly on a wet surface. Bare feet grip quite well, but soft rubber soles designed specifically for sailing tend to grip a lot better. Note that bare feet can be hopeless on a boat slip covered with seaweed.

Purpose-made sailing boots will be needed if sailing a cruiser in wet or cold conditions. Rubber boots are no substitute!

WARM GLOVES

Hand protection

Most dinghies and yachts have control lines made of synthetic material that is hard on the hands and can burn if it slips through your palm. Narrower diameter ropes are very difficult to grip with bare hands. Sailing gloves with reinforced palms are strongly recommended.

Cold hands are only likely to be a problem in very low air temperatures when wind chill may freeze your fingers. Dinghy sailors need to find gloves that provide the right compromise between thermal protection, waterproofness and the high degree of suppleness required to control the boat.

Sun protection

If you don't wear skin protection it is easy to get sunburned while sailing. A cooling breeze masks the heat of the sun, which is reflected off the water. Before you know it, your skin is burned, even though with that breeze blowing you may still be feeling delightfully cool. And if you haven't had enough water to drink, this may cause dehydration. Always protect your head and body with a hat and suitable clothing, and keep drinking water when in strong summer sun.

WATER BOTTLE

Eye protection

Sun reflecting off the water, together with the bright hull and sails, produces a lot of glare. Wear sunglasses that provide a high level of UV protection. They will not only improve your vision, but also help to ensure the long-term health of your vision.

UV-PROTECTIVE
SUNGLASSES

Protection after falling overboard

Despite being a sport that takes place exclusively on water, very few people drown when sailing. Dinghy sailors should wear a buoyancy aid or PFD (personal flotation device), which is mandatory in some countries and at virtually all organized events. A buoyancy aid is shaped like a foam-filled vest, and will help keep your body afloat.

In many countries where sailing is popular it is mandatory for yacht owners to provide lifejackets for everyone on board. The skipper should decide when it is essential to wear a lifejacket; at other times the decision is up to you. The principal advantage of a lifejacket over a buoyancy aid is that all lifejackets are designed to float an unconscious person face-upwards in the water.

Below: **A buoyancy aid or PFD (personal flotation device) is ideal for dinghy sailing or daysailing in a keelboat. A lifejacket is recommended for use on a yacht.**

INFLATABLE LIFE JACKET

Webbing belt

Optional crotch strap

Dinghy Sailing

Enjoy the ride

You can enjoy dinghy sailing as helm or crew. Both roles are important but there are different responsibilities for each. On some boats it's a 50:50 partnership; on others the helm has total control. It's up to you to decide which role suits you best.

The helm

The helm has responsibility for two major controls: the rudder, which steers the boat, and the mainsheet, which regulates the amount of drive for its principal sail.

On a single-handed boat, such as a Topper or Laser, the helm has total control. Responsibilities include:

❂ Steering with the tiller extension.
❂ Sheeting the mainsheet in or out to keep the mainsail at the correct angle to the wind; to help the boat change course upwind or offwind; to prevent heeling to windward (on top of yourself) or leeward.
❂ Adjusting controls to change the amount of fullness in the mainsail to suit stronger or lighter winds.
❂ Lifting the daggerboard partway up for maximum control when sailing offwind; pushing it right down to provide forward drive and minimize leeway when sailing upwind.
❂ Leaning out and hiking over the side to keep the boat as upright as possible.
❂ Moving weight fore and aft to trim the boat correctly. The stern should be lifted by sitting forward when sailing upwind or in light winds; the bow should be lifted by sitting back when sailing offwind.
❂ Tacking and jibing.
❂ Righting the boat after a capsize.
❂ Launching on the beach and landing back on the beach, possibly with no assistance.
❂ Rigging and derigging the boat.
❂ Ensuring the boat is stored correctly: protected by its over-cover and securely tied down.

Below: **Single-handed sailing puts you in absolute charge of the boat, but you will never be lonely in a popular class like the Laser.**

The crew

On a double-handed boat the helm and crew work together. As well as helping with rigging, launching and managing the boat during maneuvers, the crew has specific roles, some of which may be shared with the helm:

Below: **Sailing two-up on a dinghy like the 29er provides ultimate thrills. Both crew play a vital role — if one makes a mistake, they both take a swim!**

TIP

Try to get experience at both ends of the boat. Helming a single-handed dinghy and crewing a double-handed dinghy can provide two very different sailing experiences. Sailing is social. Whether you prefer to helm or crew, sail in a class where you will make friends.

- Sheeting the jib in or out to match the mainsail. On high-performance skiffs and catamarans, the crew frequently takes over the mainsheet upwind, which provides better sail control.
- Managing the spinnaker. This includes hoisting (on some boats the helm pulls the halyard), sheeting, jibing and dropping the sail, which performs a major role in performance offwind.
- Adjusting the major mainsail controls, which are accessible by both crew and helm.
- Lifting and lowering the daggerboard or centerboard.
- Leaning out and hiking to keep the boat upright. The crew can change from hiking to sitting in more easily than the helm.
- Moving weight fore and aft to trim the boat correctly. The crew should keep close to the helm, moving fore and aft in unison.
- Looking ahead and providing information on wind and waves for the helm — the crew gets the best view to spot gusts and changes in wind direction.
- Deciding tactics during a race — it's easier for a crew to look around at the big picture, while the helm concentrates on driving the boat.

Which is best?

Single-handed sailing is great if you like to sail alone. You don't need to find a crew, but there's no one to talk to and no one but yourself to blame if things go wrong! Double-handed sailing is great for the helm, if you want responsibility for how the boat is sailed and where it goes. Double-handed sailing is great for the crew on any high-performance boat with a spinnaker, as the crew's role is vital in managing the boat.

Sailing is fun

Always remember, sailing is a sport. We do it for fun and relaxation, not to get tense and annoyed. Never shout at your crew! Never shout at your helm! Keep calm and in control.

Choosing a dinghy

How do you make the right choice when there are so many different dinghies available? First, decide your priorities so you can then make a shortlist of suitable boats.

Left: **The Topper is a very popular junior racing class that can also be enjoyed by lighter weight adults.**

Do you want to race?

Dinghy racing is the best way to improve sailing technique. It not only forces you to make a big effort to learn to manage the boat, but also ensures you have a reason to go sailing on a regular basis. You can meet like-minded people and make new friends by joining a sailing club, which will organize racing for its members over weekends, summer evenings and during special regattas. A major advantage is that a sailing club will also provide safety cover on the water for its members.

Any dinghy can be raced: you just need to find another dinghy to race against. Some dinghies, however, though designed specifically for racing, remain suitable for recreational fun. These classes have the backing of active class associations, which organize events in many different locations and may also run major regattas, including world championships.

Right: **The Xenon combines a sophisticated rig and hull shape with durable molded construction for low-cost sailing enjoyment.**

Choice of a suitable racing dinghy may depend on local sailing clubs. They will promote specific classes, which helps guarantee good competition each time you race. Ideally, each class will race as a one-design fleet in which the first boat to finish wins, but clubs may also organize handicap racing for different types of boats, to boost the number of competitors.

One-design dinghies

Most modern dinghies and cats are "one designs." All boats are identical, except for minimal changes to specification allowed. Typical one-design classes include all Laser, RS and 49er/29er racing dinghies.

Many older classes have been updated to keep pace with the times and now allow more modern materials and construction or a more sophisticated modern rig. Thus a boat designed more than half a century ago (such as the Finn, Optimist or GP14) can be brought up to date and made more rewarding to sail. Dinghies constructed originally with marine plywood panels now allow for slight variations in hull shape.

Development class

A development class has few rules, often just maximum length and beam, with no restrictions on sail size or weight. Development classes were popular early on but restrictions became necessary to keep costs under control. The National 12, Merlin Rocket, International 14 and International Moth — which encourage different hull designs — are all superb but highly specialized racing machines.

Above: **Family sailors need a stable boat with plenty of space. The Omega provides good performance with a crowd on board.**

Do you want to cruise?

If you have no interest in racing, your first requirement will be a stable boat that handles easily and performs well. Size will be governed by how many people you want to sail with. A small single-hander may suffice, or you may need a big boat like a Wayfarer or Topaz Omega, which has room for four people. Many of the classic dinghies make excellent choices for dinghy cruising. They tend to be more stable than modern racing dinghy designs and are widely available second-hand for those on a tight budget (see page 159). Be aware that the bigger the boat you choose the heavier and more difficult it will be to handle on dry land. Pulling a dinghy back up the boat slip is a necessary part of sailing, but make sure it doesn't ruin your enjoyment of the sport!

Choosing a dinghy (2)

New or second-hand?

There are plenty of good offers available if you want a brand new boat. Look out for all-inclusive packages that include everything you need in addition to the boat and sails. At the very least you will require a launching dolly and top cover for the boat. You may also need a matching road trailer and under-cover to protect the bottom of the boat. Further useful extras may include padded bags to protect the rudder and daggerboard, which can be surprisingly fragile on high-performance boats.

Buying second-hand provides lots of bargains, with dinghies available at all prices. However you may need expert advice to ensure a trouble-free purchase. Check everything that is being sold with the boat,

including the condition of sails, rigging, control gear and foils, which frequently get damaged. Repairing dinghy equipment can be expensive. Check for rusty bearings inside trailer wheels, which may seize up as you drive back home.

Below: **Like all rotomolded dinghies, the Laser Vago is extremely tough and almost maintenance free, but you still need to beware of scratches!**

Below: **This all-wood Solo is a beautiful boat, but will require extra time, maintenance and money to keep it in top condition.**

TIP

Match the type of hull construction to your budget, but consider buying second-hand to make a big savings over the cost of a new boat. If you buy second-hand, check the sails, foils and fittings carefully — replacements may be very expensive.

Older wooden dinghies are prone to rot, but can generally be repaired. They also require regular maintenance with varnish and paint. Older fiberglass dinghies may suffer from faded gel coat and cracks in the gel coat (which may be cosmetic or more serious, indicating failure at a major stress point). The mast base, rudder pintles and daggerboard case are typical damage areas. Fiberglass may delaminate, breaking away from the central foam core and letting water soak into the boat, which will get heavier with age, so check the weight of the boat if possible.

What is your budget?

If you are on a tight budget, there are two alternatives. Either buy second-hand, or look at a molded plastic boat such as the Topper, Pico or RS Vision. The more you pay for a boat, the more refined it should be in terms of construction, equipment and performance. At the top of the scale you can expect the stiffest and lightest possible hull built in epoxy laminate with carbon or crafted in wood, matched with superlight carbon spars, stretch-free laminate sails, the very best control gear and superb handmade foils for ultimate racing performance. In the mid-range, you should expect foam sandwich construction, offering a good compromise between weight and stiffness, and a sophisticated rig with aluminum spars.

What type of construction?

Rotomolded plastic is very durable and has excellent impact resistance. On the minus side, it's heavy and any damage is difficult to repair.

Polypropylene is particularly vulnerable to scratches if you drag your boat up the beach! All plastic boats will slowly fade and lose their sheen through exposure to UV light.

Fiberglass is vulnerable to small "dings" in the gel coat, and impacts such as a collision may penetrate the central foam core. However, this is quite easy to repair and to achieve a near perfect match with the existing hull color. All fiberglass boats will slowly fade through exposure to UV light. Unlike rotomolded plastic or polypropylene, you can paint a fiberglass hull.

Above: **Sophisticated epoxy foam sandwich construction ensures that this RS800 is both light and stiff. This type of construction needs careful handling, but can provide top performance for many years.**

Wooden dinghies can look unbeatably beautiful. The downside is that they are considerably more expensive than fiberglass and plastic dinghies. They also require more maintenance and careful handling to prevent scratches to paint work or varnish. Any level of damage repair is possible but will tend to be pricey.

How many crew will it hold?

Many dinghies are specifically designed to be sailed by either one or two crew members. Recreational single-handers such as the Taz or Pico may carry more than one; recreational double-handers such as the Vision or Omega may carry more than two crew. Modern dinghies generally display their maximum permitted capacity.

Do you want to crew or helm?

There is always demand for crews, particularly among dinghy racers. One major advantage of crewing is that you can enjoy all the fun of sailing without having to own a boat. You can also learn sailing skills from an experienced helmsman, and take advantage of the great range of dinghies available that provide exciting performance for both helm and crew.

Single or double-handed?

Both provide a lot of fun, but there are specific advantages to sailing double-handed or on your own.

Single-handed advantages

❂ Single-handed boats tend to be cheaper than double-handers due to their smaller size and simpler rig.
❂ You don't need a crew, so there's no one to organize, let you down when you want to go sailing, or shout at when things go wrong.
❂ If you race, you are totally in control and have only yourself to blame for not winning.
❂ There is a wide choice of single-handed classes, many of which get big turnouts at regattas.
❂ All types of single-hander are available, from a novice junior boat like the Tera to a high-performance skiff such as the RS700.

Double-handed advantages

❂ You don't get lonely when you sail. It's fun to enjoy the sport with a crew and work as a team.
❂ A double-handed boat can provide more exciting performance, whereas the asymmetric spinnaker and trapeze are only usable by expert sailors on single-handed boats.
❂ You can share the time and effort needed to rig, launch and retrieve the boat from the water.
❂ You may be able to share the cost of owning a double-handed boat.

Above: **The Contender has a single sail and trapeze and is a great racing machine if you like to sail alone.**

Above: **The OK dinghy is a classic single-hander with an unstayed rig. Originally built in marine plywood, modern OKs have foam sandwich construction and carbon spars.**

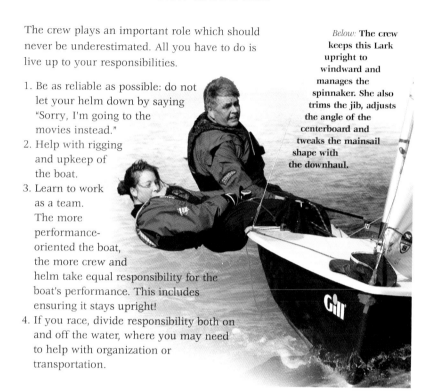

Below: **The crew keeps this Lark upright to windward and manages the spinnaker. She also trims the jib, adjusts the angle of the centerboard and tweaks the mainsail shape with the downhaul.**

How to be a crew

The crew plays an important role which should never be underestimated. All you have to do is live up to your responsibilities.

1. Be as reliable as possible: do not let your helm down by saying "Sorry, I'm going to the movies instead."
2. Help with rigging and upkeep of the boat.
3. Learn to work as a team. The more performance-oriented the boat, the more crew and helm take equal responsibility for the boat's performance. This includes ensuring it stays upright!
4. If you race, divide responsibility both on and off the water, where you may need to help with organization or transportation.

Below: **The Buzz provides fun for two crew with a single trapeze, mainsail, jib and asymmetric spinnaker.**

What is your skill level?

There is a wide gulf in the ability level required to sail a novice boat like a Pico and a high-performance skiff like a 49er. Experience will teach you how to set your level.

A beginner will need to start sailing in a fairly stable boat with power and speed that are easy to control. How quickly you progress will to some extent depend on the weather conditions when you sail.

Below: **Sailing in a warm force 4 breeze with flat water is likely to be a lot less challenging than sailing in a cold, dense force 4 with waves and tide.**

Why choose a catamaran?

In simple terms, cats are faster than dinghies. Two slim hulls are easier to drive through the water than one wide hull. Connected by two aluminum beams, they form a wide "platform" for the crew, which helps provide sufficient leverage to hold down a big and powerful rig — particularly if the crew hang out on trapezes. When the windward hull is flying just off the surface of the water, the cat's wetted resistance is minimized and performance is maximized, both upwind and downwind.

Below: **Wow! That looks difficult, but it's actually very stable and easy to sail a cat like this Hobie 15 at 45 degrees. However it's not a good way to sail fast!**

What are cats made of?

Most racing cats will have fiberglass foam sandwich hulls, which provide the best compromise of stiffness and weight.

Each hull is built in two-part molds that allow bulkheads to be incorporated. This creates a light, stiff structure combined with the foam core, with the two halves of the hull mold-bonded together and ready for fittings to be attached. Rotomolded polyethylene is used to build durable cat hulls at the lowest possible cost. Popular models include the Dart 16, Hobie Twixxy and Topaz 16CX.

How much wind?

The amount of wind required to start sailing will depend on a mixture of factors:

- Sail power, determined by area, height and efficiency of the rig.
- Width and weight of the cat's platform.
- Weight and leverage of the crew.

Most cats need force 3 to start sailing fast, will be at full potential speed in force 4, and will be maxed out in force 5, when crew skill and ability to depower the rig become essential.

The most stable sailing platform

One good reason for choosing a cat is that the crew's "platform" provides a much more stable base than any dinghy when sailing at speed. This makes cats ideal for learning and experiencing the delights of the trapeze, which is both more efficient and more pleasant than hiking over the side.

Right: **The Topaz 14 Xtreme combines low-cost rotomolded hulls with a high-aspect rig, providing lots of power for one sailor on the trapeze.**

Above: **Many recreational cats have shallow skegs on each hull that are sufficient to prevent sideslip, but many racing cats have removable daggerboards for extra lift.**

A cat also provides a great way of learning to handle an asymmetric spinnaker, with the mouth of its chute projecting in front of the boat where it is clear of the forestay and bridle. This ensures the spinnaker hoists, drops and will not snag.

TIP

Cats are best in wide open areas of water, so make sure you have enough space. Some sailing clubs encourage cats; others think they sail too fast or take up too much space.

The stable cat platform is a huge bonus when the crew is jibing the spinnaker or trimming the sheet out on the trapeze wire, plus there is the major advantage that the spinnaker provides lift, which helps prevent the leeward bow from nose-diving.

Curiously, the spinnaker doesn't make a big difference to the cat's speed through the water downwind and probably makes it slower upwind, due to the extra weight and clutter. However, a spinnaker provides the power for a cat to bear away on the apparent wind and sail deeper downwind than with two sails, reducing the distance it has to cover. The bottom line is that trapezing and spinnaker sailing provide loads of extra fun for cat sailors!

What to wear for dinghy sailing

Dinghy sailing in most conditions requires a wetsuit, the top choice for keeping warm. To keep you warmer still, items such as a dry top can be worn over the wetsuit. Other essential items are dinghy boots, gloves and hiking shorts. Safety equipment such as a buoyancy aid and trapeze harness also need to be worn.

Safety equipment

Buoyancy aid

Buoyancy aids are available in vest or pull-on styles, with more or less buoyancy to support heavier or lighter weights. The buoyancy aid should be a close fit that does not obstruct your upper body when sailing. If you capsize and are in the water, the buoyancy aid should stay secure around your body, without floating up over your head.

Trapeze harness

If the boat you sail has a trapeze, you will need a trapeze harness, which is worn over the wetsuit and under the buoyancy aid. The harness has a hook or spreader bar, which must be adjusted so that it is pulled in as close as possible to your body.

Below: **The trapeze harness is normally worn underneath the buoyancy aid. Sailing shoes are vital for good grip on the deck.**

How effective the wetsuit is at keeping you warm will depend on a number of factors:

- ✿ The fit. A close fit that molds to your body, preventing cold water washing around the inside, is vital. To achieve this, the neoprene must be supple and stretchy and specifically cut for a male or female fit. When trying on a wetsuit make sure you can bend and stretch in any direction and that the neck is comfortable.
- ✿ The thickness. The thicker the neoprene, the warmer and more constrictive it will be. Most wetsuits combine thicker body panels with thinner leg and arm panels — maybe 5 mm for the body and 3 mm for arms and legs.
- ✿ How waterproof? Neoprene is a waterproof material but a wetsuit cannot be fully watertight. The more cold water is able to flush through the inside of the wetsuit, the colder you will become. To prevent this, the best quality wetsuits have sealed stitching, which will not let the water through, and a carefully shaped tight fit at the ankles (or thighs on short-leg wetsuits), wrists (or arms on short-arm wetsuits) and neck. The zipper will let water inside the suit so an effective barrier is provided by full-length neoprene flaps.

Dinghy clothing

Super stretch paneling

3 mm neoprene construction

Reinforced knee panels

WETSUIT

Side pockets

Neoprene waistband

HIKING SHORTS

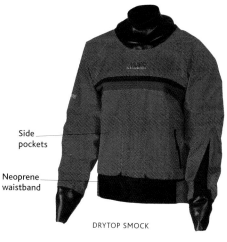

DRYTOP SMOCK

Adjustable strap

DINGHY SHOES

Molded sole

Types of wetsuits (steamers)

A wetsuit with full-length legs and a back zipper provides the best compromise for dinghy sailing. A "convertible" has removable neoprene arms — a useful feature. A "shortie" wetsuit is good for performance sailing in warmer weather, but leaves your knees unprotected.

Boots or shoes

Dinghy boots are recommended for most dinghy sailing. The design should feature a tough and gripping molded rubber sole combined with a neoprene sock, which helps to protect your ankles. Side zippers will make the boots much easier to get on and off. Dinghy shoes use the same neoprene and rubber and are more comfortable to wear in hot weather, but provide no ankle protection.

Hiking shorts

To hike effectively you need support. Hiking shorts with stiff reinforcement under the thighs can be worn over a wetsuit.

Drytop

A wind- and waterproof drytop can be worn over a wetsuit, providing increased protection in colder weather. Make sure it is a loose fit so you can move easily.

Drysuit

A drysuit is a loose-fitting one-piece suit that is totally waterproof, with soft rubber seals at the wrists, ankles and neck keeping all water out. Drysuits can be worn with a thermal base layer and mid layer, and are a top choice for winter sailing.

Gloves

Short finger gloves with a reinforced palm are the best choice for dinghy sailing, enabling greater dexterity than any full-finger gloves.

What else do you need?

It won't be easy to move your dinghy manually, so you will need a launching dolly to move it to the water. A trailer or combination dolly is useful for this purpose. You also need a means of protecting the dinghy from the weather, a range of tools for maintenance and accessories for ease of sailing. Comprehensive insurance is a sensible precaution and third-party insurance is mandatory if you aim to race.

Dolly

All dinghies require a launching dolly to push the dinghy to and from the water. The dolly should have a galvanized steel, rustproof frame with a shaped support for the hull and inflatable tires to make it easy to pull or push. If you launch over a sandy beach or shingle, larger tires will be helpful.

Trailer or trailer-dolly

To transport a dinghy by road, a trailer with a heavy-duty galvanized steel frame and mast support, roadworthy wheels and tires, and supports for the hull is essential.

The trailer will need to be equipped with a license plate, with brake, signal indicator and reversing lights, plus straps to hold the boat down. The car must have a suitable trailer hitch and a power socket for the trailer lights.

Purpose-built trailer-dollies provide the perfect combination. The dolly slides on and off the trailer on rollers and is secured to the trailer at the front. The dolly always supports the boat. Never immerse trailer wheels in the water. The bearings may seize, particularly if exposed to salt water. Always launch and retrieve a dinghy on its

dolly, which has no bearings. Different states and provinces have different towing regulations and maximum permitted speeds.

Covers

For protection in the boat park, a dinghy needs a waterproof top cover which may be available in boom-up or boom-down design. A bottom cover will protect the hull from road dirt when trailing.

Foils on high-performance dinghies tend to have fragile tips and edges. They should be stored and protected in padded bags designed for the rudder and

Above: **When trailing, the boat is protected by top and bottom covers. A trailer with license plate, brake lights and signal indicators is a legal requirement if you trail on road. Effective straps are vital to ensure the boat is securely held on its trailer.**

Opposite: **The launching dolly should support the hull, with guides to hold it in place when the boat is semi-afloat. Most modern trailers are part of a combi-trailer system — this means the boat and its dolly can be pulled directly onto the trailer.**

daggerboard. Carbon masts will slowly deteriorate when exposed to UV light so a mast sock cover is recommended.

Insurance

Third-party insurance is mandatory at most sailing events and is strongly recommended for all dinghy sailing. Comprehensive insurance against theft, loss or damage is likely to be worth the additional premium: boat repairs and replacement can be very pricey.

Optional extras

If you buy a new dinghy, a wide range of optional extras may be available: a different colored hull and waterline, padded foot straps, top-rated blocks and control gear, additional control systems, high-performance foils (these are stiffer and lighter), carbon spars (in place of aluminum) and carbon reinforcement in the hull.

Accessories

✪ A wind indicator is invaluable for showing the exact direction of true wind. It can be mounted on the bows or front of the mast on a single-handed dinghy with just a mainsail, or on the top of the mast when the dinghy has a jib.

WIND INDICATOR

✪ A waterproof sailing watch allows you to keep in touch with the time and provides a vital countdown facility if you go racing.

WATCH

✪ A compass attached to the deck or mast allows you to spot wind shifts and may be required to plot a course. Conventional and digital dinghy sailing compasses are available.

✪ A GPS will settle all questions on how fast you can sail and can also be used for long-distance dinghy cruising or racing. A small waterproof GPS unit can be worn on your wrist, stored inside your buoyancy aid pocket or be attached to the mast at deck level.

COMPASS

✪ It is advisable to carry a purpose-designed safety knife when you go sailing. This can easily be carried in the pocket of a buoyancy aid. A stainless steel multitool is invaluable when rigging or packing a dinghy onto a trailer. At the very least you will need some kind of tool for undoing stiff shackles.

GPS

SAILING KNIFE

Dinghy design and construction

The first rise in dinghy sailing took place soon after the end of the Second World War II. Many new dinghy designs appeared during the late 1940s and 1950s, and many still remain popular as classic classes today.

Classic classes

All the early dinghy designs were built in wood using three principal construction techniques:

Clinker hulls: built with overlapping horizontal planks covering a frame, as originally used for dinghies such as the Merlin Rocket and National 12. This method was most suitable for professional boatbuilders.

Cold-molded hulls: built with thin diagonal wooden veneers glued together over a male mold to provide the shape of the boat, as originally used for dinghies such as the Firefly and Finn. This method was only suitable for professional boatbuilders.

Plywood hulls: built with marine plywood panels joined together in a "chined" box shape, with the plywood twisted to form curves if required. This method was equally suitable for professional and DIY boatbuilders, who could build a dinghy cheaply with modest woodworking skills. Many classic dinghy classes are still built with plywood hulls as a better-looking but more expensive alternative to fiberglass. Considerably more maintenance and care is required than for a fiberglass boat, although epoxy varnish and paint can provide a finish that will last for several years.

Right: **The Merlin Rocket is one of the great classic classes. Early boats were built of wood with overlapping clinker planks; the number of planks was eventually reduced, with the option of marine plywood or foam sandwich construction, as shown here.**

FIREFLY

NUMBER OF CREW: **2**
LENGTH: **12 ft** BEAM: **4.6 ft**
MINIMUM HULL WEIGHT: **163 lb**
MAINSAIL AND JIB: **117.1 ft²**
IDEAL CREW WEIGHT: **243–320 lb**

The legendary Uffa Fox designed the Firefly in 1946. Originally built using hot-molded construction, the modern Firefly is built in fiberglass although wooden boats can often be bought second-hand. The Firefly can provide very exciting racing on a budget, making it a popular choice for dinghy team racing at university and world championship levels.

MERLIN ROCKET

NUMBER OF CREW: **2**
LENGTH: **14 ft** BEAM: **7.2 ft**
MINIMUM HULL WEIGHT: **216 lb**
MAINSAIL AND JIB: **107.2 ft²**
SPINNAKER: **107.6 ft²**
IDEAL CREW WEIGHT: **309–375 lb**

Unlike most dinghies, the Merlin Rocket, which first appeared in 1946, is a "development" class. Any design that fits within the measurement rules is allowed, these having been updated to keep pace with the times. Hundreds of different Merlin Rocket designs have been produced since the early years when all boats were built with planked wooden construction. Modern Merlin Rockets provide a highly refined sailing experience, with hulls built in lightweight foam sandwich construction. A few extremely expensive boats are still made from wood.

OPTIMIST

NUMBER OF CREW: **1**
LENGTH: **7.5 ft** BEAM: **3.7 ft**
MINIMUM HULL WEIGHT: **77 lb**
MAINSAIL: **38.6 ft²**
IDEAL CREW WEIGHT: **88–110 lb**

Originally designed by Clark Mills in 1947 as a boat for children, this has the simplest possible plywood construction and a "sprit" rig that allows the mast, sprit and boom to fit inside the boat for easy storage. The Optimist is established as the world's most popular racing class for under-16-year-olds, who can start sailing it from around 7 years of age. Most modern Optimists are built in lightweight fiberglass construction, though they are also available in both plywood and aluminum.

GP14

NUMBER OF CREW: **2**

LENGTH: **14 ft**   BEAM: **5 ft**

MINIMUM HULL WEIGHT: **293 lb**

MAINSAIL: **138.3 ft²**

SPINNAKER: **90.4 ft²**

IDEAL CREW WEIGHT:**265–330 lb**

Jack Holt designed the General Purpose 14-foot dinghy in 1949, using simple plywood construction. Thanks to its sturdy, stable hull shape, the GP14 remains popular for dinghy cruising or racing and is fitted with a symmetrical spinnaker. Most modern GP14s have fiberglass foam sandwich construction, though wooden boats are also professionally built.

FINN

NUMBER OF CREW: **1**

LENGTH: **14.8 ft**   BEAM: **4.9 ft**

MINIMUM HULL WEIGHT: **265 lb**

MAINSAIL: **107.6 ft²**

IDEAL CREW WEIGHT: **176–243 lb**

Richard Sarby designed the Finn as a new Olympic single-handed class in 1949. Finns were originally built in molded wood veneer, with an instantly recognizable unstayed wooden mast bending in a graceful curve. Modern Finns have fiberglass hulls, carbon masts and laminate sails to bring their performance up to date.

ENTERPRISE

NUMBER OF CREW: **2**

LENGTH: **13.3 ft**   BEAM: **5.2 ft**

MINIMUM HULL WEIGHT: **207 lb**

MAINSAIL AND JIB: **115.2 ft²**

IDEAL CREW WEIGHT: **265–330 lb**

The Enterprise, designed by Jack Holt in 1956, is instantly recognizable thanks to its bright blue sails. Over 23,000 Enterprises were built in the first 50 years of the class, originally in plywood construction and more recently in fiberglass foam sandwich. Some combine this with wood.

SOLO

NUMBER OF CREW: **1**

LENGTH: **12.4 ft**   BEAM: **5.1 ft**

MINIMUM HULL WEIGHT: **154 lb**

MAINSAIL: **90 ft²**

IDEAL CREW WEIGHT: **143–220 lb**

Jack Holt designed the Solo as a single-handed racing dinghy in 1956. Originally built in plywood construction, modern boats are available in fiberglass foam sandwich, all-wood or "composite" construction, which combines a fiberglass hull with a wooden deck. This class is very popular for racing on inland water, but also has well-attended national and world championships at coastal venues. Unlike pure one-designs, there is a free choice of foils and sailmakers, which helps make the Solo extremely varied.

FIREBALL

NUMBER OF CREW: **2**

LENGTH: **16.2 ft**   BEAM: **4.5 ft**

MINIMUM HULL WEIGHT: **175 lb**

MAINSAIL AND JIB: **123 ft²**

SYMMETRICAL SPINNAKER: **140 ft²**

IDEAL CREW WEIGHT: **280–348 lb**

Peter Milne designed the Fireball in 1962. It was a radical boat, looking more like a low-slung rocket than a boat, and was a precursor of the skiff designs that became popular after another three decades. Originally built from almost flat plywood panels, the Fireball was equally suitable for professional or DIY construction, providing one of the fastest dinghies available at a very low price. The class still remains very popular worldwide, but top-quality epoxy foam sandwich has become the hull construction method of choice.

MIRROR

NUMBER OF CREW: **2**

LENGTH: **10.9 ft**   BEAM: **4.6 ft**

MINIMUM HULL WEIGHT: **100 lb**

MAINSAIL AND JIB: **58.1 ft²**

SYMMETRICAL SPINNAKER: **70 ft²**

IDEAL CREW WEIGHT: **176–220 lb**

The last of Jack Holt's great designs was the Mirror, launched in 1963. The Mirror was designed to be built using "stitch and glue" construction developed by Barry Bucknell: marine plywood panels are stitched together using wire ties with fiberglass tape and resin sealing the joins. This method made the Mirror accessible to many thousands of DIY enthusiasts. The Mirror also featured an unusual gunter rigged mainsail with a gaff (a spar to hold the top), which allowed all the elements of the rig to be stored inside the boat. More than 70,000 Mirrors have been built, with the class enjoying a new lease on life as a junior racing boat. Mirrors are still built in wood, but fiberglass foam sandwich versions have become increasingly popular. The class approved major updates to design in 2006 when an optional Bermudan rig was allowed, followed by a revised cockpit layout.

Fiberglass dinghies

From the 1960s, most new dinghies were molded in fiberglass. This new material had the benefit of lower production costs and allowed curved hull shapes, which were difficult to build in wood. It also claimed to be maintenance free.

Fiberglass, also known as GRP (glass-reinforced plastic), is a laminate formed from strands of glass cloth and resin. Molds are built for the hull and deck to produce multiple moldings for the hulls.

Glass cloth is laid in the mold and "wetted out" with polyester resin, after which a chemical reaction turns it into a hard laminate. Using the correct amount of resin is a precise skill. Too much and the boat will be heavy; too little and the hull may have voids in the laminate.

Foam sandwich

A more refined form of construction is foam sandwich, also known as FRP (foam, reinforced plastic). The hull or deck is built with three layers:

1. The first layer is a fiberglass laminate, which becomes the outer skin of the hull with a gel coat providing the surface color.
2. The second layer is provided by sheets of foam, which are cut to fit the shape of the boat. This central layer of foam enables the hull to be stiffer and lighter than a hull formed from a single thick fiberglass laminate.
3. The third layer is a fiberglass laminate, which becomes the inner skin of the hull with a gel coat and non-slip finish providing the surface color inside the cockpit.

Epoxy laminates

Epoxy resin can be used to build a superior laminate to polyester resin, staying stiffer and lighter for longer. The downside is extra cost. Building boats with epoxy resin requires considerably greater skill, using techniques such as "vacuum bagging," which sucks excess resin out of the wet laminate. Epoxy resin is invariably used to build high-performance boats in conjunction with foam sandwich construction. The laminate may be built with different types of glass, carbon or Kevlar cloth to provide maximum stiffness at minimum weight.

Watch out for...

A fiberglass dinghy is much easier to look after than a wooden dinghy, but is not maintenance free. It will need regular washing with fresh water to remove any salt stains, can be cleaned with acetone and should be protected from UV light. Over a period of years, the outer gel coat will fade and may need repainting. A polyester laminate will gradually become heavier and deteriorate due to water seeping into the laminate.

Classic fiberglass dinghies

420

NUMBER OF CREW: **2**
LENGTH: **13.8 ft** BEAM: **5.3 ft**
MINIMUM HULL WEIGHT: **176 lb**
MAINSAIL AND JIB: **140.5 ft²**
SYMMETRICAL SPINNAKER: **97 ft²**
IDEAL CREW WEIGHT: **243–320 lb**

The 420, designed by Christian Maury in 1960, was one of the first dinghies to be built only in fiberglass. It is established as a popular international youth racing class for teenage sailors, who sail with a symmetrical spinnaker and single trapeze. It provides an ideal trainer for the larger 470.

NUMBER OF CREW: **2**

LENGTH: **15.4 ft** BEAM: **5.5 ft**

MINIMUM HULL WEIGHT: **265 lb**

MAINSAIL AND JIB: **136.7 ft²**

SYMMETRICAL SPINNAKER: **153.9 ft²**

IDEAL CREW WEIGHT: **243–320 lb**

Andre Cornu designed the 470 in 1963 exclusively for fiberglass construction. It looks similar to a scaled-up 420 and became an Olympic double-handed class with conventional symmetrical spinnaker for women and men.

470

LASER

NUMBER OF CREW: **1**

LENGTH: **13.9 ft** BEAM: **4.7 ft**

MINIMUM HULL WEIGHT: **130 lb**

MAINSAIL: **76 ft²**

IDEAL CREW WEIGHT: **143–187 lb**

The Laser is the world's biggest selling sailboat and an Olympic class, originally designed by Bruce Kirby in 1971. The Laser is an absolute "one design." All boats are exactly the same, although slight changes to the specification have been permitted since the Laser first appeared. The winning formula for the Laser is that it is not only extremely simple and comparatively cheap, but also fun and fast to sail. Hull and deck are fiberglass with a small cockpit and simple daggerboard. The rig has a two-part mast, which slots into the deck without a forestay or shrouds for support.

LASER RADIAL AND LASER 4.7

NUMBER OF CREW: **1**

LENGTH: **13.9 ft** BEAM: **4.7 ft**

MINIMUM HULL WEIGHT: **130 lb**

MAINSAIL: **61.4 ft² and 50.6 ft²**

IDEAL CREW WEIGHT: **143–165 lb**

Two other versions of the Laser are available, both using exactly the same hull and fittings. The Laser Radial has a radial cut sail that is smaller and easier to handle than the full-size rig. It is raced as the women's single-handed Olympic class and as an international youth class. The laser 4.7 has a smaller sail, making laser sailing more accessible to lightweights and teenagers.

Polyethylene dinghies

Rotomolded plastic dinghies began to appear in the 1990s and have become established as a favorite choice for low-cost recreational sailing.

Polyethylene is the principal material used to produce rotomolded (rotational molded) boats. It requires considerable investment to build specialized aluminum molds, but allows the manufacturer to produce hulls far more quickly and with less manpower than any other form of dinghy construction. The plastic granules are heated and rotated in a combined hull and deck mold, ensuring that melted plastic covers the entire surface.

Most rotomolded dinghies have plastic inner and outer skins with a central sandwich to add rigidity. Polyethylene is heavier than fiberglass and it is not possible to build internal bulkheads to provide support in key areas of the hull. Technical expertise is required to ensure the rotomolding program varies the thickness of the plastic around the inside of the mold, with thicker layers for high-stress areas.

As well as being cheaper than fiberglass, rotomolded hulls are exceptionally durable and tough. However, they are generally heavier and less stiff than fiberglass, and so provide less responsive sailing for those used to racing dinghies with top performance. A novice won't notice this until they are more experienced.

Molded plastic dinghies

TOPPER

NUMBER OF CREW: **1**
LENGTH: **11.2 ft** BEAM: **3.9 ft**
MINIMUM HULL WEIGHT: **95 lb**
MAINSAIL: **56 ft²**
IDEAL CREW WEIGHT: **70+ lb**

The Topper, designed by Ian Proctor in 1976, is virtually unique in being injection-molded in polypropylene. With a two-part mast and simple unstayed rig, it was originally conceived as a "car toppable" boat, hence the name. After three decades it has become popular as a junior racing class. It gets a huge turnout at major events including the annual world championship on Lake Garda. The original Topper had a transom-mounted mainsheet, but for racing a center mainsheet has become the most popular choice. Its major advantage is that it is virtually maintenance free.

LASER PICO

NUMBER OF CREW: **1–2**
LENGTH: **11.5 ft** BEAM: **4.5 ft**
MINIMUM HULL WEIGHT: **132 lb**
MAINSAIL: **54.9 or 68.9 ft²**
OPTIONAL JIB: **11.7 ft²**
IDEAL CREW WEIGHT: **70+ lb**

Jo Richards designed the Pico in 1995 as a purpose-built rotomolded boat suitable for novices of all ages. The Pico is extremely tough and durable, has enough space in the cockpit for two children or one adult, and is widely used by sailing schools.

LASER FUNBOAT

NUMBER OF CREW: **1–2**
LENGTH: **12.8 ft** BEAM: **4.1 ft**
MINIMUM HULL WEIGHT: **154 lb**
MAINSAIL: **51.7 ft²**
IDEAL CREW WEIGHT: **77+ lb**

An unusual concept for a fail-safe training dinghy, the Funboat bridges the gap between dinghy and catamaran with a hull that looks like a sledge and is extremely difficult to capsize. It was designed by Yves Loday in 2000.

RS FEVA

NUMBER OF CREW: **2**

LENGTH: **11.9 ft** BEAM: **4.7 ft**

MINIMUM HULL WEIGHT: **139 lb**

MAINSAIL: **59.2 or 70 ft²**

JIB: **22.6 ft²**

ASYMMETRIC SPINNAKER: **75.3 ft²**

IDEAL CREW WEIGHT: **176–330 lb**

The Feva, designed by Paul Handley and RS in 2002, was conceived as a modern rival for the Mirror, to provide sailors with all the thrills of sailing with an asymmetric spinnaker. It has quickly become a popular junior racing class.

RS VISION

NUMBER OF CREW: **2+**

LENGTH: **15.1 ft** BEAM: **5.7 ft**

MINIMUM HULL WEIGHT: **275 lb**

MAINSAIL: **96.9 ft²**

JIB: **34.4 ft²**

ASYMMETRIC SPINNAKER: **135.6 ft²**

IDEAL CREW WEIGHT: **308 lb**

A family dinghy with optional trapeze, the Vision was purpose-designed for rotomolded construction by Phil Morrison in 2003. It has enough space for two adults and two children.

TERA

NUMBER OF CREW: **1**

LENGTH: **9.4 ft** BEAM: **4 ft**

MINIMUM HULL WEIGHT: **77 lb**

MAINSAIL: **51.7 or 39.8 ft²**

IDEAL CREW WEIGHT: **308 lb**

Paul Handley designed the RS Tera in 2005. This rotomolded single-hander for junior sailors is a multipurpose boat with a choice of two rigs and the facility to row with a pair of oars.

LASER VAGO

NUMBER OF CREW: **1–2**

LENGTH: **13.8 ft** BEAM: **5.1 ft**

MINIMUM HULL WEIGHT: **190 lb**

MAINSAIL: **86.1 or 100.3 ft²**

JIB: **28.6 ft²**

ASYMMETRIC SPINNAKER: **122.5 or 140 ft²**

IDEAL CREW WEIGHT: **165–330 lb**

Designed by Jo Richards in 2005, this is a versatile one or two-person rotomolded dinghy with asymmetric spinnaker and trapeze.

TAZ

NUMBER OF CREW: **1–2**

LENGTH: **9.7 ft** BEAM: **3.9 ft**

MINIMUM HULL WEIGHT: **100 lb**

MAINSAIL: **42.8 ft²**

IDEAL CREW WEIGHT: **143 lb**

The Taz is a rotomolded beginners' boat designed by Rob White and Ian Howlett in 2002. It can be sailed by one or two children, is car toppable and has the option of a small jib.

TOPAZ OMEGA

NUMBER OF CREW: **2+**

LENGTH: **15.2 ft** BEAM: **6.5 ft**

MINIMUM HULL WEIGHT: **308 lb**

MAINSAIL: **123.8 ft²**

JIB: **37.7 ft²**

ASYMMETRIC SPINNAKER: **137.2 ft²**

IDEAL CREW WEIGHT: **265+ lb**

A large rotomolded dinghy designed by Ian Howlett in 2004, the deep, spacious cockpit is ideal for a family.

TOPAZ VIBE

NUMBER OF CREW: **2**

LENGTH: **12.3 ft** BEAM: **5.2 ft**

MINIMUM HULL WEIGHT: **154 lb**

MAINSAIL: **73.7 ft²**

JIB: **23.8 ft²**

ASYMMETRIC SPINNAKER: **90.5 ft²**

IDEAL CREW WEIGHT: **165–330 lb**

A smaller sister to the Xenon, this was designed by Ian Howell and Rob White in 2006.

TOPAZ XENON

NUMBER OF CREW: **2**

LENGTH: **14.8 ft** BEAM: **6.6 ft**

MINIMUM HULL WEIGHT: **260 lb**

MAINSAIL: **129 ft²**

JIB: **37.7 ft²**

ASYMMETRIC SPINNAKER: **137.2 ft²**

IDEAL CREW WEIGHT: **220–308 lb**

A two-man rotomolded dinghy designed by Ian Howlett in 2005, this performance-oriented class is raced in the annual Champion of Champions event for dinghy sailors.

Asymmetric spinnakers and skiffs

The introduction of asymmetric spinnakers in the early 1990s helped to make dinghy sailing more accessible than ever as a high-performance sport, boosted to the maximum by developments from Australian skiffs.

Asymmetric spinnakers

The principal attraction of an asymmetric spinnaker is that it is simple and a lot of fun to use. Unlike a conventional spinnaker, the asymmetric is an easily handled sail that is launched and retrieved from a chute in the front of the boat.

It is relatively straightforward to jibe (the crew simply allows the sail to move around the front of the boat before pulling in the sheet on the new side) and it provides unparallelled performance on a reaching course with the wind blowing across the boat, acting as an oversized free-flying jib attached to a pole that extends from the bow.

An asymmetric spinnaker is not designed for sailing directly downwind like a symmetrical spinnaker. Instead the crew have to sail a series of downwind reaches, making a zigzag course from jibe to jibe, using the apparent wind angle to ensure optimum speed.

Skiffs

The skiff concept was developed in Australia, where extreme high-performance designs such as the Sydney Harbour 18s combined narrow, flat-bottomed, lightweight hulls with hugely powerful oversized rigs and the use of racks and trapezes to keep the boat upright. Skiffs are designed to plane upwind and offwind, sailing from jibe to jibe on a reaching course. The size of the rig and sails reflects the performance of the boat and ability of the crew, topped by the 18-foot (5.5 m) skiff, which has three crew powered by unlimited sail area!

Skiffs and asymmetric dinghies

B14

NUMBER OF CREW: **2**
LENGTH: **14.8 ft** BEAM: **10 feet**
MINIMUM HULL WEIGHT: **137 lb**
MAINSAIL AND JIB: **185 ft²**
ASYMMETRIC SPINNAKER: **314 ft²**
IDEAL CREW WEIGHT: **298–364 lb**

Designed by Julian Bethwaite in 1984, the B14 was billed as the fastest no-trapeze, twin-crew dinghy in the world. It owes its performance to the combination of a very light hull with small wetted surface area and a large powerful rig, including a huge spinnaker. Wide aluminum racks provide the crew with enough leverage to keep it upright.

49ER

NUMBER OF CREW: **2**
LENGTH: **14.8 ft** BEAM: **10 ft**
MINIMUM HULL WEIGHT: **137 lb**
MAINSAIL AND JIB: **185 ft²**
ASYMMETRIC SPINNAKER: **314 ft²**
IDEAL CREW WEIGHT: **298–364 lb**

Julian Bethwaite designed the 49er as a new twin-trapeze Olympic class in 1995. This superb skiff requires an athletic and hugely experienced crew, working together to keep the boat under control. The lightweight hull is built in epoxy foam sandwich, with "wings" to increase leverage. The oversize rig is fitted with carbon spars. To keep 49er crews on their toes, a new bigger rig was launched for the 49er in 2008.

RS200

NUMBER OF CREW: **2**

LENGTH: **13.1 ft** BEAM: **6 ft**

MINIMUM HULL WEIGHT: **172 lb**

MAINSAIL AND JIB: **124 ft²**

ASYMMETRIC SPINNAKER: **89 ft²**

IDEAL CREW WEIGHT: **254–320 lb**

An asymmetric hiking dinghy designed by Phil Morrison in 1995 as a smaller sister to the RS400, this highly maneuverable boat provides excellent one-design racing for twin-crew teams.

29ER

NUMBER OF CREW: **2**

LENGTH: **14.4 ft** BEAM: **5.6 ft**

MINIMUM HULL WEIGHT: **154 lb**

MAINSAIL AND JIB: **129 ft²**

ASYMMETRIC SPINNAKER: **172 ft²**

IDEAL CREW WEIGHT: **231–309 lb**

29ER XX MAINSAIL AND JIB: **161 ft²**

ASYMMETRIC SPINNAKER: **205 ft²**

IDEAL CREW WEIGHT: **265 lb**

Julian Bethwaite designed this smaller, lower cost skiff in 1997, built in fiberglass foam sandwich. The 29er is fitted with a single trapeze and raced as an international youth class for teenagers. It's a challenging boat,

easy to capsize and tricky to sail well. The 29er XX (launched in 2005), has exactly the same hull but a much bigger rig, twin trapezes and an all-carbon mast.

LASER 2000

NUMBER OF CREW: **2**

LENGTH: **14.6 ft** BEAM: **6.1 ft**

MINIMUM HULL WEIGHT: **220 lb**

MAINSAIL AND JIB: **127 ft²**

ASYMMETRIC SPINNAKER: **106 ft²**

IDEAL CREW WEIGHT: **265–397 lb**

Phil Morrison designed the Laser 2000 in 1998. A stable fiberglass dinghy which is comfortable and easy to handle at novice level, its performance can be transformed by a big asymmetric spinnaker on a windy day. It's equally popular for learning to sail and racing.

RS800

NUMBER OF CREW: **2**

LENGTH: **15.7 ft** BEAM: **6.2–9.5 ft**

MINIMUM HULL WEIGHT: **137 lb**

MAINSAIL AND JIB: **178 ft²**

ASYMMETRIC SPINNAKER: **226 ft²**

IDEAL CREW WEIGHT: **275–353 lb**

Designed by Phil Morrison in 1999 as a twin- or single-trapeze

skiff with racks and an asymmetric spinnaker. The design was updated in 2007, with a revised cockpit layout and modified rig for female crews.

RS700

NUMBER OF CREW: **1**

LENGTH: **15.4 ft** BEAM: **6.3–7.6 ft**

MINIMUM HULL WEIGHT: **123 lb**

MAINSAIL: **138 ft²**

ASYMMETRIC SPINNAKER: **172 ft²**

IDEAL CREW WEIGHT: **231–309 lb**

A single-handed skiff designed in 2000 by Nick Peters and Alex Newton, the fiberglass foam sandwich hull has aluminum racks to increase leverage. Variable width is used for equal competition for different crew weights.

INTERNATIONAL CANOE

NUMBER OF CREW: **1**

LENGTH: **17 ft** BEAM: **3.3 ft**

MINIMUM HULL WEIGHT: **110 lb**

MAINSAIL AND JIB: **108 ft²**

ASYMMETRIC SPINNAKER: **Unlimited**

IDEAL CREW WEIGHT: **132–187 lb**

Despite the fact that its design dates from 1948, the International Canoe is one of the most extreme dinghies. The sailor perches on the end of a long sliding seat to keep the very narrow hull upright. Modern International Canoes are mainly carbon fiber to a standard design, with an unlimited size asymmetric spinnaker.

RS500

NUMBER OF CREW: **2**

LENGTH: **14.2 ft** BEAM: **5.2 ft**

MINIMUM HULL WEIGHT: **170 lb**

MAINSAIL AND JIB: **102 ft²**

ASYMMETRIC SPINNAKER: **151 ft²**

IDEAL CREW WEIGHT: **145–220 lb**

This single-trapeze, double-handed dinghy was designed by Phil Morrison in 2006 to provide equally attractive skiff-style performance for teenagers or adults, with a reasonable degree of stability.

Rigging a simple dinghy

A small dinghy such as a Topper, Pico or Laser has the simplest possible rig that is very quick to assemble. Rigging for all these dinghies follows the same procedure, with slight variations.

Rigging a simple dinghy

Unpack the components
- Sleeved two-part mast made of aluminum or fiberglass tube.
- Boom made of aluminum tube.
- Sail made of Dacron with an optional set of plastic battens.
- Daggerboard, rudder, tiller and tiller extension.
- Ropeset including downhaul and outhaul lines for the mainsail, boom vang, traveler line and mainsheet with blocks.

Assemble the mast and sail
- Place the boat on the beach or on its dolly, angled so that the bow is pointing directly into the wind.
- Push the two halves of the mast together. Avoid getting sand or grit in the joint, as this may make it difficult to pull the mast apart.
- Unfold the sail and lay it out on the ground. Align the luff tube or sock along the edge of the sail with the wind direction, with the bottom corner (tack) closest to the wind and the top corner (head) furthest from the wind.
- The sail on a dinghy like the Laser needs three stiff battens to support the roach (see pages 16–17). Push each batten, thin end first, into its pocket in the leech, ensuring the outer end is locked into the sail.
- Pull the luff tube down over the mast. Note that unlike most other luff-tube dinghies, the Topper also has a main halyard, which attaches to the top of the sail and passes down through the luff tube.

Put the mast in the boat
- Roll the sail so that it is tightly wrapped round the mast.
- Lift the mast vertically then lower its mast base into the deck socket. Both the Pico and Topper have a locking system to hold the mast in place.

Complete the rigging
- Attach the boom to the mast, just below the tack of the sail. The Pico and Topper both have a plastic jaw that fits over the mast. The Laser has a more conventional gooseneck pin that fits into the mast.
- Attach the traveler line to the stern of the boat.
- Attach one end of the mainsheet to the boom. Pull the mainsheet through the blocks on the boom, traveler line and cockpit floor. Secure the free end of the mainsheet with a figure-eight knot.
- Making sure the boat is pointing into the wind, unfurl the sail and attach the outhaul line to the clew. This will hold the boom in a horizontal position beneath the foot of the sail.
- Pull down and tension the downhaul (also known as a

Below (left to right): **1.** Sort out all the components before you start rigging the boat. **2.** Most mainsails need battens. **3.** Make sure the battens are securely locked into their pockets. **4.** Pull the luff tube of the sail down over the mast, and ensure the base of the mast is free of dirt. **5.** Lift the mast vertically. If it's windy you may need an extra pair of hands to keep it steady. **6.** Drop the mast into its deck socket. **7.** The mainsheet is connected to the traveler line at the transom.

cunningham) line, which is attached to the tack of the sail.
- Attach the boom vang between the mast and boom.

Ready to go
- Lay the daggerboard in the cockpit, ensuring it is attached to the shock-cord retainer, which will prevent it from falling out of the boat.
- Drop the rudder onto the stainless steel pintles (pins) on the stern of the boat. The rudder must lock on to the pintles so that it can't fall off in a capsize.
- Insert the tiller into the rudder head, ensuring it is free to move from side to side beneath the mainsheet traveler line. Attach the tiller extension.

- Make sure the drain plug and any drainage hatches are secure.
- Tension the outhaul, downhaul and boom vang to remove wrinkles from the sail.

Below: **Attach and tension the downhaul, outhaul and boom vang which will help control the shape of the mainsail.**

Rigging a twin-crew dinghy

Most dinghies specifically designed to be sailed by two crew have a more complex rig supported by wire shrouds and a forestay. Rigging is similar for all twin-crew boats, but there are many variations in the process for different designs.

Twin-crew dinghy rigging

Putting up the mast

On most boats the mast of a twin-crew dinghy can be left up for the whole season. It only needs to be lowered if the dinghy is being road trailed or put into winter storage.

Putting up the mast normally requires two people. Depending on the boat, the mast may range from very light (especially carbon) to quite heavy. Make sure that shrouds, forestay and any trapeze wires are untangled.

- Lift up the mast and place its base on the mast step, which may be located at deck or cockpit floor level. Some dinghies have a mast gate, or belt and screw, which will lock the mast in position while shrouds and forestay are attached.
- If there is no mast gate, one person must hold the mast steady while the other attaches the two shrouds to adjustable fittings (chain plates) on the sides of the boat.

- Attach the wire forestay to the chain plate. Some dinghies have a conventional wire forestay, which attaches to a chain plate on the bow. Others rely on a wire inside the luff of the jib as the forestay, which holds up the mast, so a length of rope can act as a temporary forestay before the jib is attached.
- Many dinghies have a roller furling jib. The tack (bottom corner) of the jib is attached by a shackle to the roller on the bow.
- The head of the sail is attached to a furling swivel on the end of the jib halyard, which is pulled up the mast. The jib can be furled when not in use.
- Pull down hard on the halyard, either using a multi-purchase block or lever system. This produces rigid tension on the jib luff and prevents it from being blown into a curved shape.

Rigging the mainsail

Make sure the boat is secure on its dolly with the bow pointing directly into the wind.

- Place the rolled mainsail in the cockpit so that the luff (identified by its thick "bolt line" edge) is next to the mast.
- Unroll the mainsail and insert the battens. Lock them securely.
- Attach the main halyard to the head of the sail. Pull on the halyard and feed the bolt line into the slot on the mast.
- One person should pull the halyard while the other feeds the bolt line into the slot, ensuring it doesn't jam.
- Pull the mainsail to the top of the mast and secure the halyard.
- Undo the boom vang so it is slack while hoisting the mail sail.

Below (left to right): **1. Step the mast and attach the shrouds and forestay. 2. The RS500 shown here has an adjustable forestay. 3. Attach the luff of the jib to the forestay. 4. Attach the halyard to the head of the jib. 5. Pull up the jib halyard until** it is taut. **6. Unroll the mainsail. 7. Attach the halyard, feed the bolt rope into the mast slot and start pulling up the halyard. 8. As it goes up, make sure the bolt rope feeds into the mast slot. Lock the halyard when the sail can go no higher. Make sure** the boom vang is released to allow the mainsail to be fully raised.

Rigging the boom

✪ The boom is attached to the mast by a "gooseneck" fitting. It will be held in a horizontal position when the mainsail is raised. The angle of the boom is controlled by a kicking strap that pulls down or a GNAV (reverse "vang"), which pushes down against the sail.

✪ A center mainsheet connects twin blocks on the boom to a jamming block in the cockpit floor where it is led through a jamming cleat. This allows the helm to leave the mainsheet in a locked position.

Attaching the foils

✪ The rudder slides down on pintles mounted on the transom and should be locked in position.

✪ The tiller is inserted into the rudder head, where a pin may be used to lock it in position. The tiller extension can be attached with a twist-grip fitting.

✪ The daggerboard should be laid in the cockpit, ready for use by the crew. If the boat is fitted with a centerboard, it must be fully retracted.

Final rigging

✪ Attach jib sheets to the clew of the jib and lead them through blocks or fairleads on either side of the boat.

✪ Tension the downhaul and outhaul lines to remove creases for the mainsail. Apply sufficient boom vang tension to prevent the boom lifting, or undo it fully if conditions are windy during the launch.

Below: **The downhaul is used to tension the luff of the mainsail and can be adjusted while sailing.**

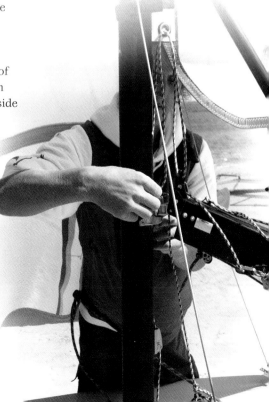

Rigging a catamaran

The "platform" of a catamaran, formed by the hulls, beams and trampoline, is normally left fully assembled. Raising or lowering the mast for trailing or storage is straightforward, but requires two people to pull and push it upright due to the extra weight of its elliptical-shaped spar.

Raising the mast

Make sure the catamaran is level, either resting on its trailer or on the ground. Two people will be needed to raise the mast — due to the elliptical wing shape on a cat, it tends to be considerably heavier than on a dinghy. Make sure that shrouds, forestay and trapeze wires are not tangled.

- ✪ Lay the mast across the two beams with the mast base pointing forward.
- ✪ Attach the two shrouds to shroud plates on each hull.
- ✪ Remove the security pin from the mast base, which is then locked onto the mast step ball, in the middle of the forward beam.
- ✪ With the mast base secure, one person can walk the mast upright, lifting it hand over hand, while the other guides it and keeps it steady by pulling on the forestay.

✪ When the mast is upright, the forestay is attached to the chain plate or roller-furler on the wire bridle which is connected to the bows of both hulls.

Tensioning the rig

Most cats have one or two trapeze wires on both sides of the boat. Each wire has a trapeze ring on the end. A shock-cord and line connects the trapeze ring to the boat, ensuring the trapeze wire stays taut when not being used. Cats perform best with the mast raked back at an angle of about 10 degrees; trapeze wires can be used to tension the rig on land.

- ✪ One person pulls back on the trapeze wire on one side, while the other person moves the shroud further aft on the chain plate.
- ✪ Repeat on the other side.

Attaching rudders and tillers

Catamarans have a separate rudder on each hull. It is quite time-consuming to attach or detach rudders, so they are generally left on for the season. The tillers on each rudder are connected by a longitudinal tiller bar, which slots down over a pin at each end.

- ✪ Fix the rudders with conventional dinghy pintles, or secure by a full-length stainless steel pin designed to cope with heavier loads.
- ✪ The tiller bar has an adjustable-length mechanism to ensure that both rudder blades are parallel. You can normally judge this by eye, or measure the distance between the leading and trailing edges of each blade.

Cat rigging

Hoisting the mainsail

The mainsail of a cat has full-length battens to maintain the shape of the sail under heavy load.

✪ Unroll the sail and tension each batten to remove wrinkles before hoisting the sail.

✪ Attach the main halyard and feed the head and bolt rope into the slot in the trailing edge of the sail. One person will need to feed the bolt rope into the slot while the other pulls on the halyard. Due to full-length battens in the sail, it may feel quite heavy and difficult to pull to the top of the mast.

✪ Most cats have a system that locks the head of the sail to the top of the mast. Pull the sail up as far as it will go, and then pull it down by a half inch or so until it locks, either with a stainless steel ring (which drops over a peg) or a ferrule (which jams against a pair of jaws). Luff tension is vital for best performance on a cat and is provided by a multi-purchase downhaul.

Below: **A fully powered-up cat has heavy loads on its rig and rudders. Make sure everything is perfect before you set sail.**

Attaching the mainsheet

✪ Attach the multi-purchase mainsheet to the rear beam and lead it through the traveler control. This allows a continuous control line to be used for both the mainsheet and the traveler adjustment.

Below (left to right): **1. Lift the mast with shrouds attached. 2. Use the trapezes to tension the shrouds. 3. Unroll the sail and attach the halyard. 4. One crew pulls the sail up while the other guides it into the mast. 5. Make sure the mainsheet is untangled. 6. Always check the drain plugs. 7. A pin holds the tiller extension onto the tiller bar — make sure it is secure.**

Rig controls

Sailing a dinghy requires more than just steering the boat. There are also rig controls, which are all operated by lines. The primary control is the mainsheet, which adjusts the angle of the mainsail, while secondary controls such as the cunningham and kicking strap change its shape.

Putting shape into sails

A mainsail is not a simple triangle of cloth with three straight sides. To provide best performance, the sail must have an aerodynamic curved shape. All the individual panels that are joined together to create the sail are cut with curved sides to promote the correct shape.

❂ The leech has a curved "roach" (the area outside a straight line between tack and head) to increase the size and power of the sail. Battens must support this area.
❂ The foot of the mainsail on a modern dinghy is only attached to the boom at the tack and clew, allowing a slightly curved shape that helps wind flow across the bottom panel of the sail. The mainsail on older dinghies may have a straight foot that is attached to a slot along the full length of the boom.
❂ The luff is cut with a curve, designed to match the way the mast bends when you go sailing.

Managing sail shape

As soon as you pull the mainsheet in, the mast will start to bend backward and sideways. The sophistication of the mast and rig controls will determine how much control you have over the way it bends and affects sail shape. An unstayed mast made from parallel-sided aluminum or fiberglass tube will provide minimal control; a fully stayed mast made from tapered aluminum or carbon fiber with varying wall thickness can provide a high degree of control, with spreaders, lower and upper shrouds helping to dictate the degree and direction of bend.

Above: **The mast of this Xenon bends in a curve that pulls the mainsail into a flatter shape, which helps to depower the sail in stronger winds.**

What are rig controls for?

You do not want to go sailing with exactly the same power in light, moderate and strong winds. In light winds you need more power to drive the boat; in stronger winds you need less power to control the boat and keep it upright. This is particularly important when sailing toward the apparent wind on a beating or

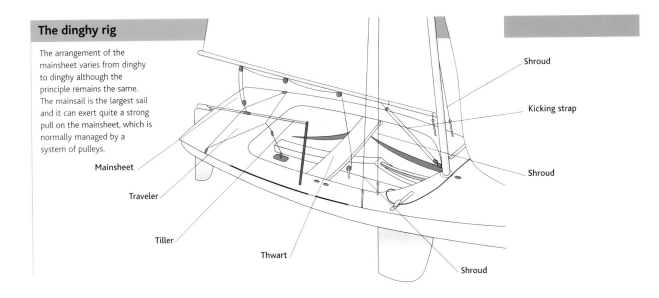

The dinghy rig

The arrangement of the mainsheet varies from dinghy to dinghy although the principle remains the same. The mainsail is the largest sail and it can exert quite a strong pull on the mainsheet, which is normally managed by a system of pulleys.

Mainsheet

Traveler

Tiller

Thwart

Shroud

Kicking strap

Shroud

Shroud

Left: **Too much power! For a quick solution, the helmsman should ease off the mainsheet. For a longer term solution, the crew should pull down the cunnigham to flatten the sail and open the leech.**

Above: **The modern Finn has a highly sophisticated rig with a carbon mast. Sail shape can quickly be changed from flat to full with a closed or open leech.**

mainsail while the boat is sailing and can be operated by dual control lines led to each side of the boat. Pulling down on the cunningham bends the mast, moving sail draft (curvature) forward and opening the leech, making it easier to handle in stronger winds.

On a catamaran the cunningham is replaced by a multi-purchase downhaul control that is used to bend the mast and flatten the sail.

Boom vang

The boom vang, or kicking strap, is a control line between mast and boom. Its original role was to hold the boom down at a horizontal angle, preventing it from riding up when sailing downwind with the

reaching course. When sailing downwind with the wind, full sail power can be used in most conditions.

Rig controls allow you to increase or decrease the amount of fullness (draft) in the mainsail, move the fullness forward or backward, and increase or decrease the way the mainsail twists from the bottom to the top of its leech.

Mainsheet and jib sheets

The sheets control the angle of each sail to the wind. Pulling the mainsheet in as hard as possible will also tighten the leech, which helps the boat point higher to windward in light or moderate winds.

Cunningham

The cunningham is a downhaul control line attached to the luff of the mainsail, approximately 12 inches (30 cm) above the boom. It is named after Briggs Swift Cunningham II, who skippered the *Columbia* to victory in the 1958 America's Cup. The cunningham allows the crew to adjust the amount of leech tension in the

> **TIP**
>
> When you hoist the mainsail in the boat park, you have to pull the curved luff up a straight mast. This explains why the bolt line may not slide up the mast as easily as you might expect.

mainsheet eased. As a sail control, the boom vang plays an important role in regulating sail twist, bending the mast and tensioning the leech.

Below: **Perfect trim. Helm and crew are sailing this Merlin Rocket to windward beautifully. They adjust the sail shape as a perfect balance to their weight.**

Dual control lines can be led to both sides of the boat for instant adjustment while sailing. On a catamaran, the boom is held down by mainsheet tension at the back of the boat. A boom vang is not required.

What is a gnav?

Gnav is vang spelled backward. It performs exactly the same function as a boom vang, using an aluminum strut between the mast and boom. Unlike a boom vang, the gnav is above the boom, which has the major advantage of leaving the forward area beneath the boom unobstructed. The angle of the gnav is adjusted by sliding it along a track mounted on the top of the boom.

Below: **The sail of this Phantom provides a beautiful foil for light winds with minimal cunningham and boom vang tension.**

Above: **The gnav is an upside-down boom vang that frees up the area below the boom directly behind the mast.**

Outhaul

The outhaul control line is led from the clew of the mainsail along the boom. If it is tightened, the outhaul will flatten the lower section of the mainsail and move the area of maximum draft further aft. The outhaul is not so easy to adjust while sailing and plays a minor role in the sail control of many boats.

What is sail twist?

The leech of a sail will twist from the bottom to the top. If you look at a sail from behind, the bottom panel is always twisted at a closer angle to the wind than the top panel.

When to use sail controls

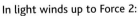

In light winds up to Force 2:

- ✪ No cunningham and boom vang tension are needed
- ✪ Outhaul can be tensioned to promote better airflow over the flattened lower part of the sail.

Adjusting the amount of twist is useful for maintaining control of the boat. The top part of the mainsail can be transformed into a flat blade, which effectively creates no power and greatly reduces the heeling of the boat in stronger winds.

The amount of sail twist is governed by mainsheet and boom vang tension. Tightening the mainsheet pulls the sail inward at the bottom and downward at the top. The downward pull of the kicking strap is used to provide more precise control over sail twist.

Right: **The slot between jib and mainsail accelerates wind flow. A wider slot makes the rig easier to control as the wind increases.**

TIP

On a catamaran, sail twist can be controlled by using mainsheet tension at different positions on the full-length traveler across the rear beam. This allows the mainsail to be sheeted hard in at any angle to the apparent wind.

oderate winds below Force 3:

oderate amount of boom vang tension can be used promote mainsail leech twist, reducing wer in the top of the sail, making the boat easier hold upright

• cunningham tension is required

e outhaul can be eased to provide maximum wer at the bottom of the mainsail.

In strong winds over Force 4:

✪ The object is to completely depower the top of the mainsail for sailing toward the wind

✪ Maximum boom vang, cunningham and outhaul tension is used to bend the mast. This stretches and flattens the sail, moving all power forward. The top half of the sail twists open and becomes a flat, powerless blade aligned with the wind.

Where to sail

Launching off a sandy beach onto smooth water with a fair wind and warm sun sounds like sailing perfection. But everything is not always as it appears. The sand may be too soft to push your boat to the water, the water may shelve steeply from the shoreline, rocks may be hidden beneath the surface, or perhaps there's no one to help if things go wrong!

Safety cover

Always sail with safety cover when you are learning, and, if possible, when you are experienced as well. Safety cover should be provided by a qualified safety boat driver who knows how to handle a rescue boat in close proximity to a dinghy, which may be capsized with crew in the water. Beware of rescue by a well-meaning but inexperienced powerboat driver: an experienced powerboat driver will be able to manage the propeller and the movement of the boat without inflicting injury.

Golden rules for safety boat drivers are:

- The driver must always wear a kill cord, which will cut the ignition if he or she leaves the controls.
- The engine gearshift must be in neutral if the boat is anywhere near people in the water. Better still, turn off the ignition.

Sailing clubs

Join a sailing club and enjoy the following benefits:

- The club will be situated in a good sailing location. If you have problems with rigging, launching, landing or simply don't know if it is safe to sail, other members can help.
- The club will provide storage for your boat and changing facilities. Most clubs will also provide catering and organize off-water social events.
- The club will organize regular racing and sailing courses for its members. This is a great way to improve and to make friends.
- The club will provide reliable safety boat cover during events.

Learn to sail on vacation

Beach club vacations with organized dinghy sailing provide great opportunities. You can learn to sail in a warm location with lessons from professionals. You can try a wide range of equipment with a safety boat on hand. Be aware though that the different vacation operators vary greatly. For instance, a specialized sailing company will likely provide top levels of equipment and lessons suitable for all standards. Beach club vacations

Below: **Some facilities have slipways and pontoons.**

Above: **A shallow launch ramp with a smooth surface clear of seaweed or slime is the easiest place to launch and retrieve a dinghy.**

Below: **There's nothing better than sailing where it's sunny and warm. These sailors are waiting for the afternoon breeze.**

cater to a broader recreational market and are not likely to have the same choice of dinghy or cat sailing gear.

Warm weather and a relaxed atmosphere can give a great introduction to sailing. Dinghy sailing back home may be different and more challenging, with tidal waters and difficult weather, but you can rest assured it will be just as much fun.

Safety boat cover

You should find quality safety boat cover:
- ✪ On sailing vacations at beach clubs and similar operations.
- ✪ On a sailing course staged by a school, club or activities center.
- ✪ During a regatta or organized sailing event.
- ✪ During organized racing by a sailing club.

Right: **Avoid sailing without safety cover — you never know when it might be useful!**

Inland and coastal sailing

You can sail a dinghy inland (such as on a lake or reservoir) or on an open sea. Sailing inland has the benefit of fresh water, but the wind may be unpredictable. Sailing on the sea can provide unlimited space, but the tide and waves make conditions more challenging.

Inland water

Advantages:

✓ It is very pleasant to sail on clean fresh water, which gives the boat and its equipment a free wash instead of leaving sticky, salty residue.

✓ No sandy beach also means no sand in your boat or in your sailing equipment.

✓ A small lake or reservoir is comparatively safe, with a compact area for safety cover. If you get into trouble and can't make it back, your boat will be blown to the nearest leeward shore.

✓ The water level won't drop and rise due to tides and there won't be tidal flow. (This isn't the case when sailing on a river, which may have strong tidal flow and rise and fall.)

✓ Lakes and reservoirs used for sailing are often in beautiful areas, so they can provide great sailing with stunning scenery.

✓ With limited space, inland sailing locations are often excellent for tactical racing.

✓ If you live inland, the perfect stretch of inland water may be close to home.

Left: **A big advantage of inland water is no tide. The water will generally be at the same level when you sail back to shore!**

Below: **Inland sailing venues can provide huge areas and stunning locations.**

Coastal water

Advantages:

✓ There are no limits on how far you can sail, apart from common sense and practicality. There is also plenty of space without being hemmed in by other boats.

✓ Sailing in a harbor, bay or along the coast provides plenty of variety and interest.

✓ The challenge of tides will spice up your sailing.

✓ Open water with waves is very enjoyable for the more experienced, high-performance sailor.

✓ Sandy beaches can be beautiful places when you launch and land in a boat.

Disadvantages:

✗ Sand and salt spray get in your boat and in your clothes.

✗ Tides can provide a major challenge. When there is a high tidal rise and fall, sailing access may be limited. If you get the timing wrong, there may be a very long way to drag your boat over sand or mud.

✗ Sea conditions will change with the tide. At high tide, there may be tricky waves breaking on the beach. You may not be able to sail against strong tidal flow, which will sweep your boat in the wrong direction.

✗ An onshore wind will pile up waves on the beach, making it difficult to launch or land. An offshore wind can be dangerous: light and flukey inshore, but blowing hard offshore.

✗ Rescue cover will be limited, unless you are sailing in a club event or with an organized group.

✗ Most coastal harbors have lots of traffic, and require knowledge of buoys, navigational channels, markers and shipping lane regulations.

Disadvantages:

✗ You may run out of space. High-performance dinghies need large areas of water to perform.

✗ Unless you sail well away from the lakeshore, the wind will be affected by hills, trees, buildings and any other obstructions on the windward shore (where the wind is blowing from), which may create a gusty, shifty pattern. A small lake surrounded by trees will have rapid changes in wind speed and direction, but many sailors enjoy that for tactical racing.

✗ There may be a muddy shoreline and mud where you launch. The water may not be perfectly clean, with the chance of algae and other growth.

✗ In winter, freshwater lakes and reservoirs can become very cold. Drysuits should be worn; capsize is best avoided — if possible!

Below: **Salt spray must be washed off your boat and out of your clothes when you come back to shore.**

TIP

Sailing on fresh water is cleaner but can be colder than sailing on salt water!

Launching a dinghy

There are a number of factors to consider when launching. Which is the best direction for the wind to be blowing? Do you need to think about tides? What surface is best to launch your boat from? Are there any dangers to avoid?

Offshore wind

The wind is blowing away from the shore. This will tend to flatten any waves, so the water appears flat. Close to the shore the wind may be light and gusty as it blows past buildings, trees and other obstacles. Further out it will get stronger the further from the shore you sail. This can be a real danger if you capsize or cannot control the boat. You will be blown out into stronger winds and rougher water, making it more difficult to safely get back to shore.

Onshore wind

The wind is blowing onto the shore. In any strength of wind this will push up waves, which break on the beach. Launching will be difficult, as you have to beat away from the shore, with each wave driving the boat back. Landing may be difficult, particularly if breaking waves are big enough to roll the boat over.

Cross-shore wind

This is the perfect wind direction for launching or landing your boat. The wind is blowing from the side, so you can sail out on a beam reach, tack or jibe, then sail back in on a beam reach.

Tidal effects

There may be a big difference between launching and landing at different states of the tide. At low water, there may be a lot of sand or mud to pull your boat across. At high water, the sea may have

reached a steeply shelving part of the beach where it is impossible to hold the boat while standing in the water.

Left: **Cross-shore wind, blowing parallel to the shore, is perfect for launching and landing. But deep water could make it difficult to hold on to this Hobie 16.**

Below: **The wind here is onshore. The crew will push the bows away before getting in, ensuring their Laser 2000 avoids the moored dinghies.**

TIP

Be courteous to other people on the beach, swimming or in the launch area. They may not understand that you are struggling with the boat.

When you prepare to launch, be aware of which way the tide is flowing and when it will change. If the tide flows in the same direction as the wind, the sea will be relatively smooth. If the tide flows against the wind, the sea will be heaped up into short, uncomfortable waves.

Left: **When the tide goes out, there may be a lot of mud. Time your sailing accordingly! Despite the low tide, these Taz sailors have sufficiently solid ground to push their boats down to the water on dollies.**

Pulling a dinghy overland

Pulling a light boat across hard sand is easy; pulling a heavy boat across soft sand may be impossible. If the dolly wheels start to sink, get more helping hands. Gravel is very difficult to pull a dinghy over. The boat must be firmly secured to its dolly. Rubber mats or tracks are laid down by sailing clubs to overcome this problem. Concrete is perfect, but becomes slippery if seaweed is not cleared away. Wear sailing boots or shoes for grip; beware of slipping and falling under the boat.

Obstructions and dangers

When launching a dinghy beware of the following:

❂ Keep clear of swimmers when launching or landing your boat.

❂ Watch out for moored boats.

❂ Look out for small powercraft: a jet-ski driver may be going too fast with no comprehension of "rules of the road."

❂ Check for underwater obstructions (such as a rock or reef) that may be covered by the tide. Consult a chart or ask a local sailor with experience.

❂ Make sure the rudder and tiller are clear of seaweed or other obstacles.

Left: **Places to land and launch can get busy. Never barge in; offer to help with other people's dollies.**

Leaving the shore

Are you ready to sail? Launching a dinghy with two crew has the advantage that one crew can hold the boat while the other pulls the dolly back to the shore. If you are launching single-handed, seek help from a volunteer who doesn't mind getting their wet feet!

Ready to sail

Rig the dinghy as close to the water as possible, with the bows pointing into wind. If the wind is light, it should be possible to pull the dinghy to the water's edge with the mainsail hoisted. Beware of the dinghy blowing over as you pull it down the boat slip or beach; the bow must be kept towards the wind, with the launch crew ready to hold down the boat's windward side if necessary. The mainsheet must be uncleated so that it can run free, and the kicking trap loosened.

Before you launch, make sure the boat is correctly rigged, with everything secure and stowed. Don't forget the drain or plug, which is usually in the transom of the boat. This must be securely tightened. Make sure the rudder blade is locked in the fully lifted position. If possible, always fit the rudder before launch. It can be very difficult to engage the pintles when the boat is swinging around on the water.

Launching with two crew

When launching with two crew:
- Use the dolly to pull the dinghy into deep enough water where it will slide off and float — normally about knee height for the crew.
- One crew should take the dolly ashore. Leave it in a safe place above the tidal waterline, without being an obstruction for people on the shore.
- The other crew must hold the boat. If it is a stable design, you can hold it by the bow and let it blow downwind. If it is unstable, like a skiff, you may need to hold it by the windward shroud, keeping it pointing at a slight angle toward the wind.
- The crew should be first to get on board, either over the windward side or over the transom of an open cockpit boat.
- Standing or sitting in the middle of the boat, the crew should partly lower the centerboard or partly insert the daggerboard, which will be required to prevent the boat going sideways once the sails are sheeted in.

Above: **With the wind blowing onto the shore, the crew pull their RS Vision bows-first into the water until it is deep enough to slide off the dolly.**

Using the launching dolly

Launch the dinghy on a shore or boat slip with a launching dolly. When in the water get your crew to hold the boat by the bow and to wind, while you climb in and hoist the sails.

Launch into the water

You can also launch the dinghy stern-first, whereby the dinghy will swing off with its stern downwind. Stern-first can also ease the removal of the dolly.

Remove the launching dolly and return it to the dolly park

TIP

If you sail a popular class, all dollies may look much the same. Mark your dolly so that you can identify it every time: a strip of colored insulating tape wrapped around one of the bars works well.

Above: **The crew of this RS800 inserts the tip of the daggerboard in its case, while the helm steadies the boat by holding the windward rack.**

Below: **When you leave the shore, it's vital to get the rudder fully down as soon as possible. Check everything is working.**

- ✪ Depending on the depth of water available, the crew should also partly lower the rudder blade.
- ✪ When the crew is ready, the helm pushes the boat into a beam reach position, grabs the tiller extension to control the rudder, and gets in over the windward side. At the same time, the crew balances the boat and unfurls the jib, sheeting in to help the dinghy bear away and gather speed.
- ✪ As soon as the boat has sailed into deep enough water, the helm must lower the rudder blade and lock it in the fully down position. It is not possible to steer the boat properly with the rudder blade partly lifted, as this will create very heavy weather helm. The crew must also lower the centerboard or daggerboard to the fully down position for maximum control.

Launching single-handed

If you are alone, get someone to help retrieve the dolly while you hold the boat.

- ✪ Pull the boat into thigh-deep water, holding the bow into the wind. When you are ready to go, move quickly to the back of the boat and push the rudder halfway down. Then grab the side of the boat just behind the mast and push the daggerboard halfway down.
- ✪ Push the bow away from the wind so that the boat is on a beam-reaching course.
- ✪ Step up into the cockpit, while pushing away with your back foot.
- ✪ Sheet in the mainsail to move away from the shore. As soon as the water is deep enough, let go the mainsheet to slow down the boat and push both daggerboard and rudder all the way down.

Sailing away from the shore

If the wind is blowing cross-shore, you should have no problems sailing away on a beam reach. If the wind is blowing more offshore or onshore, different techniques may be required for a smooth getaway.

Launching in an offshore wind
The main problem is that with the boat pointing toward the beach, you need enough space to turn around without hitting the shore. Make sure there is plenty of space to leeward, so the boat can turn in an arc. Decide whether turning to port or starboard will get you away from the shore quickest.

- Hoist the mainsail onshore. With the wind blowing from behind you, push the boat stern-first down the beach. Ensure the rudder blade is locked fully upright.
- Push the trolley into deep enough water to slide the boat off. The crew should hold the bow, while the helm gets on board and lowers the rudder to the fully down position: this should be possible with the stern in deeper water.
- The centerboard or daggerboard should be partly lowered to ensure the boat will pivot

following a change in rudder direction. With the board up, the boat would just slide sideways.
- When you are ready to go, the crew must push the bow as far as possible to leeward (away from the wind), jumping on board once the boat begins to accelerate as the wind blows from the side. To help the bow bear away quickly, the helm should unfurl the jib and "back" it by pulling in the windward sheet. The wind blowing against the wrong side of the jib will push the bow away from the shore quickly.
- As soon as the boat is facing away from the shore, let go the windward jib sheet, straighten out your course and sheet in on the new side.

Below: **Make sure everything is ready before you start sailing. Check to see how much space you need to avoid other boats.**

Launching in an onshore wind
It can be tricky to sail away from the shore in an onshore wind, when waves may push your boat back onto the beach.

Check the angle of the boat when the bows point into the wind. If the starboard side of the boat is nearest to the beach, sail away on a starboard tack and vice versa.

- It may be possible to launch the fully rigged boat by pulling the dolly bows-first into the water, if the water isn't too deep.
- Alternatively, you can launch the dinghy stern-first in an onshore wind with the mainsail lowered and jib furled. The crew should push the boat out to the deepest possible water before jumping on board, then hold the bows while the helm climbs on board to hoist the mainsail.
- Before attempting to sail away, lower the rudder and centerboard or daggerboard as far as possible; ideally the rudder should be fully down.

Left: **Wait your turn to leave in an onshore wind, when speed and power are needed to get away.**

✪ Catamarans have a launch dolly with a single axle and two large wheels. Push the dolly under the hulls so that it is at the balance point close to the shrouds.

✪ Launch the cat stern-first. Then sit on each bow to lift the sterns and let the cat slowly sail backward away from the shore. The crew can then climb onto the trampoline and make the turn.

Above: **Cat sailors have a novel way of leaving the shore in an offshore wind — simply sail out backward, with both crew sitting on the bows!**

✪ Keep plenty of power and speed to sail through waves. Turn the bow toward each wave, and then bear away to accelerate as soon as the wave has passed. This will make your passage more comfortable and less bumpy.

Launching a cat

When launching in an offshore wind, it can be difficult to turn the boat without sailing back onto the shore. One way to overcome this is to reverse away from the shore.

What if there's no jib?

A single-handed dinghy won't have a jib to help it turn. Push the bow offwind until it is pointing away from the shore; allow a wide arc to leeward to guarantee completing the turn. Pump the rudder to speed up the turn.

Getting off the shore

Getting away in an offshore wind: Give a shove off and move into water deep enough to put the centerboard or daggerboard and the rudder fully down.

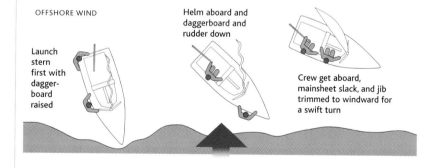

OFFSHORE WIND

Launch stern first with daggerboard raised

Helm aboard and daggerboard and rudder down

Crew get aboard, mainsheet slack, and jib trimmed to windward for a swift turn

Getting away in an onshore wind: With the wind blowing toward the shore you need to move away from the launch place. When you can maneuver, turn the boat and pick up the wind in the sails.

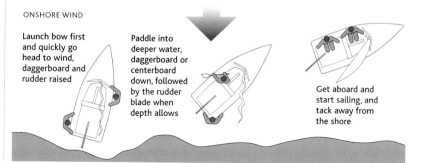

ONSHORE WIND

Launch bow first and quickly go head to wind, daggerboard and rudder raised

Paddle into deeper water, daggerboard or centerboard down, followed by the rudder blade when depth allows

Get aboard and start sailing, and tack away from the shore

Sailing on a reach

Start sailing in light winds up to a maximum of force 3, using a stable, easily handled dinghy. Begin by sailing on a reaching course, with the wind blowing across the boat.

Wind on the beam

A beam reach (with wind blowing at 90 degrees across the boat) provides a great combination of stable and efficient sailing. The wind produces maximum airflow on both sides of the sails, which can be balanced by the crew leaning out to windward. Power from the sails and lift from the centerboard or daggerboard, drive the boat forward instead of sideways, which lessens the amount the boat will heel and allows it to sail faster in the right direction.

Sheeting

Pull the mainsheet and jib sheet just far enough in to stop the sails flapping. Do not oversheet, which will stall the airflow across the sails and reduce power. Telltales on the

Right: **Keep the boat flat when sailing on a reach. It will sail faster and be easier to steer, with less weather helm. Either hike out or ease the mainsheet.**

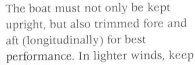

sails should be streaming aft. If you are sailing with mainsail and jib, the lower part of the mainsail next to the mast may be backwinding. This is normal, caused by wind flowing through the slot between main and jib; it will not affect performance. Fair-leads are used to adjust the position of the jib sheets to control the slot.

Trim

The boat must not only be kept upright, but also trimmed fore and aft (longitudinally) for best performance. In lighter winds, keep weight forward to lift the stern and prevent dragging, which will slow the boat down. As the wind increases and the boat accelerates, move weight back. When sailing double-handed, both crew should sit close together on the side of the boat, close to the shrouds.

The joy of planing

In force 3–4 winds the boat should start "planing." A wonderful sensation, it feels as though the boat is skimming across the surface instead of pushing through water. This takes place when the hull leaves its stern wave behind and powers along on top of its bow wave. There is much-increased speed and the wake behind the stern becomes flat. The crew must move back to lift the bow. If the boat drops off the plane (slowing down and the bow dropping) the crew should move forward again. Hiking straight legged helps distribute the center of effort.

Left: **Perfect trim, both sideways and fore and aft. The crew of this National 12 demonstrate how a dinghy should be sailed.**

Keep it upright

Try to sail as upright as possible. When a gust hits, ease the sheets or hike out to prevent the boat heeling. If the boat heels too far:

- It will sail slower, due to the side of the hull dragging in the water.
- It will slide sideways, due to the daggerboard or centerboard providing less resistance.
- It will develop weather helm (the tiller wants to pull away from you) as the rudder blade loses contact with the water.
- It will be a struggle for the crew to control the boat while hanging over the side.

How to hike

Hiking or sitting out is a major feature of dinghy sailing. Your weight provides a counterbalance to wind in the sails tipping the boat. Sit up on the sidedeck and put your feet under the foot straps, with the tips of your boots sticking out the other side. Modern dinghies have good ergonomics that allow you to slide in or out over the side. When the boat heels, drop your body over the side of the boat; the foot straps will ensure that you are secure.

How comfortable it is to hike will depend on your fitness and strength, as well as leg reach from the side of the boat to the foot straps. If you intend to race you will need to take hiking seriously; the more you lean out in a breeze, the faster the boat will go! Hiking shorts are recommended to make this more comfortable.

Above: **Watch the sail and watch your course. If the tiller starts pulling, ease off the mainsheet. The crew of this Comet Treo are enjoying a relaxed fun ride with wind on the beam.**

Below: **Sailing on a well-powered reach is physical. The best sailors really work the boat by constantly moving their bodyweight in and out, fore and aft.**

Left: **Bows flying, crew aft and planing fast. This Streaker lives up to its name with a good dose of speed on a reach.**

Sailing into the wind

If you want to head in the direction from which the wind is blowing, you need to sail the boat as close to the true wind as possible. For novices, "beating to windward" can be the most challenging course.

Above: **Modern dinghies such as the Xenon like to be sailed flat and fast, without "pinching" into the wind.**

TIP

Use both hands when pulling in the mainsheet. It is quicker, more efficient and much more stylish than using one hand to pull the mainsheet through the jamming cleat. Holding the tiller extension across your body with your backhand, pull in a length of mainsheet with your front hand. Hold the sheet taut with your backhand while grasping the tiller extension, and use your front hand to pull the mainsheet in again.

Wind from ahead

You cannot sail directly into the wind (this is the "no sail" zone) but you can sail towards the wind on a course known as "beating." Depending on the design of boat, skill of the crew and sea conditions it's possible to sail at an angle of 30–45 degrees to the apparent wind. The closer the angle, the higher the boat will point toward its target.

Wind blowing from ahead flows over both sides of the sails, which provides forward drive, aided by the dynamic lift and lateral resistance of the daggerboard or centerboard. However, the wind wants to push the boat backward and sideways all the time. Wind in the sails and daggerboard or centerboard resistance will make the boat heel over. Resist this by hiking out and depowering the mainsail.

Sheeting

In very light winds the mainsheet and jib sheet should be pulled in. As the wind increases, the mainsheet and jib should be pulled in firmly. Telltales should be streaming aft.

For best performance, holding the sheets is recommended, but for learning or leisure sailing, it is much less tiring to lock the sheets in their jamming cleats. The jib sheet can generally be left cleated when a gust hits, but the helm will need to uncleat the mainsheet with a quick upward flick to ease the sheet. Practice pulling the mainsheet through the jamming cleat. Pull the mainsheet down to lock the sheet; pull it up to unlock and let go.

Trim

Keep weight well forward when sailing upwind, pushing down the bow and lifting the stern.

Above: **In light winds, sit still and concentrate on keeping the boat moving upwind.**

Keep it upright

If a gust hits, you have two choices. Either ease the mainsheet to lose power and let the boat come upright, or "luff" by steering into the wind. The closer you sail toward the wind, the less heeling effect it will have on the sails. However with less sail power, the boat will slow down.

Pointing high and low

Pointing very high with the sails backing is known as "pinching to windward." It can work well with traditional dinghy designs with narrow-bottomed hulls, and may be useful in the final approach to a

racing mark. Pinching does not work on modern skiff-style designs with flat-bottomed hulls, which need to be sailed fast at a greater angle to the wind: if you attempt to pinch, you will slow right down. Performance to windward relies on VMG (see above).

Velocity made good (VMG)

Two boats wish to sail to a spot directly upwind. They will have to tack, beating to windward in a zigzag course, to arrive there. Boat A points at 30 degrees to the wind and sails at an average speed of 4 knots. Boat B points at 40 degrees to the wind and sails at an average speed of 7 knots.

Boat A has a VMG of 3.5 knots and Boat B has a VMG of 5.6 knots toward the windward mark. Boat B should reach the spot first thanks to better VMG. It takes about an hour longer for Boat A to get to the mark.

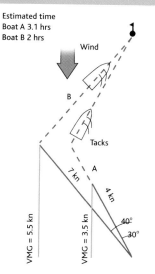

Estimated time
Boat A 3.1 hrs
Boat B 2 hrs

Wind

B

Tacks

7 kn   A

4 kn

VMG = 5.5 kn

VMG = 3.5 kn

40°

30°

The number and timing of the tacks each crew chooses to do is key to successfully meeting a mark. Every boat has an optimum angle to the wind. Find your own boat's optimum angle of performance and practice sailing! It may vary depending on the strength of the wind and other factors such as the tide.

TIP

On a dinghy you steer with the tiller extension. Hold the tiller extension with a downward grip like a dagger! This will enable you to hold the end of the tiller extension across your body.

Below: **Don't let the boat heel too far, or it will slip sideways instead of making good progress upwind. On some dinghies, it might help to put a reef in the mainsail.**

Sailing away from the wind

If you want to head in the direction to which the wind is blowing, you need to sail with the wind behind. It sounds easiest to run straight downwind, but it may be better to follow a broad-reaching course.

Running dead downwind

Sailing with the wind directly behind can pose problems:

- The wind cannot flow over both sides of the sail. It is just pushing the boat along, with decreased sail efficiency.
- There is no side-on stability. If there are waves, the boat may start rolling. The crew of a double-handed dinghy can limit the way the boat rolls by careful weight distribution, sitting on both the windward and leeward side. A single-handed dinghy crew may need to crouch toward the cockpit to balance the boat.
- On a double-handed dinghy, the mainsail will blanket the jib. This can be cured by pulling out and sheeting the jib on the windward side (known as "goosewinging").

- "Goosewinging" is very effective at using all the sail area, but only works well if you "sail by the lee." This means you have to bear away slightly (pull the tiller toward you) so that the wind is blowing over the leeward side of the stern, instead of from directly behind.
- If you don't steer the boat correctly when running by the lee, there is a danger it will jibe: the wind catches the mainsail on the wrong side, and the boom slams across. This may cause capsize.

Above: **Beware of the boat rolling to windward when you sail deep downwind. Pull in the mainsheet or push the tiller away to counteract this.**

Left: **The wind is blowing over the stern, with the boat heading a few degrees off sailing directly downwind. If the helmsman veers away any further, the mainsail will blanket the jib.**

> ## TIP
>
> If the boat starts rolling, pull the mainsheet to put some power into the sail, or steer a course that is closer to the wind. Also, be sure to redistribute the weight in the boat quickly.

Sheeting downwind

On a double-handed dinghy, the mainsheet should be let out until the boom is by the leeward shroud. The boom on a single-handed dinghy should be let out at a similar angle up to around 80 degrees from center. Letting the boom out at right angles to the boat will destabilize the boat when there is any breeze.

Trim downwind

- Keep weight forward to ensure the stern doesn't drag. Move aft if the boat starts to sail fast.
- Be ready to move weight to either side of the boat to reduce rolling in waves.

Try a broad reach

If you don't like the idea of rolling downwind or experiencing an unexpected jibe, there is a simple solution: luff up toward the wind.

Steer on a broad reach with the wind blowing across the windward side of the stern. This will power up the jib on the leeward side, and give side-on stability that will stop rolling, providing a faster and more comfortable ride for the crew who can both sit up on the windward deck. The obvious drawback is that you are not sailing directly downwind to the spot you want to reach. Instead, you will need to sail a zigzag course with a series of broad reaches.

Below: **Running dead downwind in a moderate wind. The helm kneels in the cockpit to balance the boat.**

Modern dinghies with asymmetric spinnakers have much better VMG if they are sailed this way, covering a greater distance than a direct downwind dinghy but arriving first due to much better speed.

Sheet in the sails so that telltales are streaming horizontally and the boat is sailing at a good speed. A dinghy should plane easily on a broad reach. Be ready to move weight back to keep the bow flying. Sailing on a very broad reach may not provide a lot of side-on stability; beware of the boat rolling to windward in a lull.

Below: **Sailing by the lee, you can goosewing the jib onto the opposite side. This is the most effective way of running downwind with mainsail and jib.**

Below: **The boom vang holds the boom down when the mainsheet is eased. In windy conditions, letting the boom ride up will help depower the mainsail.**

How is a catamaran different?

Cats require slightly different sailing techniques from a dinghy. The "platform" formed by two hulls, two crossbeams and a trampoline make a cat more cumbersome to maneuver on dry land, but a lot more stable for the crew as soon you launch the cat onto the water.

Launching a cat

Catamarans have a launch dolly with a single axle, two cradles and two large wheels. The best types have huge tires, which are great for pushing the boat across softsand.

- Lift one bow to raise the whole boat high enough to push the dolly underneath. The cradles should be positioned under each hull by the shroud at the approximate balance point of the whole boat.
- Push the cat on its dolly by holding the bridle wire (connecting the two hulls to the forestay) or bows.
- Slide the cat off the dolly into the water, then take the dolly ashore. Leave it well above the high-water mark.

Sailing into the wind

- Don't "pinch" when sailing upwind in a cat. Always sail free and fast, and go for VMG (see page 99).
- Sheet hard in with the mainsheet traveler on the centerline.
- In light winds, keep weight right forward to lift the sterns.
- In force 2–3, the windward hull will begin to lift off the water. Sailing a cat is quickest with the hull just "kissing" the water. Flying the hull high may feel good, but will slow you down.

Far left: **One crew pushes the dolly under the hulls, while the other holds up the hull, which is sufficient to lift the whole front of the boat.**

Left: **A cat is very stable for launching. One crew drops the rudders and attaches the mainsheet, while the other holds the forestay bridle.**

Sailing away from the shore

Sailing a cat away from the beach is straightforward. It is very stable and it's easy to jump on board. Most recreational cats have fixed skegs, so unlike dinghies you don't need to fiddle with daggerboards. Cats also accelerate quickly, which gets them rapidly away from the shore; ideal with an onshore wind.

Launching a cat in an offshore wind can be problematic because of its tendency to accelerate quickly, coupled with its inability to turn as tightly as a dinghy. This can make it difficult to turn the boat away from the launch area.

An excellent way to overcome this is to reverse out. Launch the cat stern-first with the sails hoisted. Make sure the sterns are pointing downwind, which is the way you want to go. Hop up onto each bow, and straddle them like a horse. This will lift both sterns, allowing the cat to sail slowly backward away from the shore. Keep both legs dragging to steer the cat and slow it down. When the cat is far enough out, the crew can move onto the trampoline, take control of the sails and rudder, and sail away.

✪ Use body weight on the side or out on the trapezes (standard on most cats) to keep the windward hull flying just above the water. If you can't hold the hull down, pull on the downhaul, which will depower the sail. Pull hard for maximum effect.

Right: **Sailing into the wind, the windward hull should lift so that it's flying just above the water. Always sail a cat fast and free.**

Sailing away from the wind

✪ Never sail directly downwind on a cat. Drag from the two hulls, together with reduced airflow over the sails, makes this very slow.

✪ Always sail on reaches, with the wind blowing across the boat to produce maximum drive. Follow a zigzag course from jibe to jibe toward your goal.

✪ Use apparent wind to steer a course with maximum VMG (see page 99). For force 3 and above, employ the technique known as "hotting it up." Steer toward the wind to build up power, lift the windward hull and accelerate. As the boat accelerates, the apparent wind direction moves further ahead.

✪ Bear away on the apparent wind, to sail more of a true downwind course.

✪ When a cat accelerates on a reach, you need to move weight back so that both crew are by the rear beam.

✪ Beware of the leeward bow diving under the water at speed. If the bow keeps dipping, the cat will decelerate and may pitchpole, rolling end over end.

Left: **A useful catsailing technique is to steer upwind to fly the windward hull and increase speed, then bear away on the apparent wind with the hull still flying.**

How to tack

If you want to sail toward where the wind is blowing from, you will need to change tack. Fluid and fast tacking is a vital element of dinghy sailing. The tacking maneuver is relatively easy, but a perfect tack relies on knowing how to changeover hands. A lot of practice and good communication is required.

Turning the boat

The technique required for tacking a dinghy is straightforward, with the boat turning from tack to tack through an angle of about 60 degrees.

- Sail to windward with the sails sheeted in.
- Push the tiller away slowly, making the boat spin around on its centerboard or daggerboard.
- As the bow passes through the eye of the wind (when it is "head to wind") the crew moves across the cockpit to the new windward side. The jib sheet must be let off so that it will run free, with the mainsheet uncleated and eased.
- The helm straightens out the rudder as the boat bears away on the new course, and sheets in the mainsail at the same time.
- The crew sheets in the jib. Both crew lean out on the new windward side to counteract heeling.

Handling tiller and mainsheet

Most modern dinghies have a centre mainsheet; the lead of the sheet is in the middle of the boat, just forward of the helm who holds the sheet with his leading hand. Good technique is required to change hands during a tack, while keeping control of the tiller and mainsheet throughout the manoeuvre. The length of the tiller extension will help determine how it is achieved: practice will make perfect, so keep trying!

- Hold the tiller extension across the front of your body, using a "dagger" grip with the backhand.
- Uncleat the mainsheet to ease the mainsail as you push the tiller away to steer into the tack.
- Pivot your body through 180 degrees, facing forward, as you cross the cockpit. As you do this, keep hold of the mainsheet in your front hand and continue to steer the boat around with your back hand.
- Let your "dagger" grip twist around the tiller extension as you move to the new side, swiveling the tiller extension forward so that it doesn't hit the boom, which will be in the middle of the boat.
- Twist your body around to sit up on the new sidedeck, still holding the tiller extension with the same hand, which is now holding the tiller extension behind your back. The other hand is still holding the mainsheet.

Right: **1.** To start the tack, steer the boat up into the wind. **2.** If the wind is light, rolling it to windward will make the tack more dynamic, turning the boat quickly and powering up the mainsail on the new side. Note how the helmsman has flipped the tiller extension under the boom, just before he moves to the new side. The crew lets the jib backwind to help pull the bow around. **3.** The helm pivots across the boat facing forward, then sits on the side, with the tiller extension held behind his back. When the boat has settled down, he changes his front and back hands.

The perfect tack

✪ Move the mainsheet hand across your body so that you can grasp the lower half of the tiller extension. This now becomes your back hand holding the tiller extension. For a moment you will hold both the tiller extension and mainsheet in the same hand, before flicking the tiller extension past your back shoulder and across your body and grabbing the mainsheet with your new front hand.

Transom mainsheet

Many classic dinghy classes were fitted with a mainsheet led from the transom. If you tack with a transom-led mainsheet, you will need to pivot through 180 degrees, facing toward the stern as you change sides. The obvious disadvantage is that you can't watch where the boat is heading!

Above: **Perfect tiller extension control, as the helm of a Merlin Rocket walks through a tack.**

Going into a tack

1. The crew of this Enterprise are sailing at good speed going into the tack. 2. The helmsman steers into wind, while the crew keeps the jib sheeted in to pull the bow around. 3. The helm pivots facing backward, while moving across the boat as the crew sheets in the jib on the new side.

How to tack (2)

What happens if the boat stops as the bows turn into the wind and won't keep turning onto the new tack? Keep practicing, don't get "stuck in irons" and before long you will be a master at powered-up roll tacks!

Left: **Note how the jib is still sheeted as this RS200 tacks, helping to pull the bow through the eye of the wind without stalling.**

Stuck in irons – with jib

If you steer the boat into a tack and it stops head to wind, you are "stuck in irons." The boat will sit still, and then start to drift backward. Keep the jib sheeted in on the old side until the bow has swung through the eye of the wind, and only then let go to sheet in on the new side. If you have already let go of the jib sheet and the boat stops head to wind, "back" the jib by pulling in on the old side so that the wind can blow against it and blow the bow around.

A dinghy without a jib is more prone to get stuck in irons. Make sure you have plenty of "way on" as you turn into the tack. The boat should be up to speed and not about to stall, so the momentum will help carry it through the turn.

Push-push, pull-pull (no jib)

If you get stuck in irons on a single-handed boat such as a Pico or Laser:

- Push the boom and tiller away at the same time. Pushing the boom will backwind the sail so that it fills on the other side and drives the boat backward; pushing the tiller will allow the boat to reverse, so that it turns away from head to wind.
- Pull the tiller and pull in the sail. Pulling the tiller will help the boat bear away on the tack; pulling in the sheet will power the sail to drive the boat forward.

Roll tacks

In lighter winds, the technique known as "roll tacking" can produce a quicker and more powerful turn. Instead of relying on the rudder, an aggressive change of crew weight plays the major role in spinning the boat through the turn. The rolling action powers up the sails and provides faster acceleration on the new tack.

- Steer gently into the tack, with the boat heeling to leeward (away from the wind), which will make it want to turn toward the wind.
- Stay on the windward side and roll the boat into the turn as the boom crosses the centerline.
- Ease the mainsheet and move quickly onto the new windward deck, with the new leeward side heeling right over as the boat points in the new direction.
- Lean out and sheet in the sails in one dynamic movement, bringing the boat upright and powering it up at the same time.

Below: **The roll tack is a dynamic movement that rolls the boat through the tack. Note how the helm will be holding the tiller extension in his new front hand when he sits on the side, ready for the changeover between the tiller and sheet hands.**

How to tack a catamaran

Catamarans tend to tack slowly, due to the drag from one hull pivoting around the outside of the turn. High-performance cats with daggerboards tend to tack quite easily; recreational cats with skegs or asymmetric hulls may get stuck head to wind if you don't use the right technique.

- ✪ The cat should be sailing at speed before the helm steers into the tack with the mainsheet in. Don't ease it out yet.
- ✪ Steer carefully. The two rudders will act like a brake if you slam them over too fast.
- ✪ Keep the jib sheeted in.
- ✪ Stay on the windward side of the boat until the jib has backed, with the wind blowing on the other side, which will push the bows through the tack.
- ✪ Keep the jib sheeted on the old side until the cat is correctly lined up for the new tack at about 40 degrees to the wind.
- ✪ The helm must steer carefully through the tack, pivoting to face backward while moving to the new side of the boat.
- ✪ While moving across the boat, ease the mainsheet by about 12 inches (30 cm) to loosen the mainsail and allow the full-length battens to pop onto the new side.
- ✪ Bear away carefully as the crew sheets in the jib on the new tack, pulling in the mainsheet as the cat accelerates back to full speed.

Right: **Straighten out the course and sheet in carefully to allow the cat to accelerate smoothly on the new tack.**

Tacking in a cat

Above: **Note how the helm is kneeling on the side ready to tack — this is a good catsailor's position as he pushes the tiller away.**

Above: **Always ease off the mainsheet as you go through the tack on a cat, or the boat may stall head to wind.**

Above: **The helm pivots around, facing aft, onto the new windward side, before bearing away on the new tack.**

How to jibe

Jibing a dinghy is changing tack with the wind blowing from behind instead of ahead. The mainsail is powered up throughout the turn, making it vital to keep the boat under full control. In stronger winds, it can be a difficult maneuver: making a mistake often leads to a capsize.

Worried about jibing?

People worry about jibing. During a tack, the boat turns into the wind and loses virtually all power in its sails, so it is fairly easy to maintain control. During a jibe, the boat turns away from the wind with the result that the sail is powered up all the time. Jibing in light winds is easy, but in stronger winds, a jibe becomes more dynamic. The boat sails through the turn at speed, and when the boat gybes the jibes sweeps across the cockpit like a scythe. It is easy to lose control and capsize the boat.

Turning the boat

You may be sailing on a run or on a broad reach. You must:

⚙ Steer precisely through the turn.

⚙ When the wind direction changes from directly behind to blowing on the new windward side, help the mainsail to jibe by pulling the boom across.

⚙ Straighten up on the new tack while the boat is still sailing on a downwind course.

Jibing

⚙ Prepare for the jibe. If you are sailing double-handed, make sure the crew is ready and knows what will happen.

⚙ Pull the tiller to bear away into the jibe, with the mainsheet eased. Heel the boat to windward to help it turn in lighter winds.

⚙ The helm pivots to face forward in the cockpit, swiveling the tiller extension to ensure that the rudder will steer the boat through a smooth arc.

⚙ With the wind blowing from directly behind, the helm grabs the mainsheet as it falls off the boom.

TIP

The boom can swing across the cockpit at high speed. Don't get hit on the head! Beware of accidental jibes! The crew should take care not to get caught by the boom vang: keep well behind it, but keep clear of the mainsheet at the same time.

✪ In the moment when the wind swings to the new windward side, the helm gives a sharp tug on the falls of the mainsheet. This should be enough to flick the boom and mainsail across the cockpit to the new side. Both crew duck under the boom as it swings across at speed.

✪ As the boom swings across, the helm changes sides, swiveling the tiller extension to keep steering in a smooth arc, while holding the mainsheet with his or her front hand.

✪ The helm pivots to sit on the new windward side, using the same hand technique as a tack. Sit well forward with the extension held behind your back, grab the lower half of the extension with your old sheet hand, flick the extension across the front of your body and grab the mainsheet with your new front hand.

✪ If you are sailing double-handed, the crew should change position by moving into the cockpit during the jibe. Let off the old jib sheet and pull it in on the new side as the boom swings across the cockpit. Move your weight to balance the boat and prevent it tipping over when the sails power up on the new tack.

Left: **With the jibe successfully accomplished, sheet in the mainsail and power up on a new broad reach.**

Jibing a catamaran

It is easier to jibe a cat than a dinghy, because you have a much more stable platform with two hulls. Jibing technique is similar, with the main exception that the mainsheet is mounted on the rear beam.

✪ The helm steers into the jibe.

✪ As the wind swings behind, the helm pivots to face aft and kneels by the middle of the rear beam.

✪ The helm grabs the falls of the mainsheet to swing the mainsail to the new side.

✪ The helm keeps steering carefully through the arc of the turn, before straightening out the course as soon as the mainsail has jibed. Check the transom to ensure the main is clear.

Cat jibing

1. You can let the boat heel slightly to windward going into the jibe, which will help the hull carve around.

2. Duck as the boom comes across and straighten the course to keep sailing downwind with the boat held flat.

3. Don't let the boat round up onto a reach or heel to leeward, which will often lead to a capsize.

How to jibe (2)

Why do dinghy sailors capsize when they jibe? Normally it is caused by lack of control. Work out what the problems are and you won't make any mistakes.

Boom control

Decide when the moment is right to grab the falls of the mainsheet, then give a tug and send the boom on its journey across the cockpit. Consider having the crew control the boom by holding the boom vang to offset a powerful swing. If you leave the boom to move on its own, it will wait until the boat has turned far enough for the wind to hit the back of the mainsail. The result is that the boom will swing over, violently and hard.

This may be dangerous for the crew (one good reason to sail wearing a helmet) and the momentum as the boom crashes across to the new side can cause the boat to tip right over. The helm may lose control of the steering, and the boat will keep turning onto a beam reach. With wind on the beam, the boat will capsize.

Don't turn too far

Keep control by jibing through the smallest possible angle. You only need to turn the boat through an arc that's big enough to jibe the mainsail onto the new tack. From there you can choose your direction: either keep sailing downwind, or head up onto a reach.

In light winds, it is possible to jibe through 180 degrees (from a beam reach to a beam reach) without much trouble. But as the wind gets stronger, letting the boat turn too far is asking for a capsize. Lack of steering control is the usual problem. The helm makes a mess of swinging the boom across the cockpit, so it crashes to the new side. In the heat of the moment he or she forgets how quickly the boat is turning and lets it spin right around until the bows are almost into the wind on the new tack, with the wind blowing the rig and boat over.

Don't trip

Some dinghies tend to trip on their centerboard or daggerboard as they jibe, which makes the boat heel over. On traditional dinghy classes, it's normal to jibe from run to run with the centerboard partly or fully retracted. On single-handed dinghies such as the Laser, it's normal to jibe with the daggerboard pulled up halfway. Make sure the top of the daggerboard is clear of the boom and boom vang. On modern dinghies with asymmetric spinnakers, it's normal to leave the centerboard or daggerboard fully down.

TIP

Always grab the "falls" of the mainsail (the two or three strands of rope that drop from the blocks on the boom) to pull the boom across. Hold them all together, so that you are giving the boom a highly effective tug.

Below left: **The disadvantage of jibing or tacking with a transom mainsheet is obvious — the helm can't see where the boat is going during the few seconds it takes to turn the boat.**

Below: **Jibing an Enterprise with a traditional transom mainsheet. The helm has to face aft, as the crew pulls on the boom vang to help flick the boom across.**

TIP

Keep control of the rudder: straighten out your course as soon as the mainsail has jibed. Be prepared to sail an "S" to regain control of stability.

Don't slow down

If you are sailing fast in a strong wind, try not to let the boat slow down when you jibe. The faster you sail through the jibe, the lighter the apparent wind will be, which makes it easier to keep control.

TIP

Steer from sailing deep downwind on one tack to sailing deep downwind on the other tack. Keep the angle of the jibe tight and then adjust your course.

Left: **Stay low and concentrate on steering through the jibe, ready to flick the boom across at the precise moment when the stern switches through the eye of the wind.**

Coming back to shore

At the end of a great sailing session it is time to sail back, land on the shore and pull your boat out of the water. It is important to plan ahead before you make your final approach to the shore. The tide or the wind may have changed and there may be more people around.

Has anything changed?
Tides:

If you are sailing in a tidal area, the water could be a lot higher or lower than when you launched. If the water is higher, the angle of the beach may have changed from a gently shelving to steeply shelving shore. When you jump out of the boat, the water may be a lot deeper than you expect. If the water is lower, rocks and other underwater obstructions may be dangerously close to the surface. When you land, the dolly may be a long way up the beach, which is tricky if you are sailing single-handed. It may also be a long way to pull the dolly across soft sand or mud.

Wind:

Has the wind changed direction since you launched? An offshore wind in the morning may have changed to an onshore sea breeze in the afternoon. Flat water has now become waves breaking on the shore, which could make it tricky to land.

People and boats:

Did you launch early in the day? If you return on a fine summer's afternoon you can expect to have to maneuver past swimmers by the shore, sunbathers on the beach or other dinghies jostling for position on the boat slip.

Approaching in a cross-shore wind

As with launching and sailing off the beach, landing should be straightforward in a cross-shore wind.

⊛ Sail in toward the beach on a beam reach. Look ahead to make sure your landing spot is clear. If the slipway is blocked by other boats or there are children swimming in the water, change your landing spot or wait for the jam to clear.

⊛ If you have a furling jib, roll it away to slow the boat down. When sailing on a beam reach, remember that you can only slow right down by luffing (pushing the tiller away) toward the wind.

⊛ Leave the rudder right down until you are ready to stop the boat and get over the side. You should aim to sail into water which is little more than thigh deep. If you partially lift the rudder, the boat will develop strong weather helm and become difficult to steer.

⊛ The daggerboard or centerboard will require more depth than the rudder, but leave them down for as long as possible for best control. You can still steer the boat with the board partly retracted.

⊛ As the boat enters shallow water, slow down by gently luffing into the wind.

⊛ Stop before the rudder blade touches the bottom! Turn the boat directly into the wind so that it will come to a dead halt.

⊛ The crew should jump over the side and grab the windward side shroud or forestay to hold the boat steady. The helm must raise the rudder and lock it, before

Below: **1. Approach the shore and slow down with the daggerboard or centerboard partly retracted. 2. Turn into wind to stop and let the crew hop over the side. 3. Grab the bow and hold the boat so it is facing** into wind. **4. Push the dolly under the boat so it is fully supported and level. 5. You may have to tie the dolly handle to the bow.**

pulling up the centerboard or pulling out the daggerboard.

🟤 The helm should retrieve the dolly. Walk it into water that is deep enough to pull the dinghy onto its support. When you do this, the dolly must be aligned with the wind.

🟤 Depending on wind strength, it may be necessary to drop the mainsail before you pull the boat and dolly up the beach. If the mainsail is hoisted, the bow must be kept pointing into the wind when you drop the sails.

TIP

If the mainsail is hoisted, let off the cunningham and boom vang controls to reduce power in the sail. Make sure the mainsheet can run free.

Above: **How are you going to get ashore? A small dinghy such as the Taz can be carried up the beach by a couple of willing adults.**

Coming back to shore (2)

Approaching in an offshore wind

The wind will be blowing off the shore, with flat water likely to make the approach straightforward. But the wind will not let you sail straight to the shore. You will need to sail a zigzag tacking course toward the shore, pointing the boat a little way from your destination on your final approach. This means you can sail in on a close reach, with the option of heading up or bearing away.

- Be aware of leeway on the final approach. If the beach is gently shelving, the daggerboard or centerboard may need to be partly lifted when the boat is still some way out.
- When you are close to the shore and don't need to point high, furl the jib to slow down. To lose more speed, ease the mainsheet until the mainsail starts flapping.
- Fully retract the centerboard or pull out the daggerboard before the rudder touches the bottom.

The crew should immediately jump out on the windward side and hold the boat by the shroud or forestay.

Approaching in an onshore wind

When the wind is blowing onshore, waves may make the approach difficult and there could be problems stopping the boat. The solution is to reduce speed to a minimum.

- In light winds, you may be able to sail into shallow water and turn the boat through 180 degrees so that it stops with the bow pointing into the wind. Be aware that the water could be a lot deeper at the bow than the stern, making it difficult for the crew to hold the boat, particularly if there are waves.

Below: **If you try to catch the bow of a boat, make sure it is moving slowly. Don't get trapped in deep water with big waves between the bow and the shore.**

✪ Sailing toward the beach in stronger winds, you can furl the jib to slow down but you can't let out the mainsail. Luffing side-on to the wind will depower the mainsail but also turns the boat side-on to the waves, making it unstable. And your boat will be heading in the wrong direction!

✪ The solution is to drop the mainsail before making the final approach (only possible on a double-handed dinghy with a conventional main halyard).

✪ Turn the boat head to wind in flat water before you get into waves, which will build up closer to the shore. Drop the mainsail quickly and stow it in the cockpit.

✪ Lift the centerboard or dagger-board, and then back the jib to help turn the boat and sail in towards the beach. On the final approach, furl the jib or let the sheet go so that you slow right down.

✪ Alternatively, if it is mandatory for your boat to have paddles, simply drop the sails and paddle ashore.

✪ The crew can jump out on the windward side, grab the side of the boat and let it turn into wind while the helm raises the rudder.

Below: **Approaching the beach in an onshore wind is not a problem in light winds. But in strong winds it may be necessary to drop the mainsail and stow it in the cockpit, before making a final approach at slow speed. Note that this Merlin Rocket has no rudder! The helm has removed the fixed rudder for the final approach, and is just steering with the sails.**

Landing single-handed

With no crew to help pull up the daggerboard or hold the boat, you have to plan ahead before making the final approach.

☸ When the wind is cross-shore or offshore, ease the mainsheet to slow the boat down, while keeping enough speed to steer.

☸ Most single-handed dinghies have a daggerboard. Pull it halfway up on the final approach, then let off the rudder downhaul, attached to the side of the tiller.

☸ As you sail into shallow water, lift the daggerboard higher to make sure it can't hit the ground.

☸ Turn the boat into the wind and get out over the windward side. Pull out the daggerboard and lay it in the cockpit. Pull up the rudder blade fully.

☸ In light winds, you may be able to leave the boat in shallow water and run ashore to get the dolly. In strong winds, you'll need help.

Sailing in on waves

If the wind is blowing onshore, you will need to luff onto a beam reach to depower the sail and slow down, jump out, and spin the boat so that it is facing into the wind. When it is very windy and there are waves, sail in with the daggerboard lifted and rudder blade released, keeping your weight well back in the boat to avoid pushing the bow into a wave. Look for a flat spot between the waves to luff, jump out and grab the boat. If there are breaking waves, it may be impossible to use a dolly. The boat needs to be carried quickly to shore.

Landing a cat

Above (left to right): **Waiting to be pulled back up the beach; the crew has gone to fetch the dolly.**

Above: **Is anyone going to help you when you reach the shore? It's handy, even in a light wind.**

Above right: **Most single-handers are light enough for one person to pull up the boat slip. The Phantom is made of superlight epoxy sandwich construction.**

Landing a catamaran

☸ Furl the jib to reduce power on the final approach.

☸ It is very difficult to steer a cat if the rudders are not right down, so leave them down until you stop and the crew have jumped out over the windward side. Rudder blades on cats are designed to pop up if they hit the bottom.

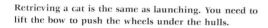

Retrieving a cat is the same as launching. You need to lift the bow to push the wheels under the hulls.

A cat is surprisingly easy to pull or push with a dolly as long as the surface isn't too steep.

- While the crew holds the cat, the helm lifts the rudder to the full-up position, unhooks the mainsheet from the clew and lets off the downhaul, to depower the sail.
- If you are landing in an onshore wind, consider lowering the mainsail and making the final approach under jib alone.
- Push the wheels under the hulls and secure them to the shrouds on each side with tethers before pulling the cat ashore. If there are waves breaking, help may be required.

Packing up

If you are sailing on salt water, hose the boat down with fresh water before derigging and packing it up. Salt can corrode fittings and build up damaging deposits over time.

- Remove the drain plug in the transom and drain any water in the hull by tipping the boat.
- Let the sails dry before you put them away. Always roll or flake the mainsail and jib before putting them into a bag.
- Store rudder and daggerboard foils in padded bags for protection.
- Use an overall top cover to protect the boat and prevent it degrading in UV light. Make sure the cover will keep rain out of the cockpit.
- Dinghies in boat parks can get blown over in a gale. When you leave the boat, tie it down securely to ground anchors on either side.

Right: **If you have been sailing on salt water, always wash your boat thoroughly with fresh water to get rid of all salt residue.**

Dinghy capsize

There can be few dinghy sailors who have never capsized. It is all part of the learning process. Once you have mastered sailing in a more stable dinghy, capsize should become a rare occurrence.

Double-hander capsize

There are three disadvantages to capsizing:

- You will probably get very wet!
- You may get cold (though not if you wear the right clothing for the conditions).
- You may get tired, particularly if conditions mean you capsize

several times. If that happens, be prepared to signal a rescue boat for help.

Knowing what to do

You will know when a capsize is inevitable. The boat passes the point of no return, and the actual capsize is slow enough for you to plan your next movement. An experienced sailor will always try to place a leg over the upper side of the boat as it goes over, then swing over the other leg and stand on the centerboard with the boat on its side. This is known as a dry capsize! However,

Single-hander capsize

As the rig drops down onto the water, step over the side of the hull onto the centerboard. Regain your balance. Assess the situation, check the mainsheet is uncleated and undo the boom vang.

Hold the gunwale with both hands and lean back. A small single-hander will start to right itself straight away. If the rig does not lift off the water, step further back on the centerboard for more leverage and try again.

Once the rig has lifted off the water, it will start to lift quite quickly. When it has reached 45 degrees, be prepared to place one leg over the deck.

Quickly step over with the other leg as the boat comes up. If necessary, move rapidly to the other side to stabilize the boat. Get your bearings, make sure everything is ready and the bow is pointing into the wind, then sail away.

Below (left to right): **1. The crew is in the water and the helm checks that she is unhurt. 2. The helm stands on the centreboard and pulls on a righting line. 3. The helm and crew ensure that the** **mainsail and jib sheet are uncleated and can run free and the centerboard is fully down. 4. As the helm pushes down on the hull to right the boat, the crew is in the water, ready to be scooped back into the** **cockpit. 5. As the rig lifts off the water, the helm steps over the side of the dinghy at the same time as the crew rolls back into the boat. 6. Helm and crew can now stabilize the boat and sail off.**

on a two-handed boat only one person (normally the helm) can enjoy this luxury. The crew is relegated to falling in the water.

The perfect capsize in a single-hander

- ✪ You know it has become inevitable so, as the rig drops down onto the water, step over the side of the hull onto the centerboard.
- ✪ Hold on and get your balance.
- ✪ Make sure the mainsheet is uncleated.
- ✪ Grip the gunwale with both hands and lean back. A small single-hander like a Pico or Laser will start to right itself immediately. If the rig doesn't lift off the water, you need more leverage. Step further back on the centerboard and try again.
- ✪ Once the rig has lifted off the water, it will start to lift quite quickly. When it has reached 45 degrees, be prepared to pop one leg over the deck.

- ✪ Step over with the other leg as the boat comes upright: do this smartly! If necessary, move your weight rapidly to the other side of the boat to stabilize it.
- ✪ Get your bearings, and sail away.

The perfect capsize in a double-hander

- ✪ For the helm, the technique is similar to a single-hander. Just step over the side onto the centerboard as the boat capsizes.
- ✪ The crew should slide gracefully into the water between the mast and the cockpit. Don't fall into the sail: you may fall through it or sink the rig and invert the boat. And do not hang on to the top side: your weight may pull it right over and invert the boat, making capsize recovery more difficult.
- ✪ As soon as the dinghy has capsized, both crew should check that the other is alright.
- ✪ Next, they must ensure that the mainsheet and jib sheet are uncleated and can run free.

- ✪ If the spinnaker is hoisted, this must be pulled back inside its chute.
- ✪ The extra size and weight of the hull and rig of a double-handed boat can make it more difficult to pull up from a capsize. The helm may need to stand further back on the centerboard and lean back by pulling on a righting line. Some dinghies have righting lines under the gunwales. Or use the spinnaker sheet or jib sheet.
- ✪ The crew must be ready to get scooped back into the cockpit by floating alongside without pulling down on the hull.
- ✪ As the rig lifts off the water, the crew should roll into the cockpit just before the helm steps in from the other side.
- ✪ At this point helm and crew are on different sides, perfectly positioned to stabilize the boat and then recommence sailing.

Dinghy capsize (2)

Capsize problem solving

Recovery from a capsize does not always go smoothly. The boat may be difficult to pull back upright, keep capsizing or turn upside-down. All of these problems can be solved with practice and clear thinking about what to do next. One of the positive aspects of righting a capsized boat is that you can generally take your time, assess the situation and enjoy a brief rest.

Losing the boat

Don't let go when the boat capsizes. Because modern dinghies float high on their sides, they also blow surprisingly quickly downwind. If you fall in the water, grab something like the tiller or a sheet. You may not be able to grab the hull because it is so smooth.

If you become separated from the boat, try to swim back before it starts to blow downwind. If you are sailing single-handed and can't catch the boat, indicate that you need help by crossing your arms above your head. If you are sailing double-handed and one crew becomes separated, it should be possible to right the boat single-handed, then sail over to pick up the other crew. If not, indicate that you need help by crossing your arms above your head.

Capsize checks

- As soon as the boat capsizes, check the other crew are okay.
- Make sure the mainsheet and jib sheet aren't cleated and can run free.
- Check the board is fully down. A loose daggerboard may slide out; a loose centerboard may swivel back into the hull.

Reaching the daggerboard

Modern dinghies are very buoyant, due to the thick double bottom creating a self-draining cockpit. They also tend to be a little wider than older dinghy designs. That's great for most purposes, but when a

Above: **Reaching up to the centerboard or daggerboard can be difficult if the boat floats high, like this Mirror.**

Below: **Don't lose the boat! Hang on so you can scramble aboard when it comes upright after a strong wind capsize.**

modern dinghy capsizes it also tends to float very high on its side.

If you don't manage to flip your legs and hop onto the board as the boat capsizes, you will need to swim around to the board, which may be quite high above the water. This is no problem on a small single-hander — a quick grab on the end of the board can suffice to pull back upright. But it may be a problem on bigger dinghies when it's necessary to climb onto the daggerboard to pull the boat upright. Pulling yourself up is strength-sapping, particularly when the daggerboard is slippery and may be sharp enough to inflict cuts and bruises if you're not wearing a wetsuit. If you wear a trapeze harness, take care that the hook doesn't damage the board.

Left: **Swimming the bow around so that it is pointing toward the wind will make the boat easier to pull upright.**

Difficult to right

A capsized dinghy will normally blow downwind of the rig, which acts like a sea anchor. If the boat is difficult to pull upright, pull the bow around until it's pointing into the wind. That should allow the wind to blow under the rig, helping lift it off the water. As the boat comes upright it should be pointing on a close reach, making it less likely to keep rolling over through 180 degrees.

Stowing the spinnaker

If you capsize with the spinnaker hoisted, pull it back into the chute or bundle it into the bag before you attempt to right the boat. You generally cannot right the boat with the spinnaker hoisted.

Below: **If you capsize with a spinnaker, you must stow it in the bag or chute. Unless the wind is very light, you cannot right the boat with the spinnaker hoisted.**

Capsize problem

Don't pull the boat upright if the wind will then blow straight onto the leeward side of the sails. Swing the bow around into the wind. It will blow across the windward side of the rig as you pull the boat upright. If you are sailing double-handed, helm and crew should be prepared to put their weight in both leeward and windward sides of the cockpit as necessary. If you are sailing single-handed, be prepared to throw your weight across the cockpit.

Inversion

Because they float high in the water, buoyant modern dinghies can turn upside-down. This may happen if the crew stands on the rig, which will sink down, or if they cling to the top of the boat and pull it right over. Ideally, the mast should be sealed, providing the rig with some buoyancy, but many masts leak through fittings and halyards.

If the boat inverts, swim clear. If you are caught underneath the boat, stay cool and push yourself down and out to the side.

When the boat is upside-down, it is quite easy for one crew to climb up on the gunwale and grab the end of the daggerboard. If they then lean backward and then slightly forward, this will lift the transom and allow

The roll

The 180-degree roll can be a problem in a strong breeze, and soon becomes frustrating and exhausting. You use a lot of effort to pull the boat upright, but the momentum keeps going as the rig swings through 90 degrees and the boat capsizes on top of you!

Pulling a boat upright

Above: **1. If the boat is upside-down, make sure the daggerboard or centerboard is fully out.**

2. One crew stands on the gunwale and pulls back — this is enough to float the rig to the surface.

the boat to pivot into the wind as the rig slowly rises toward the surface. When the boat is on its side, resume normal capsize drill.

Getting trapped

Fatal accidents are extremely rare, but have occurred when a sailor has got trapped beneath the rig or boat. If you wear a trapeze, beware of the hook snagging on a shroud, elastic or control line. This is most unlikely to happen, but the immediate solution is: don't panic, work out the problem, and unclip the hook. If you are wearing a sacrificial hook (recommended), pull the release and let it go. If not, undo the quick release buckle on the side of the harness and wriggle out.

Prevention is better than cure. Make sure all elastics and control lines are taut and there is no excess line in the cockpit that you could get tangled in. Avoid wearing bulky clothes that may snag and make it more difficult to get out from under the rig. A close-fitting buoyancy aid is ideal and makes it much easier to move in the water. Carry a safely secured knife for emergency use, sharp enough to cut through lines.

Trapped?

It is possible to get caught under the mainsail when the boat capsizes, or under the hull if the boat inverts.

If you are caught under a Dacron mainsail, it is relatively easy to push the material up to get an airspace, before moving out from underneath the sail. Mylar laminate sails are more rigid and less forgiving. Don't panic: just swim or push yourself out past the leech.

3. The second crew is ready to stand on the daggerboard in the normal capsize position.

4. He pulls the boat upright while the crew in the water holds on to the bow. If your crew is too heavy to lift into a high floating boat, pass them a line at the transom and help pull them up by their lifejacket.

Capsizing to windward

Beware of sailing into a wind shadow (typically created by a large moored yacht), which will suddenly cut off the wind from your sails.

If your dinghy capsizes to windward, don't panic. Just slide back into the water in the space between boom and boat, so that you don't end up under the mainsail.

Filling with water

On many dinghies, you can sail off on a broad reach until the self-bailers in the cockpit floor have drained the water. This will be quicker if the self-bailers work in conjunction with hinged transom flaps. Some dinghies sail too slowly for self-bailers to be effective after a capsize. In that case you will need to bail out the water by hand. Remember to always carry a suitable bailer and make sure it is securely attached to the boat.

Filling with water

Some dinghies (particularly older designs) have single bottoms that do not drain water out of the cockpit. The advantage is that the boat should float fairly low in the water when capsized. The disadvantage is that when righted, the cockpit may be half full of water.

Left: **There is a lot of water to shift if you capsize in a classic dinghy like an Optimist. All you can do is bail like crazy.**

Capsizing to windward

When you are hiking out, or trapezing, and the sails suddenly lose power your boat will roll to windward and may capsize. The solution is to look ahead and predict what is going to happen, so you can be ready to bear away with the wind or move your weight into the middle of the boat.

Left: **Aaargh! Capsizing to windward is not much fun, as the boat comes over on top of you. Just stay cool and stay in the space between boat and boom.**

If you are sailing an older dinghy, check that the buoyancy compartments do not leak, as this could sink the boat. It can be a problem on home-built marine plywood dinghies, but the joints between the buoyancy compartment and hull can be resealed with fiberglass tape.

Many dinghies have one or two drainage plugs in the transom. There may also be a plug in the cockpit floor and in the base of each buoyancy tank. Always check that the plugs are pushed or screwed right in before you launch the boat. When you pull the boat back out, remove the plugs and tip the boat on its dolly to ensure any water is drained from inside the hull. (It is a wise precaution to remove exterior plugs from an unattended boat, in case someone decides to "borrow" them: this sometimes happens in the boat park!)

Capsizing is exhausting

Endless clambering up onto a capsized boat is exhausting. It can be a vicious circle: you get exhausted, therefore you capsize again; you get more exhausted and capsize yet again.

Exhaustion

In normal circumstances you can capsize and continue sailing, but it's a good time to consider if you feel physically OK. If there's any feeling of exhaustion, head for the beach before you capsize again. If you keep capsizing, summon help so that you can get a tow back to the beach.

Other dangers

If you are sailing in tidal waters, check where the flow is sweeping your capsized boat. In some situations, you may need to right the boat and start sailing as quickly as possible: for instance, if you are being swept into a busy channel or into water "racing" around a headland.

Getting dunked in the water during a capsize will make you far more vulnerable to the effects of wind chill. If you're feeling cold, it's time to head for the shore.

Be careful when a RIB or powerboat driver offers to help. The driver may be willing but untrained. It can be extremely difficult to maneuver a powerboat close to a capsized dinghy or cat, particularly in waves. Beware of the propeller, which is potentially lethal. Check that the driver puts the gearshift into neutral when anywhere close to a crew in the water, rigging or sails.

Left: **Be careful close to a powerboat such as a RIB. The driver must put the gearshift in neutral to ensure the propeller is not turning.**

Catamaran capsize

The wide base of a catamaran is a lot more stable than a dinghy at rest, but beach cats can and do capsize — particularly if you're sailing the boat hard and fast.

How do you capsize?

There are two ways a cat is likely to capsize. First, it may be blown over sideways like a dinghy. But the crew of a cat have much greater leverage than a dinghy, so this type of capsize is normally easy to prevent by letting go of the mainsheet or traveler.

Second, the cat may "pitchpole": a typical high-speed catsailing capsize. The cat is sailing fast on a reach. The leeward bow drives down into a wave, but does not surface quickly enough to prevent the boat from decelerating. Momentum keeps driving the rig forward, while the apparent wind direction swings behind and increases as the cat decelerates. The leeward bow is driven deeper into the water until the cat tips over and capsizes.

Below: **The point of no return. All you can do is slide gracefully down the trampoline as the cat goes over.**

Below: **Aieeee! Cat capsizes can be fast! Be prepared to be flung off in a pitchpole, like the crew of this Hobie.**

Going over

When a cat capsizes, there is more distance to fall. If possible, both crew should slide down the trampoline into the water; avoid jumping onto the fully battened sail.

If the cat pitchpoles, the capsize may be fast and quite violent. Both crew will be thrown forward. Watch out you don't swing around the front of the boat if you are on a trapeze. If this happens, beware of hitting the spinnaker pole — you may damage it or it may damage you! As an antidote, brace your legs or grab something solid to prevent being thrown forward.

Capsized

In the event of a capsize, remember the following:

✪ First check that both crew are OK.

✪ Do not let go of the capsized cat, which will quickly start to blow downwind. Grab a sheet or control line to maintain contact.

✪ If the mast is sealed the cat should float on its side. Do not stand on the rig; this may invert the boat.

✪ Swim around and climb onto the lower hull. This is normally a lot easier than it might sound!

✪ Both crew can take a rest here and hold the underside of the trampoline.

Getting the cat upright

The width of a cat can make it difficult to pull back upright. The rig, with its elliptical mast, is heavy to lift off the water, and you also need to pull the top hull up to a vertical position.

The cat will naturally blow downwind of its rig, but it is easiest to pull the cat back upright with bows pointing into the wind. This will allow wind to blow under the mast and mainsail. To get the cat into this position, the crew should move forward to sink the bow and lift the stern, thus encouraging the bows to pivot towards the wind.

The big pull

✪ Before you try to pull the cat upright, make sure the mainsheet and jib sheets are uncleated so that they will run free. If the spinnaker is out, it must be pulled back into the chute.

✪ All beach cats should be fitted with a righting line that the crew can easily grab. This line is permanently stowed in its own trampoline bag, tied to the cat platform close to the mast foot.

✪ Pull the righting line out of its bag, throw the free end over the top hull and catch it on the other side. Then lean back and pull. The righting line should be knotted so that it's easy to hold onto. To make it easier still, take a turn round your trapeze hook.

✪ In most situations, both crew will need to lean back on the righting line to provide enough leverage to pull the cat upright.

Below: **When the cat is on its side, the crew can stand on the lower hull. Note the righting line, which is attached just below the mast base and led over the top hull for the crew to pull back on.**

Catamaran capsize

Coming upright

When the rig lifts off the water and the top hull swings past a vertical position, the capsized cat will accelerate through 90 degrees as it swings fully upright. Watch out for the windward hull as it falls from above and hits the water. You do not want to be under it, but that's easy to avoid. As the windward hull hits the water, both crew should be ready to grab the forward beam to steady the boat, or grab the bar (called a dolphin striker) under the forward beam, which is easier to hold.

Getting back on

Most cats have at least one trapeze handle on each side. Use this to pull yourself back onto the trampoline. Swim around the outside of the hull to the windward side. Grab the trapeze handle, lie back in the water, lift your feet onto the deck and pull yourself up. It's easier than it sounds!

Alternatively, you can climb over the back beam, but it can be tricky with the tiller bar in the way. Climbing over the front beam is possible with a dolphin striker as a step, but becomes difficult if the cat starts moving forward through the water.

Below: **This is the best way to get back on the trampoline. Grab the trapeze handle, put your feet on the side and then pull yourself up.**

Above (left to right): **1. If the cat is upside-down, climb onto the upturned trampoline. 2. Lead the righting line over one hull. 3. Pull from the bow, which will pivot the cat and allow the rig to float upward. 4. Let the cat pivot so it is pointing toward the wind. 5. Take a breather before pulling back hard to lift the rig off the water. 6. As the cat comes upright, prepare to grab the front beam or dolphin striker (the reinforcement strut under the mast). 7. Climb back on board. Well done!**

Upside-down

One advantage of an upside-down cat is that it will only drift slowly with the wind. Another is that you can sit quite comfortably on the upturned boat and take a rest.

To start getting the cat upright, you first need to pull it up onto its side, into the normal capsize position. The procedure for this is:

✪ Lead the righting line under the deck of the windward bow (nearest the wind) and over the bottom of the hull.

✪ Take the free end of the righting line toward the bow of the leeward hull (furthest from the wind) so that you can pull diagonally across the bottom of the upturned boat.

✪ With the leeward bow pushed down, the windward stern will lift off the water and the rig will float toward the surface. Once the cat is on its side, continue to right it in the normal way. This may prove impossible if the mast is stuck into the bottom or the cat

has filled with water, in which case a rescue boat may be required to help pull the cat back upright. Cross both hands above your head to show you need help.

TIP

If the cat inverts, keep clear of the trampoline. If you get caught underneath (which is most unlikely) don't panic. Just push yourself out to the side.

Common-sense seafaring

Check the forecast carefully if you want to go dinghy sailing, and learn to make the most of conditions on a sea-breeze day. Look where you're going and keep to the right side of a channel. Stick to the rules and sail safe!

Watch the weather

Weather forecasts are widely available on the Internet, TV, radio, in newspapers and by phone. They are also surprisingly accurate. Don't ignore them. Always check the forecast wind speed and direction before you leave. Inshore waters forecasts or specialized websites tend to be more accurate for sailors than land forecasts — and remember, the wind blows stronger across open water.

Hotting up the wind

Perfect sailing conditions can be provided by a sea breeze. This is created when there is a marked difference in air temperature between land and sea. The sun heats the land; hot air rises and draws in cold air from the sea, creating an onshore breeze.

Below: **A sea breeze provides perfect afternoon conditions for cats and skiffs that perform at their best in fresh winds.**

Left: **Stormy skies with wind building. No problem if there is safety cover close at hand.**

- ❂ If the sea breeze blows in the same direction as the gradient wind, which is created by a high- or low-pressure weather system, the sea breeze will be strong. If the sea breeze blows against the gradient wind, both winds may cancel each other out and leave no wind at all! At this point you will be becalmed.
- ❂ A sea breeze will normally start to blow after midday, building in strength through the afternoon to a peak of force 4–6, depending on weather conditions and terrain.

Having mixed with stronger, higher winds, the sea breeze will die away in the evening, to be replaced by a light offshore breeze that is drawn off the cooler land.
- ❂ The direction of the sea breeze will normally change, veering from an onshore to a sideshore breeze by the end of the day.
- ❂ Local topography may accelerate the sea breeze through gaps and over hills, creating particularly strong winds.

Rules of the road

Remember who gives way:

- ✪ Port gives way to starboard.
- ✪ Allow plenty of room when passing another boat.
- ✪ If you are converging on the same tack, the leeward boat (sailing closer to the wind) has the right of way.
- ✪ Sailing boats do not have the right of way just because they are racing. It may be courteous to give way, depending on the situation.
- ✪ Power gives way to sail, but not if the power craft is in a channel or constrained by its draft.
- ✪ Always make your intentions clear.
- ✪ Your ultimate responsibility is to avoid a collision.

Buoys and channel markers

- ✪ Channels are color coded for different parts of the world. In the U.S., you should leave red (port) markers to the right when returning to sea, and green (starboard) markers to the left. This can be remembered by the mnemonic, "Red, right, returning."
- ✪ Keep to the right side of a channel, both sailing in and sailing out.
- ✪ As a dinghy sailor, it makes sense to stay out of the main channel when there are large boats around. Don't get stuck in the wind shadow of a ferry.
- ✪ If there is tidal flow, it will be strongest in deep water and slackest in shallow water.

Right: **Keep out of the main channel — between the buoys — when entering or leaving a harbor. This will help you keep out of the way of bigger boats.**

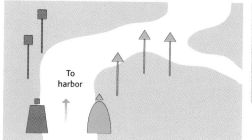

Above: **System A buoyage — when entering a harbor, the port hand marker (red) is on the left and the starboard hand marker (green) is on the right.**

In North America the buoyage system (system B) is different from other parts of the world: port hand buoys are green and starboard buoys are red.

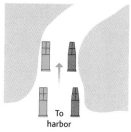

Left: **Starboard tack boat (foreground) has right of way over port tack boats when beating to windward. Get it right! You must know the rules.**

Too much wind

When the wind gets stronger, dinghy sailors have the choice of reducing sail area or sail power to maintain control, keep sailing and avoid capsizes.

Reefing a dinghy

It is possible to "reef" the sails (reduce the sail area) on many learner and recreational dinghies.

Single-handed dinghies

Dinghies with no shrouds and a luff tube mainsail — such as the Topper or Pico — have a simple reefing system that is dependent on having no battens in the sail.

- Rig the sail with the cunningham attached to tension the luff.
- You can either rotate the mast to roll the sail, or hold the clew and wrap the sail around the mast.
- When the required amount of sail area is left, attach the boom vang and outhaul and tension the sail, pulled as flat as possible. The reefed sail shape will be adequate, but not very efficient.

Double-handed dinghies

Dinghies with shrouds can be fitted with a sophisticated "slab reefing" system. This is available on modern recreational dinghies such as the RS Vision, Laser Vago and Topaz Omega. The bottom panel of the mainsail is pulled down onto the boom. Good sail shape is maintained, but power making the sail heel over (called the heeling moment) is greatly reduced due to the sail being smaller and lower.

Slab reefing is easy to manage on dry land. It can be done on the water, but will be considerably more difficult. Caution is the best advice. It is much easier to take a reef out when the wind is too light than to put a reef in when it's too strong!

- The dinghy must be turned head-to-wind.
- The mainsail is fitted with two reefing lines, which pull down the luff and leech and effectively remove a "slab" from the bottom of the sail. On more sophisticated systems, a single control line pulls the luff and leech lines down together, while the boom is held horizontal by a gnav.
- Let go the mainsheet, ease off the halyard and pull down luff and leech lines until the eyes that they pass through have been pulled down tightly onto the boom. Ease off the boom vang or gnav in order to re-tension the main halyard.
- The reefed "slab" can be tucked neatly alongside the boom, using elastics to hold it in place.

Far left: **The sail of a Taz can be rolled around the mast and secured by the downhaul to reduce its size.**

Left: **The Laser Vago has a reefing system for the mainsail using lines, which pull down a horizontal slab in the sail.**

Above: **Many dinghies can sail under mainsail alone with the jib furled for easy handling in stronger winds. This Comet Trio also has a reefable mainsail.**

Furling jib

Most dinghies can be sailed under mainsail with the jib furled. This will reduce power and make the boat easier to handle single-handed. The dinghy will not point as high or sail as fast upwind, and may be more difficult to tack without getting stuck head-to-wind.

Balance the boat!

If the bow is digging into the water in stronger winds, move the crew weight further back. Half-raise the centerboard or daggerboard so that the rig has less to "push" against, which will reduce heeling.

Depower the mainsail

Most high-performance and dedicated racing dinghies have no reefing option. Instead, you need full tension on the cunningham, boom vang and outhaul control lines. This will flatten the mainsail, twist the top half so that it acts like a flat blade with no drive, and move all remaining power to the front of the sail where it is most easily controlled in strong winds.

Below: **The crew move aft to prevent the bow digging into the water in a fresh breeze, but never let the transom drag if you slow down.**

Over the side

Man overboard (MOB) is a major safety issue, even when you're sailing close to the shore. Picking up the person as quickly as possible relies on good boat handling skills and a cool head.

Man overboard!

Crew can fall out of a dinghy for several reasons. It might be due to foot straps breaking when they are hiking, the harness coming undone when out on the trapeze, losing their balance when the boat heels over, or getting knocked off the side by a wave. You need to act quickly.

☻ The person in the water should be wearing a buoyancy aid and suitable clothing for the water temperature, but will still need to be picked up as quickly as possible. If there are waves, the big danger is losing sight of them. It is vital to keep watching the person's position in the water while you turn the boat.

☻ Let the sheets fly to slow the boat down the moment the person falls out of the boat.

☻ Turn upwind and tack the boat around to return to the MOB.

☻ Furl the jib so that you can control boat speed with the mainsail. Sail toward the man overboard so that your final approach is on a close-reaching course, leaving enough space to turn head-to-wind beside them.

☻ Bring the boat to a dead stop, with the person in the water as close as possible to the windward shroud. Take care not to run them over.

☻ The person being rescued may be able to climb over the windward side. Alternatively, they should climb in over the transom.

Above: **The person in the water needs to get their breath back before they attempt to climb back into the boat. Just hold on to the gunwale and float with the buoyancy aid.**

Overboard alone tactics

If you are sailing single-handed and fall over the side, there will be no one to sail back and collect you! As you fall out, hang on to the mainsheet and don't let go. The boat will only sail a short distance before it capsizes, and you can pull yourself in, take a deep breath and right the boat.

Making their pick up

Try to keep watching the man overboard as you tack to head back on a reach to a point downwind of the person in the water. Aim to turn upwind so the boat will come to a dead stop, head to wind, with the person overboard by the windward shroud, where you can grab them or they can hold the boat. Depending on your level of sail control, you may need to furl the jib or let it flap in the final approach.

Wind

Let the sheets fly to slow the boat if required.

Tack around to head back

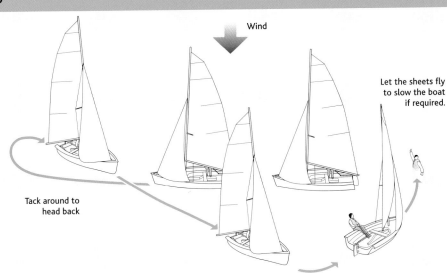

Recommended safety equipment

- A cell phone in a watertight case. In case there is no signal, consider also carrying a handheld marine VHF.
- A handheld, waterproof GPS for information on position and speed.
- A safety knife that will cut through rope, shock-cord or trampoline mesh (a folding knife, which can be stowed in the front pocket of a buoyancy aid, is recommended for each crew).
- Extra clothing, including spray jackets, sailing gloves and fleece hats, stowed in a waterproof compartment.
- Water, to prevent dehydration. A water bottle can be attached to the base of the mast, or held by a cage in the cockpit.
- Power food bars for a quick and easily digested energy hit.
- A small pack of flares for use in inland or coastal waters.
- One or two paddles in case of light winds.
- A towline at least 30 feet (9 m) long.
- Basic tools, including pliers and shackle key. A stainless steel multi-tool could be very useful. Make sure it is attached to the boat!

CELL PHONE WITH WATERTIGHT CASE

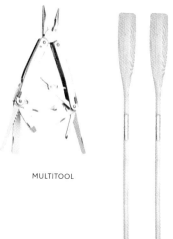

MULTITOOL

PADDLES OR OARS

Overboard off a cat

Cats sail faster than dinghies. This means they cover a greater distance before they can turn around and sail back toward the MOB.

- Keep the cat flat on the water and do not risk a capsize. The cat will probably be impossible to pull back upright with one crew, and will quickly blow downwind of the MOB when it is on its side.
- Keep watching the person in the water.
- Jibe instead of tack. It's a quicker and more reliable way of turning a cat.
- The MOB should climb back onto the windward hull by the shroud, not over the forward beam. They should lie back in the water, grab the trapeze handle with the nearest hand, lift a foot onto the hull, and pull up onto the trampoline.

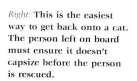

Right: **This is the easiest way to get back onto a cat. The person left on board must ensure it doesn't capsize before the person is rescued.**

HOBIE 15

Dinghy skills

Coming alongside a pontoon or rescue boat, or picking up a mooring, are extremely useful dinghy handling skills. You need to make a controlled approach and bring the dinghy to a dead stop at just the right moment.

Coming alongside a pontoon

Reservoirs and lakes often have a pontoon by the side of the launching area. This can be convenient for mooring alongside if you're waiting for the boat slip to clear or want to make a brief visit ashore.

⊗ Dinghies are seldom equipped with fenders to protect the hull, so check the pontoon has suitable fendering first.

⊗ Try to approach on a course that allows you to turn head-to-wind in the final approach, and come to a dead stop as you come alongside.

⊗ If it is only possible to come alongside on a downwind course, drop the mainsail before making the approach, then furl the jib to slow right down as the dinghy comes alongside.

Above: **The wind is blowing along the pontoon, allowing this Lark to lie alongside with the mainsail hoisted. If the wind is blowing off or onto the pontoon, the mainsail must be lowered and the jib furled.**

Mooring up

Always try to come alongside head to wind, unless there is fast-flowing tide. If the tide is stronger than the wind, you may need to drop the mainsail, furl the jib and point the bows into the tide to stop the boat.

Make a wide approach to the mooring, so you can turn and pick up the mooring with the boat stopped head to wind. The crew needs to have a boat hook ready to pick up the mooring. There is often a "pick up line" attached to a small buoy, which makes it easier to attach to the heavy mooring.

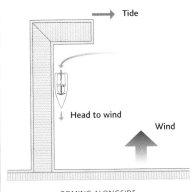

COMING ALONGSIDE

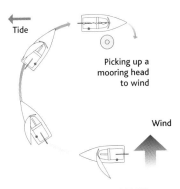

Picking up a mooring head to wind

STOPPING ALONGSIDE A MOORING

⊗ If the wind is blowing across the pontoon, choose the leeward side. Otherwise, drop the mainsail before making the approach to ensure the dinghy can't be blown hard against the pontoon.

⊗ Check the current when coming alongside a pontoon on a river. If there is a strong current, always turn into it to slow down and stop the boat. Drop the mainsail if the wind is blowing from behind. If the current is flowing at right angles to the pontoon, approach on the down-tide side.

⊗ As the dinghy comes alongside, the crew should be ready to step onto the pontoon. For a brief stop, hold the dinghy by the shroud. If longer, secure the dinghy to the pontoon with a bow line and stern line. Drop the mainsail and retract the centerboard if you leave the dinghy.

Coming alongside a boat

You may need to come alongside a rescue boat. Rigid Inflatable Bottom boats (RIBs) with soft inflatable sides make this easy — there is nothing to scratch or damage your dinghy. If you come alongside a solid-hulled boat, make sure it has low enough fenders on.

⊗ Approach slowly on an upwind course so that you can bring the dinghy to a dead stop as it pulls alongside. Most RIBs have grab lines along each side.

● Always approach on the leeward side of the boat, so that the mainsail is blowing away from it. If you approach on the windward side, the dinghy may be blown over on top of the boat.

Mooring a dinghy

It can be useful to pick up a mooring. Make sure the mooring buoy has a ring or grab handle so that you can secure a bowline.

● The final approach should be made at slow speed on a reaching course, so that you can bring the dinghy to a dead halt, head-to-wind, with the buoy on the windward side where it is easy to grab hold of it: about level with the front of the centerboard or daggerboard case. If the dinghy is still moving, it won't be possible to hold on to the buoy — you will need to let go and try again.

● The crew should secure a line to the buoy, either with a bowline or by leading the end of the line back to the dinghy.

● Retract the centerboard or daggerboard and drop the mainsail in the cockpit, so that the dinghy is stable on the mooring.

Above: **Coming alongside an RIB is easy because it has rubber inflatable sides. Come alongside head to wind, slowly.**

Below **These Hobie cats can be left for a short time on moorings, with downhaul eased right off to depower the mainsail, mainsheet removed from the clew and both rudders lifted. It is still necessary to watch them from the beach.**

Dinghy skills (2)

Sailing without a rudder or sailing backward is an impressive way of showing off a surprisingly useful set of seamanship skills. Learn how to master them — you may be glad of them one day!

Sailing without a rudder
You may need to sail a dinghy without a rudder for several reasons:

❂ Your dinghy is fitted with a "fixed rudder." Some high-performance dinghies have a fixed rudder inside the rudder stock. The advantage is that the fixed blade cannot flex or move inside the rudder stock. It is absolutely rigid, and much lighter than a lifting rudder. The disadvantage is that you have to stay out of shallow water, or sail without the rudder when launching and coming ashore.

❂ You have capsized, and the rudder has fallen off its pintles and sunk to the bottom. (You can prevent this by ensuring the security clip has locked the bottom pintle so that it cannot slide off.)

❂ The rudder has become damaged, most likely through running aground at speed. This could break the lock-down mechanism or even shatter the blade.

How do you steer?
Steering without a rudder is surprisingly easy in light winds and flat water, if your dinghy has a mainsail and jib. More wind will make it progressively more difficult; waves may make it impossible.

There are two tools to steer the boat: trimming the sails and heeling the hull over. Pull in the mainsheet to put more power into the back of the boat, making it steer toward the wind. Let go of the mainsheet and pull in the jib to put more power into the front of the boat, making it steer away from the wind. Heel the boat to leeward (away from you) to change the underwater shape and encourage the boat to steer toward the wind; heel the boat to windward (toward you) to encourage the boat to steer away from the wind.

Right: **This Merlin Rocket uses a fixed rudder that has a stiffer foil and is lighter than a conventional lifting rudder. The disadvantage is that you have to remove the rudder in shallow water and will need to steer the boat with body movement and sail trim.**

TIP

You can also steer the boat toward the wind with a single-handed boat, though it is not so effective. Partially raise the daggerboard to encourage the boat to turn more easily, and use heeling as the primary tool to steer the boat, aided by sheeting in or letting out the sail.

Above: Going, going, gone! Beware of the daggerboard falling out of the boat in a capsize. It must be secured by a safety leash.

What if the main foil breaks?

It's unlikely, but the centerboard could snap off or get jammed when retracted into its case. More likely is that you capsize, invert the boat and the daggerboard slides out and sinks to the bottom. This can be avoided by ensuring the daggerboard handle has a security line attached to the boat.

If the worst happens and you are left with no foil, the main difficulty will be making progress upwind — the bow will just bear away.

Above: Body movement and sail trim are all that's being used to steer this Laser Bahia on a straight course. With skill, you can also tack or jibe without the rudder.

Below: The crew holds out the boom while the helm steers in reverse. The jib is sheeted on the windward side, so it is backwinded. You can also reverse under mainsail alone.

All you can do is move crew weight right forward and sink the V-shaped part of the boat as much as possible, which will provide a flat shape to resist leeway.

Reversing under sail

You can also sail a dinghy in reverse, but only in fairly light winds. There may be a situation where there is no way to escape from a tightly packed mass of boats, particularly if you're launching when the wind is blowing straight offshore. This is also useful to get seaweed off the rudder and board.

To get the boat moving in reverse, turn it so that the bows are pointing into the wind. Then hold the boom out against the shroud, or at right angles on an unstayed boat, so that the sail blows backwards.

Sit well forward to lift the stern, which allows it to take over as the "bow." If the mainsail is pushed out on the starboard side, it will tend to turn the boat to starboard when sailing in reverse. Only use a little tiller angle to counter this and steer the boat.

Using a trapeze

Trapezing a dinghy is great! It allows you to stand out on the side of the boat, suspended by a wire, using maximum leverage to hold the boat upright. What's more, it's nowhere like as difficult as it looks!

The trapeze harness

You need a harness to be comfortable. It should fit snugly over your wetsuit or drysuit, but under your buoyancy aid, which should be cut high enough to leave plenty of space for the hook.

Most harnesses are fitted with aluminum or plastic "spreader bars," which are designed to spread the pull from the trapeze wire across your hips. These harnesses are adjusted to fit with straps, which have quick-release buckles so that you can undo them in a hurry — for instance if the harness hook gets caught during a capsize. Some harnesses have a hook mounted on a small central plate laced to each side of the harness. This style is more fiddly to put on and adjust, but can feel more comfortable.

Practicing a trapeze

Right: **A harness is attached to the body over your wetsuit and under your buoyancy aid. Note the hook for attaching to trapeze wires.**

If you want to trapeze in high-performance, flat-out fashion, you will need a harness with full back support. For a more relaxed, sit-up style, back support is not required.

Safety first

A "sacrificial hook" allows you to press a button or pull a lanyard to detach the hook from the spreader bar. This could be a lifesaver if the hook gets caught on a wire during a capsize.

How trapeze wires work

The trapeze wires are attached to the mast, normally at the same height as the spreaders, on each side of the boat. Each wire is connected to a stainless steel "ring," which holds the hook. When not in use, each wire and ring is held taut by a shock cord attached to the deck or trampoline.

Trapezing height

Trapeze rings can normally be adjusted for height, using a short control line to vary the distance between the trapeze ring and wire. The lower you trapeze, the more effective your leverage will be. However, it's easier to learn with the trapeze ring set high.

It can be useful to adjust the height of the trapeze ring while sailing; for instance, pulling the ring higher so that your body clears the waves, or lowering the ring when you move aft on a broad reach.

Going out on the wire

The best conditions for learning to trapeze are on flat water with a steady wind around force 3. Lighter, gusty winds make trapezing difficult. You want enough power to go out on the wire without fear of pulling the boat over to windward, which could make it capsize on top of you.

- Sit on the side of the boat, with your feet tucked under the straps.
- Grasp the plastic handle above the trapeze ring with your front hand. Slip the ring onto the hook with your back hand.
- Sit back in a semi-hiking position to take any slack off the trapeze wire. If it is still slack, adjust the ring to a higher position so that it won't fall off the hook.
- Make sure the helm has the boat well powered up, so that it will take your weight on the

Below: **1.** Sit on the side and pull the trapeze ring onto the hook. **2.** Hold the trapeze handle with your back hand, take your weight on the wire and step out on your back foot. **3.** Follow with your front foot and try to relax. **4.** Straighten both legs to get body weight away from the boat and let go of the handle. **5.** Keep your feet slightly apart with legs flexed. **6.** Holding the jib or spinnaker sheet helps balance. Bend your legs if the wind drops and the boat heels to windward. **7.** Crouch as you come back in. **8.** Drop both feet back onto the cockpit floor. **9.** Take the trapeze ring off and let it go on its shock cord.

wire without rolling to windward.

⚙ Hold the jib sheet with your back hand and move your body out, taking the weight on the trapeze wire as you put your front foot on the side of the boat.

⚙ Step out immediately with your back foot, pushing off the side with your back hand into a crouched position with both feet on the side of the boat.

⚙ Straighten your legs with your feet close together. You are now trapezing!

Trapeze techniques

Learn to relax on the trapeze and keep your balance at all times. Don't be afraid of capsizing — stay cool, unhook and get off the side.

Coming in off the wire

- Bend both legs so that you're in a crouched position, and grab the trapeze handle with your front hand at the same time.
- Slip the back foot off the side of the boat and into the cockpit, supporting your body with your back hand.
- Follow immediately with your front foot, so that you are sitting on the side of the boat in a semi-hiking position.
- Knock the trapeze ring off the hook with your back hand; let go of the handle with your front hand.

Below: **You need good balance to tack from wire to wire on a skiff! Stand up, unhook and walk across the boat, ready to hook onto the new side.**

Best trapezing technique

- Stand with the balls of your feet on the side of the boat. Face forward. Keep your feet together.
- The trapeze wire will pull you forward, particularly if you move back when the boat is sailing on a reach. Use your front leg as a brace, with your back leg slightly bent to adjust your balance.
- As soon as you are out on the wire, let go of the handle. The trapeze wire and hook will hold your weight.
- Hold the jib sheet with one or both hands. Keeping it taut is useful for keeping your balance.
- If you lose your balance, grab the the helmsman's buoyancy aid so that you don't swing forward.

Above: **Trapezing on a spinnaker reach in force 3. Note the way the crew keeps his feet close together, leaning aft and looking forward.**

- Stand by the shroud when beating upwind. Move further aft when the boat bears away onto a reach. Just step back along the side of the boat, keeping your front legs braced against increased forward pull from the trapeze wire.
- Avoid getting tangled in the shock cord that holds the trapeze wire taut. The shock cord should be aft of the shroud for most trapezing positions.
- If waves keep hitting your body, pull the trapeze ring to a higher position. A wave could knock your feet off the boat, leading to a capsize.

Rolling over

One crew out on the wire provides a lot of leverage. The taller and heavier the crew, the greater the leverage. If there is a lull in the wind, the boat will roll over to windward. The crew on the trapeze must anticipate this and react by bending their legs into a semi-crouched position, or coming right in off the trapeze. In marginal winds it is fairly easy for the crew to push weight in or out, with the helm keeping his weight in and concentrating on keeping full power in the sails. It is easier for the crew to go in and out on the wire when there are lulls and gusts in the wind, leaving the helmsman to stay out on the wire and steer the boat.

Left and below: **As the helm steers into a tack, ready to swing out on the new side, the crew of this Olympic 470 leaves it to the last second to move positions.**

What happens if you capsize on the trapeze?

It is important to disengage the trapeze hook from its ring before the boat goes right over. All that's needed is to think clearly as the boat capsizes.

1. Do not panic.
2. Crouch down as the boat goes over, unhook from the trapeze ring and slide down the outside of the hull. Get straight back onto the boat if possible.
3. Try not to fall forward onto the sail; you may go straight through it.
4. Get weight off the side as soon as possible to avoid pushing the boat into a fully inverted capsize.
5. If the boat capsizes to windward (on top of you) concentrate on getting the hook off the trapeze ring. If you are under the mainsail, get out by moving toward the stern of the boat.

Left: **The trapeze hook can be useful when it comes to pulling a cat back upright. Take the strain on the righting line, with a couple of locking turns around the hook.**

Trapezing at speed

Cats and skiffs provide the highest performance on a trapeze, with the opportunity for both helm and crew to experience sailing on the wire.

Trapezing on a cat

Cats are more stable than dinghies, which makes them excellent for learning to trapeze. You can get out on the wire in light winds, with no fear that the cat may roll over to windward like a dinghy. Most cats have at least one trapeze; many have two for crew and helm.

On a dinghy, it helps to push with your feet while moving out on the trapeze. On a cat, there is nothing for your feet to push against on the flat trampoline or windward deck, so moving out on the trapeze requires a committed push with your back hand.

Feel the power!

A cat can accelerate very quickly; brace your back leg to counteract this. Sudden deceleration is likely to pose bigger problems out on the wire. The cat is blasting along at speed, the leeward bow drives into a wave and the cat slows suddenly with the result that the crew is thrown violently forward. In the worst case, the crew will slingshot around the front of the boat, which can lead to a capsize, and bruises!

A slingshot is most likely to happen on a reach, when the crew has moved right to the stern of the windward hull to keep the leeward bow flying. You need a dynamic posture, facing forward with the front leg straight and braced and the back leg well bent. If you start to fly forward, don't hesitate to grab the helmsman. Some cats have a foot strap to anchor the crew's back foot by the rear beam. Others have a "retaining line" with a small hook, which connects the end of the beam to the crew's trapeze ring to stop him being thrown forward.

Capsize on the wire

If the cat capsizes when you are out on the trapeze, there is a long way to fall. Unhook, crouch on the side and slide down the top of the trampoline into the water. Don't stay on the windward hull; this will push the cat over into an inversion. Don't fall into the mainsail either; you may break battens, rip the sail or injure yourself. Beware of getting stuck under the trampoline. Swim clear as quickly as possible.

Twin wiring

Many cats and some high-performance dinghies have twin trapezes. The crew should trapeze lower, providing the helm with a clear view forward. Sailing upwind, both crew go out on the wire and stand close together.

Left: **Use weight on the trapeze so the windward hull is skimming the surface. It's easier for the crew to go in and out, while the helm stays out on the wire.**

Left: **When three-sail reaching with a spinnaker, cats generally develop optimum VMG with one crew on the wire and one sitting in on the trampoline.**

Left: **Try to hang on if the leeward bow drives under the water on a full bore reach. Despite looking critical, this SL16 bobbed up and continued sailing, without a capsize.**

Above: **Best practice is to keep your feet close together like the helm of this Hobie 15, not like the crew who appears a bit wobbly!**

Sailing on a reach, VMG (velocity made good) may be maximized with one or both crew out on the wire. On cats, it normally pays for the helm to sit, which allows better control and allows the cat to sail deeper downwind. On skiffs, it frequently pays for both helm and crew to stay out on the wire.

Helming from the wire

The technique for moving out and coming back in on the trapeze is similar for helm and crew: step out with the front foot first, and then follow immediately with the back foot. The helm has to maintain control of the rudder at the same time.

As you go out or in on the wire, "lock" the rudder in the straight-ahead position by pushing the tiller extension down hard with your back hand on the side of the boat. If you are sailing a cat, it will be locked against the hull; if you are sailing a skiff, it will be locked against the rack or wing.

With both crew out on the wire, it can be a big help if the crew takes over the mainsheet sailing upwind. The helm can concentrate on steering the boat; the crew can use both hands to trim the sheet, so the boat keeps sailing flat at full speed. The crew passes the mainsheet back to the helm when they tack.

Left: Helming a dinghy from the wire is a balancing act, particularly when sailing on a broad reach. Note how this Contender sailor stands right on the stern to lift the bows while the boat is planing.

Sailing with a spinnaker

Do you want to sail with a symmetric or asymmetric spinnaker? Both have advantages, but the more modern asymmetric is a lot simpler to use.

Asymmetric versus symmetric

Virtually all dinghy spinnakers had a symmetrical shape until the asymmetric shape was developed in the early 1980s. Since then, all new dinghy and cat designs have been fitted with asymmetric spinnakers.

Why are symmetrics so good?

✺ The symmetrical spinnaker looks like a puffed-up triangle with equal-length sides. It is designed primarily for sailing downwind and is extremely effective on a dead run with the spinnaker boom pulled back against the shroud. It can also be flown on a close reach with the spinnaker boom against the forestay.

✺ The symmetrical spinnaker is a demanding sail to master. One corner is attached to the sheet and the other corner is attached to an identical rope known as the "guy." This is led back through the end of the spinnaker pole, which is attached to the mast and can be angled backward or forward through 90 degrees, as well as moved up and down. Sailing with a symmetrical spinnaker is rewarding if you get everything right, but can be unforgiving if you get anything wrong.

Why are asymmetrics so good?

✺ The asymmetric spinnaker looks like a puffed-up triangle with three different-length sides. It resembles an oversized jib, flown from the end of a pole that sticks straight out from the bows. Unlike the symmetrical spinnaker, it only has one clew, which allows the crew to sheet the sail on either side.

Below: **The 420 has a classic symmetrical spinnaker, but still packs a punch on a three-sail reach with the crew out on the wire on a breezy day. Note how the two clews are set almost level, with the spinnaker pole trimmed to just the right height and pulled back off the forestay.**

Below: **The V3000 has a superlight hull that planes effortlessly when powered by its big asymmetric spinnaker on a broad reach. But unlike the 420, it cannot be used for running directly downwind.**

☼ The asymmetric spinnaker is designed for sailing at full bore on a reach, with its power providing increased speed, which tightens the angle of the apparent wind. This allows the crew to bear away and sail deep downwind, while sailing a zigzag course from jibe to jibe. It is not designed for running straight downwind, although some asymmetric dinghies are fitted with a spinnaker pole, which can be angled to the windward side to provide more conventional downwind performance. Asymmetric spinnakers are also not good on a close reach, when there will be too much power in the sail, pushing the boat over and driving it sideways.

☼ The asymmetric spinnaker is easy to master, so long as you learn with one of modest size. It is simple, straightforward and relatively forgiving. Jibing is easier than than with a symmetric spinnaker.

Spinnaker care

☼ Spinnakers are made from light-weight, rip-stop nylon. This is extremely strong, but if it snags it will tear easily. Make sure that anything sharp (such as pins, rings or shackles), are well covered with insulating tape.

☼ Most modern dinghies and cats have a "chute" from which to launch the spinnaker, replacing the traditional spinnaker bag in the cockpit or on the trampoline. The chute is either solid molded plastic or a taut mesh. When pulling the spinnaker back into the chute,

Safe hoisting and dropping

When the wind is astern of the dinghy there is least pressure on the spinnaker. As soon as the boat moves onto a broad reach, you move into a zone where the spinnaker will catch the wind and power up. Do not hoist or drop the spinnaker in this zone if at all possible.

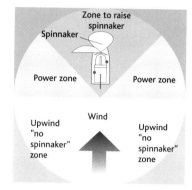

Below: **When all the control lines are attached, pull the spinnaker into its chute and then try a dry land hoist to check it has been done correctly.**

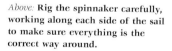

Above: **Rig the spinnaker carefully, working along each side of the sail to make sure everything is the correct way around.**

beware of it snagging. If it jams, don't pull harder and harder; try to work out what has gone wrong — you might be standing on the halyard!

☼ Use spinnaker tape to repair small tears. Available from chandlers, it sticks easily to a dry, clean sail with all salt removed.

TIP

The symmetrical spinnaker is excellent for inland locations where space may be limited and it's much more efficient when sailing directly downwind, but you still have the option of reaching. The asymmetric spinnaker is at its best on open water where you can enjoy a high-speed blast without any worries about running out of space while jibing downwind.

Rigging a spinnaker

Unlike the mainsail or jib, the spinnaker is a free-flying sail, which is hoisted and dropped while you are sailing at speed. When setting up the spinnaker, it's vital to ensure you've got everything right.

Setting up an asymmetric spinnaker

- Use bowlines to attach the halyard, retrieval and tack line.
- Identify the tack, clew and head.
- The spinnaker is launched and retrieved by a continuous loop line. One end is attached to the head of the sail and acts as the halyard. The other is attached to a patch on the outside of the sail and acts as the retrieval line. The retrieval end of the line is led through one or two rings on the outside of the sail, which helps feed the sail into the mouth of the chute when it is pulled down.
- The tack of the spinnaker is attached to the tack line at the end of the spinnaker pole.
- The spinnaker sheet also forms a continuous loop. Double it over and push the end of the loop through the ring in the clew, then

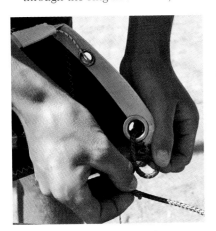

Above: **The tack of an asymmetric spinnaker is attached to the spinnaker pole by a short tack line. Use a bowline.**

pull the two free ends through to lock the sheet tight. Lead the free ends outside the shrouds and through the spinnaker blocks. Ensure each sheet is fed in the correct direction so that the ratchet on the block will lock with the sheet under tension. Tie the two ends of the sheet together with a double figure-eight knot to make a continuous loop.

- Check that the spinnaker can be launched and retrieved successfully. Only the head and clew should be visible when the sail is pulled back into its chute.
- Check that the spinnaker can be jibed from side to side: the sheet must pass outside the jib luff and spinnaker retrieval line. Attention to detail is all important.

Setting up a symmetric spinnaker

- Identify the head. Run your hand down the port (red) and starboard (green) sides of the sail to ensure each clew is on the correct side of the boat.
- If the dinghy is fitted with a chute, a continuous loop is used as the halyard and retrieval line.

TIP

Always do a test hoist on dry land when the wind is light. Check the spinnaker is the correct way up — it's embarrassing to hoist upside-down!

Asymmetric spinnaker setup

- Attach one end of the sheet to the starboard clew with a bowline. Lead it back, outside the starboard shroud and through the starboard spinnaker block, then across to the port-side spinnaker block. Make sure the sheet passes through each block in the correct direction for sheeting and easing the sail. Lead the free end forward outside the port shroud, and tie it to the port clew with a bowline.
- Pull the spinnaker into the chute, then check to ensure it can be hoisted and retrieved successfully. The pole isn't connected to the spinnaker until the hoist. It is stored alongside the main boom, from where it can be pushed forward by the crew.

Below (left to right): **1.** Hoist the asymmetric spinnaker to make sure that halyard, retrieval line and sheets are correctly attached and will launch on the correct sides of the shrouds and forestay.

2. If all is well, use the retrieval line to pull the spinnaker inside its chute.
3. The spinnaker sheet should be continuous, attached to the clew with an overhand knot at the halfway point.

4. Both free ends of the spinnaker sheet should be tied together with a secure double knot so you can grab the sheet at any point.

Spinnaker bags

On some dinghies the spinnaker is stowed in a bag at the front of the cockpit. There is no retrieval line. Instead, the crew has to grab the sail and bundle it into the bag.

With the bag system, the spinnaker cannot be launched from the bow. It is always preferable to launch it to leeward (downwind), but the bag system means it may be on the wrong side. Some racing crew overcome this problem by having a bag on each side of the cockpit, so that they can plan to drop the spinnaker on the correct side for the next leeward hoist. It's easier to drop the spinnaker on the windward side than trying to drag it under the boom.

Right: **Some boats have a spinnaker bag by the mast. This keeps weight and complexity out of the bows, but requires greater crew skill when launching or stowing the spinnaker.**

Asymmetric control

Learn to launch an asymmetric spinnaker and sail at full bore on the apparent wind, always under control.

Launching an asymmetric

Unless the wind is very light, the helmsman must bear away downwind to hoist the spinnaker. As the spinnaker is hoisted, it will be blanketed by the mainsail. This ensures there is no danger of the partly hoisted spinnaker filling with wind and blowing the boat over sideways.

✿ Bear away downwind, then sail a straight course with the boat absolutely level.

✿ The crew hoists the spinnaker on the halyard, which pulls the spinnaker pole out of the bow at the same time. Make sure the sheets will run free. Stand in the cockpit with the halyard immediately in front. When the helm is ready for the hoist, pull in the halyard hand-over-hand.

Concentrate on hoisting the spinnaker as quickly as possible, so that it cannot drop into the water or fill with wind when half-hoisted.

✿ The halyard is pulled through a cleat, which will jam automatically. Make sure it is hoisted all the way to the top if you hoist the spinnaker on land, and mark the halyard where it passes through the cleat. Then every time you hoist on the water, you will know when it is fully up.

✿ Take the leeward spinnaker sheet and start to pull it in as the helm heads up onto a broad reach to power up the sail. If it is twisted, a jibe will often set it straight.

Sailing on apparent wind

✿ The asymmetric spinnaker is a very powerful sail. You need to find the right balance between generating maximum power and maintaining control. This will provide the best VMG (velocity made good) as you sail downwind. As the boat accelerates, the effect of apparent wind will allow the boat to be sailed downwind on a full speed reach.

Below: **The helmsman of this RS200 steers deep downwind on a broad reach, ensuring that the mainsail blankets the spinnaker while it is being hoisted by the crew.**

Left: **Loads of power and speed for this Laser 2000 on a force 5 day. You can see the helm is bearing away on the apparent wind, heading deeper downwind to keep the boat upright. If the boat heels any more, it may luff out of control, or "broach."**

Perfect trim

❂ Sailing downwind with an asymmetric spinnaker, the crew should move well back to take weight off the bows, either hiking or out on the trapeze. Hold the spinnaker sheet with both hands and watch the luff (leading edge of the spinnaker) like a hawk. Pull the sheet in to stop the sail flapping, and then ease it until the luff begins to curl. This will provide maximum power. If there is no curl in the luff, the sail is too tight, which will interfere with airflow. Ease the sheet. If the luff is collapsing, the sail is too loose, which will depower the sail. Pull in the sheet.

❂ Push the tiller away to steer toward the wind and power up the spinnaker, so that you are sailing at full speed on the apparent wind.

❂ The boat will only respond to steering with an asymmetric when it is kept flat. If the boat heels over, it will slow down and may turn up toward the wind, out of control. When a gust hits and the boat starts to heel, bear away immediately to hold it flat on the water. If the wind drops and the boat slows down, head up to increase power and speed. The wind is never constant in speed or direction, so you will always sail a "wiggly" course with an asymmetric spinnaker: luffing to build power, bearing away to keep control.

❂ The crew needs to trim the spinnaker sheet virtually all the time. The helm must steer to follow the spinnaker, luffing when power decreases, bearing away when power increases.

Below: **The spinnaker helps lift the bow of this Comet Trio on a flat-out reach. The furled jib decreases sail area and allows clear air flow into the spinnaker. Note how the helm has opted to sail downwind and sit inboard, which makes it easier for him to control the boat.**

TIP

If you capsize with an asymmetric or symmetric spinnaker, pull it back into its chute (or spinnaker bag) before you attempt to right the boat.

Jibing an asymmetric spinnaker

Learn how to jibe and drop an asymmetric spinnaker under full control. Avoiding common mistakes that can make it all turn out wrong is just a matter of thinking clearly, steering carefully, staying on a downwind course and holding the boat flat throughout the turn. After that, it's easy to do the drop.

Jibing with an asymmetric spinnaker

The great thing about asymmetric spinnakers is that they are very easy to jibe as you blast at full speed downwind, going from tack to tack.

What does the helmsman do?

- The helmsman should keep the boat as flat as possible throughout the jibe, while concentrating on steering through a steady turn.
- Keep the boat moving fast to minimize apparent wind, which will reduce power in the mainsail. For instance, if you sail through a jibe at 10 knots in 20 knots of true wind, the apparent wind will be 10 knots as it swings behind the boat. But if you slow down to 5 knots, the apparent wind will increase to 15 knots and make the mainsail more difficult to control during a jibe.
- Beware of luffing too high on the new tack when the mainsail changes sides. Be ready to bear away to keep the boat heading downwind, under control, before luffing to build power in the spinnaker.

What does the crew do?

- The spinnaker is kept under control during the jibe by being pulled back against the jib.
- As the helmsman begins steering into the jibe, grab the new sheet and pull in any slack. Hold the old sheet as you move across the boat, which will help flatten the spinnaker as the stern of the boat passes through the eye of the wind.
- Let go of the old sheet and quickly pull in the new one as you move onto the side of the boat, ready to power up for the new reach.
- Trim the spinnaker sheet until the luff has a slight curl. Focus on getting the trim correct.

Dropping an asymmetric spinnaker

- It is vital to bear away downwind. This allows the crew to come into the middle of the cockpit to let go the halyard and pull in the retrieval line, with the mainsail blanketing the spinnaker for optimum control.

Above: **Note how the Laser 2000 is kept flat as the helm bears away dead downwind and the crew pulls in slack on the spinnaker sheet for the new jibe.**

Above: **As the boat changes direction past dead downwind — with wind over the stern on the port side — the helm should flip the boom across with a yank on the falls of the mainsheet.**

⚙ The crew can pass the spinnaker sheet to the helmsman or just stand on it — with the boat sailing downwind, there won't be much power in the sail.

⚙ Pull in any slack on the retrieval line before letting the halyard go. This is vital to keep the spinnaker drop under control.

⚙ Flick the halyard out of its cleat to let it go, and then quickly pull in the retrieval line hand-over-hand. Stop when the spinnaker has been pulled right back into the chute.

Problems with the drop

Either the spinnaker won't pull back all the way into its chute, or it drops into the water and gets run over by the boat. This can lead to a really nasty mess, with the spinnaker wrapped around the daggerboard.

⚙ Always tension the retrieval line before the drop. This will help gather the sail, ensuring it fits easily into the chute and will not drop over the bows.

Right: **Don't drop the spinnaker in the water — it should be going into the chute and not get run over by the boat! The helm needs to be steering deeper downwind; the crew needs to be quicker retrieving.**

⚙ The quicker you pull that retrieval line, the less chance there is of the spinnaker dropping under the chute. Throw both hands back behind your body as you pull the line in.

⚙ Make sure the continuous halyard/retrieval line cannot snag. It must run free, without a bundle of knitting jamming in a block.

⚙ Check you're not standing on the halyard/retrieval line or that the halyard hasn't locked back into its cleat — two common mistakes!

⚙ If the spinnaker will not pull into the chute, pulling harder may tear the sail. It is much better to go for a quick re-hoist, and then drop the spinnaker again.

Above: **Perfect!** Keep steering downwind with the boat held flat, letting the crew sheet in on the new side before luffing onto a new reaching course.

Above: **No!** These guys tried to flip the boom too early, lost control of the steering and are due for a capsize.

Symmetric spinnaker control

The classic style of spinnaker is a more difficult sail to manage than the modern asymmetric. Practice will be needed to keep it under control, particularly in stronger winds.

Left: **The crew of a Cadet attaches the inner end of the spinnaker pole to the mast, while the helm stands with the tiller between his legs — a great position to keep the boat balanced.**

Bottom: **The symmetrical spinnaker requires greater skills than the asymmetric spinnaker, due to having a removable pole and sheets led to both corners, one of which acts as the "guy."**

○ Pull the spinnaker pole forward from the boom and clip the outer end to the guy. Attach the uphaul/downhaul or slide it into position in the middle of the pole, then clip the inner end to the mast.

○ Two pairs of hands are needed to pull the halyard and hold the sheet and guy while the spinnaker is hoisted. A symmetric is generally a lot smaller than an asymmetric spinnaker, so the hoist is quicker. One good method is for the helmsman to stand with the tiller between his legs, using both hands to pull up the halyard quickly, with the crew ready to pull in on the sheet and guy as soon as the spinnaker is hoisted.

Managing the spinnaker pole

The spinnaker pole has to be handled by the crew during hoists, jibes and drops. This is different from most asymmetric systems, which automatically launch or retract the spinnaker pole during hoists or drops. During asymmetric jibes the pole is usually left alone. The pole is attached in three places.

○ The outer end is clipped onto the "guy," which acts as the sheet on the windward side of the boat.

○ The inner end is clipped onto the mast.

○ The center is attached to the uphaul/downhaul, which is used to control the vertical angle of the pole. The outhaul/downhaul may be permanently attached, so the boom simply slides through a ring.

Hoisting the spinnaker

If you are launching the spinnaker from a chute, which is in front of the jib, the hoist can be made on either tack. If you are launching from a bag in the cockpit, you can only do this on the leeward side, where it will be blanketed by the mainsail.

Trimming the spinnaker

○ The spinnaker should be set at approximately right angles to the wind. The guy is used to lock the spinnaker's position, with the end of the pole pressing against the windward clew.

Jibing a spinnaker

Above (left to right): **1.** Going into a jibe, the crew unclips the spinnaker pole from the mast, then clips it to the new guy. **2.** The crew unclips the end of the pole from the old guy and prepares to clip it to the mast. **3.** As the wind starts to blow from the new side, the helm flips the boom across. With the pole clipped onto the mast, the crew pulls back on the guy, ensuring the pole is at the correct angle and height for the new course, and then starts trimming the sheet.

Below: **Who said symmetrical spinnakers are boring? Cranked up on a broad reach, these 420 sailors are having a lot of fun.**

✪ Pole height should be adjusted with the uphaul/downhaul so that both windward and leeward clews are level. This will change with the wind angle: the end of the pole needs to be raised for a reach and lowered for a run.

✪ Trim the spinnaker sheet with the guy locked by a cleat. For maximum power, trim the sail so that the luff is just curling.

✪ Sailing on a reach, the guy will obstruct the crew. A hook or "twinning" control line is used to pull the guy down to deck level by the shroud.

Jibing the spinnaker

The standard method of jibing the spinnaker is to move the pole from side to side, while the boat is sailing almost directly downwind with the boom on the new side.

✪ Unclip the pole from the mast.
✪ Clip the end of the pole to the old sheet, which becomes the new guy.
✪ Unclip the other end of the pole. The old guy will fall away, ready to take over as the new sheet.
✪ Clip the free end of the pole to the mast.

Dropping the spinnaker

Sail deep downwind to blanket the spinnaker. If the boat has a chute, let go the halyard and pull smartly in on the retrieval line. Then unclip and stow the pole. If the boat has a bag in the cockpit, the drop is easiest on the windward side. Take off the pole, then pull the spinnaker down by its leech and bundle it into the bag.

Dinghy care

Look after your boat and it will look after you. Forget about it and it will get run-down, waste money and may even let you down.

No salt!

If you have been sailing on salt water, always wash off the salt or it will corrode fittings, abrade sailcloth and speed the deterioration of your boat. Use a hose to wash everything, and then leave the boat and its sails to air-dry but do not let sails "flog."

Clothing care

Soak your wetsuit, boots, buoyancy aid and anything else in fresh water to get rid of any salt. Otherwise it won't dry properly, zippers will corrode and seize up, everything will feel sticky and the colors will fade.

Above: **Find a clean space to work on your boat and make sure everything is packed so it will be in top condition next time you go sailing. Beware of tar on the beach or dirt on the grass!**

Below: **A Dacron sail can be rolled or folded, but avoid hard creases. A Mylar laminate type of sail can only be rolled. If it is creased, it will crack.**

Hang your wetsuit or drysuit on a hanger in a cool, dark closet. Check drysuit seals and replace any that look ready to tear. Wax the heavy-duty drysuit zipper to ensure it will open and close easily.

Neoprene boots can get smelly, generally caused from wearing them on a hot day. Water won't wash the smell away. Use a proprietary cleaner to kill the bacteria inside.

Boat cleaning

If a hose is unavailable, a sponge or wet cloth and a bucket of water should be sufficient to properly clean the hull and deck. Acetone, carefully applied and wiped on with a rag will remove deeper grime. Avoid domestic cleaning products, which may leave a slippery residue. Specialized boat cleaners include non-slip polish.

Sail care

Wash dirty sails with warm water and detergent, then rinse with cold, fresh water. Do not attack sails with something like a hard-bristle brush, or use chemicals or bleach.

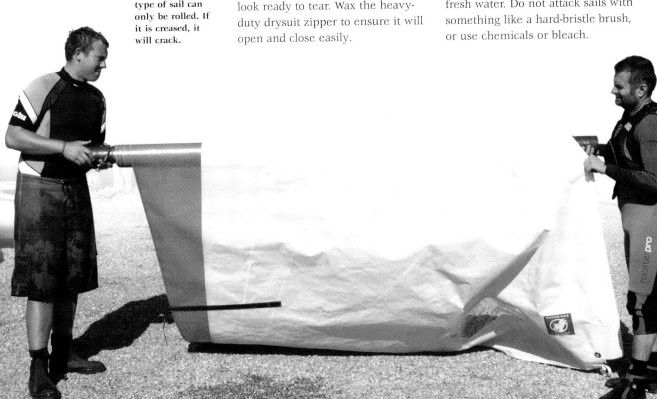

Allowing a sail to flap hard in the wind to dry, known as "flogging," can damage the coating of a Dacron sail or delaminate a Mylar sail over time. The mainsail is not a problem, since it is held fairly rigid by the mast, boom and battens. But the jib will flog in stronger winds so you should roll it up or drop it instead.

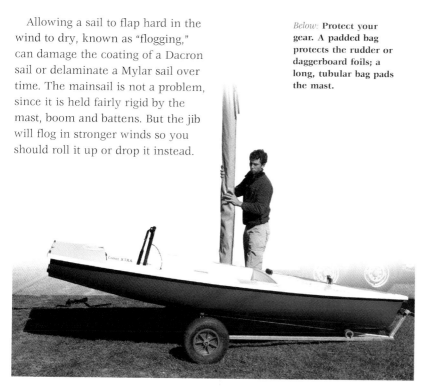

Below: **Protect your gear. A padded bag protects the rudder or daggerboard foils; a long, tubular bag pads the mast.**

Secure the cover with all the straps pulled tight under the hull. Make sure water cannot leak inside. If you have a boom-up cover, there is often a problem with rain getting in by the mast. Leave the dinghy bows-up, or with self-bailers open, so that water drains straight out.

Make sure the dinghy is securely attached to ground anchors. Dinghies blowing over in the winter cause carnage. For extra safety, consider lowering the mast. Be aware of your next-door neighbor!

Home storage

Make sure the boat is supported so it cannot sag — especially for a polypropylene or polyethylene hull, which could deform. Support the mast so it is absolutely straight.

Sails deteriorate in strong sunlight so store them out of the light. If you leave the dinghy in a boat park with the jib rolled, use a protective zip-up sock to cover the sail. Roll laminate sails from head to foot; flake Dacron sails in a series of folds. Take out the battens or release batten tension.

Avoid storing a sail that is still wet. Spinnaker cloth is particularly susceptible to mildew, which will be difficult to remove.

Boat park storage

Drain all water out of the boat. Unscrew inspection hatches and dry the inside of the hull with a sponge. Remove the drain plugs to allow air to circulate inside the hull. Just remember to put them back next time you go sailing!

Below: **When road towing, use top and bottom covers to protect the hull.**

Dinghy damage

Make regular checks to keep all your dinghy equipment in top condition. It will reward you with safer and less expensive sailing throughout the

Left: **Look at all that string! This Merlin Rocket has highly complex rig controls and there is a lot to replace when it all wears out.**

✪ Check the boat thoroughly and replace anything that is not in perfect working order.

✪ Sheets and control lines fray if the same area is regularly gripped by a ratchet block or rubs against a fair-lead. The frayed area will slow the rope down as you ease or tension it, and may also break. Replace it as soon as possible.

✪ Shock cord is used to keep things under tension, such as trapeze wires, foot straps or the continuous halyard/retrieval line for the spinnaker, and to hold the rudder or daggerboard down. Shock cord eventually stretches and loses its recoil.

their spring. Wash out any salt to prevent corrosion and give them a spray with silicone. If a spring wears out, the whole cleat will need to be replaced.

✪ Shrouds are strong, but individual wires can break — a particular problem with roller-furling forestays. The top swivel often doesn't turn as freely as the bottom one, straining individual wires and eventually breaking them. Replace the shroud or risk the mast falling down.

✪ Check for corrosion or weakness where the shrouds and forestay are attached to the mast. Then check the chainplates and forestay connection at the bow.

✪ Centerboards, daggerboards and rudder blades are prone to "dings" caused by hitting the bottom. The more fragile the foil, the worse the ding will be. You can ram a molded plastic foil into the ground and only get a few scratches, but the same impact will knock the bottom right off a lightweight laminate foil.

✪ Do not ignore damage; it will only get worse. Minor dings can be repaired with gel coat filler rubbed back to a smooth finish with wet and dry sandpaper. If a bigger chunk has been knocked off the foil, build up the area with marine epoxy filler, then power-sand it to the correct shape.

Right: **A beautiful glass-sheathed, laminate wood foil requires careful handling. If you let it hit the bottom, the leading edge will get damaged.**

Far right: **Boat fittings will loosen with extended use. Check the rudder is a tight fit inside its stock and that the pintles are secure in the transom.**

Buying second-hand

If you want to buy a second-hand dinghy, find out what are the most likely things to go wrong. Major problem areas can include:

☀ If the pintles come loose, access to tighten or replace them can be very difficult on some boats.

☀ Running aground at speed can split the back of the daggerboard case. Check carefully inside.

☀ The mast base is a high-stress area, particularly on unstayed dinghies where the mast slots into a hole in the deck. If it is cracked inside, repair may be impossible.

☀ If the laminate is sub-standard, the foam will absorb water, put on weight and start to disintegrate. Not good news for any boat!

☀ Beware of buoyancy tanks that leak around the seams. Water gets inside and can be difficult to get out.

☀ Battens will eventually cut or wear their way out of their pockets, normally sticking out at the inner end when under tension. Repairs needed!

☀ Trailers sometimes get pushed into the water. Salt water will eventually cause seized bearings in the wheels, most likely when you're a long way from home.

Hull dings

☀ Polyethylene and polypropylene hulls are not suitable for amateur repair, so it is just as well they are bang-proof, although the plastic can scratch badly.

☀ Fibreglass is more susceptible to minor impact damage, but is reasonably easy to repair. Fibergalss repair materials should only be used in dry, dust-free conditions with a reasonably warm temperature.

☀ Damage to the gel coat outer skin can be repaired with a correctly color-matched two-part gel coat. Sand the damaged area smooth before applying the gel coat.

☀ More extensive damage, which may require cutting through fibreglass into the foam core, is best handled by professionals, as it's important to get everything absolutely right.

Dinghy and cat racing

Racing is fun. It is also the best way to improve sailing ability and make friends at the same time. You can race at all levels, from complete novice to full-time professional.

Where should I race?

Racing is organized by sailing clubs and dinghy classes. Clubs organize local race series for their members, mostly on weekends and summer evenings, plus regattas. Class associations organize regional and national events and championships, where the sailors race at different venues hosted by a local club.

Right: **Turning around the leeward mark on a windward-leeward course. The leading 49er has jibed around and is starting to beat back up the course; the pursuing 49er has just dropped its spinnaker in the final approach to the mark.**

How should I race?

Boats frequently race together as a class: whoever finishes first is the winner. Different classes may also race together on handicap. In the U.S., the Performance Handicap Racing Fleet (PHRF) system, based on each yacht's relative speed, is used in yacht racing. Cats use a handicap based on boat measurements.

Left: **Racing is crowded! These tightly bunched Cadets show why it is vital to get clean wind.**

What should I race?

- Hiking dinghies need least space and are excellent for racing on inland water where the wind may be shifty. Fast tacking and maneuverability provide great tactical racing.
- Trapeze dinghies need more space to show off their pace. They are recommended for larger lakes and reservoirs, or open waters.
- Skiff-style dinghies need even more space to maximize use of their asymmetric spinnakers, zigzagging on a series of gybes to race downwind.
- Cats need the most space. They are slow to tack or maneuver, but

Left: **Insurance is required to enter a race. With fast-closing speeds, accidents are possible, though injuries are rare.**

very fast in a straight line. As with skiff-style dinghies, cats must sail a zigzag course downwind.

- Race organizers will require third-party insurance coverage.

The racing course

A race should ideally test sailors on different points of sailing: upwind, downwind, reaching and mark rounding. A local club may set a course using existing buoys and channel markers. However, for a championship or national event, the organizers will "lay a course" with their own buoys, using a specific layout. These buoys or marks need to be rounded in a certain order.

Windward–leeward course

The simplest type of course has upwind (windward) and downwind (leeward) legs, with racers sailing a number of times around the course. The start line is at the leeward end of the course and also acts as the finish. A spacer leg with a short beam reach is often incorporated to prevent collisions when boats turn around the windward mark at the top of the course.

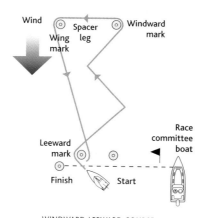

WINDWARD-LEEWARD COURSE

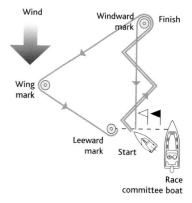

CLASSIC COURSE

Classic course

The traditional Olympic racing course was a "triangle and sausage" incorporating a beat to the windward mark at the top of the course, a reach out to the "wing mark," a reach on the opposite tack to the leeward mark at the bottom of the course, a beat to the windward mark, a dead run to the

leeward mark and a final beat to the finish by the windward mark. The sequence of triangles or sausages can be changed, as can the number of laps. Modern variations include the P-shaped or trapezoid course, which can be tailored to provide a suitable mixture of beating, reaching and running.

The rules of the road state who has right of way in order to avoid collisions on the water. More specific rules are required when racing.

Watch out!

There is greater risk of collision at several stages of the race:

- Boats will be very close together at the start, when they jockey to get away ahead of everyone else.
- Boats will be crossing on different tacks when sailing upwind toward the windward mark.
- Boats will be crossing on different jibes when sailing downwind toward the leeward mark.
- Boats will be squeezed together when rounding marks.
- Boats will be overtaking on reaches.

Racing Rules

The Racing Rules of Sailing are updated by the ISAF (International Sailing Federation) every four years. If you break a rule (for instance, not giving way on port tack or barging in when turning around a mark), you must do a "penalty turn" as soon as possible. The penalty turn must be through 360 degrees, requiring a tack and jibe. Some race organizers require a 720-degree penalty turn.

If you break a rule and continue racing without a penalty turn, another boat may protest. A protest committee will decide the outcome, which may be disqualification.

Below: **As with any sailing situation, port tack must give way to starboard tack. In this instance, the port-tack Cadets are all well clear.**

The racing rules

Right of way

- *Rule 10*: *When boats are on opposite tacks, a port-tack boat shall keep clear of a starboard-tack boat.* The port-tack boat can either tack, slow down or bear away under the stern of the starboard-tack boat. This also applies to sailing downwind — the port-tack boat must jibe out of the way.

Above: **Boats that have an overlap to windward must keep clear. The Topper with the blue and white sail cannot bear down on the Toppers to leeward.**

- *Rule 11*: *When boats are on the same tack and overlapped, a windward boat shall keep clear of a leeward boat.* An "overlap" is when any part of one boat overlaps the other: when the bow of one boat is level with the helmsman of the other boat. A boat that is attempting to overtake on the windward side cannot force the leeward boat to change course.

- *Rule 12*: *When boats are on the same tack and not overlapped, a boat clear astern shall keep clear of a boat clear ahead.* "Clear astern" or "clear ahead" means there is no overlap between the boats.

Tacking

⚙ *Rule 13*: *After a boat passes head-to-wind, she shall keep clear of other boats until she is on a close-hauled course. During that time rules 10, 11 and 12 do not apply. If two boats are subject to this rule at the same time, the one on the other's port side or the one astern shall keep clear.*

This rule deals with the problem of a port-tack boat that tacks (or jibes) at the last moment to avoid a starboard-tack boat, with the result that the starboard-tack boat has to take avoiding action. The port-tack boat must complete its tack and be sailing with the mainsail sheeted in on the new side, while it is in clear water.

Avoiding contact

⚙ *Rule 14*: *A boat shall avoid contact with another boat if reasonably possible.*

Even if you have right of way, avoid collisions at all costs!

Marks or obstructions

⚙ *Rule 18*: *When boats are overlapped, the outside boat shall give the inside boat room to round or pass the mark or obstruction, and if the inside boat has right of way the outside boat shall also keep clear.*

Left: **Tack or dip? In a port-starboard situation, you have to decide if it's best to tack or bear away a few degrees to dip under the stern of the starboard-tack boat.**

This rule is used to avoid collisions when boats pile around a mark on the course. An overlap must be established before the boats reach the "two-length zone," which extends in a circle two boat-lengths from the mark.

The message is: you cannot push in at the last moment; you have to wait your turn to round the mark. But if a boat on the inside establishes an overlap before the two-length zone, the outside boat must give it enough room to round the mark.

Below: **Turning around a mark, boats on the inside must be given room. The two Hobie Cats have to go wide to leave space for the two RS Fevas which arrived within two boat-lengths of the mark first.**

✿ *Preparatory:* One sound signal. Four minutes to go. Code Flag P is hoisted (the "Blue Peter" with blue background and white square).

✿ *One minute:* One long sound signal. One minute to go. Code Flag P is dropped.

✿ *Start:* One sound signal. The class flag is dropped.

Most boats, if not all, will start on starboard tack as they begin to beat toward the windward mark. Making a perfect start requires experience and a cool head.

The start line

The race organizers lay a start line, positioning their committee boat at one end to start the race and an outer limit mark at the other end.

The first leg of the race is normally directly upwind. This theoretically gives all boats the chance of an equal start as the wind is coming from ahead.

The length of the start line should be approximately equal to the length of all the boats added together, plus an additional 25–50 percent to provide a little more space. The start line should be set at right angles to the wind. Ideally, the port end of the line will be angled forward by 5–10 degrees.

This "line bias" helps to ensure that boats are spread out along the full length of the line at the start. It is extremely difficult to set the start line at a perfect angle to give everyone an equal chance, particularly if the wind keeps changing direction. Too much bias

to port, boats will be able to sail across the fleet on port tack. Too much bias to starboard means all boats will be bunched at the starboard end, trying to squeeze around the committee boat with the rest of the line empty.

Countdown

You need a countdown timer synchronized with the "warning signal" to make a perfect start. Wear it on your wrist or attach it to the port side of the boom, to give both crew a clear view.

✿ *Warning:* One sound signal. Five minutes to go. The class flag is hoisted on the committee boat.

The perfect start

The bow of your boat hits the line as the starting signal sounds. Your boat is sailing in the correct direction, at full speed, in clean wind. You have assessed port and starboard bias and worked out which end of the line is most favorable, ensuring you cross at the optimum point.

Above: **Perfect! Leave the start line at full speed, with no boat ahead or directly to windward. The green Cadet is well away.**

Hare and tortoise

A "pursuit race" can provide a lot of fun for a fleet with a mixture of different boats. Handicaps are calculated in advance over a specific timescale during which the boats will race around the course. The slowest boats start first, followed by progressively faster boats, with the fastest boats starting last of all. At the end of the period, the race is completed when the leading boat finishes its lap of the course.

Countdown flags

Learn to recognize the flags that identify the countdown to the start. Sound signals are referred to as guns, although normally a horn or whistle is used. Sound signals are used to draw your attention to the flags, which tell you what to do.

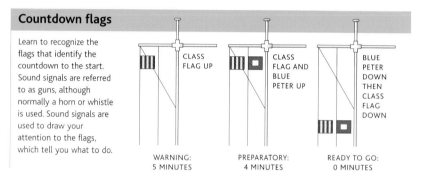

The imperfect start

Your boat is boxed in with boats ahead and to windward making a terrible mess of the wind. The result is your boat cannot sail fast or point high. The solution is to tack as soon as possible, getting away from other boats and finding clean wind.

The premature start

Do not cross the line too early. If any part of your boat is over the line when the starting signal sounds, you are "on the course side," known as OCS. You must go back and recross the line, without interfering with other boats. The committee boat will signal one or more boats are OCS by making one sound signal and hoisting Code Flag X (blue cross on white background).

Flag signals

In some situations, half the fleet or more may be over the start line. The committee boat will signal:
• a General Recall with two sound signals and the First Substitute flag (yellow on blue triangle). All the fleet must return and wait for the start sequence to recommence.
If there are further general recalls, more draconian rules may be used.

• Round the Ends rule: any boat that is OCS within one minute of the start must go around the end of the start line to restart. This is indicated by Code Flag I (black circle on yellow background).
• Black Flag rule: Any boat that is OCS within one minute of the start is disqualified from the race.

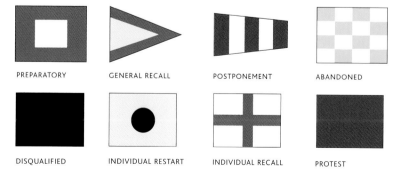

Racing around the course

A series of stages lead around the course based on beating, reaching and running, with windward and leeward turning marks at either end.

Racing upwind

The first leg of the race is normally a beat to the windward mark. The object is to get there first. To do that you have to sail fast in clear wind and choose the right side of the course.

If you are sailing close behind a boat that is to windward or leeward, it will interfere with your wind. Tack as soon as possible so that you can sail in clean wind. Then, if necessary, tack back again.

"Covering" is a tactic where one boat keeps a rival boat in its wind shadow. Every time the other boat tacks to break cover and find clean wind, the leading boat tacks to reestablish cover and stay ahead.

Boats can tack up the middle of the course (known as the "rhumb line"), from side to side all the way across the course, or up one side of the course that may be favored by better conditions (for instance, more consistent wind, smoother water or more favorable tide). The wind may, of course, change direction. If the wind shifts to the right, the right side of the course will become closer to the windward mark, and vice versa.

Turning around the windward mark

Sound advice is to always make the final approach to a mark on starboard tack. On port tack, you

Above: **Toppers cross the start line and start the first beat to windward. Many will soon tack onto port in order to clear their wind.**

run the risk of being caught by a long line of starboard-tack boats. But if you can find a slot to tack around the mark, a late approach on port tack could be a winning maneuver.

Boats will tend to bunch up in the final approach to the windward mark, which may create a big problem with turbulent wind.

Below: **Bearing away around the mark from a beat to a run. The crew is getting ready with the spinnaker pole.**

If conditions are crowded, don't attempt to give the windward mark a close shave that requires pointing the boat as high as possible. Delay tacking so that you have sufficient space to leeward to handle the effects of wind shadow. There is nothing worse than hitting or missing the mark, and having to go around it again.

At the top of the course, you will either bear away onto a beam reach or start to head downwind. Keep the boat flat on the water, so that it will bear away easily. Prepare to move weight back as it accelerates on a reach. Don't let the boom hit the mark or you will have to go around again!

Racing downwind

If you are racing a dinghy with an asymmetric spinnaker, or any catamaran, it is quickest to reach from jibe to jibe. If you are racing a dinghy with a symmetrical spinnaker, or a single-handed dinghy such as a Laser, it is quickest to sail along the rhumb line directly downwind.

Below: **Sailing back after the race. If you did badly, learn from your mistakes and vow to do better next time!**

Beware of port-starboard crossings when reaching at high speed under spinnaker. The starboard-tack boat always has right of way — collision can cause a lot of expensive damage.

Boats racing downwind can be affected by wind turbulence. If you are running downwind, a boat directly behind will cause wind shadow and may be able to overtake. If you are reaching across the wind, a boat ahead and to windward will cause wind shadow and be impossible to overtake.

Beware of "luffing." It is permitted for a boat to luff above its "proper course" (directly to the next mark) to prevent a boat to windward from overtaking. It is not permitted to luff beyond head-to-wind. The other boat

Above: **Sailing directly downwind, it can be difficult to avoid being "blanketed" by boats coming up behind. The Cadet with the blue spinnaker is in danger of being overtaken.**

must also be given enough time to change its course without a collision.

Boats will change course from a reach or run to a beat. Go in wide so that you can come out tight, with the daggerboard or centerboard fully down and the sails sheeted right in.

The finish

The race continues to the finish, which may be at the top of the course after another beat, or at the bottom of the course after another downwind leg.

Cruising

4

Choosing a yacht

If you visit a marina or look through a yachting magazine, the choice of yachts can overwhelm. So many look much the same. But look a bit harder and you will discover yachts of all shapes and sizes, pristine to jaded, with hulls made of fiberglass, wood, steel, aluminum or even concrete!

What is the best size?

In the 1970s a 25-foot (7 m) yacht would have been considered a good size for cruising with family and friends. Since then, size has increased along with people's aspirations. Yachts of around 35 feet (10.5 m) have become normal for family cruising, and 50-foot (15 m) boats have become a common sight. Most range from about 28–40 feet (8.5 to 12 m) in length, and have white fiberglass hulls and single-mast Bermudan rigs.

Right: **The Cornish Shrimper is a delightful modern pocket cruiser in a traditional style, complete with tan sails and a gaff mainsail.**

Left: **The Parker 275 is a small yacht with a lifting keel and rudder, which allow it to be moored in shallow water or launched on a road trailer.**

Left: **Top of the class. Swan is a legend to which many owners aspire. This is one of the classic designs — a 48-foot (14.6 m) Swan specially designed for members of the New York Yacht Club.**

Why have a cruiser?

⚙ A bigger yacht should sail or motor faster, as it has a longer waterline length. When sailing, a few extra knots of speed can make a big difference to arrival times.

⚙ A bigger yacht should provide the crew with a more pleasant ride in rough water. The bigger the boat, the less it will be affected by waves. Novices will be less likely to be scared by the boat's motion and hopefully will be less inclined to feel seasick!

⚙ A bigger yacht will have more space in the cockpit and down below, thus allowing the crew to live on board without getting in each other's way. This is particularly important in bad weather, since the last thing you want when you are cold and damp is to be cramped in the cabin. Extra space will allow greater home comforts, such as larger double cabins with standing headroom, larger dining area, a better galley with more storage space, an en suite shower, and toilet compartments. It also has practical advantages such as affording a larger navigation area.

What needs to be considered?

✪ Everything gets more expensive as yachts move up in size. For instance, bigger sails require more material, more powerful winches and stronger, longer halyards, sheets and control lines. More space on board also creates more demand for expensive, complex appliances and toilet facilities.

✪ The annual cost of owning a yacht tends to increase in direct proportion to its size. Most marinas or harbor masters charge a fixed rate per foot or per meter. More cans of antifouling are needed to treat the underwater area of the hull. When things need fixing, repairs can be very expensive. The bigger the yacht, the more you will tend to pay.

✪ Larger yachts generally have deeper keels, although this will depend on the type of yacht. Deep keels require deepwater anchorages and moorings, while smaller yachts can enjoy the benefits of being closer to shore.

✪ A larger yacht can be difficult to manage short-handed. You have to manage bigger sails when sailing, and a bigger boat when entering or leaving a marina.

✪ Larger yachts require more space when turning in a marina. However, a large modern yacht with bow thrusters may be much easier to maneuver than a small traditional yacht with a long keel.

Right: **Marina berths provide plenty of choice around the world, although some areas have long waiting lists for larger berths.**

Below: **You don't need to have a huge yacht to be comfortable or have fun. This is the cabin of the Shrimper, only 19 feet (5.8 m) long.**

Choosing a cruiser

All yachts are a compromise. Some are primarily designed for family use, which means they should be equally comfortable in a marina or under sail. Others are designed to give the best possible sailing performance, which means sacrificing some comfort and space.

Above: A classic wooden yacht is very beautiful, but needs a lot of time spent on maintenance and a lot of expense!

Above: You can find great value among older yachts. This 28-foot (8.5 m) Twister is a long keel classic, built first in wood and then in fiberglass.

Above: Family cruising is always fun with great weather! Chartering a yacht is highly recommended.

What type of yacht is best?
Traditional wooden yacht

Most wooden yachts are old, although a handful of modern boats are built, at huge cost. Typically, a wooden yacht follows a traditional long keel design with a narrow hull that doesn't have a lot of space inside. For traditionalist perfection, a wooden yacht may also have a wooden mast and boom. It may also have a complex rig such as yawl or ketch with a mizzen mast near the stern, a schooner with a second mast forward, or a gaff with a spar supporting the top of the mainsail. Wooden yachts are often beautiful boats, standing out from fiberglass houseboats. Unfortunately, they can be time consuming and expensive to maintain.

Classic long keel yacht

The long keel yacht tends to be sturdy and dependable, with good seakeeping qualities. It is not particularly fast compared to modern fin keel yachts, will tend to heel more if the yacht has a deep hull, and may be difficult to maneuver under engine. The narrow beam will also constrict cabin space. But a long keel classic is a fine boat for an enthusiast. Sturdily built in fiberglass with proper timber trim, yachts built in the 1960s and 70s have excellent second-hand value.

Family cruiser

This is the most popular category of yacht. The aim is to find the best possible compromise between sailing performance, easy handling and onboard comfort for the crew. Virtually all family cruisers are built in fiberglass, with a long fin keel and Bermudan rig. The wider and deeper the hull, the more storage and accommodation is available.

Performance cruiser

The accent here is on sailing performance, combined with live-aboard comfort. A performance cruiser will tend to have less space below than a family cruiser, with a deeper keel and taller rig boosting its performance. This type of yacht is likely to be more rewarding to sail and suitable for racing, but there will be a premium price to pay and more crew will be needed to manage the sails.

Blue water yacht

This is the type of yacht for sailing around the world. It doesn't need to be big, but it does need to be sturdy and dependable. Traditional blue water yachts have full-length keels, while modern ones tend to have long fin keels. In addition to wood or fiberglass, hulls may be built in aluminum or steel for maximum strength. Ferro-cement enjoyed a brief period of popularity as a rugged "build it yourself" option.

Lifting keel yachts

Some yachts have lifting keels and rudders that swivel or retract vertically. This allows the yacht to motor and moor in shallow water inaccessible to a yacht with a conventional keel. Principal disadvantages are extra cost and additional maintenance. There will also be a slight loss of space inside the yacht where the keel is housed. Lifting keel yachts can be used as "trailer sailors" if they are small enough to be launched and retrieved on a boat slip.

Multihulls

Cruising catamarans can provide very spacious accommodation, with cabins in the hulls and a large saloon spread across the central bridge deck. Unlike a yacht, a cruising cat will not heel over and is designed so that there is no danger of capsize. A cruising trimaran will tend to provide considerably better sailing performance, particularly upwind, but has comparatively cramped accommodation in the main central hull.

Below: **Hallberg Rassy is a Swedish range designed expressly for cruising. They are solid, dependable and built to last a lifetime.**

Right: **Cruiser-racers combine racing performance with cruising comfort. Power comes from a big sail area — difficult if you are short on crew.**

Above: **A lifting keel such as that on the Parker 275 has excellent sailing performance and can moor in very shallow water. One disadvantage is that the keel box uses up cabin space.**

Right: **The Dragonfly 800 is a small cruising trimaran with great sailing performance yet cramped accommodation.**

Inside a cruiser

Modern yacht interiors are a compromise between practicality at sea and comfort on a berth. This page describes a modern cruising yacht of around 32 feet (10 m) length.

Companionway

The entrance to the yacht interior is through a companionway at the cockpit's front. This is closed by a sliding top hatch and slatted washboards or doors, which must be able to withstand breaking waves in extreme conditions when the crew take refuge inside. There should be firm handholds outside and inside the companionway, with a set of steps down to the main saloon. The steps can be removed for access to the engine, under the cockpit floor.

Saloon

This main living area of the yacht is straight ahead as you come down the companionway steps. The saloon has a central table, with saloon berths either side to provide enough room for the number of people sleeping on board to sit around the table, the social hub of the yacht. This table can often be lowered to transform a side seat into a double berth opposite a single berth.

Galley

Normally by the companionway, modern galleys have pressurized hot and cold water, and large cooling lockers to store perishable food. A fridge requires a lot of electric power, which means plugging into a shore supply when in a marina or running the engine from time to time when at anchor or at sea.

Above: **The galley maximizes space for food preparation, cooking and storage.**

Below: **Extremely compact, the head offers sink, shower, storage and toilet.**

Backstay

Coach Travel

Hatch Coaming

W

Binnacle

Wheel

Cockpit

Engine control lever

Cleat

Fairlead

T

Fridge

Galley

Storage

Companionway

Aft cabin

Head

Locker

Above: **The Bavaria 32, almost 34 feet (11 m) in length, is popular with charter companies.**

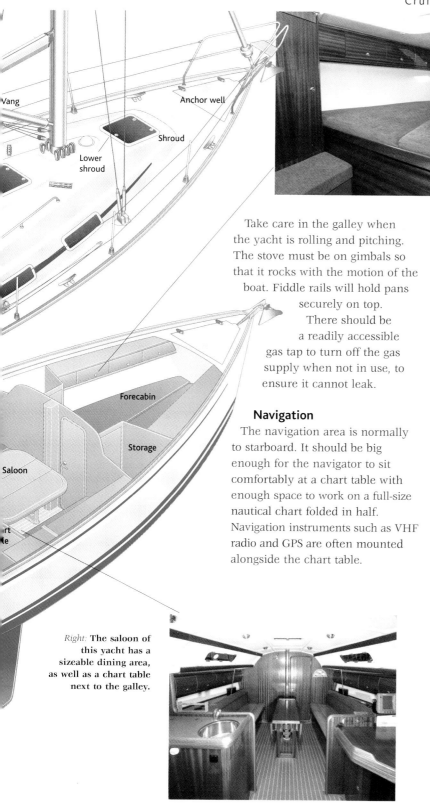

Left: **The forecabin of a Bavaria 32 has plenty of space for two, along with storage.**

Vang

Anchor well

Shroud

Lower shroud

Forecabin

Storage

Saloon

Take care in the galley when the yacht is rolling and pitching. The stove must be on gimbals so that it rocks with the motion of the boat. Fiddle rails will hold pans securely on top. There should be a readily accessible gas tap to turn off the gas supply when not in use, to ensure it cannot leak.

Navigation

The navigation area is normally to starboard. It should be big enough for the navigator to sit comfortably at a chart table with enough space to work on a full-size nautical chart folded in half. Navigation instruments such as VHF radio and GPS are often mounted alongside the chart table.

Right: **The saloon of this yacht has a sizeable dining area, as well as a chart table next to the galley.**

Aft cabin

The yacht may have a single or double aft cabin with wide berths. There should be secondary engine access from this part of the boat.

Forecabin

There are generally berths to port and starboard, with a removable infill providing the option of a V-shaped double berth. The forward hatch provides ventilation and light. This is a comfortable place to sleep on a mooring, but isn't so great at sea when the boat is pitching.

Heads

Marine lavatories, or heads, are connected to the outside of the hull by seacocks, which can normally be left open. Most work on a pump system: you pump in sea water to flush out the bowl. Today, all have a holding tank so that sewage can be disposed of out at sea. Beware that too much paper and anything unexpected can block the pipes — not a fun task to remedy! A sink can provide pressurized hot and cold water, as well as a shower, with an electric pump to remove water from the bilges. Environmental standards vary worldwide. Consider pumping out only while docked to avoid fouling the water, and use only "green" cleaning products.

On deck

When the crew are "on deck" they have access to the cockpit, sidedecks, foredeck and coachroof. Most of the crew's time will be spent in the cockpit, which provides shelter and comfort. Moving onto the foredeck or sidedecks is generally for jib handling or mooring the boat.

Below: **The cockpit provides a comfortable seating area for the crew with easy access to the main cabin. A sprayhood is a very useful extra.**

Left: **The helmsman's wheel is mounted on a binnacle with the main compass housing, just aft of the cockpit on this Sweden Yachts 390.**

The cockpit

The cockpit is the hub of a yacht, from where the crew control the boat. On modern yachts, all sail controls are led back to the cockpit area or coachroof on either side of the companionway. Winches for the headsail or spinnaker sheets are mounted on the coamings at the sides. The roller-furling line for the headsail is led back along the sidedeck to a jamming cleat within easy reach of the cockpit. The mainsheet may be led to a traveler in the cockpit, or back along the coachroof. Winches and jammers for halyards, reefing lines and boom vang are normally mounted on the coachroof.

The helmsman's position is at the back of the cockpit. On smaller yachts up to about 23 feet (7 m), a tiller is used for steering. This tiller can sometimes be raised vertically, so that it is out of the way when not in use. On larger yachts, the steering wheel is mounted on a pedestal known as a binnacle, which also has a housing for the main compass. Some yachts have two linked steering wheels on either side of the boat. This allows you to steer on the high side when heeled over.

Benches on either side of the cockpit should provide enough space for all the crew to sit. If the yacht is heeling, it is more comfortable to sit on the windward side — brace your feet to ensure you don't slide down to leeward!

The coachroof should help protect the crew from wind and spray. A folding spray hood may be installed to increase protection, but forward visibility will be restricted. The helmsman must have a clear view forward at all times, particularly when maneuvering in a marina.

The tubular steel bars of the stern pulpit (the sturdy railing at the back of the boat), encloses the stern to provide additional protection.

Sidedecks

The sidedecks provide a walkway to the foredeck and mast area. On most yachts the decks will be fiberglass with a nonslip finish.

A "luxury" finish is provided by teak planking laid on top, which looks great. In good weather, it is normal for the crew to sit up on the windward side.

Above: **Sidedecks provide a walkway on either side of the coachroof, which is fitted with grab handles.**

Coachroof

You will need to step up onto the coachroof to work at the mast, particularly when lowering the mainsail. Beware — the shiny sloping sides on a fiberglass coachroof may not offer a very good grip.

Foredeck

The crew must access the foredeck for mooring and anchoring. It may have a fiberglass or teak non-slip finish. The tubular steel bars of the pulpit (which encloses the bow of the boat) give additional protection.

Storage

Cockpit lockers have ample storage for warps, fenders, an inflatable dinghy, brushes, buckets, tools and everything you might need on deck. When accessing a locker, make sure the lid is secured in the open position: the wind could blow it down onto your head.

Most yachts have a small dedicated locker in the stern to supply the gas stove. Always close off the gas tap at the tank when not in use.

Below: **Teak planking provides a luxurious deck finish. Note how the coachroof merges into the foredeck, making it easy for the crew to move around the boat.**

Deck hardware

Specialized hardware ensures that yacht sailing is enjoyable and physically possible for most people. You don't need to be super-fit or super-strong to control the sails or drop the anchor at the end of the day!

Winches

The sails on a yacht can generate massive loads. On yachts from about 23 feet (7 m) long, a small winch mounted on the coachroof winds up the mainsail and headsail halyards, after which the halyards can be locked by a clutch. The same winch may be required to tension reefing lines. Larger two-speed winches, mounted on either side of the cockpit, wind in the headsail sheets. "Self-tailing" winches are designed to be operated by one person who winds the winch, while a groove in the top of the winch grips the tail.

Handles

A removable handle fits in the top of each winch, but a heavier, longer handle will be required to wind a heavier load. Winch handles are normally stowed in pockets on either side of the companionway in the cockpit. When you insert a handle, make sure it is locked into the winch and try not to drop it over the side!

Blocks

- ✪ All control lines under heavy load are led through blocks.
- ✪ The mainsheet has top and bottom blocks, which provide multi-purchase control of the mainsail.

- ✪ The headsail sheets controlling the jib (which does not overlap the mast) or genoa (which does overlap the mast) are led through blocks on the sidedecks or sides of the coachroof. These blocks are normally mounted on a track, which allows their position to be moved forward (tightening the leech) or backward (tightening the foot). This is necessary to maximize performance when changing to a different sail.
- ✪ The control line that furls the headsail is led from the bow to the cockpit, passing through a series of small blocks on the toe rail on one sidedeck.

Above: **The large primary winch in the foreground is used for the starboard side headsail sheet which has the highest loads. This kind of winch may have two or three speeds, activated by reversing the handle or pressing a button in the top.**

Above: **The headsail roller furling line is led aft along the port side deck to the cockpit, passing through a locking clutch and turning block.**

⚙ Turning blocks are used to guide control lines (halyards, reefing lines, boom vang downhaul) from the base of the mast to the cockpit end of the coachroof.

Cleats and clutches

⚙ Mainsail and headsail sheets must be ready for immediate adjustment, but other control lines (halyards, reefing lines, boom vang, headsail furling) can be locked for a long period.

⚙ A jamming cleat has jaws that lock the line: different sizes of cleat are used for different diameter lines.

⚙ A clutch provides a more sophisticated solution when a line is under load. You can wind the rope in with the clutch in the "locked" position (handle back) and you can unlock the rope (handle forward) under full load.

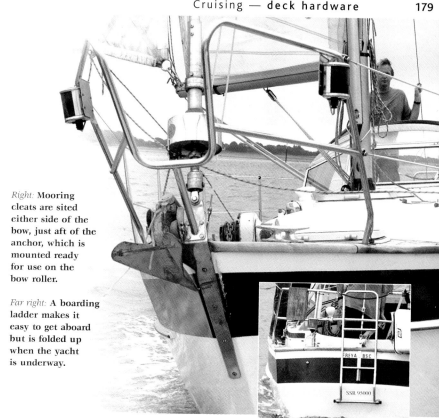

Right: **Mooring cleats are sited either side of the bow, just aft of the anchor, which is mounted ready for use on the bow roller.**

Far right: **A boarding ladder makes it easy to get aboard but is folded up when the yacht is underway.**

Mainsheet traveler

Yachts have a mainsheet traveler that allows the mainsheet to be moved from side to side. This is useful for a more direct pull on the boom when reaching, or to get the mainsheet away clear of the cockpit's middle.

Mooring cleats

Typically two conventional horn-shaped mooring cleats are positioned on either side, at the bow and stern of the boat; sometimes with a third halfway between, or "midships."

Binnacle and wheel

The wheel is mounted on the binnacle and connected to the rudder by wires or rods, which require occasional maintenance. If the connection fails, an "emergency

tiller" can be locked onto a steering post, right above the rudder. The bigger the wheel, the easier it will be to turn the rudder.

The main engine control levers for forward/neutral/reverse and speed are often fitted to the binnacle, where they are easy for the helm to hand.

Anchor

⚙ The principal anchor may be stowed in a locker in the bows, accessible from the foredeck, or stowed in the bow roller, with a locking pin and lashing to hold it secure. Chain and rope is stowed in the chain locker in the bow.

⚙ On larger yachts, the anchor may have an electric windlass to pull up the chain. The windlass uses a lot of energy, so the yacht engine must be run in neutral to back up power.

⚙ A secondary anchor should be stowed in a cockpit locker, together with chain and rope.

Hatches

There are normally one or two hatches in the forward coachroof or bows, giving light and ventilation to the saloon and forward cabin. Hatches usually should be closed when sailing.

Boarding ladder

Most yachts have boarding access at the stern. The boarding ladder folds up and down for use and storage.

Deck safety gear

Modern yachts are designed to be as safe as possible. The deck is fenced with lifelines, which help reduce any danger of falling over the side. When working on deck at night or in bad weather, always clip to a secure point for safety.

Stanchions and lifelines

Stanchions are strong aluminum posts that are screwed to the deck. Lifelines or guardrails are horizontal wires that pass through the top and middle of the stanchions to make a protective "fence" around the sides of the boat. A small section of guardrail can be unclipped to enable crew to get on board.

Toerail

Most yachts have a heavy-duty aluminum toerail all the way around the side of the decks. As well as being useful to brace your feet against, this also reinforces the joint between hull and deck. Cutouts at

> **CAUTION**
>
> If you are wearing a harness, do not clip it onto the lifelines or stanchions. They are not designed to provide secure support.

Above: **The pulpit encloses the forestay and bow area, and provides working access to the anchor.**

the bows and stern provide fair-leads for mooring warps, while a central cutout can be used for springs, which prevent the boat moving fore and aft when moored side-on.

Pulpit

The pulpit may have port and starboard navigation lights on either side. Designed to keep the foredeck crew safe (particularly if changing a headsail), the pulpit must allow sufficient access to lower and lift the anchor on its bow roller.

Left: **The aluminum toerail runs along the side of the boat, reinforcing the bond between hull and deck. Note the cleat at the widest point that is mainly used for springs.**

Stern pulpit

The stern pulpit ensures that no one can inadvertently fall over the back. There is occassionally a removable guardrail for access to the stern boarding ladder.

Grab rails

Remember the old sailor's maxim: "One hand for yourself and one for the boat!" A yacht should have grab rails along the sides of the coachroof, perfect for when you move along the sidedeck.

Harness attachments

Heavy-duty rings are sometimes bolted into the sides of the cockpit as harness attachment points. To move forward, the harness clip can be attached to the jackstay (made of webbing or plastic-covered wire), which extends along each sidedeck. This allows crew to move right along the deck without unclipping the harness.

Safe sailing!

- Ensure that there are enough lifejackets for everyone on board.
- Stay in the cockpit when possible: it is the safest part of the boat.
- If the mainsheet track is in the cockpit, keep well away from it, especially during tacks and jibes.
- Beware of the boom at all times. Being hit by the boom could cause a serious head injury, so try to keep your head below boom level at all times.

- If you need to go forward, stay low and hold on with one hand.
- If the skipper asks the crew to wear harnesses, follow his advice. Make sure you are hooked onto a secure anchor point.
- Keep out of the way of the wheel or tiller, particularly during a maneuver. Remember that the tiller will sweep across the cockpit during a tack or jibe.
- When the boat is sailing or motoring, make sure no lines can fall out of the cockpit and over the side. Stow the loose ends of halyards and control lines in separate coils.

Right: **It's fine for an experienced sailor to step onto the coachroof when the wind is light. But no matter how calm it seems, you should always be ready for the boat to pitch or roll.**

Below: **Beware of the boom when moving around the deck. Helm and crew must be aware of what the other is doing. It is potentially safer to move along the windward side if you want to get to the foredeck.**

What to wear on deck

You need to dress correctly for sailing. Specially designed sailing gear will provide comfort and safety from your feet to the top of your head! Although quite expensive, it is a good long-term investment.

Shoes

Don't go sailing in bare feet. It's OK if you are careful and the boat has a teak deck, but there is so much opportunity for injuring your feet or slipping. Deck shoes specially designed for sailing are strongly recommended. Try to avoid wearing them ashore, which will soon wear out the nonslip soles.

Boots

If it is cold or wet you will need sailing boots. They should be easy to pull on and off, totally waterproof and have excellent grip. As with shoes, avoid wearing them on shore. Traditional rubber sailing boots do a good job. More stylish leather sailing boots are more expensive, but more comfortable and last longer as well.

Gloves

Sailing gloves with leather palms are recommended for handling lines. They provide far more grip than bare hands on narrow control lines.

Sunglasses

There is a lot of glare on the water. To see clearly and protect your eyes, you need high-quality sunglasses with efficient UV-resistance. Use a strap to prevent losing them overboard.

Waterproof jacket

A specially designed waterproof jacket is vital if you are sailing in strong winds, rain, spray or cold weather. Be aware that there is a huge price range. Jackets for "ocean"

Rollaway hood

Size-adjustable waterproof cap

CAP

WINDPROOF FLEECE

Elastized braces

High collar to keep spray and wind out

Rollaway hood

Fully lined

Articulated knees

INSHORE JACKET

Super stretch panel

GLOVES

Adjustable ankle cuffs

OVERALLS

BOOTS

DECK SHOES

use can cost considerably more than jackets for "coastal" use, but the latter are adequate for occasional sailing. The price difference pays for superior waterproofing, breathability and durability. Even the cheapest jacket should be waterproof with good durability.

Features to look for include deep, fleece-lined pockets in the sides of the jacket to keep your hands warm, a heavy duty zipper, a high collar that completely encloses your neck, a built-in hood that can be pulled tight around your face, and double wrist cuffs and reflective panels on shoulders, back or wrists.

Waterproof overalls

If it is cold or there is any chance of getting splashed by waves, you will need waterproof overalls specifically designed for sailing. Features to look for include breathable material for best performance with layers; chest-high cut with adjustable braces; reinforcement on knees and seat and adjustable ankles. Waterproof overalls are often fitted with a vertical front zipper for easy access. Women-specific designs are available with a back zipper, though these have a reputation for leaking.

Fleece

Choose a windproof fleece as a mid-layer. This is vital for yacht sailing in most climates!

Pants and shorts

Pants or shorts in breathable synthetic material that will dry quickly when wet are ideal, as are reinforcements to pant knees and seat, tapered ankles for wearing in boots and zippered heavy duty pockets so nothing can fall out.

Shirts

Choose shirts or T-shirts made of synthetic material, which will act as a breathable base layer when worn with a fleece or jacket.

Hat or cap

Wind chill rapidly draws heat from your body, not least through major heat loss from your head. Keep a thermal beanie-style hat in the pocket of your waterproof jacket. A cap with a visor will shield your eyes somewhat from the sun.

Sun protection

The wind increases the effect of the sun, so use a high SPF sunscreen.

Right: **It's easy to get cold when not active on deck especially if there is a lot of spray coming over the side. It really helps if you dress correctly for the conditions.**

How a yacht is rigged

Standing rigging, spars and sails provide the power that drives a yacht on the wind. There is a big choice of rig variations, but for cruising the popular choice is a Bermudan sloop with an easily handled headsail.

Different rigs

- A Bermudan mainsail is triangular and common on modern yachts; a gaff mainsail nearly square with the gaff itself supporting the top. A Bermudan sloop has a single mast and boom supporting a mainsail (behind the mast) and headsail (in front of the mast).
- A yawl rig has a shorter mizzen mast behind the rudder at the stern of the yacht. A ketch rig has a shorter mizzen mast forward of the rudder at the stern of the yacht. The mizzen balances the boat, which can be sailed without the mainsail if required. A yawl or ketch looks beautiful, but adds complexity and cost to the rig.
- A schooner has a second shorter mast nearer the bow. One or both can be used at the same time. Sail handling is easier due to the smaller size of the sails, but a schooner also adds cost and complexity to the rig.

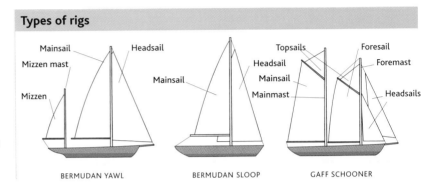

Types of rigs

BERMUDAN YAWL — Mainsail, Mizzen mast, Headsail, Mizzen

BERMUDAN SLOOP — Mainsail

GAFF SCHOONER — Topsails, Foresail, Headsail, Foremast, Mainsail, Mainmast, Headsails

Spars

The mast, boom and spinnaker pole (for booming out the spinnaker) are knows as spars. Aluminum spars are standard on most yachts. Carbon fiber provides lighter weight, but is much more expensive. Some traditional yachts still have wooden spars, which are very heavy and will require varnishing.

Below: **This Twister is sailing under reefed mainsail and jib hanked onto an inner forestay. The genoa (a headsail that overlaps the mast) is completely furled.**

Above: **During the sailing season, the mainsail is permanently attached to the boom. Hoist it with the boat head to wind.**

Mainsail

- The mainsail is attached to the mast and boom and provides the principal power of the yacht. It is normally stowed on the boom inside a cover during the sailing season, and hoisted each time you want to go sailing.

- The size of the mainsail can be reduced by reefing. There are two or three slab reefs, which pull down and shorten the sail.
- Some larger yachts have "in-mast" or "in-boom" roller furling, which allows the mainsail to be rolled out for sailing and rolled back in for storage. It's neat, but it is complex and expensive, it requires maintenance for fail-safe operation and a partly rolled mainsail has a less efficient shape than a mainsail with its area reduced by slab reefing.

Headsails

- A genoa is a very large headsail that overlaps the mast when it is sheeted in. A jib (also known as a "working jib") is a smaller headsail that does not overlap the mast.
- A genoa enhances performance due to the "slot effect," which accelerates airflow past the leeward side of the mainsail. However, the larger the headsail the harder the winching required to sheet the sail in. High-aspect jibs (also known as "blades") can give excellent performance and are quicker and easier to wind in.
- On a masthead rig, the forestay is connected to the top of the mast. On a fractional rig, the forestay connects to a point lower down the mast. The fractional rig combines a smaller headsail with a larger mainsail for easier handling. It also allows the mast to curve backward, which pulls the mainsail forward and flattens its shape, thus depowering the sail in stronger winds.
- Roller-furling is fitted to most cruising yacht headsails. This allows the sail to be rolled up on a

Right: **This yacht has a masthead Bermudan sloop with a large, overlapping genoa that will require a lot of hard winding every time the boat tacks.**

K

3882

mooring, and partly rolled to reduce the amount of sail. However, with a partly rolled sail there will be loss of windward performance since an efficient shape cannot be maintained.

- The alternative to roller reefing is a headsail attached to the forestay by hanks (pistons) or with a bolt rope pulled up a luff groove.
- A storm jib is a very small headsail for extreme conditions. It must be hoisted separately and is normally attached to the forestay by hanks. Most people will never use a storm jib but it's nice to know that it's on board!

Standing rigging

Principal support for the mast is provided by the forestay, backstay and shrouds. Secondary support is provided by lowers (lower shrouds, which support the bottom half of the mast), cap shrouds (which prevent the top half of the mast from bending sideways) and spreaders (which spread the load toward the sides of the boat). The rigging is

Above: **Solid rod rigging is a stylish, higher performance alternative to stranded wire shrouds. The "tubes" in the foreground prevent sheets chafing on the shrouds.**

attached to chain plates at deck level, with bottlescrews to adjust individual lengths. Stainless steel stranded wire rigging is standard for most cruising yachts, although more expensive solid rod rigging is an option.

The mainsail

The mainsail is the principal sail and is attached to both the mast and boom. To cope with changes in wind strength, it is vital that its size can be increased or reduced quickly and efficiently by means of reefing.

Boom attachment

- ❂ The yacht's mainsail is too large and cumbersome to derig every time you stop sailing; it is attached to the boom throughout the season. It is secured along the foot of the sail by a bolt rope, or halyard, fitted into a slot in the boom, or has a "loose foot" with attachments at tack and clew.

- ❂ The mainsail is stored on top of the boom by "flaking" the sail in a series of zigzag folds and securing the folds with lengths of webbing or shock cord known as "sail ties," at intervals along the boom. Flaking the sail neatly takes patience, and is easier with at least one crew member and the captain. A sail cover should be used to protect the sail from UV degradation and rain.

- ❂ Some cruising yachts are fitted with lazyjacks, which make stowing the mainsail much easier. The lazyjacks are a web of light lines between the mast and boom that "catch" the sail as it is lowered. The lazyjacks may be attached to canvas panels that run along both sides of the boom. These panels can then be zipped shut along the top.

Mast attachment

The mainsail is attached to the mast by sliders on a track. When the sail is hoisted or lowered by the main halyard, the sliders move smoothly up or down. When lowering the sail, one crew may need to stand at the mast and pull individual sliders down by hand.

Above left: **The mainsail provides maximum power when sailing with the wind behind the beam. Here the mainsail has a "loose foot" and is attached to either end of the boom.**

Above: **The mainsail is flaked in a series of folds on top of the boom. Sail ties hold it in position until it is time to hoist the sail.**

Slab reefing

Depending on the size of the mainsail it is normally possible to take in two or three reefs. You lower the mainsail to make a smaller triangle, with the top of the reef sitting parallel with the boom.

Reefing lines

- ❂ Each reef has a color-coded reefing line attached and ready to use.

Above: **The mainsail's luff is attached to the mast by a series of sliders. When dropping the sail, you may need to pull the sliders down the track.**

✪ At the front of the boom, the reefing line is led up the luff to a block or cringle (metal eye) at the height of the reef. The line is then led back down to turning blocks on the deck that direct it to a clutch on the coachroof.

✪ At the back of the boom, the reefing line is led up the leech to a block or cringle at the height of the reef. The line is then led back to a block on the boom, forward to the front of the boom, and down to turning blocks on deck and then to a clutch on the coachroof.

✪ Some yachts only have reefing lines on the leech. One crew has to stand by the mast in order to pull the reefing cringles down onto hooks either side of the boom.

Battens

The mainsail has stiff battens that help support the "roach" (the sail area outside a straight line between the head and clew of the sail) when the sail is dropped. Battens fit into pockets and are left fully tensioned in the sail. Over a period of time, batten pockets will need repair.

Reefing the main

Most yachts have a system of slab reefing. Sometimes a reef is put in while in harbor, but it is often done on the water when the sails are already hoisted. Before starting to reef, the mainsheet and boom vang should be eased and the topping lift tensioned.

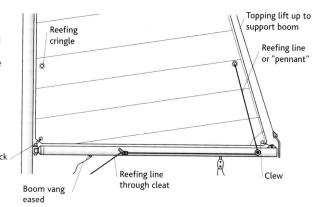

Reefing cringle

Topping lift up to support boom

Reefing line or "pennant"

Tack

Boom vang eased

Reefing line through cleat

Clew

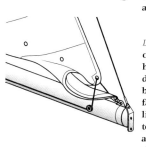

Left: **The reefing line is pulled tight, to pull down the leech and create a reef. The equivalent amount of sail is pulled down at the luff. The topping lift is pulled up taut to support the boom as the sail is lowered.**

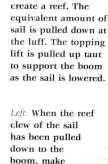

Left: **When the reef clew of the sail has been pulled down to the boom, make fast the reefing line. Ease the topping lift and tighten the kicking strap.**

Right: **This Westerly Konsort has full-length battens, which help keep the sail's shape, and ensure it drops in neat folds when lowered.**

Raising the mainsail

The mainsail is normally the first sail to be set and the last to be dropped. During hoists and drops, the yacht must be pointing directly into the wind and under full control.

Briefing

The skipper or mate briefs the crew and explains what will happen when the mainsail is raised or lowered. Be aware of any dangers that might be created by the boom moving from side to side, the sail flapping, or the crew getting in the way and obscuring the helm's vision.

Where to hoist

The yacht must be pointing head-to-wind while the mainsail is being hoisted. This will take a few minutes. During this time the yacht must be moving forward slowly under engine power, so that the helmsman can keep it pointing into the wind (around 2 knots). If the yacht stops moving forward, the bow will be blown off to one side. If the mainsail is hoisted while the yacht lies to an anchor or mooring,

Above: **Hoisting the mainsail, the skipper motors slowly forward, keeping the yacht pointing into the wind. Allow plenty of sea space, so you can allow yourselves more time.**

the yacht will naturally face head-to-wind, but a gusty wind may still blow the bow from side to side, which will make the hoist awkward.

The yacht only moves in a fixed direction while the mainsail is being hoisted, so the helm must plan ahead and allow plenty of sea space. It will be difficult to change course with the sail partly hoisted.

Always plan to hoist the mainsail in flat water. Do not wait until you leave the protection of land and get into waves. A rolling yacht with the boom crashing from side to side makes hoisting unpleasant, and can be dangerous.

During the hoist, the helm's view may be obstructed. Beware of other boats on moorings and channel markers and buoys.

Prepare the sail

Remove the sail cover from the boom. This is best done before you leave the mooring or marina berth. Starting at the mast, fold the cover back along the boom and stow it in a cockpit locker.

Yachts with lazyjacks normally have a fixed cover that stays on the boom while sailing. Simply unzip the cover along the top to expose the sail.

Make sure the boom vang is eased right off. Be ready to uncleat the mainsheet and let it run free. Warn the crew that the boom and traveler may swing around.

Attach the halyard

Always attach the halyard to the head of the sail before you get underway. If the engine suddenly fails, you may need to hoist the mainsail in a hurry.

Let off the halyard clutch on the coachroof to provide slack, but don't let the halyard run free. One crew should go forward and clip the snap shackle on the end of the halyard to the head of the sail. Pull the halyard down and take a single turn around a cleat to secure it. Close the clutch and tension the halyard to pull it tight to the mast, so it can't wind itself around the shrouds or radar or other lines or equipment.

Ready to hoist

Sail ties will need to be removed from the sail (unless the boom has lazyjacks). It's good practice to close the companionway hatch so that there is no danger of falling through the hole! Keep a good lookout forward — the helm's vision may be obscured.

Above: **Make sure the mainsheet is cleated, so the boom cannot swing when you are attaching or removing sail ties.**

Right: **When you remove the sail ties, the mainsail may obscure the skipper's vision. Keep a good lookout to warn of dangers ahead.**

Setting the mainsail

With the crew ready and everything prepared, it's time to hoist. Pull the mainsail up, but be prepared to stop or let the sail back down if there are snags.

Hoisting from the cockpit

- If the halyard is attached to the sail and pulled down under tension, it must be slackened off and then retensioned. Never let the halyard fly loose in the wind: it can easily take a wrap around the spreaders, and may be tricky to flick back into position.
- Make sure the clutch is closed, then start to pull the halyard hand-over-hand. When the load begins to feel heavy, take two turns around the winch and continue to pull in hand-over-hand. When the load gets heavier, take at least one more turn around the drum and then take a turn around the self-tailing jaws.
- Put the handle in the top of the winch, then wind steadily until the head of the sail has reached the top of the mast. Take the rope off the winch, coil and stow it neatly.

Beware lazyjacks!

The ends of the battens can catch on the lazyjacks as you hoist. The helm must steer the boat to keep the mainsail between the lazyjacks as it is hoisted. If a batten snags, the mainsail will need to be dropped back down until it is free. So watch the sail as it goes up.

Above: **Sail control lines are led down from the mast or boom to turning blocks on the deck, and routed back to the cockpit. The hook pulls down reefs on the luff.**

Topping lift

The topping lift is an adjustable line that carries the weight of the boom when the mainsail is not hoisted. When the mainsail is fully up, slacken the topping lift sufficiently to allow the boom to be sheeted right in. Remember that the topping lift must be fully tensioned before you drop the sail.

Boom vang

Tension the boom vang by pulling it back through the clutch once the mainsail is hoisted. The boom vang prevents the boom from riding up when you sail offwind.

Dropping the mainsail

The drop is the reverse procedure of the hoist. Beware of reduced visibility for the helm as the sail is dropped and gathered.

- The yacht must be pointing into wind while the sail is dropped. This is not as critical as with the hoist, but it will help keep the sail and boom under control.
- Let off the mainsheet and ease off the boom vang. Tension the topping lift so that the boom cannot drop down.
- Take two turns around the winch with the halyard and prepare to let off the clutch.

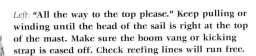

Left: **"All the way to the top please." Keep pulling or winding until the head of the sail is right at the top of the mast. Make sure the boom vang or kicking strap is eased off. Check reefing lines will run free.**

- One crew should go forward to the mast to help pull the sliders down the track.
- When everyone is prepared for the drop, let off the clutch and begin to ease the halyard. Never let it run! Keep the drop under control and work in time with the crew at the mast.
- As the sail is lowered, it may help to pull in the mainsheet to stop the boom from waving from side to side.
- When the sail is fully lowered, tension the mainsheet and pull

the end of the boom up higher with the topping lift if necessary.
- If the rig has lazyjacks, the mainsail will have fallen in folds. All you need do is zip up the bag.
- Without lazyjacks, the sail will need to be "flaked" on top of the boom. Ensure the boom is secure and centered for this. Pack the sail as tightly as possible and secure with sail ties.
- Remove the halyard snap shackle from the head of the sail; secure it to the end of the boom and tension.

- Do not secure the halyard alongside the mast: it will make a horrible clanking noise against the aluminum if there is wind. Beware of letting go of the halyard: it can be very difficult to catch!
- Put the sail cover on.

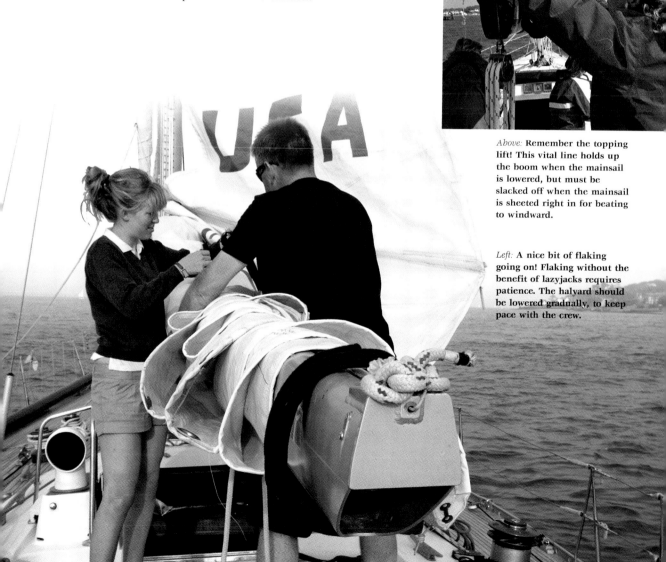

Above: **Remember the topping lift! This vital line holds up the boom when the mainsail is lowered, but must be slacked off when the mainsail is sheeted right in for beating to windward.**

Left: **A nice bit of flaking going on! Flaking without the benefit of lazyjacks requires patience. The halyard should be lowered gradually, to keep pace with the crew.**

Handling the headsail

Most cruising yachts have a large roller-furling headsail. The sail can be rolled up or partly rolled if you wish to sail with reduced sail. It's an easy system of sail management, but there are compromises on performance.

How is the sail attached?

⚙ A roller-furling headsail is attached to an aluminum luff groove, which rotates around the forestay. The bolt rope in the luff of the sail is pulled up the luff groove by the headsail halyard, with the sail unrolled.

⚙ The sail can conveniently be left hoisted and rolled for the whole sailing season. Some owners store the rolled sail inside a long, sausage-shaped bag, which helps prevent UV degradation.

⚙ The two headsail sheets are attached to the clew of the sail with bowlines. Make sure they are pulled tight.

Below: **The bolt line on the luff of the headsail slides up a luff groove, which will rotate around the forestay when the roller-furling system is activated.**

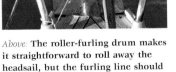

Above: **The roller-furling drum makes it straightforward to roll away the headsail, but the furling line should be kept taut and under control.**

Top: **When you furl the headsail, aim to roll it as tightly and neatly as possible. Then lock the furling line and tension both the headsail sheets.**

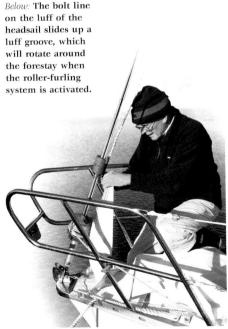

Unfurling the sail

⚙ You can unfurl the headsail when the boat is heading in any direction, but it's best on a reach, when the unrolled sail will be blown out to the side.

⚙ The furling line must be able to run free when the sail unfurls. Flake out the line to ensure there will be no snags when the sail unfurls.

⚙ Take two clockwise turns around the leeward headsail winch with the sheet. When the furling line clutch is unlocked, pulling the sheet will start unrolling the headsail. Wear gloves to control the furling line, which is paid out hand-over-hand. Pulling the line against a winch or cleat should provide sufficient friction if it starts pulling hard. Always try to avoid letting the headsail unroll with an uncontrolled bang.

Furling the sail

⚙ Unless the wind is very light, you will probably need to lead the furling line around a winch and wind it in to begin the rolling process. The furling line has a narrow diameter: keep it under tension and wear gloves.

⚙ Two crew need to work together. One winds in the furling line while the other eases off the sheet. Don't just let the sheet go. Keep enough tension to ensure there are tight rolls. As the sail rolls away, the load will lessen and you can pull in the furling line hand-over-hand.

 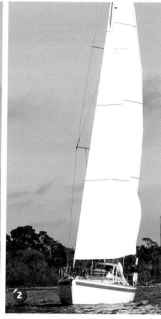 

Right (from left to right):
1. The headsail is unfurled by unlocking the clutch holding the furling line and pulling in on the leeward sheet taken around a winch. 2. As more sail is exposed, the headsail will start to blow open. The furling line must be able to run free, with no chance of snagging in the clutch. 3. The sail is fully unfurled and the crew sheets it in for a beat.

⚙ When the sail is fully rolled, it should be tight and neat. If not, unroll the sail and try again. Keep rolling until the sheets have taken a couple of full turns around the sail. Lock the furling line, pull both sheets until they are taut, and then cleat them securely.

reduced, the headsail block should be moved forward on its sliding track. If the sail is increased, move the block aft. This can only be done when there is no tension in the sheet. To judge if the block

is in the right position, check to see if the leech and foot of the sail have a similar curve. If the leech is too full, move the block forward; if the foot is too full, move it back.

Reefing the sail

⚙ If it is windy, you may only want part of the sail to be unrolled. Take a cautious approach. Pull out a length of furling line and then lock the clutch before pulling on the sheet to unroll the sail.

⚙ If you want to reduce headsail area, go through the furling procedure. There will be a heavy load on the furling line: it must be taken around a winch and the rolls must be as tight as possible.

⚙ As the size of the sail changes, you will need to change the lead of the sheet. If sail area is

Right: **If you reduce the headsail, the sheeting angle should be moved forward to allow for a shorter foot.**

Reefing

Sails are reefed to keep the boat in proper balance. If the rudder feels heavy and the boat is heeling right over, it's time to reduce sail area.

Balance the sails

The mainsail is the main "engine" of the yacht. Its size and power must be balanced by the headsail when you reef. Think of it like a weathercock, with the mast acting as the central spindle. If you furl away three-quarters of the headsail, a full-size mainsail will put too much power behind the mast and create weather helm, which means the boat wants to head up into the wind and is difficult to steer.

Below: **This is as far as any yacht should heel. If the leeward deck starts going under water, it will slip sideways and slow down — well past time to shorten sail.**

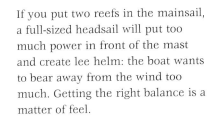

Reducing sail area

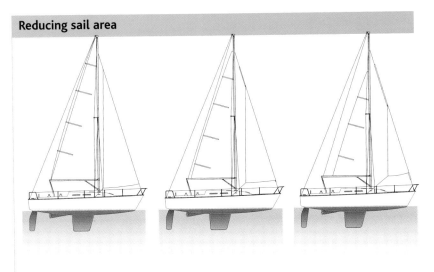

Full sail on a typical fractional rigged Bermudan cruising yacht should provide perfectly balanced sailing up to force 4.

As the wind increases, both the boat and rig can be made more manageable by reducing sail area, with one reef in the mainsail and a partly rolled headsail.

Strong winds may require two or three reefs in the mainsail, with the headsail rolled to a small size, which keeps the boat in balance and does not cause weather (heading up) or lee (bearing away) helm.

If you put two reefs in the mainsail, a full-sized headsail will put too much power in front of the mast and create lee helm: the boat wants to bear away from the wind too much. Getting the right balance is a matter of feel.

Be cautious — reef early

- Check the wind before you sail. If it looks windy, the mainsail should be reefed during the hoist or before you go. Remember, it's a lot easier to shake out reefs when the wind is too light than to take in reefs because it's too strong.
- Be cautious when you unroll the headsail, too. Unlock the clutch, pull out seveal feet of furling line, lock the clutch and see how the sail feels. If there is not enough sail area, unroll some more. It may be easiest to lead the furling line around a winch, undo the clutch and ease away under load.

Do not heel right over

In a breeze, a yacht will heel over. An angle of 10–20 degrees is normal. If the boat heels much more, it will start to slide sideways and slow down, plus it will become very uncomfortable for the crew. Solve this problem by reefing. Most yachts will lose suprisingly little speed.

Reefing the mainsail

- ⚙ Many yachts have a twin-line reefing system for the mainsail, allowing the crew to reef without leaving the cockpit. On others, a crew has to go to the mast and pull the reef cringle down onto a hook on the side of the boom.
- ⚙ The yacht should be heading into the wind when you reef. If you are sailing downwind, turn into the wind. Be prepared for it to suddenly get a lot rougher.

Ready to reef

- ⚙ Identify the leech and luff reefing lines, which are color coded for each reef.
- ⚙ Let off the boom vang.
- ⚙ Take two turns around the winch with the halyard.
- ⚙ Ease the mainsheet and take up slack on the topping lift so the boom can't drop into the cockpit.

Reef

- ⚙ Let off the halyard clutch.
- ⚙ Ease the halyard enough to pull the luff reefing line down tightly to the front end of the boom.
- ⚙ Pull the leech reefing line down tightly to the aft end of the boom.
- ⚙ Lock the halyard and then wind it back up to tension the luff fully.
- ⚙ Ease off the topping lift and tension the boom vang.

Taking a reef out

- ⚙ Head into wind. Ease the boom vang and mainsheet; tension the topping lift.
- ⚙ Take three turns around the winch with the halyard. Let off clutches for both reefing lines and ensure the lines can run free. Wind up the halyard with the mainsheet slack and the boat head-to-wind. Beware of snagging the lazyjacks as the sail is hoisted. When it is fully up, close both reefing clutches, take the halyard off the winch, coil and tidy the lines.
- ⚙ Ease off the topping lift and tension the boom vang.

Above: **This is how some yachts reef, by tying each one in with a reef knot. It makes for a tidy sail.**

Right: **On some yachts you need to pull down the luff by hand, in order to pull the cringle (metal ring) over the reefing hook on the boom, before retensioning the sail.**

Left: **Lazyjacks allow the reefed sail to be neatly enclosed by the sides of the boom bag.**

Sailing upwind

Sailing a yacht toward the wind is a skill. You don't get the same "seat of the pants" response as sailing a dinghy. But the principle is the same: set the sails correctly and keep the boat balanced.

away a few degrees. If the leeward telltales are lifting, try easing the sheet out or head up a few degrees.

Setting sails for reaching upwind

Pull the mainsheet in until the mainsail stops flapping. Never over-sheet the sail as this will reduce power. Pull the headsail sheet in until the headsail stops flapping and the telltales stream backward. Wind will be funneling down the slot between the headsail and mainsail, causing the mainsail to "backwind." This is normal and pulling the main in tighter will only reduce drive.

How close can you sail to the wind?

Beating to windward, you want to sail as close to the wind as possible,

Below: **The slot between the mainsail and headsail accelerates the wind. The mainsail may start backwinding as the yacht drives forward, but it doesn't impair performance.**

Watching the wind

Most yachts have a windvane at the top of the mast, but you can't keep looking up and staring at it without getting a crick in the neck! Electronic wind direction instruments in the cockpit show where true and apparent wind is blowing from, but only provide a two-dimensional picture of how close and how effectively the boat is sailing toward the wind.

The best way of gauging performance is the simplest: watch the telltales on the headsail. Telltales are strips of wool or plastic near the luff of the sail, showing how wind is flowing over the sail. If the telltales are streaming back on both sides of the sail, everything is going well. If the telltales on the windward side of the sail are lifting, try pulling the sheet in more or bear

Above: **Sailing on a close reach with sheets eased provides good speed and an easy motion through the water.**

Above: **Many yachts will find a comfortable "groove" when sailing upwind, indicating that the sails are well balanced with no hard pull on the rudder either way.**

Left: **A good view of the telltales on the leading edge of the headsail can be a great help when steering upwind. Telltales should stream horizontally on both sides.**

but you also want the boat to feel comfortable and make good speed.

The closest you can expect to point is around 30 degrees to the wind. Realistically, a course of around 45–50 degrees is more likely. A deep fin keel and tall slim sail help a yacht point up well; a shallow fin keel and partly rolled headsail will "fall off" to windward.

Setting sails for beating upwind

When beating to windward, the sails should be pulled in tight, but not too tight, or you may depower the boat. The mainsheet traveler is best in the middle position. Sheeting in the headsail is more critical. Watch the end of the leeward spreader. On most rigs, the headsail should be very close without touching it. If it touches (probably due to insufficient wind) ease the sheet. If it is more

than a few inches away (probably because the crew has given up winding in a strong wind) wind the sheet in some more.

Be ready to bear away slightly if the telltales start to fly high on the windward side. Use the lower telltales for most precise feedback. It is not possible for the leech (trailing edge) of the headsail or mainsail to stay in a straight line from top to bottom. The sail will naturally "twist" open toward the top and be angled more into the wind. This is why telltales higher in the sail will stream differently from telltales lower in the sail.

Steering upwind

The tiller or wheel should feel reasonably light, with slight weather helm (heaviness) providing some "edge." If weather helm feels heavy,

the boat is out of balance. You may need to ease the mainsheet or reef the mainsail. Lee helm means too much power from the headsail.

Keep the boat moving

Part of the skill of sailing to windward is keeping the boat moving at a steady speed and getting a balance between direction and speed. Heading straight into waves will slow the boat right down. In larger waves, the only way to keep up speed is to bear away and sail at a wider angle to the wind.

Tacking

To sail toward the wind, you will need to change tack. It's a straightforward maneuver that relies on good communication between the helmsman and crew.

Why do you need to tack?

You cannot sail directly toward the wind. The closest a yacht can point toward the wind is about 30 degrees, but that is a very "high" course. How many times you tack depends on local conditions. In a large sea area with a consistent wind pattern and no tidal flow, one change of tack may suffice. In a crowded area with changeable wind and different tidal effects, a yacht may make several tacks, in a zigzag course toward its goal.

The arc of the tack

In order to tack, you need to steer the bows of the boat through the eye of the wind. The boat must keep turning throughout the whole arc of the tack, first luffing toward the wind, then pointing into it, and finally bearing away from the wind.

If the boat points at 40 degrees to the wind on one tack, it will need to tack through an arc of about 80 degrees to sail on the new tack. However, if you turn a little further (for instance, through 90 degrees), it will allow the boat to accelerate on the new tack, before luffing as close to the wind as possible but without stalling the boat.

Who does what?

The helmsman (helm) briefs the crew, tells them when he is tacking and then steers the yacht through the tack. The mainsheet can stay sheeted throughout the tack. There is normally no need to touch it. The headsail sheet must be let off on the old tack and pulled in on the new. This is managed by two cockpit crew, one on each side of the boat, but it's possible for one experienced crew to let off and pull in the sheets on a medium-size yacht.

Changing tack

- ✪ The helm decides when to tack after checking that the area to windward is clear. Watch for waves, which may stop the boat head-to-wind, and look for a flat patch. If in doubt, postpone the tack.
- ✪ The helm announces: "Ready to tack?" One crew goes to the

headsail winch on the leeward side, takes the sheet out of the self-tailing jaws and holds it. The other crew goes to the headsail winch on the windward side, pulls the slack headsail sheet in until it is taut, takes two turns around the winch and holds it firmly.

- ✪ Both crew announce: "Ready!"
- ✪ The helm announces: "Lee-ho" (traditional) or "Tacking" (modern). He turns the wheel or pushes the tiller to leeward to steer the boat into the wind.
- ✪ The boat must keep turning and not stall head-to-wind. Do not let go of the leeward sheet. As the boat passes through the eye of the wind, it will catch the back of the headsail and help push the bows round on to the new tack.
- ✪ Let go of the sheet when you are certain the boat has turned through the eye of the wind. Ease it and then flick it off the drum.

Left: **On starboard tack, this yacht is sailing as high into the wind as it can go. Changing course to starboard will mean a turn of at least 60 degrees in order to sail on port tack.**

Above (left to right): **1. When the crew are "ready" give the instruction "Lee-ho" and turn smoothly into the wind. 2. The sails should be kept sheeted in as the yacht turns head-to-wind. 3. Letting off the headsail sheet at the last moment allows the headsail to "back," which ensures the bow continues to turn onto the new course.**

Right: **Having steered through at least 60 degrees, the helm can straighten out the course while the crew sheets in the headsail on the new side. If they find it difficult to winch the sail in, help by briefly luffing toward the wind to depower the headsail.**

❂ At the same time, the other crew pulls in hand-over-hand on the new sheet. The headsail should be pulled most of the way in before it starts to power the boat. As the load gets heavy, put two more turns on the drum. Jam the sheet around the self-tailing jaws, put in the handle and wind the sail in tight for the new beat.

❂ The helm should center the wheel or tiller to stop the boat from turning further as the headsail is being wound in. If the crew is finding it hard work, the helm should luff toward the wind to briefly depower the headsail and make winding easier. Bear away when winding is finished.

Sailing offwind

Sailing with the wind behind the beam is what most sailors enjoy most. The yacht will sail at its fastest on a broad reach, the motion will be easy and the apparent wind will feel warm and light.

Watching the wind

When sailing with the wind well astern, keep checking the windvane on top of the mast and electronic wind-direction instruments in the cockpit to avoid accidental jibing (taking the stern through the wind unexpectedly). Telltales are useful for checking the set of the headsail on a broad reach, but aren't effective sailing downwind.

When jibing is safe

✪ If you are running with the wind right behind (a "dead downwind" course) don't jibe by mistake — especially in strong winds when an uncontrolled jibe could be dangerous.

Below: **Keep heads low and beware of the mainsheet when sailing offwind. The skipper must take care not to steer into an accidental jibe.**

✪ Prepare a "preventer." Attach a rope (of headsail sheet diameter and strength) to the end of the boom. Lead the rope forward and secure it so that it will hold the boom in a fixed position. For instance, the preventer can be led through the fair-lead in the toe rail at the bows on the leeward side, and then secured to the nearest deck cleat. The preventer should hold the boom if the helm inadvertently steers into a jibe. It is essential that the preventer is tied in such a way that it can be released under strain.

✪ Beware of sailing "by the lee" which is when the wind is blowing over the stern from the leeward (wrong) side. If the boat rolls, changes course on a wave or you are just steering badly, the mainsail and the boom may crash across in a sudden unexpected jibe.

✪ If in doubt, head up a few degrees so that the boat is sailing on a broad reach. This will be faster, more stable and much easier for the helm. Even though you are not heading in exactly the right direction, it may be better to jibe (sail a zigzag course) to reach your goal.

Setting sails for reaching offwind

✪ Sailing on a beam reach or broad reach, the mainsheet should be eased until the mainsail starts to flap, and then pulled in a touch. The further offwind the course, the more the mainsheet should be eased, but avoid letting the mainsail touch the shrouds.

Left: **On a broad reach, the headsail should be trimmed so that the windward (inside) telltales are streaming horizontally, with the mainsail sheeted in far enough to prevent backwinding.**

Above: **Sailing offwind reduces apparent wind and makes everything seem much warmer and more pleasant, but all that can change when you start to head back upwind and it feels colder and windy.**

Ensure the boom vang is pulled right down to hold the boom perpendicular.

☁ Trim the headsail so that the telltales are streaming back on both sides. If the windward telltales are lifting, wind in the sheet. If it's the leeward telltales, ease out the sheet.

☁ The yacht will sail at its fastest on a broad reach, but if it heels too far with sideways slip this will slow you down. Reducing sail (by reefing the mainsail and rolling the headsail) will make the boat feel more comfortable and allow it to sail at a better speed.

Steering downwind
Unlike steering upwind, when only small corrections should be needed, the helm may need to be more active sailing downwind. If the wind is fresh there will be following sea (wave pattern moving in the same direction as the boat), which will literally push the stern from side to side. The helm must anticipate and react to keep the boat sailing as straight as possible, with constant course correction. This can be quite tiring, so it's good to let each crew take short spells on the helm.

Goosewinged
The most effective way to sail directly downwind is to "goosewing" the headsail, which means pulling the headsail out on the windward side. It works best if there is a pole, attached to the mast and clew, to hold out the sail. If not, the helm must sail by the lee without jibing, which requires concentration and skill. The main boom must have a preventer attached in case of an unexpected accidental jibe.

Safety downwind
Beware of the boom. The cockpit crew should keep low in case of an accidental jibe, especially when going on deck. And hold on with one hand — the boat may roll unexpectedly.

Jibing

Changing tacks when sailing downwind is known as jibing. The wind, blowing over the stern, continues to power up the mainsail as the boom swings from one side to the other. This makes the jibe a dynamic maneuver that the crew must carefully manage in a breeze.

Managing a jibe

Controlling the boom

Before a jibe, the boom is normally right out for downwind sailing and if not controlled could swing through an arc of more than 150 degrees: from the shrouds on one side to the shrouds on the other; before a tack, the boom is normally sheeted in tight as for upwind sailing so that it can only swing through a small arc.

During a tack, the boat turns head-to-wind, which depowers the sails. The yacht's momentum should keep it turning, but it may also be necessary to "back the headsail" to push the bows round.

By contrast, during a jibe, the boat turns with its stern to the wind. If the boom is let out against the shrouds (the normal position for downwind sailing) the mainsail will be fully powered throughout the jibe. The mainsail must be carefully managed to prevent the boom crashing from one side to the other. The headsail, on the other hand, is easy to manage, as it will be blanketed by the mainsail throughout most of the jibe.

In dinghy sailing, it is normal practice to let the boom swing in a wide arc right across the boat. On a yacht, the distance of the arc and the weight of the boom make a "free swinging jibe" too difficult and dangerous to control in all but the lightest winds. The boom could be lethal if it hits someone and could cause severe damage to the mast.

How do you jibe?

It is vital that the helm briefs the crew and maintains careful control of the jibe. Always turn through a narrow arc during the jibe, and then steer onto the new course when the boat has settled down. If you attempt to jibe in a wide arc the boat will be difficult to control.

Changing jibe

⊕ One crew will need to manage the mainsheet; the other will need to manage the headsail sheet.

⊕ The helm decides when to jibe.

⊕ Check that the area to leeward and ahead is completely clear. During the jibe, the helm's vision may be obscured by the headsail. Beware of waves picking up the stern during the jibe, which will affect steering. Choose a flat patch of water for maximum control.

⊕ The helm announces: "Ready to jibe?"

⊕ If a preventer has been rigged on the boom, this must be removed. The mainsail crew starts pulling in the mainsheet. Depending on the size of the yacht, it may be possible to pull the sheet in hand-over-hand, or wound in on the winch, ensuring that the clutch is closed. The helm steers deep

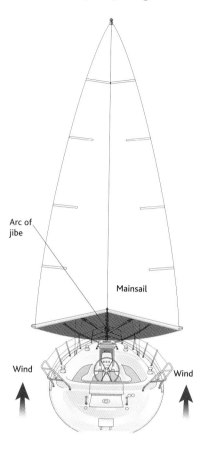

Above (left to right): **1. Pull in the mainsheet before you jibe, so the boom can only swing through a narrow arc. 2. Turn the rudder to steer into the jibe. 3. Let the headsail sheet go as the stern swings** through the wind. **4. The boom will swing across; straighten the course so the boat remains sailing deep downwind. 5. Sheet in the headsail and ease out the mainsail on the new side.**

Above: **The arc of the mainsail during a jibe. In anything but light winds the boom should be pulled in tight using the mainsheet to prevent it from swinging right across the boat when you jibe.**

downwind to take pressure off the mainsail, but not risking a premature jibe.

✪ When the mainsheet is pulled right in, the crew announces "Ready!" The second crew, standing by the leeward headsail sheet, also announces: "Ready!"

✪ The helm announces: "Jibe-ho" or "Jibing" and bears away to run directly downwind, then run by the lee (the wind blowing over the leeward side of the stern)

until the boom swings to the new side. He first checks for any heads or bodies in the way of the boom.

✪ As the boom swings across, the helmsman continues turning the wheel (or pulling on the tiller) to settle onto the new course. The mainsheet crew eases the mainsheet out to match the course. The headsail crew takes the sheet off the winch and pulls it in on the new side.

Above: **When the wind is directly behind you can goosewing the headsail onto the windward side, but you may need a pole to hold it out.**

Cruising with spinnakers

The traditional symmetrical spinnaker made of lightweight rip-stop nylon is very efficient for sailing directly downwind. A yacht sailing under spinnaker on a breezy day looks fantastic, but requires expertise.

Hoisting a spinnaker

✪ The spinnaker is hoisted from a bag carried onto the foredeck and secured to the guardrail. The bottom corners of the sail are connected to the sheet (leeward side) and guy (windward side). These two identical sheets both have snap shackle connectors. They are led aft (outside the shrouds) to turning blocks at the stern toe rails, then forward to cockpit winches for the crew to trim. The guy is always on the windward side, where it is led through the outer end of the spinnaker boom, supporting the tack of the sail. When you jibe, the old guy becomes the new sheet and vice versa.

✪ The inner end of the spinnaker pole is attached to the mast. An uphaul/downhaul control line keeps it horizontal.

✪ The guy acts as a control line for the spinnaker boom, which sets the correct position of the spinnaker. If the yacht is sailing directly downwind, the spinnaker boom is pulled as far back as possible so that it is against the shroud. If the yacht is sailing on a reach, the boom is let forward; on a beam reach it will almost be parallel with the boat, but should never rest against the forestay. With the boom in a set position, the crew trims the spinnaker sheet, which requires constant attention. The sheet should be eased until the leech (windward side) starts curling, and then pulled in.

✪ The spinnaker is a high-flying sail, which can take control of the boat. Both bottom corners (tack and clew) should be level. This is achieved by adjusting the height and angle of the spinnaker pole.

Jibing a spinnaker

✪ Various methods are used for jibing the spinnaker, including using two booms or dipping the end of the pole in the gap between mast and forestay.

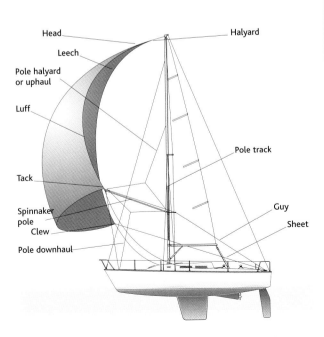

Below: **The spinnaker is made up of the halyard, sheets, pole, uphaul and downhaul. All the control lines (including the guy and sheet, uphaul and downhaul) are kept in place whether the sail is raised or not.**

Head
Leech
Pole halyard or uphaul
Luff
Tack
Spinnaker pole
Clew
Pole downhaul
Halyard
Pole track
Guy
Sheet

Below: **Problems setting the spinnaker in very light winds — 5 knots of breeze is all it takes to fill the superlight rip-stop nylon.**

On smaller yachts, the "end forend" method is widely used.

- As the helmsman steers into the jibe, the foredeck crew unclips the inner end of the spinnaker boom from the mast, grabs the sheet (which will become the new guy) and clips it into the pole's free end. He pushes the boom out on the new side, unclips the old guy (which will become the new sheet) and attaches the end of the pole to the mast.
- The cockpit crew must control the spinnaker sheet and guy to give the foredeck crew sufficient slack at the right time. The helm must steer carefully through the jibe, timing the mainsail's swing to blanket the spinnaker at the phase when the foredeck crew is changing ends on the spinnaker boom.

Dropping a spinnaker

- The spinnaker is a powerful sail. To keep control during the drop, the helm must steer so that the mainsail helps blanket the spinnaker. The speed of the drop is critical. The halyard must be lowered at just the right speed for the crew to gather it in without the spinnaker falling in the water.
- When it's time to drop the sail, the cockpit crew grabs the sheet close to the clew of the spinnaker, pull in the foot and pull down the sail under the boom, which is bundled straight down a hatch or companionway.
- When the spinnaker is lowered, the halyard, sheet and guy can be clipped to the pulpit with the lines tightened.

Asymmetrical spinnakers

- Most cruising yachts have asymmetrical spinnakers, also known as gennakers, reachers or cruising chutes. These sails act like a headsail made of lightweight material with a curved luff, but not attached to the forestay. They are effective on a broad reach, but fairly ineffective dead downwind unless a boom is used to hold the sail out.
- The tack of the sail is attached to the bow or to a pole that protrudes from the bows and may be pulled out when the sail is launched. The clew is attached to port and starboard sheets, which are led back to the cockpit. The spinnaker sheets must pass outside the forestay to allow the spinnaker to swing around the front of the forestay when the boat jibes; neither sheet must pass between mast and forestay.

Socks or snuffers

- The spinnaker can be hoisted by halyard from a bag on the deck, but a more controllable method is to hoist it inside a tubular sock. An uphaul pulls the sock to the top of the mast to let the sail fly; a downhaul pulls the sock down to snuff the sail, before it is dropped like a sausage on to the deck.

Below: **The cruising chute is very effective on a broad reach, but unlike a symmetrical spinnaker is not suitable for running directly downwind.**

Using the engine

Most yachts have diesel or gas engines to provide reliable power and economic fuel consumption. The engine is vital for docking, passage making when there is no wind, and providing electricity for equipment and lights.

Below: **1. A folding propeller reduces drag while sailing. 2. A fixed-blade propeller creates maximum drag under sail. 3. A feathering propeller reduces drag and is efficient in reverse.**

Engine access

- The engine is usually housed under the cockpit sole. Access for maintenance is behind the companionway steps; there may also be an inspection hatch in the aft cabin.
- Battery switches for the engine are normally close to the companionway. Separate batteries are used to start the engine and provide auxiliary power for the yacht. This ensures that the engine battery will not run flat.
- The engine control panel, with starter, rev counter and warning lights, is often on the side of the cockpit, within easy reach of the helm. The combined throttle and gearshift control may be mounted on the side of the cockpit or on the binnacle.

Below: **Access to the engine may require removing the companionway steps. Some yachts will have a secondary access panel in the side cabin.**

Propeller types

Which propeller works best?

- The traditional yacht propeller has two or three fixed blades that require no maintenance apart from cleaning. Also effective in reverse, it has the best forward propulsion if the blades are perfectly pitched. Disadvantages include extra drag from the propeller, which will spin while the boat is sailing (unless placed in "astern" position). Unless the yacht has a shaft lock, this also makes an annoying noise.
- A folding propeller has two or three blades that fold flat while sailing. This creates minimum drag and is therefore the top choice for racing yachts. However, it has poor reverse thrust and maintenance is required.
- A feathering propeller has three twisting blades. This type can provide the best possible reverse

Motorsailing

Moderate engine revs can give a big boost to sailing performance by increasing apparent wind. This is particularly useful in marginal conditions when a yacht is sailing slowly and not able to point high upwind. Motorsailing is like a magic wand. You can suddenly point high and 'sail' at maximum speed. In addition, the 'wind' in the sails will help prevent unpleasant rolling. But you can't motorsail directly into the wind. You will have to drop the mainsail, roll the headsail and put up with an unpleasant motion.

Right: **Motorsailing in calm conditions. Ths sails stabilize the boat and stop it from rocking too much.**

thrust, combined with low drag and reduced prop walk (see page 209). Maintenance is required.
- ✪ The position of the propeller relative to the keel and rudder has a major effect on the boat's handling under power in reverse.

Filling the diesel tank
- ✪ The filler for the diesel tank is normally in the sidedeck, close to the cockpit. Check that the filler is marked "diesel" and not "water" before you fill the tank! Don't allow water or dirt to get into the diesel tank. Beware of diesel spills, which will be slippery on deck and need to be cleaned up.
- ✪ Check the engine manual to find out how many gallons per hour the engine will use at cruising revs. Keep a note of engine hours

— diesel fuel gauges on yachts can be inaccurate and should not be trusted. If you allow the engine to run out of fuel, you'll have to bleed air out of the fuel

system before you can start it again. This requires some expertise and will be difficult if the yacht is rolling.

Regular checks
- ✪ Check engine and gearbox oil levels.
- ✪ Check that belts are tight and hoses are in good condition.
- ✪ Check fresh cooling water level.
- ✪ Check raw water and fuel filters.
- ✪ Check grease gland for straight-through propeller shaft.
- ✪ Check cooling water is being pumped out as soon as the engine has started. The exhaust will be to one side at the stern.
- ✪ It is worth taking a small engine maintenance course from your local club to become familiar with the requirements of your engine.

Boat handling under power

All yachts behave differently under power. Motoring in a straight line is not a problem, but things can be trickier in a marina. There is restricted space to turn the boat, and motoring astern may be unpredictable.

Left: **Most yacht engines have a single lever control. Backward is reverse, upright is neutral and forward is ahead. Push the red button in on this engine and move the lever forward to get high engine revs out of gear.**

Beware of the wind

Yachts are affected by the wind when maneuvering at slow speed. You need to keep power on to keep the yacht moving in a specific direction, especially on a windy day. If the propeller stops pushing the yacht ahead, the bow will start to blow downwind.

Keel and propeller

The position of the propeller between rudder and keel will have a major effect on how a yacht handles when motoring astern. The keel configuration is equally important. Some traditional long keel yachts are virtually impossible to steer while motoring astern. With experience, skippers learn how best to maneuver traditional yachts.

Above: **If the boat slows right down, the wind will start to blow it off course. If the wind is blowing from starboard, the bow will blow off to port.**

Engine control

* The main control lever combines the throttle and gearshift. A red button (or similar) at the base of the lever is pressed in to select neutral for starting. Use the throttle to increase engine speed in neutral. With the engine running smoothly, pull the lever back to the vertical position; the red button will click "out," which enables the lever to engage gears. (This is true of the majority of yachts, but some may need to have the button engaged for forward and reverse gears.)
* Push the lever forward to engage forward gear and increase speed; back for reverse gear. Always pause with the lever in the vertical neutral position when shifting between these gears.
* Keep revs down and never use full throttle, other than for safety.

Prop walk

- Prop walk drags the stern in the direction in which the propeller is rotating. For instance, a clockwise spinning propeller will drag the stern to starboard when motoring ahead. In reverse, the propeller will spin in the opposite direction and drag the stern to port.
- Prop walk has most effect when maneuvering at slow speed. Moving ahead, it's fairly easy to control your course with the rudder; when reversing, it may quickly pull the stern in the wrong direction, which will be impossible to correct without motoring ahead.
- It helps to know which way prop walk will push the stern in reverse. You can simulate this

Above: **Allow for prop walk when reversing, to ensure the yacht is able to travel in a straight line entering its berth. It's an advantage if you can face aft while steering.**

PROP WALK

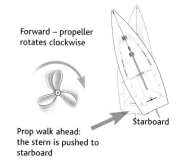

Forward – propeller rotates clockwise

Prop walk ahead: the stern is pushed to starboard

Starboard

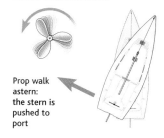

Reverse – propeller rotates counterclockwise

Prop walk astern: the stern is pushed to port

with the yacht tied up alongside the dock. Put the engine into reverse; the stern will be pushed away from turbulent water streaming off the propeller.

Think ahead

- Think ahead and ask, "What if?" Maneuvering in a marina is like playing a game of chess.
- Work out how you will leave or enter a berth and brief the crew. If you are not sure, seek advice from the harbor master.
- Have all lines and fenders ready before you need to use them.
- Check wind direction and tidal flow, and assess how it will affect maneuvering your boat.

Left: **The key to handling a boat well under power is understandng "prop walk." The stern tends to be pushed sideways in the same direction as the propeller rotates.**

- Avoid getting into a dead-end position, unable to turn and being blown against the quay or other boats.
- Avoid busy times when leaving or entering a marina. Try to arrive early before the main rush, while there is still plenty of free space.
- Task someone to watch for other boats on the move, and always check for other yachts moving before casting off your own lines.
- If visiting a new dock, radio ahead to the dock master for instructions and berth location.

Entering a marina

It is easier to leave a marina than to arrive. If you are sailing in a new area, you may have no experience of the harbor you are about to enter. Careful preparation will make the challenge of docking a lot easier.

Left: **Get fenders and lines ready in the final approach to a marina, and watch how other boats moor up.**

Below: **Leave plenty of time to attach fenders; you may need them on both sides.**

for example, "B27" and describe its location. If you don't know where to go, temporarily moor alongside the visitors' pontoon and report to the harbor office for instructions.

Attaching fenders

Ensure fenders are secured before entering a berth, at the correct height for the pontoon, and cushioning the yacht's widest part. One crew can stand ready with a "roving fender," to plug a gap. If going stern-to to the dock, attach one large fender to the transom.

Attaching ropes

❂ Place coiled mooring ropes inside the lifelines at the bow and stern. Lead the end of each rope over the lifelines, through the fair-lead and onto the deck cleat, and secure it with a bowline. The coil of rope will run outside the lifelines when led to the dock.

❂ When coming alongside or berthing stern-to, be prepared to step ashore with the coil of line. If someone is waiting to catch the

Before you arrive

❂ Every yacht should have a "pilot guide," which will provide information on marinas, harbors and anchorages in the sailing area. Study it and make a plan for the final approach. Note specific instructions or hazards.

❂ Call the harbor master by VHF or cell phone. The pilot guide will provide information on VHF channels and phone numbers. Request berthing instructions before you enter.

Brief the crew

Tell the crew where you intend to berth and what will happen. If you are not sure where you will berth (for instance, port-side or stern-on to the dock), have fenders and warps ready on both sides.

Final approach

When you approach a marina or harbor, keep to the starboard side. If the harbor master expects you, he will tell you which berth to head for:

Right: **When harbors appear very crowded, look for a berth on the outside. Remember that it's not as easy as driving round a parking lot — allow space for the boat to turn and for the effects of the wind and tide.**

Sunsail Odyssey 45

mooring lines, pass or throw the coil. When throwing a coil, it is imperative that it does not fall short. Do not attempt to throw the entire coil. Separate the coil between your left and right hands, throw the lighter coil and let coils slip off your other hand at the same time.

✪ Be careful when going ashore. Don't fall between the boat and the dock! The helm should have enough control of the boat to allow the crew to safely step ashore with stern and bowlines.

✪ As soon as you are on the dock, be ready to take a turn round the cleats nearest to the bow and stern. Never attempt to "hold" a yacht without using a cleat: if the wind or tide catches the boat, it will pull you off the dock.

✪ Pull in gradually on the bow and stern lines to bring the yacht close alongside. At this stage, you may need to move to different cleats, better placed to hold the yacht.

✪ Secure the bow and stern lines and attach springs. Either:

1. Use the ends of the mooring lines as springs (see page 214);
2. Lead mooring lines back to the yacht;
3. Attach mooring lines to the dock with bowlines and keep the rest of the length on deck.

Hands and feet

Beware when fending off. Never risk putting your hands or feet between two yachts or a yacht and the dock. A roving fender may be crushed, but won't feel any pain!

Top left: **Attach the fenders, making sure they are at the correct height to protect the widest part of the boat.**

Top right: **Have lines coiled ready for you to pass or take them ashore.**

Below: **"Piles" are widely used in countries such as Holland. The yacht is moored bows-on with stern lines attached to piles on either side.**

Berthing in a marina or harbor

The object is to stop the boat in exactly the right spot, which will enable the crew to secure the mooring lines. Wind, tide and tightly packed boats can make this difficult. If in doubt, ask the marina staff for assistance or look for a berth with an easier approach.

Below: It can be a tight squeeze with boats on either side. Use the engine control carefully in reverse to avoid hitting the pontoon.

Arriving alongside

✿ Approach the pontoon with enough speed to provide steerage, but not too fast. Use reverse gear to stop the yacht alongside.

✿ To make things as easy as possible, aim to arrive at slack tide when tidal flow will have minimum effect.

✿ If there is tidal flow through the marina (for instance, in a river) it is preferable to come alongside against the tide, which will stop the yacht and hold in the stern while the crew secure the bowline. If you come alongside in the same direction as the tide, it will drive the yacht forward and push out the stern. In that situation, it is vital to secure the

✿ With little or no tide, it is best to come alongside with the bow pointing into the wind for control. Secure the bowline and the stern will be blown alongside the dock.

✿ In a crowded marina, you may have to reverse alongside the pontoon. Always reverse into the

tide or wind (whichever is strongest) and secure the stern line while the bows are pushed or blown alongside.

✿ If the wind is blowing onto the pontoon, aim to stop the yacht parallel to it, a few feet away. The wind will then blow the yacht

Approaching the pontoon

1. Approach the pontoon with lines ready and fenders out.
2. Take the bow line ashore and fasten it to the cleat.
3. Take the stern line ashore and fasten to the cleat.
4. Attach the fore and aft springs (see page 214).

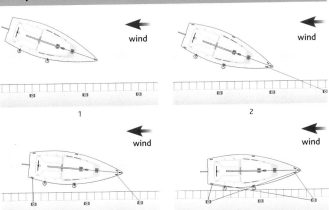

alongside. Beware of coming alongside a leeward pontoon which is on the outside of a marina with no protection from wind and waves: it may be uncomfortable lying alongside, or dangerous if the wind increases.

- If the wind is blowing away from the pontoon, head toward it at an angle of about 30 degrees. The wind should blow the bows out and allow the yacht to come alongside parallel to the pontoon, enabling at least one crew member to get ashore with a line.

Right: **Reversing alongside a berth. Note the skipper is facing backward. If you catch hold of a boat in this way, be careful it doesn't pull you off the dock!**

Arriving stern-first

- Line up the yacht carefully before reversing into your berth, which may be a narrow gap between two moored yachts. Consider how prop walk will kick the stern to one side and wind may blow the yacht sideways. You need power to reverse in a straight line. If you slow right down, the bow will start to blow downwind.

- If you need to drop the anchor, make sure it is far enough out to hold.
- The crew must be ready to fend off on both sides. Get the stern lines secured as soon as possible, then hold the yacht off the dock with a little forward power. This will enable the crew to tension the anchor, or pull in and secure the lazy line, which is attached to the pontoon, adjacent to the yacht's stern.

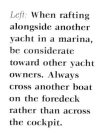

Left: **When rafting alongside another yacht in a marina, be considerate toward other yacht owners. Always cross another boat on the foredeck rather than across the cockpit.**

Rafting alongside other yachts

- Harbors can become crowded in high season when it may be necessary to moor alongside a raft of other yachts. The procedure is straightforward. Bowlines, stern lines and springs connect yachts. Care needs to be taken not to overlap shrouds and spreaders with the neighboring yacht, in case the two roll together and clash. Fendering is vital on both sides of the boat. To keep the raft stable, take long bow and stern lines to the dock. Smaller yachts should berth on the outside — a larger yacht could "bend" the raft.
- Etiquette is required when berthing alongside. Be considerate to your neighbors. If you need to cross their boat, go across the foredeck but avoid falling down the hatch!
- Yachts on the inside may wish to depart the following morning. Careful planning is required if there is a lot of wind or tide, to avoid chaos.

How a yacht is secured

Different methods are used to secure yachts in marinas and docks. Depending on the location, it may be necessary to berth alongside, stern-to or bows-on to a dock, pontoon or harbor wall.

Berthing alongside

- Yachts are frequently berthed alongside narrow finger pontoons attached to the main pontoon of a marina. Each pontoon has large horn cleats or mooring rings, suitably spaced for a yacht's bow line, stern line and springs.
- Fenders are hung from the lifelines or toe rail to protect the sides of the yacht. Ensure they protect the yacht's widest part.
- The yacht is secured by a bow and stern line led to the pontoon. These are attached to cleats ahead of and behind the yacht.
- Springs are diagonal lines that prevent the yacht surging forward or backward, particularly in a tidal location. A spring attached to the bow is led back to a cleat on

the pontoon to prevent the yacht moving forward. A spring attached to the stern is led forward to a cleat on the pontoon to prevent the yacht moving backward. Springs can also be led fore and aft from the middle of the yacht.

Controlling the line on a cleat

1. Turn the line around the back of the cleat and pull.
2. Start creating a "figure-eight" by wrapping the line around the cleat.
3. This produces enough friction to hold the line.
4. A twisted locking turn can be added to make the line more secure (but take care not to do this on lines that need releasing quickly).

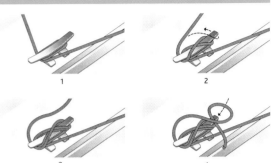

Lying against a pontoon

This is the basic arrangment for lines where a boat lies alongside a pontoon. It may vary depending on how the cleats are arranged in the harbor.

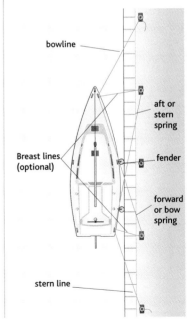

bowline

aft or stern spring

fender

forward or bow spring

Breast lines (optional)

stern line

Left: The stern line holds in the stern. The two springs prevent the yacht moving forward and aft, although in this instance the stern spring could be a little tighter.

Left: **Mooring bows-on is recommended if it's shallow close to the dock.**

Below: **Mooring stern-to. The stern is secured by two stern lines; the bow is held by an anchor or lazy line.**

Using cleats

- A yacht pulls hard. Always take a turn around a suitable heavy-duty cleat when you need to hold the bow or stern stationary.
- When securing a mooring rope, take two turns round the main body of the cleat. Follow with figures-eights across the horn.
- Leave your ropes neatly on the dock. Coil loose ends or lead them back to the yacht.

Watch the tide

Marinas in tidal areas have floating pontoons that move up and down with your yacht. Harbor walls do not move. All mooring lines will need to be adjusted as the tide rises and falls. If the harbor dries out, special care will be needed to ensure the yacht is in a position to sit alongside without toppling over!

Berthing stern-to

- In areas like the Mediterranean, it is normal to berth stern-to in marinas and harbors. This allows you to step ashore from the stern and ensures that yachts can be packed in tightly!
- The yacht is moored with two lines securing the stern to the quay. The bow can be secured by dropping the anchor or retrieving the marina lazy line.
- In a harbor, the yacht drops its anchor, reverses into the berth, attaches the stern lines, and then takes up slack on the anchor chain. It can be difficult to get the distance right. If you drop the anchor too far out, you won't have enough chain to reach the dock. If you drop it too close, the anchor will not hold the bows.
- In marinas, a lazy line attached to the dock makes the process much easier. The lazy line leads to a heavy duty mooring rope attached to a mooring block on the harbor bottom. As the yacht reverses into position, the crew attach the stern lines and grab the lazy line while the helm keeps the engine in forward gear. The crew walk the lazy line forward to the bow, pull in the mooring line and secure it to the bow cleat. The line must be taut enough to prevent the stern hitting the dock.

Berthing bows-on

The bows are secured to the dock by two bowlines, and the lazy line mooring or an auxiliary anchor holds the stern. Berthing bows-on may be the safest option if it is too shallow to risk the rudder being close to the harbor wall. It affords more privacy than berthing stern-to, but can make it very difficult to get on and off the boat.

Leaving a marina

Plan ahead and brief the crew to ensure a smooth departure. If it appears difficult to get away from the dock, don't hesitate to ask for assistance. People will be only too willing to help by holding lines or fending off when there are difficulties.

Below: **This yacht has a permanent marina berth. When it leaves, the bow and stern lines remain attached to the pontoon.**

yacht. It is advisable to place a fender between stern and pontoon. The other crew lets off the bowline, pushes the bow off the pontoon and quickly climbs on board. The stern line is allowed to run free and the boat motors away from the pontoon.

⊗ If tidal flow is against the pontoon, or a strong wind is blowing onto the pontoon, the bows will be pinned in. Leaving stern-first provides the solution. Let off both springs. One crew hand-holds the bowline, which is led back to the yacht. Place a fender between the bow and pontoon. The other crew lets off the stern line, pushes the stern off and then quickly climbs on board. The bowline is allowed to run free and the boat motors away stern-first from the pontoon. Take great care that the stern line isn't caught in the prop.

Leaving from alongside

⊗ When you turn the rudder of a moving yacht, the stern swings out; you can't steer away from a pontoon, since the yacht will bump along the side.

⊗ If you intend to leave bow-first, the bow will need to be pushed off the pontoon. Wind blowing off the pontoon or directly onto the bow will help to push it out. Tidal flow against the bow will also push it out. Let off both springs. One crew hand-holds the stern line, which is led back to the

Leaving a pontoon

1. The yacht is secured to the pontoon.
2. The engine is in gear to prevent the wind from pushing the boat back. Spring lines are removed.
3. The bowline is eased and the bow moves out. Lines are taken in.
4. The stern line is slipped. The fenders are taken on board.

If there is not much space ahead (or astern), it may be necessary to "spring" out the bow (or stern). Remove all mooring ropes apart from a stern spring. Place a fender between the stern and the pontoon and motor in reverse. Pulling against the spring will force the bows to pivot out as the boat is pulled from its stern. Reverse the procedure to force the stern out, motoring ahead against a bow spring.

Leaving from a stern-to or bows-to berth

If the bows (or stern) are secured by a lazy line, cast off the mooring rope while motoring ahead to hold the stern (or bows) off the dock. Then slip the stern (or bow) lines and motor out of the berth.

If the bows (or stern) are secured by an anchor, slip the stern (or bow) lines and pull in the anchor chain or rope hand-over-hand. Get the anchor up as quickly as possible. Make sure the helm knows when it has broken clear.

Power turns

When leaving a marina, you may need to make a sharp turn in a tight space. Use power to help the boat turn: wash from the propeller will hit the rudder and force the stern around. The bows will swing into the turn and the stern will swing out as the boat swivels around a point close to the mast.

Use prop walk to make the tightest possible turn. (This technique only works if you turn the stern in the same direction as the propeller is spinning when moving ahead.)

If the propeller is rotating clockwise, turn to port if possible, holding the rudder hard over. Give a sharp burst of throttle in forward gear to start the turn and "pull" the stern to starboard. Shift into neutral and, if necessary, engage astern after putting the rudder hard over the other way. Keep it gentle, as prop walk in reverse gear will take the stern to port. Back into neutral, rudder hard over in the original direction, and a final burst ahead should complete the turn.

Keep it tidy

Once the yacht has left the berth, the crew should tidy the boat. Coil all mooring lines and fenders and store them in cockpit lockers or on the pushpit if short on space. Beware of dropping rope over the side, where it could get tangled in the propeller. Never go sailing with warps or fenders still attached!

Top: **When you leave or enter a berth, the tender may need to be towed alongside.**

Right: **Marinas often have narrow lanes between moored yachts, but it's possible to make a very tight power turn by using prop walk.**

Anchoring a yacht

A single anchor is enough to attach a large yacht securely to the sea bottom, other than in very bad conditions. Anchor, chain, warp and bow roller all play a vital role in ensuring anchoring is safe and easily done.

Anchor design

All anchors have a main arm known as the "shank" and a hook known as the "fluke," which digs into the bottom of the sea bed.

☸ The CQR or "plow" anchor has a hinged shank and fluke, providing good holding with reasonably light weight. This design is very popular, since it can be stowed ready for use on the bow roller.

☸ The Danforth anchor has a hinged shank and fluke. It provides good holding and folds flat, making it suitable for storage on the foredeck.

☸ The Bruce anchor is a variation on the plow anchor with no moving parts. It is unsuitable for storage on deck, but can be stowed on the bow roller.

☸ The Fisherman's anchor is a traditional design that provides good holding on weed or rock but needs to be heavy to compete on all-around holding with more modern designs. With two sharp flukes and a removable stock, this anchor is difficult to use with a bow roller and clumsy to stow on deck or in a locker.

Chain and warp

☸ An anchor is attached to a combination of chain and warp. Heavy chain provides more secure holding, but adds a lot of weight to the bows of the boat, which will increase pitching. Chain is the top choice for cruising yachts. Warp may be adequate for anchoring a smaller yacht or a racing yacht, which only needs to anchor in specific situations: for instance, waiting for a favorable tide while becalmed during a race.

☸ For effective holding, the chain or warp must lie along the bottom so that there is no upward pull on the anchor. A basic formula is used for calculating how much chain or warp is required: four times the depth for chain or six to eight times the depth for warp is recommended. Remember to take account of the tide rising when calculating the depth. It is better to let out too much than too little!

☸ The chain is stored in a chain locker or anchor locker in the bows of the boat. When you drop the anchor it is important to make

Above: **The anchor is stowed on the bow roller, with the electric windlass inside the anchor locker and the chain locker below.**

Type of anchors

The essential quality for an anchor is holding power. This depends on its design, its weight, the nature of the bottom, the weight of the chain and the length of the scope.

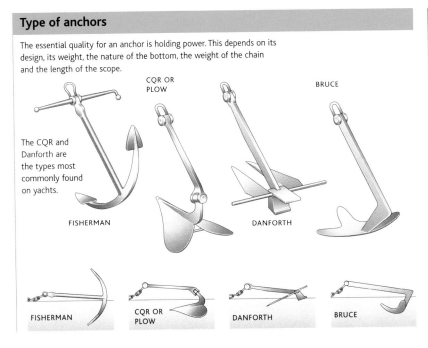

The CQR and Danforth are the types most commonly found on yachts.

CQR OR PLOW

BRUCE

FISHERMAN

DANFORTH

FISHERMAN

CQR OR PLOW

DANFORTH

BRUCE

Anchoring

Multiplying the depth of water below the yacht x4 gives an approximate guide to the right length of the chain for safe anchoring. If the anchor is held by a line, its length should be at least 6–8 times the depth of water. Scope may be adjusted as the tide rises and falls.

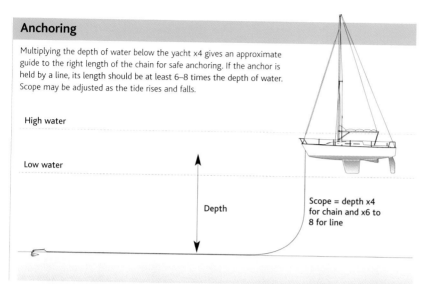

High water

Low water

Depth

Scope = depth x4 for chain and x6 to 8 for line

sure that the end of the chain or warp is secured. If using all chain, it is essential that the inboard end is secured with a piece of line long enough to emerge through the hawse hole and onto the deck. In an emergency, the line may need to be cut, and the anchor either abandoned or buoyed for later recovery. This is not the time to be wrestling with a seized shackle in the forepeak!

Anchor storage

☸ For cruising, it is very convenient if the anchor is permanently stowed on the bow roller. Remember you have a large lump of steel on the bows of the boat, so don't collide with anyone or let it overhang the pontoon when berthed in a marina!

☸ The bottom of the shank can be secured on deck by a locking pin through steel plates on either side of the roller. Tensioning the chain round the windlass or cleating the warp can secure the top of the shank. It is wise to lash the shank down.

☸ On some yachts the anchor is stowed on the foredeck or in a bow locker. Moving it on and off the bow roller can be tricky.

☸ The anchor is heavy and cumbersome, so you will need to pull out enough chain to be able

Above: **The crew operates the electric windlass with a handheld control stowed in the forecabin. The crew on the bow make sure the chain doesn't snag as it's pulled up and falls into the locker. Never put your fingers near a moving chain.**

to move the anchor, and the forestay and headsail furler will impede access to the bow roller. Place the anchor into position to drop just before you need it.

Right: **The anchor is locked ready for use in the bow roller with a steel pin. The anchor sticks out like a battering ram, so don't crash into anything!**

Controlling the anchor

A windlass is key in controlling the anchor and chain, but on a smaller yacht, lowering the anchor by hand can be quicker and just as effective.

Windlass

- Many medium-size yachts are fitted with a windlass powered by the onboard electric system. The windlass enables "hands-free" operation. You don't need to touch the chain to lower or raise the anchor — you just press a button. This is a great safety feature, but care needs to be taken.
- When lowering, the chain may snag as it is pulled up through the chain pipe out of the anchor locker. You will need to wind the chain back an inch or two to free it.
- The windlass uses a lot of power. When lifting the anchor, have the engine running in neutral at medium revs. If there is too much loading, it will blow the electricity supply, so make sure you know where the battery switch is located before operating the windlass. It is normally close to the main battery switches by the companionway. Don't expect too much from the windlass. If it is straining, stop hoisting and wait for the chain to go slack.
- The windlass can be operated by hand. Pushing the windlass lever forward or pulling it back will lock or unlock the drum that holds the chain, allowing it to spin freely. This is useful if you want to drop the chain faster than the electric motor will allow, but you must be able to "stop the drop" at any time to maintain control. The same lever can be used to crank the chain up by hand if the electric motor fails.

Dropping the anchor

- The anchor should be lowered under full control. Do not just let it all fall over the side.
- Prepare the anchor on the bow roller. Take out the retaining pin, undo any lashings and ease off the chain or warp. Ensure the anchor is securely held in the bow roller to avoid a premature drop. If you are lowering the anchor by hand (without a windlass), use a retaining line to hold the anchor back.
- The helm decides where and when to drop the anchor. He or she checks the depth sounder and decides how much chain or warp should be paid out. Ideally, it should have colored markings for each foot or fathom for the foredeck crew to count as the chain rolls out. If they are handling a lighter chain or warp,

they can pull out the required length (flaking it along the foredeck so that it will not snag) and cleat the end.
- The yacht should have stopped moving forward, and be starting to move backward when you start to lower the anchor. After the anchor hits bottom, the chain or warp should be stretched out and not just dropped in a pile.
- If it is windy or there is a strong tide running, the yacht will pull back until the chain goes taut, indicating the anchor has stopped dragging and is fully "set" in the

Left: **The anchor windlass (between the cleats) feeds the chain into the chain locker below. On this yacht, the anchor is permanently stowed on the bow roller.**

Left (left to right):
1. On an older yacht without a windlass, laying out the anchor chain on the side deck ensures it will run free. **2.** Pay the chain out hand-over-hand. Gloves are recommended. Take a turn before starting to lower the anchor. **3.** Watch how the anchor and chain are lying. When enough chain has been paid out, snub it by taking a turn around the deck cleat and let the yacht fall back on wind or tide.

bottom. In most situations, it is good practice to reverse slowly under engine to stretch out the chain, and then increase speed a little to ensure the anchor is set.

✪ Take bearings on the shoreline to check the anchor is not dragging. If the boat is pulling in one direction, you can do this by lining up two objects such as a telegraph pole and a building. If the anchor appears to be dragging, let out more chain or warp. If that doesn't work, pull it up and try again. A GPS will also indicate if a yacht is dragging.

Right: Leave room for the boat to swing. Don't get too close to boats already anchored.

Retrieving the anchor

Next to the boom, the anchor and its chain are potentially the most dangerous pieces of hardware on the yacht. Be alert to ensure that the anchor comes up smoothly without getting stuck.

Pulling up the anchor

- Anchor chain is heavy. As you pull it in, it will go taut at an acute angle to the bow. Wait for the weight of the chain to pull the yacht forward, and then continue pulling the chain in when chain falls vertically off the bow roller.
- In some situations (in strong wind or tide) you will need help from the helm, who can motor slowly ahead to take the strain off the anchor chain. Shout or use hand signals to indicate "ahead," "starboard," "port" or "stop."
- As the chain comes up, feed it down the chain pipe or give it a pull downward from inside the chain locker where it coils.
- The crew should inform the helm as soon as the anchor breaks its hold from the bottom. From that point it should be easy to pull up. If the boat is rolling or pitching, beware of the anchor swinging against the bow during the final stages of the hoist. Pull it up fast, until the shank lies horizontal on the bow roller.

What if the anchor is stuck?

- In some situations, the anchor may not break out of the bottom. Pull in as much chain as possible, and then try to drag it out by motoring astern with the chain

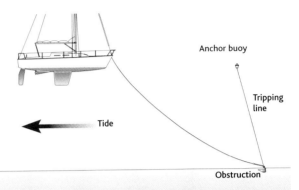

Left: **To avoid getting caught by an obstruction on the bottom, use a tripping line. Tie a line to the crown of the anchor and add a small float to the line. You may need to adjust the length of the line as the tide rises and falls.**

Anchor buoy

Tripping line

Tide

Obstruction

securely locked on the windlass or cleated. If that doesn't work, try dragging the anchor from different angles, but beware of pulling the chain across the bow, which could cause damage.

- It is unusual for an anchor to get stuck on the bottom, but it may

occur if the flukes get pulled under an obstruction such as an old mooring chain. Guard against this by attaching a tripping line to the crown of the anchor (where the flukes meet the shank). The tripping line can be attached to a fender, which will float above the

Right: **Two pairs of hands make it easier to pull up the anchor on a small yacht. Be ready to take a turn around the deck cleat if the chain comes under strain.**

anchor, or take the end of the tripping line back on board. Pulling the line vertically should help break out the anchor and release it from the obstruction.

Kedge anchor

✪ The "kedge" is a smaller auxiliary anchor normally stowed in a cockpit locker. A Danforth-style anchor, which folds flat, is ideal. The kedge normally has a long length of warp connected to a short length of chain.

✪ The kedge anchor is useful to keep the stern from swinging, or for laying a second anchor off the bow to increase holding; set it at an angle of about 30 degrees to the primary anchor. In both situations, the kedge must be rowed out from the yacht in the tender.

Above: **On this Westerly Konsort, the plow anchor is stowed on the foredeck. The anchor must be lifted through the pulpit, but it is an advantage to have no anchor sticking out from the bow roller when maneuvering in a marina.**

Laying kedge anchors

On arrival at your destination it may be useful to lay two anchors. You can lay two anchors in a single operation under motor, but in some situations the anchor needs to be laid using a tender with an outboard engine. Anchor rope is attached to the boat's foredeck, so only rope is being pulled across the water and the chain is piled up in the dinghy, ready to drop in position.

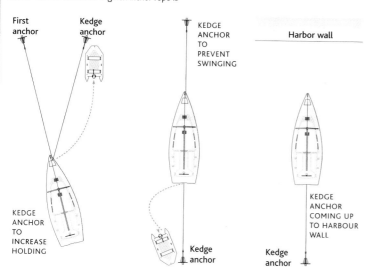

First anchor   Kedge anchor

KEDGE ANCHOR TO PREVENT SWINGING

Harbor wall

KEDGE ANCHOR TO INCREASE HOLDING

Kedge anchor

KEDGE ANCHOR COMING UP TO HARBOUR WALL

Kedge anchor

Anchor safety

✪ Always wear deck shoes or boots and gloves when handling the anchor or chain.

✪ When the chain or warp is running out, keep fingers and feet clear. It won't stop if you get in the way.

✪ Make sure you can stop the chain or warp. If you are lowering by hand, wrap the chain or warp around the base of the deck cleat and pay it out hand-over-hand.

✪ Keep children off the foredeck while you are using the anchor.

The perfect anchorage

Lying at anchor can be wonderful. Your yacht has its own space in beautiful surroundings, away from the crowded mass of yachts in a marina. But you want to be sure the anchorage is safe. It's no good going to sleep, worrying that you might be washed up on the beach.

Opposite: **These yachts appear close to the beach in an onshore wind, but the holding is good, the wind is light and the water is deep. But if the wind increases, they should be ready to leave without delay.**

Left: **Nothing can be better than your own anchorage. This yacht finds an appealing area on its own in the British Virgin Islands.**

Protection from the wind

A good location for an anchorage should provide a shield from the wind. In most situations, the wind should be blowing offshore, so you are not blown onshore. It may be possible to anchor in a light onshore wind, but if it increases, the anchorage will be uncomfortable and may become untenable.

Check the anchorage

Check the pilot book for details on suitable wind direction, holding, tidal effect, hazards and facilities ashore. Look at the chart to check low water depths (the lowest level is known as "chart datum"), buoyage, rocks or wrecks, shoal areas, and recommended anchorages (marked by an anchor symbol).

Listen to the forecast

Keep listening to the coastal waters forecast for your sailing area. If the wind is forecast to change direction or increase, consider how it will affect your anchorage. Plan ahead. It is much better to change anchorage during the day than have to leave in the middle of the night!

Work out the tide

In a tidal area, the depth will change from low to high water (or vice versa) over each six-hour period. Ensure that you have enough water under the keel at low water (unless you have a bilge keeler and intend to dry out) and enough chain or warp stretched out along the bottom at high water.

Good holding

Good holding for the anchor is vital. The chart will indicate what you can expect to find on the bottom. Mud and sand allow the anchor to dig in deeply; weed, rock and gravel provide less reliable holding. Avoid dropping the anchor on coral at all costs: the coral will be destroyed.

Allow enough scope

"Scope" is the length of chain or warp stretched out along the bottom. Remember to allow at least four times the depth for chain or six to eight times the depth for warp. To make sure the anchor is well dug in, run the engine in reverse until the yacht stops moving backward. Take three compass bearings on fixed objects to check that the yacht has

not dragged. You can also set the "anchor drag alarm" facility on the GPS. Check all is well before going ashore or turning in for the night. If the anchor chain appears to be vibrating, the anchor may be dragging across the bottom. If in doubt, pull it up and lay it again.

Above: **Make sure the anchor isn't dragging before you settle down. Fix transits on land to check your position.**

Room to swing

A yacht at anchor will swing on the tide or wind. If tide is flowing through the anchorage, the yacht will swing through 180 degrees as the tide changes direction. Ensure there is enough space all round. In many anchorages, a yacht will lie to an offshore wind during the day, and swing to a light onshore wind during the night. Check that there is enough room for your yacht to swing through 360 degrees. Motor cruisers will not have the same swing characteristics as a yacht, so yachts and boats in an anchorage may be pointing in all directions.

Rocking and rolling

✪ In poor weather, conditions on board may be uncomfortable, and there may be concerns about the anchor holding as the bow rises

and falls. As a short-term solution, let out more scope.

✪ Swell can be unpredictable, wrapping around a headland or unexpectedly rolling into an anchorage at night. Trying to ride it out will be miserable. Your best advice is to haul up the anchor and leave at first light.

Light up

To show other yachts you are at anchor, display a black anchor ball on the forestay. Always turn on the anchor light (a white light at the top of the mast) at night. Alternatively, a light temporarily attached halfway up the forestay can be used as an anchor light.

Right: **Trees on the beach help protect this anchorage in a stiff offshore breeze, ensuring it stays relatively calm.**

Picking up a mooring

Mooring buoys offer a convenient way to secure a yacht. They may be used as a temporary or permanent mooring in a river, harbor or bay.

Choosing a mooring

- Be certain that the buoy you have chosen is a mooring and not a marker for something else.
- Not all moorings are safe: they can break, particularly if too much load is placed on them.
- If you are a visiting yacht, look for "visitor" moorings. If the harbor master maintains them, the moorings should be secure. Check the pilot book for any information on maximum recommended size of yacht.

There will be a charge for mooring use but it will be much cheaper than staying in a marina. The harbor master will pay a visit to your yacht, or you may need to pay ashore.

- Visitor moorings may be provided by a local yacht club. There is often reciprocal use for members of other recognized yacht clubs.
- Local businesses such as restaurants may even provide visitor mooring; check that this type of mooring is suitable.

- Most moorings are licensed to local yachts; check with the harbor master to see if any are available for a short stay. You must be prepared to move if the designated yacht reappears, so it is unwise to go ashore and leave your yacht unattended.

Approaching a mooring

- Choose a mooring that has enough depth and will allow sufficient room for your yacht to swing on wind or tide. Beware if motorboats are moored close by: they will not swing in the same way as a yacht.
- Furl the headsail, drop the mainsail and approach the mooring under engine.
- Use the wind or tide to stop the yacht when it reaches the mooring. Assess which element has most effect — it is often the tide. If there is slack tide or no tide at all, approach into the wind.

Securing the yacht to the buoy

- The mooring buoy may have a mooring rope with a small float, or "pickup" buoy. Use the boat hook to pull the rope up through the bow roller, next to the anchor, and secure it to the foredeck cleat with the loop on the mooring rope. Dealing with mooring ropes can be messy if they are covered in weeds. If the rope is thin, keep pulling — it may have a thicker, stronger rope attached.

Picking up moorings

The way moorings are set up varies. This mooring has a mooring eye attached to a main mooring buoy and is supported by a smaller buoy. The smaller buoy is picked up with a boat hook, brought through the bow roller and fastened to the cleat using the eye.

Left: **Some sailing areas where coral is abundant encourage mooring instead of anchoring, which may damage the coral.**

Approaching a buoy

☘ You may need to secure the yacht's own bowline through the metal ring in the top of the mooring buoy. One end of the bowline is attached to the foredeck cleat. The other end is led from the cleat through the bow roller, next to the anchor roller, and down to the mooring buoy ring where it can be secured. It can also be led back up to the foredeck and tied off around a cleat. It may be preferable to lead the bowline through the fair-leads on either side of the bow.

☘ Beware of the mooring line or bowline chafing on the sides of the bow roller. Use a plastic tube to protect the line, or protect it with a towel.

Boat hook

Wooden boathooks have been superseded by aluminum boat hooks — yet most of them don't float, so keep a good grip on them! Don't drop one on the deck or coachroof, and presume it will stay there.

Can you see what's happening?

☘ In the final approach, the helm will not be able to see the mooring buoy, obscured by the bow. The foredeck crew should give directions: ahead, port, starboard, stop!

☘ Ensure the approach is dead slow and do not overshoot the buoy. The yacht should come to a dead halt with the buoy to one side of the bow, under the pulpit. If it keeps moving forward, hanging on to the buoy will be impossible.

☘ If there is tide running, the crew will need to get the mooring rope onto the deck or a bow line through the mooring without delay. Otherwise the tide will catch the bow and sweep it sideways.

Right: **Shout or indicate to the skipper during the approach. It can be very difficult to see the exact position of the mooring buoy from the stern.**

Above (left to right): **1. The mooring pickup buoy just to port of the bows. 2. The crew reaches down to hook the pickup buoy with the boat hook. The yacht must be stationary. 3. The crew quickly pulls up the pickup buoy. 4. Ensure the mooring rope is led through the fair-lead of the bow roller before slipping the loop over a foredeck cleat.**

Leaving a mooring

The yacht will be pointing into the wind or tide. The foredeck crew should let go of the mooring as soon as the helm gives the order. Unhitch the buoy and throw the line and gear clear of the boat so the helm can avoid the mooring buoy while motors slowly ahead. It is often best to drop back astern first if you can.

Using a tender

Most yachts are equipped with small, inflatable tenders. The tender can be stowed on deck or in a cockpit locker, is quick to inflate and launch, and will get crew safely ashore, provided it's not overloaded.

The bottom line

The most basic inflatables have soft bottoms that provide no directional stability for the boat. At the other end of the scale are inflatables with a rigid fiberglass bottom. These give far superior performance, but are heavier and take up more deck space. A compromise is an inflatable rib. This has extra rigidity and stability in the bottom, or rigid panels that provide a "floor." This rolls up when the tender is stowed in a locker.

Inflate and deflate

The deflated tender is packed in a sack that will fit into a cockpit locker. The tender should be unpacked and inflated on the coachroof, foredeck or dock. Make sure each compartment is pumped up hard and the valve closed. Before you lift the tender over the side,

make sure the painter (the line on the bow used to tie it up or tow it) is attached to the yacht. Drop the tender the right way up on the water.

Oar power

☻ Many small tenders have lightweight two-part aluminum oars with plastic blades. These are attached to articulated plastic rowlocks on top of the inflatable tubes. Rowing efficiency may range from acceptable to appalling. Some rowlocks flex every time you pull on the oars, slewing the tender from side to side as it moves. Also, the rower may have a plastic plank or inflatable tube for a seat. Combined with nothing to brace your feet against, this makes it difficult to pull on the oars – if you pull hard, the oars will bend!

Above left: **Go slowly when passing yachts and keep well away of swimmers.**

Above right: **The tender can be inflated on deck and then lifted over the guardrails, but remember to tie the painter on first!**

☻ Not all inflatable tenders are that bad. Some models have wooden oars and molded rowlocks that work reasonably well if the tubes are blown up rock hard. They can still be hard work to row — short, rapid strokes work best; it is much easier to row with the tide.

Lifejackets

Always wear lifejackets in a tender. This is a legal requirement in many countries. Overloading the tender with too many people in a party mood is a recipe for potential tragedy when returning to a yacht late at night.

Getting in and out

- Try to step in and out from the middle of the tender and distribute weight evenly round the sides. Sit down immediately.
- Never overload a tender: make two trips to and from the yacht.

Going ashore

- Look for buoyed lanes and landing areas when you approach a beach. It may be illegal to go near swimmers: the propellers from outboard engines of visiting dinghies are potentially very dangerous.
- Try not to drag an inflatable tender up the beach. The bottom will abrade and eventually deteriorate. Carry the tender; it will be heaviest at the stern.
- Be careful where you leave the tender. People walking on the beach may trip over the painter or outboard. Do not put an anchor out on the beach. If you have an outboard, lock it up to protect it while you are away.
- Check if the tide is rising or falling, and carry the tender above the high-water mark.
- If you leave the tender tied to a pontoon or wall, ensure it won't obstruct other boats. Tie the painter on securely. A wire and padlock is a sensible precaution after dark. Allow sufficient line for tidal rise and fall.

Above: **A perfect anchorage with the tender providing zip wire transport along the stern line to the shore. It would be wise to have oars or a paddle available.**

Light at night

- Always turn on the white anchor light, at the top of the mast, at night. This indicates the presence of an anchored yacht to other boats, but also guides you back to your own yacht after dark.
- Even with the anchor light illuminated, it can be difficult to find the way back to your yacht in a crowded anchorage. When you go ashore, take note of other yachts or features. You could leave the cabin lights on to make identification easier, or take a handheld GPS programmed with the yacht's position.
- Keep on a flashlight or handheld white light in the tender at night, so that other boats can see you.

Using an outboard motor

Many yachts have a small gas outboard motor to power the tender. It should be used sparingly, however, as two-stroke engines make an unpleasant noise and can be a nuisance to others on the water.

Keep it safe
- Never exceed the maximum recommended horsepower for the tender, indicated on the transom. An overpowered inflatable is difficult to control and is less safe.
- Never run an outboard without using the kill cord clipped around your thigh. If you fall out of the boat, the kill cord will cut the ignition and you will be safer in the water. Otherwise, the engine will keep running at the same speed, and the boat will go around in circles, which get tighter and tighter until it runs you down.

Stowage
The outboard is normally stowed in the anchor locker or on a bracket mounted on the pushpit. Store it upright, or at least horizontal, with fuel and air taps closed.

Refueling
Virtually all small outboards are two-stroke. Make sure the fuel mixture is correct when you fill the tank. It is easiest to refuel when attached to the stern pulpit. Be cautious about safety. Gas is very flammable and even fumes can be a hazard. Make sure the fuel can is securely stored in a cockpit locker with its cap closed tight.

Putting the engine on the tender
Don't drop the engine over the side! Outboards are heavy, clumsy and do not appreciate immersion, especially in salt water. If the yacht has a stern ladder and bathing platform, it is easiest to secure the tender at both ends so that it lies at right angles across the stern. Lift the outboard down carefully and lay it in the bottom of the tender. Then climb into the tender and lift the outboard onto the transom bracket. Screw the two locks tightly. For added security, link the outboard to the tender with a safety line.

Operating the outboard
- Make sure the outboard is firmly attached to the transom and that the leg is locked: it should click down onto a latch.
- Attach the kill cord to your upper leg. Make sure it holds out the ignition button.
- Turn on the fuel tap on the side of the engine. Undo the air vent on top of the fuel tank.
- Set the throttle and choke to the start position.
- Make sure the gearshift is in the upright position in neutral gear.
- Pull the starter cord back firmly and smoothly. Be careful of people sitting alongside: they don't want an elbow in their face!
- Modern outboards are very reliable, unless they have been

Below: **The best policy is to always wear a lifejacket or buoyancy aid in a tender. The driver must be attached to a kill cord when operating the outboard motor. Take the kill cord ashore.**

Above: **Adjust the painter's length so the tender tows easily and water does not flood over the bows. Beware of leaving the outboard on, as in this photograph — a lightweight tender can easily flip upside-down.** *Inset:* **The tender may need to be pulled close to the yacht or taken alongside for maneuvering in a tight space.**

neglected, have the wrong fuel or have been dropped in the water. The engine should start within two or three pulls. Close the choke and check there is a stream of cooling water spurting from the side of the engine.

❂ The gearshift has forward, neutral and reverse positions. (Simpler, very small engines turn through 180 degrees for reverse thrust.) Drop the revs down when changing gear. Use the twist throttle carefully to find a comfortable cruising speed that suits everyone. Remember that anyone sitting at the front may get splashed if you go too fast. And always take care when reversing.

Towing an inflatable tender

❂ An inflatable tender should tow well in light to moderate winds and make little difference to the speed of a cruising yacht. Make sure the painter is securely tied around the stern cleat.

❂ If there is a drain plug in the transom, open it so that water cannot collect in the bottom and weigh the tender down.

❂ Experiment with the best length for a towing line. The faster the yacht goes, the more the tender will dig in its bow, with a tendency to get swamped. Pull the painter in to lift its bows if this is a problem. You will find there is a surprising amount of strain on the painter, even at slow speed. It may be necessary to stop the yacht, pull in the tender and then try again.

❂ Don't tow a tender in rough and windy conditions: it may flip over or break the towline. Lift it out and lash it to the foredeck or coachroof upside-down. If there is a problem, deflate and store the tender in its bag.

❂ Don't risk towing an inflatable tender with the outboard attached, as it could easily flip.

❂ Avoid stopping quickly from a fast speed as this will create a backwash, which will come over the transom. Have a bailer ready to take out the water.

❂ When berthing stern-to in a marina, lead the painter forward so that the tender is towed from the yacht's bow.

Planning a cruise

The role of the skipper is to manage the yacht, ensuring that all members of the crew have a safe and enjoyable time on board. This requires sailing expertise combined with a sensitive attitude toward the crew.

The skipper's abilities

A skipper's abilities should include:

- *Navigation skills.* The skipper should know how to read a chart, plot a course, fix a position, take a bearing and use a GPS, including navigation by waypoints. He or she should also know how to interpret weather forecasts and calculate tidal flow and height in tidal areas.
- *Use of a VHF radio, including emergency procedures.* If you have a VHF radio on board, it should be DSC-equipped (digital) and the skipper should be trained in radio operation.
- *Boat handling skills to leave or enter a marina, pick up a mooring or anchor securely.* These should include engine maintenance skills, including basic repairs.
- *Sailing skills to handle the yacht in stronger winds.* These include predicting when to reef the sails, and being able to sail a safe course downwind without accidental jibes.
- *Knowledge of all safety equipment aboard, including where it is stowed and how it works.* This should range from putting lifejackets and harnesses on the crew to hammering in a wooden drain to plug a failed seacock in the hull.

Care for your crew

- The skipper must be sensitive to the ability and expectations of the crew. There is nothing worse than

Above: **The skipper should oversee navigation, but may choose to delegate passage planning. It is always wise to work on paper charts, as well as plotting with GPS.**

a gung-ho skipper who terrifies an inexperienced crew by making them sail in difficult weather, possibly putting them off sailing forever.

- Be prepared to scale down expectations. It is better to wait for the right weather and cut down distances. Aim to spend a maximum of four or five hours on the water (which, on a good day, will be equivalent under sail to little more than 25 miles (40 km)), at least until the crew's capabilities are known.

- Motoring over long distances is a poor solution to "wanting to get somewhere." Engine noise and vibration, both in the cockpit and down below, will make the trip unpleasant for anyone on board.
- Watch out for signs of crew becoming cold or seasick; these frequently occur together. If either of these happens, head for the nearest anchorage.

Talk to your crew

Good communication is vital. Brief your crew thoroughly concerning:

- *Where equipment is located on board, including lifejackets and harnesses (adjusted and ready for use by each crew member).* The skipper must decide when the crew should don lifejackets or harnesses and clip on to strong points. This is essential for crew on deck at night or in rough weather.
- *How vital equipment works, so someone else, such as the mate, can take over in an emergency.* This might include navigating the yacht, operating the engine, making a call on the VHF, stowing sails or mooring the yacht.
- *The passage plan for each day of a cruise.* Encourage at least one crew member to share navigational and passage-making duties, including decision making on where the yacht is bound.
- *How you expect the crew to manage sails.* Good communication is particularly important when reefing and jibing.

✪ *Picking up a mooring or entering a marina.* A specific briefing prior to arriving at a mooring or berth or anchoring. To avoid confusion, your crew need to know exactly what you plan to do and what is expected of them.

Let them drive!
Give all of the crew a chance to take turns on the tiller or wheel. Involve everyone in handling the yacht.

Below: **Make sure all crew are given an opportunity to steer the boat and be involved with the trip.**

Left: **Equipment on a yacht can be dangerous if not handled correctly. If unsure, ask the skipper how things work.**

Living on a yacht

Yachts come in all shapes and sizes. How enjoyable it is to live on board will be governed by factors including the amount of room available, the number of crew, weather conditions and the actual use of the yacht.

Stow everything before you sail

Take soft bags, which can be stowed easily. If there is a crowd on board, keep personal gear to a minimum. Sort out individual storage space and keep it tidy. Middle and outer layers for sailing take top preference for a quick grab; "going ashore gear" can be accessed when you have plenty of time.

Left: **A tidy life is best on board. Make sure everything is neatly stowed before you sail.**

Below: **Keep the saloon clear and pack away loose gear. Charts will slide and objects will roll as soon as the yacht starts to heel over.**

When the yacht gets underway, anything loose must be secured. Visualize what will slide if the yacht heels over. Never leave dirty dishes in the galley and keep drawers and cupboards secured.

Separate wet gear

Many yachts have a "wet locker" where waterproof jackets and pants can dry out. An alternative solution is to hang them in the heads compartment where they can drip. When the yacht is moored, open portholes or vents to allow a through draft. If the weather allows, dry wet gear on deck. Make sure it is securely fastened and cannot blow over the side.

Left: **The cabin is a small space and will soon get messy if not kept tidy.**

Using the heads

"Pumping out" the heads is an emotive issue. In many countries it is illegal close to the shore. Best practice is to use shore facilities in a marina and avoid pumping out in an anchorage. An increasing number of yachts are fitted with holding tanks, so that nothing is let out into the water until you are far from the shore.

Beware of blocking the heads. The size of a yacht's plumbing means that a blockage could easily occur. The flush system is designed to pump out a small amount of toilet paper — be modest in the amount you use and pump thoroughly. Use at least 15 strokes to pump through the water.

Pollution

Beware of polluting the water with gas, oil or any kind of household cleaners. In some counties there are hefty on-the-spot fines for skippers who leave anything sticky or foamy in the sea.

Keep the boat clean

Yachts soon get dirty with people on board. It is surprising how much accumulates in the cockpit and down below. The boat should be thoroughly cleaned at least once a day. Sweep, wipe and dust around the saloon floor. Keep the galley and heads spotless and smelling fresh. Wash down the cockpit with fresh water, if available, but close vents first. Use a brush to scrub the sidedecks and foredeck. Beware of cleaning products that may leave a slippery finish or wash into the sea as unacceptable residue, and try to use environmentally friendly products.

Watch the water

Keep clean, but don't use too much water. Most modern yachts have electric pumps to provide fresh water but the water supply is limited. If you go into a marina to refill the tanks you may have to pay the marina for it. Better to be modest in water consumption.

Do not throw garbage

Most marinas and harbors have facilities for waste disposal, so hold on to your garbage until it can be properly disposed of. Even on a hot weather cruise, plastic garbage bags can be tied shut and stowed in cockpit stern lockers. Note that used oil and or other chemicals need to be disposed of carefully.

Right: **You are not connected to sewers, so never pump unpleasant things into the sea. Always use a holding tank or the on-shore facilities in a marina.**

Cooking and catering

The galley plays a major role in enjoying life on board, whether you are in a marina or on open water.

Perfect location

Most galleys are situated by the companionway, which allows the "cook" to pass drinks or food up to people in the cockpit, or across to people sitting around the saloon table. An L-shaped layout provides good access to storage and makes it fairly easy for the cook to find a handhold or brace with their legs and hips, should the boat be heeling or rolling.

Careful of the gas

The gas tank for the stove is normally in a separate external locker in the transom of the yacht. Gas is potentially dangerous because it is heavier than air and will sink into the bottom of the yacht if it escapes. If enough gas collects in the bilges, it could cause an explosion. The gas supply should always be turned off when the stove is not in use. A gas alarm and automatic bilge pump will help ensure there is no danger from gas escaping.

Cooking underway

When the yacht is underway, it is vital that the stovetop is safe. Adjustable guardrails, which hold cooking items in place, can be used to lock a saucepan or kettle on top of each burner. If the yacht heels, the stove can be "unlocked" and allowed to swing freely from side to side on gimbals. This ensures that whatever is on top of or in the oven will stay horizontal. Never make the mistake of grabbing the stove when the boat rocks!

Beware of burns

Burns are the greatest danger when using a galley at sea. If you have hot liquids, keep the amount small so that it is safe and easy to handle. Never overfill a pan, kettle or mugs with boiling liquid, and never hold a mug or pan while pouring boiling liquid into it — put it in the sink in case of spills. If you are passing mugs of hot coffee or soup to the crew in the cockpit, do so one at a time, and get others to give you a hand. Beware of the yacht suddenly lurching — hot liquid could easily spill and scald someone. A fire blanket and extinguisher must be ready for immediate use, with the first-aid kit close at hand.

Left: **Nothing beats an al fresco lunch in the cockpit on a nice sunny day. Make the most of it!**

Left: **Cooking in the galley is a miniaturized version of cooking at home — the main difference is that your home won't suddenly rock or roll!**

Good sense

✸ It is easiest and more pleasant to eat when the yacht is at anchor or on a mooring. Time your sailing so that you can stop for both lunch and dinner, if possible. If you are unable to stop on the way, plan ahead by preparing food that can be served in a yacht that might be heeling.

✸ Fresh air and a healthy lifestyle ensure that simple food tastes great on board. You don't need to indulge in fancy cuisine when sailing, but expect healthy appetites.

✸ Alcohol is illegal to drink or have open when a yacht is underway — and no crew member should be suffering the effects of the night before. Make sure that everyone takes in plenty of other fluids, and beware of dehydration when cruising in a hot climate.

Using the fridge

Most modern yachts have a top-opening cold storage unit. The efficiency of refrigeration varies greatly. It's great to have chilled food, but there are drawbacks. The fridge will use a lot of power, so beware of flattening the batteries — it is impossible to keep the fridge cold for extended periods without running the engine. It can also be hard trying to find food or bottles in the depths of the cold storage unit — packing neatly and precisely is essential, as the bottom can get rather wet and nasty. Use the drain plug or pump to remove excess water and clean the inside of the unit regularly.

Below: **Cockpits are wonderful for a gathering after a sail. Just remember — partying is fine when you're safely moored up, but you need to be alert when sailing.**

Passage problems

Staying in a marina is like living in a floating apartment. Under sail, everything changes. The boat heels over, things slide from side to side, it's not so easy to move around and some people may feel queasy.

How far are you going?

☸ Distance can make a big difference. A short passage of 5 miles (8 km) might take an hour; a longer passage of 25 miles (40 km) should take over four hours at an average of 6 knots, or over six hours at 4 knots.

☸ The longer you are sailing, the more time there is for conditions to change. A fine morning may be followed by a fresh breeze in the afternoon, accompanied by an increasingly lively sea. If you are sailing offwind, it should be fast and fun, but if you are sailing upwind, progress could become wet, uncomfortable and slow, which may not be welcome at the end of a long day. Also, the tide may change. Beware of the tide against you, which could slow true progress to a crawl. Passage planning should try to allow for favorable tides most of the way.

Seasickness and cold

☸ Feeling sick and getting cold often go hand in hand. Most people can put up with a short trip of a few miles, even if conditions are rough. It generally takes an hour or two for the cold to seep through and for a queasy feeling to emerge.

☸ Dress up with in warm gear if heading off on a passage longer than a few miles. Wind chill will normally make you feel colder as

Left: **Make as much distance as you can when there's a good breeze and the sun shines. Be prepared to change plans to match the weather.**

Opposite: **Young sailors on this training boat may have to cope with rough weather. Keeping them busy is the best way to avoid getting sick or cold.**

time passes, so have the right clothing on before this happens. Crew may feel too queasy to go below and grab more gear.

☸ Some lucky people never get seasick. If you aren't one of those, it's worth trying seasickness or anti-motion remedies. These range from wristbands to pills.

☸ If you start feeling sick, you need something to do. Part of the problem with long passages is that you focus your mind on things like the motion of the sea. Take a turn on the tiller or wheel or help trim the sails. This may concentrate your mind enough to forget about feeling sick. Suck a hard candy: it will help you feel better and refresh your mouth. Don't sit in the cockpit, feeling worse and worse. The best

solution is to grit your teeth, go below, pull on a sleeping bag and lie down on a leeward berth.

☸ Anyone suffering seasickness will be feeling utterly wretched. The best thing is to vomit as soon as possible using a bucket in the cockpit. Hanging over the leeward side of the boat is not a great idea:

dangerous. Surprisingly, you will find other crew members are quite good at being "nurse." Once you have vomitted, you will feel a lot better. The best advice is then to get your head down in that warm berth. Drink a little water, suck a hard candy or eat plain crackers to restore some liquid and strength. Avoid acidic fruits, which do not help. The extraordinary thing is that you will definitely feel a lot better as soon as the yacht enters an anchorage, and the seasickness should disappear the moment you set foot on shore!

Left: **It is best to keep active and busy on a boat. If you feel queasy, try to keep focused on the horizon. The best way to do this is to have a turn on the helm.**

Passage conditions

We all want perfect cruising days with a fresh breeze, warm sun and kind water. But occasionally rough weather or fog may intervene and sailing through the night provides a different kind of challenge.

Right: **If you feel more secure with a lifejacket, wear one! The foam padded vest style is unrestrictive and provides extra thermal insulation.**

Below: **Be prepared for conditions to get a lot rougher when you leave the shelter of the land.**

Rough weather

✪ Do not assume that strong winds will always cause a rough and unpleasant passage. Force 6 can be enjoyable if you are sailing offwind on a sunny day, so long as the yacht is correctly reefed and well balanced. You will surf along on the small, well-spaced waves that you can expect in a coastal sailing area. By contrast, force 3 could feel extremely rough on a cloudy day, beating upwind against a foul tide streaming around a headland. It is all a matter of being in the right place, and going in the right direction, at the right time.

✪ Size helps — a small yacht will tend to be thrown around a lot more than a large yacht in rough waters. The larger yacht will also be able to sail or motor considerably faster, particularly when heading upwind.

✪ Always reduce sail ahead of time. It is much easier to furl the headsail and reef the mainsail when the wind is still reasonably light. Don't wait for conditions "to get better." You can always increase sail a bit later if you have been overcautious.

✪ Make sure that all hatches are locked shut and that everything is securely stowed above and below decks.

✪ All crew should wear a lifejacket and harness when on deck, and clip on.

✪ Keep "one hand for yourself and one for the boat." Find a secure position in the cockpit or at the wheel where you can brace yourself, and find a hand-hold.

If conditions look set to deteriorate, head for the nearest shelter or consider turning back.

Sailing in fog

Fog is horrible on a yacht. It's difficult to peer through the murk, and there is often no wind, which means you need to motor and will not be able to hear other craft clearly.

Always wait for fog to lift before leaving a mooring.

If fog comes down, keep to a slow speed and take extra care with navigation. The GPS can help find the correct route, but will be of no help in identifying other craft that may collide with you. Make sure the radar reflector is hoisted. Crew should wear lifejackets and harnesses, both above and below decks. A lookout on the foredeck should be securely clipped on. Turn on the yacht's navigation lights. If commercial traffic is a potential hazard, make for shallow water where larger vessels cannot navigate. Around the 30-foot (9 m) line is about right.

Make regular sound signals with the foghorn and listen for corresponding signals from other craft. Give one long blast and two short blasts every two minutes if under sail; give one long blast every two minutes if under power.

Sailing at night

Perspective changes at night: it can get surprisingly cold when the light drops and darkness seems to last for a long time. It is vital to keep a good lookout.

Harnesses and lifejackets should be worn in the cockpit and on deck at all times. Remember it is no use wearing a harness if you do not clip on.

Nights can be cold. Wear plenty of layers before you think you'll need them.

Identify where light switches are located. You will need a flashlight to check the sails.

Make sure appropriate navigation lights are switched on.

The skipper and crew must be able to identify navigation lights displayed by other craft. If you spot a large vessel such as a car ferry at sea, the confusing mass of its lights can make it difficult to work out where it is heading.

If you are sailing through the night, you will need to work out a watch system. Some of the crew are on deck while some can sleep below. Traditional time intervals are four hours on, four hours off. In fact, four hours is a long time to be peering into the darkness; a shorter spell may be long enough. Just before you go on watch, it's a good idea to prepare a hot drink and snack for yourself and the other crew.

Below: **Fog can be worrying when you are afloat. Listen carefully to the sounds around you, watch the GPS and if possible use radar to spot nearby craft.**

A lee cloth is designed to prevent you rolling out of a berth while resting or sleeping.

Right: **Get your night vision adjusted to the dark, but keep a flashlight on hand to check the sails. A mass of urban lights can make it tricky to spot harbor entrance lights that will guide you in!**

Man overboard

"Man overboard!" is a preventable accident that should never happen. Basic safety procedures include knowing when to wear a lifejacket and clip on with a harness to minimize any chance of tragedy.

"Man overboard!" is something you never want to experience, but if someone falls over the side, it is vital that the crew can locate and get them back on board without delay.

What causes MOB?

- Only a few man overboard incidents are impossible to predict or prevent. Anyone can fall over the side, but more experienced sailors are often at greater risk. If you've been on deck thousands of times without a harness, you're only likely to consider using one in extreme weather situations.
- Accidents happen at the most unexpected times. Getting hit by the boom is a major cause for concern; it could knock you out or clean over the side.
- Falling over the side of a moving yacht requires quick action by the crew to rescue you. But if you fall off a yacht that is moored or anchored in a tidal location you need to be cautious about the possibility of being swept away. Beware of nontidal locations where strong currents can be created by wind funneling between islands.
- If children are playing on deck, they should wear lifejackets.

Below: **A low freeboard, no guardrails and physically strong crew should make it reasonably easy to pull this person in over the leeward side of this boat. It may be useful to use steps or a hoist on a boat that has higher sides.**

Basic security

- ✿ The skipper decides when the crew should wear lifejackets or harnesses on deck. Best advice is always at night or in fog, and always in rough or difficult weather. Crew members should not hesitate to wear lifejackets when they feel the need.
- ✿ Lifejackets and harnesses must be adjusted to fit correctly and be fitted with a crotch strap.
- ✿ A harness does not achieve anything until you are clipped on. Locate attachment points between the companionway, cockpit and steering position. Jackstays (normally reinforced webbing straps secured to the deck, to which harnesses can be clipped) provide the most effective solution to moving along the sidedecks to the foredeck.
- ✿ "One for you and one for the boat" is an often quoted phrase on board: it means that if you are not clipped on, you need to have at least one hand free to hold on to something solid.
- ✿ If there is a chance you will be in severe conditions, wear a special survival suit. It provides the best protection in the event of MOB.

Over the side and clipped on

In very rough weather when the decks are flooded with water, crew need to avoid being washed over the side. If this happens and they are attached they will remain at the side the boat, but it needs to slow down. It is imperative that the crew let the sheets go, luff head-to-wind and furl/drop the sails without delay. It may be necessary to cut the lifelines to pull the person back on deck.

Below: **Hook on and hang on if you go onto the foredeck. Jackstays provide the safest means of moving fore and aft.**

Above: **Stay in the cockpit, the safest place in rough weather, but make sure you are hooked on.**

Dangers of the cold

The effects of hypothermia make cold water a killer. Predicted survival times make it clear that no time can be lost in getting a person back on board.

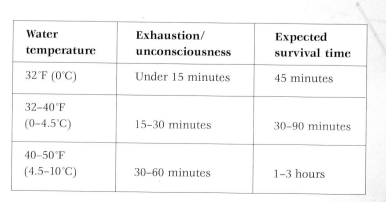

Water temperature	Exhaustion/ unconsciousness	Expected survival time
32°F (0°C)	Under 15 minutes	45 minutes
32–40°F (0–4.5°C)	15–30 minutes	30–90 minutes
40–50°F (4.5–10°C)	30–60 minutes	1–3 hours

Man overboard (2)

What the helm should do

1. Shout "man overboard!" to alert the rest of the crew.

2. Throw the lifebuoy and its danbuoy (both mounted on the stern pulpit) toward the person.

3. Heave-to by putting the helm hard over (bring the bow into wind).

4. Instruct someone to keep watching the person and to keep pointing in his or her direction. It is vital not to lose visual contact during the early stages of a rescue. If it is dark, use a spotlight. Consider using a white parachute flare to pick up retro-reflective panels.

5. GPS navigation aids have an MOB function. Hit the button to record the position where the person went over the side.

Above: **Falling overboard can happen if you have no harness or lifejacket.**

6. Alert the emergency services, but be sure to inform them as soon as the person is recovered.

7. If you start the engine while the sails are being dropped or furled, beware of any lines going over the side and snagging the propeller.

The rescue

- Start the engine as soon as the yacht is hove-to (tacked with the headsail cleated on the old side).
- If the person is close, throw a heaving line to pull in.
- If that isn't possible, furl the headsail and motor around in a circle to approach the person directly upwind. Be certain the engine is out of gear, preferably off altogether, before the casualty is alongside. Propellers can cause terrible injuries.
- Rescuing a person under sail will require greater skill. Sail away from the person on a beam reach, allowing enough distance

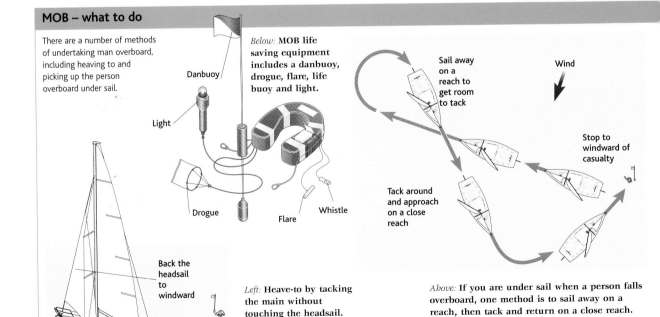

MOB – what to do

There are a number of methods of undertaking man overboard, including heaving to and picking up the person overboard under sail.

Danbuoy

Light

Drogue

Flare

Whistle

Below: **MOB life saving equipment includes a danbuoy, drogue, flare, life buoy and light.**

Back the headsail to windward

Sail away on a reach to get room to tack

Wind

Stop to windward of casualty

Tack around and approach on a close reach

Left: **Heave-to by tacking the main without touching the headsail. The jib sheet should be in tight, the mainsail eased and the tiller lashed to leeward. Start the engine but keep out of gear.**

Above: **If you are under sail when a person falls overboard, one method is to sail away on a reach, then tack and return on a close reach. If you have a spinnaker up it should be dropped immediately. Even if the plan is to pick up under sail, the engine should be started as a reserve.**

to tack and sail back on the opposite beam reach. Make the final approach to the person on a close reach, so that sheets can be eased to stall the yacht.

Getting the person back on board

⚙ Make sure the engine is in neutral when the person in the water is close by.

⚙ In light winds and flat water, pick up the person on the leeward side. In stronger winds and rougher water, this could be dangerous, as the yacht might be pushed over on top of the person.

⚙ A stern boarding ladder may be the easiest way for the person to climb back on board in calm weather. In rough weather, the transom may be rising and

falling, which would make this approach extremely dangerous.

⚙ It will be very difficult to pull a person up over the side, unless the yacht has low freeboard or is heeling over. It may be necessary to improvise a sling using lines or a small sail, hoisted by the main halyard.

⚙ Be prepared to give first aid. The person may be suffering from shock or hypothermia, and will probably be bruised from being hauled back onboard.

If you fall off a boat

⚙ If you fall off a moving yacht and are not secured by a harness, you will be rapidly left behind. If you start swimming you will become cold and exhausted,

accelerating the onset of hypothermia; also, catching a yacht sailing at a mere 1–2 knots is hard, if not impossible.

⚙ Try to remain calm and think clearly. The crew will hopefully have thrown you a lifebuoy — grab this or its floating line.

⚙ If it's rough, turn your back to the waves. This will help reduce spray getting into your airways.

⚙ Cross your legs and wrap your arms around your body to minimize heat loss, caused by cold water flowing around your body. If wearing a sailing jacket and trousers, pull the neck, wrists and ankles tight.

⚙ The state of the water will affect how easy it is to keep sight of you. If there are waves, a small head bobbing on the water may be difficult to see. The day-glo bellows of an inflated lifejacket enhance visibility by day; retro-reflective panels and a flashing light increase the chances of being spotted at night; and blowing a whistle is far more effective than yelling.

⚙ A personal EPIRB (a hand-held radio distress beacon) can transmit a distress signal from your location, which will be picked up by search and rescue agencies.

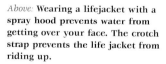

Lifejacket   Spray hood

Crotch strap

Above: **Wearing a lifejacket with a spray hood prevents water from getting over your face. The crotch strap prevents the life jacket from riding up.**

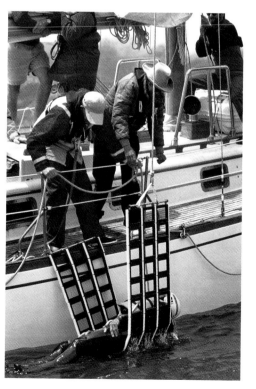

Left: **A high freeboard and guardrail make it difficult to get an incapacitated person back onto the boat. This lifting system uses the main halyard.**

Good cruising

An ideal cruising area should provide a wide choice of anchorages and harbors that are attractive and secure for overnight stops in different wind directions. The following selection of worldwide locations indicates what you can expect from a good cruising area.

What to look for

☸ *Good facilities onshore.* You want somewhere to land easily, provision the yacht, look around, eat ashore and replenish water.

☸ *Short distances between anchorages of no more than 20 miles (37 km).* You can always sail farther if conditions are great.

☸ *Protection from major swell.* This may be provided by a landmass or islands.

☸ *Straightforward navigation.* Nontidal areas make navigation considerably easier than an area with fast-flowing tides.

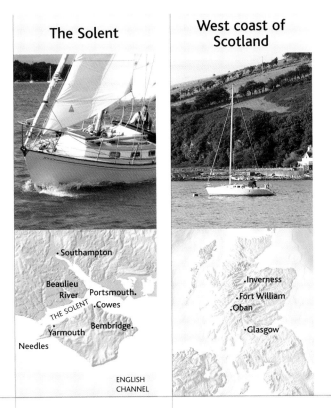

	The Solent	West coast of Scotland
Tides	Strong.	Variable.
Strengths	The Solent is the center of British yachting. All of the Solent from the Needles to Bembridge is protected by the Isle of Wight, with a tremendous variety of harbors and anchorages packed into a small area. Cowes is one of the world's leading yachting centers, with first-class facilities. Other delightful places to stop include Yarmouth, the Beaulieu River and Bembridge.	The west coast of Scotland provides wonderful cruising grounds, with deep inlets and countless anchorages. A string of islands provides excellent protection for much of the cruising area, while also increasing the number of places yachts can visit. The scenery is magnificent and there is more than enough space for everyone to go cruising.
Weaknesses	The Solent has very strong tides and frequent shipping going in and out of Southampton and Portsmouth. This is a busy sailing area that gets crowded with yachts in high season.	Good weather cannot be guaranteed! Beware of midges, which are prevalent in the height of summer.

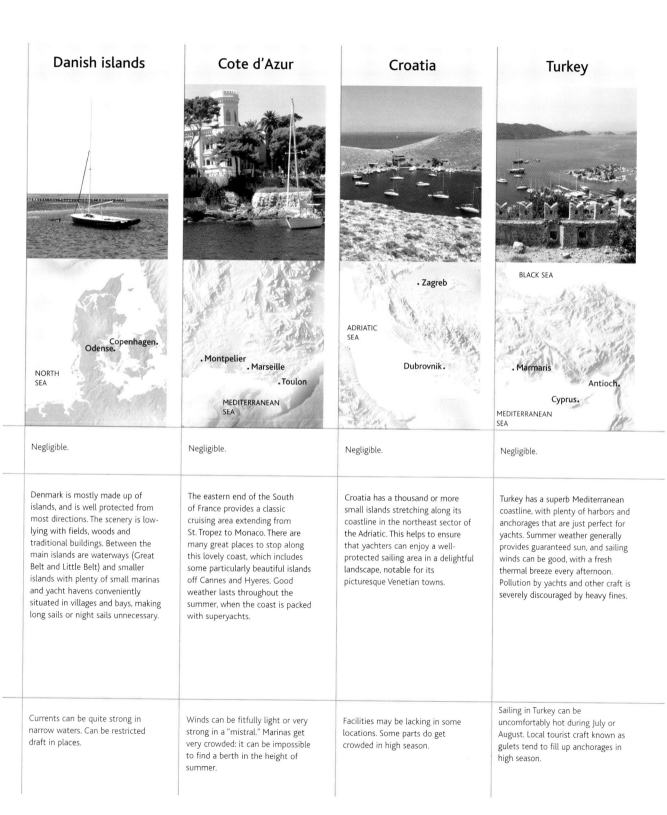

Danish islands	Cote d'Azur	Croatia	Turkey
Negligible.	Negligible.	Negligible.	Negligible.
Denmark is mostly made up of islands, and is well protected from most directions. The scenery is low-lying with fields, woods and traditional buildings. Between the main islands are waterways (Great Belt and Little Belt) and smaller islands with plenty of small marinas and yacht havens conveniently situated in villages and bays, making long sails or night sails unnecessary.	The eastern end of the South of France provides a classic cruising area extending from St. Tropez to Monaco. There are many great places to stop along this lovely coast, which includes some particularly beautiful islands off Cannes and Hyeres. Good weather lasts throughout the summer, when the coast is packed with superyachts.	Croatia has a thousand or more small islands stretching along its coastline in the northeast sector of the Adriatic. This helps to ensure that yachters can enjoy a well-protected sailing area in a delightful landscape, notable for its picturesque Venetian towns.	Turkey has a superb Mediterranean coastline, with plenty of harbors and anchorages that are just perfect for yachts. Summer weather generally provides guaranteed sun, and sailing winds can be good, with a fresh thermal breeze every afternoon. Pollution by yachts and other craft is severely discouraged by heavy fines.
Currents can be quite strong in narrow waters. Can be restricted draft in places.	Winds can be fitfully light or very strong in a "mistral." Marinas get very crowded: it can be impossible to find a berth in the height of summer.	Facilities may be lacking in some locations. Some parts do get crowded in high season.	Sailing in Turkey can be uncomfortably hot during July or August. Local tourist craft known as gulets tend to fill up anchorages in high season.

Map labels — Danish islands: Copenhagen., Odense., NORTH SEA

Map labels — Cote d'Azur: .Montpelier, .Marseille, .Toulon, MEDITERRANEAN SEA

Map labels — Croatia: .Zagreb, ADRIATIC SEA, Dubrovnik.

Map labels — Turkey: BLACK SEA, .Marmaris, Antioch., Cyprus., MEDITERRANEAN SEA

Good cruising (2)

The Netherlands	The Tyrrhenian Sea	Phuket, Thailand	Bahamas

The Netherlands

NORTH SEA

. Amsterdam

.Den Haag

The Tyrrhenian Sea

Corsica

Italy

TYRRHENIAN SEA

Sardinia

Phuket, Thailand

PHANG NGA BAY

. Phuket

INDIAN SEA

Bahamas

Florida

Abacos archipelago

Exumas district

Cuba

Tides

The Netherlands: Strong offshore; negligible on inland seas.

The Tyrrhenian Sea: Negligible.

Phuket, Thailand: Tidal range.

Bahamas: Tides.

Strengths

The Netherlands: The Netherlands provides two kinds of sailing. You can either go offshore, on the North Sea, where the long, low-lying Dutch coastline gets some protection from islands such as Texel, or explore the well-protected inland seas that are linked by canals and can provide delightful cruising for medium-sized yachts with reasonably shallow draft.

The Tyrrhenian Sea: Corsica, Sardinia and the west coast of Italy provide a wonderful cruising area with a huge variety of harbors and bays, old towns and villages and a particularly stunning backdrop as you sail around Corsica with the advantage of fine summer weather.

Phuket, Thailand: The largest island in Thailand, in an area of tropical rainforest surrounded by the blue waters of the Andaman Sea. The island has well-sheltered bays and and inlets with sandy beaches. With its light monsoon wind this area has become the center of sailing in Thailand. Phang Nga Bay to the north is a protected, very dramatic cruising area, with a variety of giant limestone sculptures rising out of green waters. There are several large islands to the east and an archipelago to the south.

Bahamas: Situated in the Atlantic Ocean, just north of Cuba, the Bahamas are famed for their hot weather, relaxed lifestyle and white sandy beaches. Only 30 islands of the 700 that make up the archipelago are inhabited. The islands are filled with boat tour operators, abundant anchorages and bustling harbors. The Abacos archipelago is considered "the sailing capital of the world" and the Exumas district is particularly fine for yacht cruising, owing to its gorgeous coastal scenery.

Weaknesses

The Netherlands: You take your chances with the weather. Strong tides and shallow water can make offshore sailing tricky. If it's windy, the inland seas can become very choppy.

The Tyrrhenian Sea: Wind can range from very light to very strong, with the potential for rough conditions at the northern and southern ends of Corsica. In high season, it may be impossible to find marina berths.

Phuket, Thailand: Threat of typhoons in the summer months. Piracy is rare but not unknown.

Bahamas: Lots of boat traffic; many "out islanders" commute. Often windy; usually 20 knots from the east.

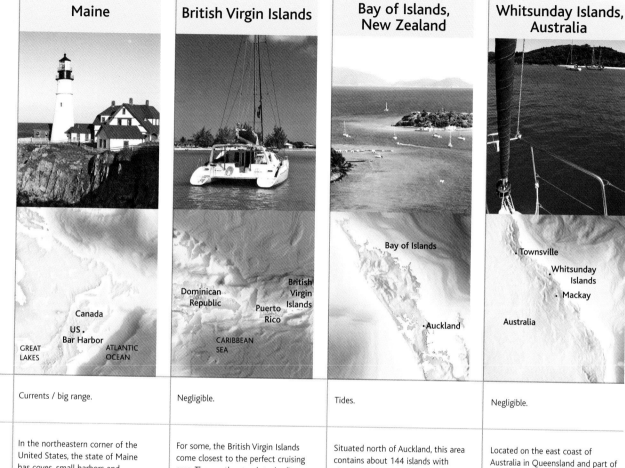

Maine	British Virgin Islands	Bay of Islands, New Zealand	Whitsunday Islands, Australia
Currents / big range.	Negligible.	Tides.	Negligible.
In the northeastern corner of the United States, the state of Maine has coves, small harbors and channels surrounded by rocky scenery. Light summer winds combine with a dramatic coastline and an abundance of birds and wildlife. Camden is the attractive base for numerous yachts, while Mount Desert Island is the largest of scores of islands.	For some, the British Virgin Islands come closest to the perfect cruising area. The weather tends to be fine on most days of the year, without being too hot. Trade winds provide a good force 4 sailing breeze: not too light, not too strong — just right! Most of the sailing area is well protected from Atlantic swell. The islands are closely packed, with a variety of anchorages only a few miles apart. Navigation is very straightforward.	Situated north of Auckland, this area contains about 144 islands with clear blue-green water in a subtropical climate. The area is famous for its historical connection with Captain Cook. The marina at Tutukaka, 80 miles (140 km) north of Auckland, is a suitable stop-off point for cruising or racing from the mainland harbors at Opua, Russell or Paihia. The area has many beautiful and secure anchorages near deserted sandy beaches, including the popular area south of Roberton Island.	Located on the east coast of Australia in Queensland and part of the Great Barrier Reef. Beautiful anchorages for exploring the coral reef and sea life of Australia. Whitsunday Island is the largest of the islands, while Hamilton Island has a large marina. Hook Island, the most northerly of the group, offers one of the best selections of cruising anchorages. The Great Barrier Reef can be visited by private yachts.
Fog occurs when the cold waters combine with the prevailing wind, especially at the height of summer. Beware of strong currents and a large tidal range.	BVI is a small sailing area, perfect for a one- or two-week vacation. For longer than a two weeks, you will need to sail farther afield.	The most popular places can be busy in summer.	The cyclone season is best avoided. Tropical heat. Stinging jellyfish are a danger in the water.

Navigation

5

Rotheneuf

S.–Coulomb

Dir.F.R.
24M
Rochebonne

RADIO MAST

Spire

SAINT-MALO

2M

nt Servan–
ur–Mer
Dir F.G.69m25M
La Balue

Barrage

WATER
TOWER (74

.46

.46

WATER
TOWER

S.–Méloir–
des–Ondes

Pylon
(R Lts)

–50

52

M

S.

de

Y TO SAINT–

What is navigation?

Traveling from one place to another, we need cues to help us navigate. Whether it's moving from one room to another, walking to the store or driving our car, we use visual cues to help us recognize where we are and to pick our route. It's the same on the water.

Traditionally the cues have always been visual. Put us in the middle of a desert or at sea and we have a problem. Navigation allows us to find our way.

Navigation using visual cues

In nautical terms, this is known as pilotage. If we can see our destination across a lake or bay, or see the banks of the river or estuary, we can just point the boat in the required direction and "go." That's fine if there are no rocks or sandbanks in the way, the visibility is good and it isn't dark. If there are obstructions, poor visibility or darkness, we will need a plan of action and hopefully some "navigation aids," such as buoys — seamarks rather than landmarks. We'll also need a "steering compass."

Navigation without visual cues

This is traditional navigation and requires positions and courses to be plotted on a paper chart so that a boat may be safely navigated to its destination. The boat's position is determined by a variety of means, and the course that needs to be steered to allow for wind and tide is then calculated. The boat is steered on this course and at regular intervals the latest position is plotted on the chart. The course to be steered is updated as required, as the boat continues to its destination.

Practical navigation

In reality, pilotage is used at the start and end of a journey, with traditional navigation used as required when pilotage simply isn't possible.

In order to carry out your chart-work, you'll need some plotting "tools" to do the job. There are a number of different types to choose from and you don't need them all.

Below: **Paper charts are expensive, so all previous work must be erased in order to use them again and again. Many people use a 2B grade of pencil, which is fairly soft and isn't too difficult to erase.**

Right: **A good-quality artist's or drafting eraser is best. Cheap erasers will simply abrade the paper.**

Left: **A pencil sharpener with**

Above: **Dividers mea[...] distance and plot latitude and longitu[...] One-handed types a[...] best for boat use.**

What tools do we need for chartwork?

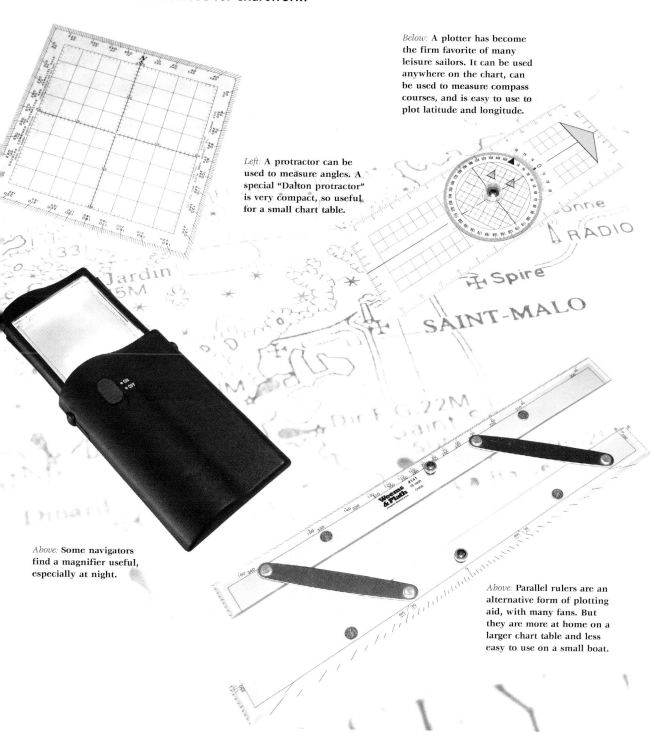

Below: **A plotter has become the firm favorite of many leisure sailors. It can be used anywhere on the chart, can be used to measure compass courses, and is easy to use to plot latitude and longitude.**

Left: **A protractor can be used to measure angles. A special "Dalton protractor" is very compact, so useful for a small chart table.**

Above: **Some navigators find a magnifier useful, especially at night.**

Above: **Parallel rulers are an alternative form of plotting aid, with many fans. But they are more at home on a larger chart table and less easy to use on a small boat.**

Navigation instruments

For basic boat navigation it is usual to install a speed/log instrument to show speed and distance, along with instruments to measure wind speed and direction as well as depth. A steering compass is also essential.

How is boat speed measured?

Most instruments measure speed through the water by means of a paddlewheel impeller that rotates as the boat moves through the water. Each revolution is counted electronically and this data is converted into distance traveled and speed through the water. The information is displayed on an LCD screen on the speed/log instrument. The paddlewheel protrudes through the hull, with the lower half of the paddle in the water and the upper part inside the "skin fitting." It can be withdrawn from the hull in order to remove marine growth. Some older instruments made use of a propeller on the underside of the hull.

The speed/log must be calibrated if it is to accurately display information, because the friction effect of the hull will cause the water flowing past the impeller to be less than the boat's speed through the water.

What is speed/log information used for?

Traditional navigation requires knowledge of distance traveled through the water in order to find the boat's estimated position where precise position fixing isn't possible, or in order to confirm a position fix.

The speed through the water reading is also used to fine-tune the boat's performance under sail and to evaluate the engine performance when under power.

Below: **A "through-hull" paddlewheel log.**

How is wind speed and direction measured?

The wind direction is measured by a windvane at the masthead. The wind speed is usually measured by rotating cups (an anemometer), also at the masthead. Data from the masthead unit is transmitted to a display for the helm.

Why do you need wind information?

Information on wind direction is necessary to sail the boat and trim the sails efficiently. It can be attained by using "telltales" attached to the shrouds, or by a "burgee" at the masthead. On a larger boat it can be more convenient to display the wind direction electronically, close to the helm. Wind speed can, to a degree, be deduced by the state of the water and its effect on the boat.

Above: **A digital boat speed/distance display.**

Wind display

The wind direction is displayed using a pointer (analog or digital) on a circular dial, with the top representing the bows of the boat. The wind speed is digital.

True wind and apparent wind

If the boat is stationary, the wind indicated (by burgee, telltale or electronic display) is the true wind. Once the boat starts to move, the indicated wind (the apparent wind) will be a combination of boat speed and wind speed. It is the apparent wind that propels the sailing boat. The sails are also trimmed to the apparent wind.

More expensive electronic wind instruments are supplied with boat speed information from the speed/log and are thus able, if desired, to display the "true" wind when the boat is moving.

How is depth measured?

A unit in the hull fires pulses of ultrasound down to the water bottom. The time taken for the pulse to travel to the bottom and back is used to calculate the depth.

The display is usually in digital form and the unit can be calibrated to show the depth below the hull unit, below the keel or below the boat's waterline, the last of these being most useful for navigation.

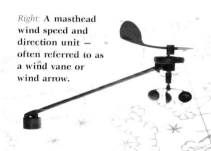

Right: **A masthead wind speed and direction unit — often referred to as a wind vane or wind arrow.**

Above: **A solar-powered, wireless digital wind display.**

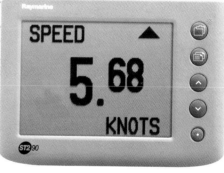

Above: **A digital boat speed display.**

Above: **A depth display unit, also known as an echo sounder.**

Right: **An analog wind direction display with digital speed.**

Keeping to a course

If you are sailing within sight of land, by day and in good visibility, you don't need a compass. However, consider what will happen if fog suddenly develops and landmarks are no longer visible.

What is a steering compass?

Any compass can be used as a steering compass, but on a boat it is desirable for it to be attached to the boat's structure, and large enough to be clearly visible to the helm.

Compasses have a pointer mounted on a magnet. The pointer aligns itself with the earth's magnetic field so that it always points toward the earth's north magnetic pole. A marine compass is mounted on a "gimbal" so that the plane of the pointer remains horizontal, even when the boat pitches and rolls.

What is compass deviation?

A compass fixed permanently in position on a boat will be influenced by the boat and its components' own magnetism, in addition to the earth's magnetic field. This may create an error in the compass reading.

Because the boat's magnetic field is aligned with the boat, as the boat changes course, its interaction with the earth's magnetic field changes, giving rise to an error that varies according to which way the boat is heading. This is called compass deviation. Magnetic items such as loudspeakers should be mounted well away from compasses, and other magnetic items should not be placed temporarily near a compass.

A steering compass can be adjusted to minimize these errors. It should be adjusted by a competent person annually.

Right: **If the compass does have deviation, then it needs to be checked on each heading (at 30-degree intervals) and a deviation card drawn up.**

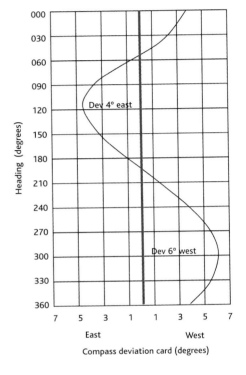

Dev 4° east

Dev 6° west

East   West

Compass deviation card (degrees)

Left: **A bulkhead compass for a yacht. The yellow lubber lines allow for parallax error on reading.**

Lubber lines

Right: **A hand-bearing compass that can be held at arm's length rather than up to the eye.**

Reading card

Above: **A compass for a bulkhead mount with a reading card that can also be viewed from inside the cabin.**

Hood

Left: **An offshore compass with a built-in hood for yachts and power boats.**

Right: **A hand-bearing compass with a neck cord, intended for use close against the eye.**

A compass correction card should be made so that the boat can be steered to the required magnetic heading (an adjustment for error will be incorporated into the navigator's calculations when working out a course for the helm to steer). In practice, an error of less than 3 degrees can be ignored because it is seldom possible to steer with such a degree of accuracy.

What is a hand-bearing compass?

A hand-bearing compass is used to "take sights" of land- and seamarks so that a bearing can be drawn on the chart from the boat to the mark to show where the boat is. They are small, easily held and used up close to the eye or at arm's length.

Because it's not attached to the boat, a hand-bearing compass has no compass deviation, but it should be used in a position where the boat's magnetic influence is minimal — i.e., well away from engines, keels or any object with a magnetic effect.

Binoculars

Binoculars are used to identify distant objects. Because the boat is continually in motion, it's very difficult to hold binoculars steady. The effect of any movement is accentuated as magnification is increased. Traditionally, marine binoculars have a maximum magnification of seven — anything more makes it virtually impossible to keep the binoculars trained on a given target.

Binoculars are specified by two numbers, such as 7x50. The first number is the magnification and the second is the diameter (in millimeters) of the large lens. The bigger the lens diameter, the larger the light-gathering capabilities — this is important if the binoculars are to be used at night.

Some binoculars are available with a built-in compass so that they can be used for taking bearings, while a more expensive option on some is to have an image-stabilization system. This allows easier use on a moving platform such as a boat, but their guarantee period is much shorter than that of traditional binoculars.

Time

A knowledge of time is needed for navigation; an accurate time check is available from your GPS set. Unless this is adjusted, it will be Universal Standard Time (UTC) or Greenwich Mean Time (GMT) — essentially the same thing.

Above and right: **Some binoculars have a built-in compass and range finder, which can be useful for taking bearings of distant or small objects and working out how far away they are.**

Above: **A traditional ship's clock, which also indicates the average state of tide. Although handsome, and easy to read at a glance, the digital clock of a GPS screen may prove more practical for serious navigation.**

Latitude and longitude

In order to navigate you need to know where you are and where you want to go. On the open sea there are no roads to follow, so charts (sea maps) have a grid of latitude and longitude superimposed on them so that specific positions can be identified.

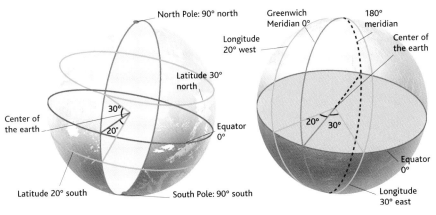

Above: **Latitude is the angle between a line drawn from any position to the center of the earth and the line joining the point on the earth's surface to the center of the earth.**

Above: **Longitude is the angle between the line joining the Greenwich Meridian and the center of the earth and the line joining the point on the earth's surface and the center of the earth.**

What are latitude and longitude?

The latitude part of the grid is formed by a series of circles, parallel to the equator. These are named by noting how many degrees they are north or south of the equator relative to the center of the earth.

The longitude part of the grid is also formed by a series of circles, but this time they all pass through both poles and are distributed around the equator, which they intersect at right angles. The zero longitude semicircle is called the Greenwich Meridian. Longitude is named degrees east and degrees west of this, increasing until the lines meet at the 180-degree (both east and west) meridian, diametrically opposite to the Greenwich Meridian. Position is defined by an intersection on the grid of latitude and longitude.

A chart has a latitude scale up each side and a longitude scale along the top and bottom borders. There is also a latitude/longitude grid superimposed on the chart.

Below: **The latitude and longitude of a position on the earth's surface.**

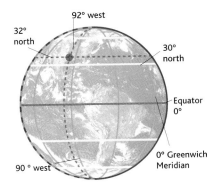

Using the plotter

To plot a specific position on a chart, first find the corresponding numbers on the latitude (the sides) and longitude (top or bottom) scales. Line up the plotter parallel to the horizontal grid line closest to the latitude mark and slide it up or down so that its top edge just meets the mark. Draw a horizontal line — the latitude — across the chart. Do the same at the second mark, moving the plotter sideways and drawing a vertical line — the longitude. The two lines cross at the specified position.

The latitude and longitude of a specific point, such as a buoy, is measured by aligning the plotter with the position of the buoy and reading off its latitude on the vertical scale and its longitude on the horizontal scale.

Using dividers

To plot a position this way, mark the required latitude and longitude on the edges of the chart. Put one point of the dividers on the latitude mark and the other on the nearest horizontal grid line. Put one point of the dividers on the same horizontal grid line but directly above or below the longitude mark, and the other point vertically above or below that, in line with the mark on the latitude (side) scale. Draw a short horizontal line at this point — this is the latitude. Do the same from the longitude mark, this time drawing a short vertical line — the longitude —

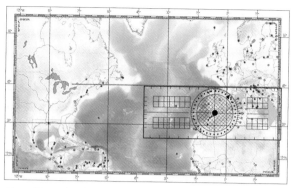

Above: **Measuring latitude with a plotter.**

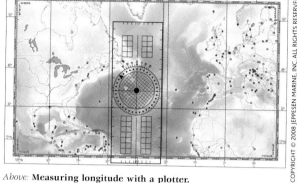

Above: **Measuring longitude with a plotter.**

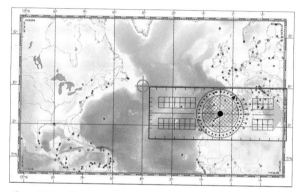

Above: **Measuring latitude of a point on a chart.**

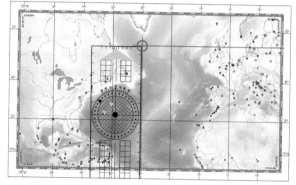

Above: **Measuring longitude of a point on a chart.**

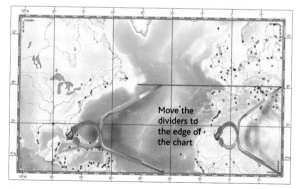

Move the dividers to the edge of the chart

Above: **Measuring latitude with dividers.**

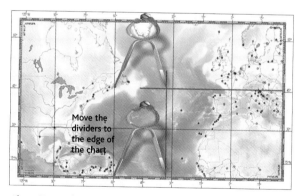

Move the dividers to the edge of the chart

Above: **Measuring longitude with dividers.**

where it crosses the latitude line. This is the plotted position.

To measure the latitude and longitude of a specific feature on the chart, place one point of the dividers on it and the other on the nearest horizontal grid line, directly above or below. Move the dividers to the edge of the chart. Place one point on the same horizontal grid line and make a mark where the other point cuts the latitude scale. Repeat this with the nearest vertical grid line and the top or bottom of the chart, making a mark on the longitude scale. Read off the latitude from the vertical scale and the longitude from the horizontal scale.

Dividers or plotter?

It's probably easier to use a plotter to draw latitude and longitude on a chart, but easier to use dividers to find the latitude and longitude of an object, such as a buoy or other feature, marked on a chart.

Distance and direction

An understanding of distance and direction is necessary for navigation. Both are obtained by measuring between two points on a chart.

How do you measure distance?

The angle between the equator and the North (or South) Pole is 90 degrees. Each degree is divided into 60 minutes, giving a total of 5,400 minutes. *One nautical mile is defined as one minute of latitude.*

The advantage of using a nautical mile, rather than a statute mile or kilometer, is that no special scale is needed. The latitude scale is always used to measure the distance.

Each minute is divided into tenths and hundredths, rather than seconds as is normal for angles. This makes their use much easier.

Because the paper chart is a flat representation of a spherical surface, the latitude scale on the chart consists of unequal divisions. You should use the part of the latitude scale closest in latitude to the distance being measured.

Measuring distance with dividers

It's usual to measure distance on a chart using a pair of dividers. Open the dividers out to the distance between two points and measure this distance against the latitude scale on the side of the chart. Alternatively, open the dividers to a convenient distance on the latitude scale, say 10 miles, and then "walk" the dividers along the line to be measured, counting the steps; measure any distance left over on the latitude scale and add it to the total.

Measuring direction on a chart

Direction is the angle between the line joining two points on the chart and the nearest meridian of longitude. The meridians depicted on the chart may or may not be parallel, which is why you must use the nearest meridian to get an accurate reading.

Right: **The difference between magnetic north and true north.**

North pole

Variation east

North magnetic pole

Variation west

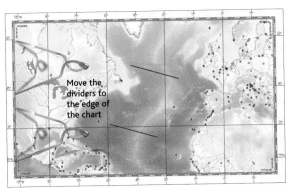

Above: **Measuring distance using dividers.** Ensure that you measure at the same level of latitude as the distance you are measuring or the result will be inaccurate.

Move the dividers to the edge of the chart

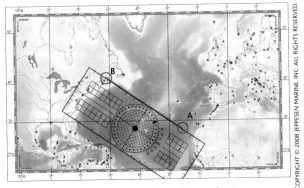

Above: **Measuring direction of point A from point B using a plotter.**

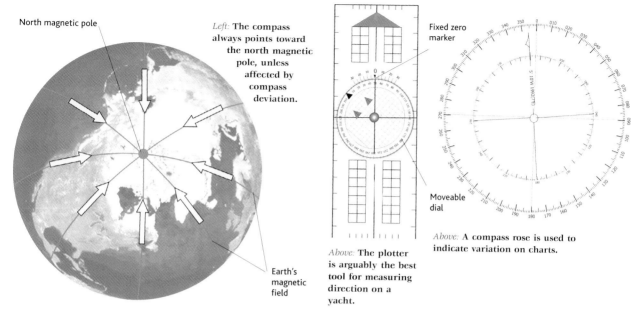

North magnetic pole

Left: **The compass always points toward the north magnetic pole, unless affected by compass deviation.**

Fixed zero marker

Moveable dial

Earth's magnetic field

Above: **The plotter is arguably the best tool for measuring direction on a yacht.**

Above: **A compass rose is used to indicate variation on charts.**

Measuring direction with a plotter

Place the plotter on the line joining the two points, with the big arrow pointing toward your destination. Rotate the central knob until the "North" indicator is pointing up and the grid on the circular central dial is aligned to the nearest part of the chart's latitude and longitude grid. Read off the true direction against the fixed zero marker at the edge of the circular dial.

What is magnetic variation?

The earth's magnetic field is aligned with the north and south *magnetic* poles. These are not in the same place as the geographic poles and in fact are slowly changing position.

A compass needle points toward the north magnetic pole, so there will be a difference between magnetic north and true north. This difference is called magnetic variation. When using a compass to steer a course, you need to know the magnetic direction rather than the true direction.

Why is magnetic variation different in different places?

If you are in London, England, and face the North Pole, the north magnetic pole is to your left. If you stand in Tokyo, Japan, the north magnetic pole is to the right. Marine charts show the magnetic variation at different places and also the amount the variation changes every year.

How do you apply variation?

There are a number of rules of thumb, but the easiest method is to apply variation as you use the plotter.

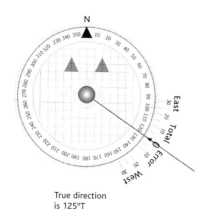

True direction is 125°T

Above: **Measuring the true direction (that is, toward the North Pole) on the zero reference line of the plotter.**

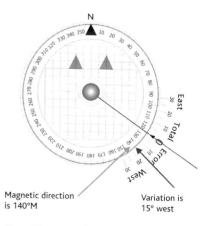

Magnetic direction is 140°M

Variation is 15° west

Above: **The magnetic direction is read off the outer scale against the magnetic variation (indicated here by the magenta arrow).**

What is a nautical chart?

Nautical charts are specially drawn for navigation at sea. They show all nautical features, such as buoys and lighthouses, and land features useful for navigation. They show the shorelines, depths, rocks and other dangers to navigating a boat, and contain important navigational information.

Who makes nautical charts?

Nautical charts are mainly produced by national hydrographic departments. In areas rarely visited by large ships, the surveys they are based on may have been made back in the 19th century with unsophisticated equipment. This means that charted positions may be incorrect by several miles, depths may be wrong due to silting or the growth of coral, and hazardous rocks may have been missed.

Chart source diagrams

Charts from major producers have a source diagram showing how various parts of the chart were surveyed and when. Only areas used by commercial and naval shipping will be regularly surveye Do not place undue faith on the accuracy of charts surveyed a long time ago.

Below: **A typical British Admiralty chart for the Channel Islands and northern France.**

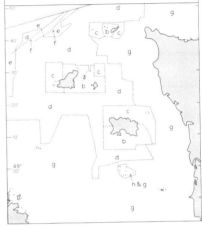

Admiralty surveys:
a 1990 1:25,000
b 1960–84 1:5000–1:20,000
c 1859–66 1:12,255–1:18,360 (leadline)
d 1859–69 1:73,000 (leadline)
e 1830–81 1:117,480–1:520,000 (leadline)
f 1936–68 Lines of soundings
French government:
g 1938–90 1:10,000–1:150,000
Compiled mainly from 19th-century leadline surveys
Aerial photography:
h 1980

Above: **This is a source diagram showing that some areas were surveyed in 1990 but others as long ago as 1830. Much care will be needed when sailing in the areas covered by the early surveys.**

Charts for leisure sailors

Leisure charts often contain additional information useful for small craft. They are based on national charts, but may use different conventions for color and symbols. They often have no source diagram.

What is map datum?

The earth is not a regular sphere, but has minor irregularities in shape. National cartographers have developed formulae, called map datum, representing the shape of the earth in their locality. Charted positions will differ by several hundred feet depending on which map datum is used.

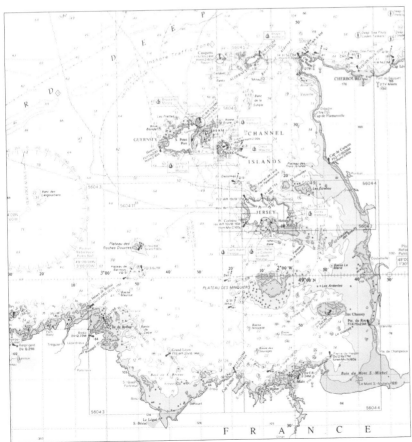

With the advent of GPS, a common world map datum named WGS84 was calculated and is now used for all new charts. All GPS positions are automatically given in WGS84 format. If the GPS position is plotted on a non-WGS84 chart, the position will not be correct.

Charts using different map datum will show how to adjust the position to allow for WGS84. Unless you are using the chart to approach dangers closely, the difference can normally be ignored.

What is chart scale?

The scale of a chart is the ratio of the distance on the earth's surface to the same distance on the chart. A 1:25,000 scale means that 1 inch on the chart represents 25,000 inch on the earth. A large-scale chart has a small number (say 1:5,000) and is used for close pilotage. A small-scale chart has a large number (say 1:1,000,000) and is used for navigational plotting.

SATELLITE-DERIVED POSITIONS

Positions obtained from satellite navigation systems are normally referred to as WGS84 Datum; such positions should be moved 0.03 minutes SOUTHWARD and 0.10 minutes EASTWARD to agree with this chart.

Left: **A small-scale chart can be used for planning and plotting.**

Lower left: **A large-scale chart can be used for entering and leaving a harbor.**

Below: **When changing to charts of differing scale, be careful to check you are clear in your mind what the units of the latitude scale represent.**

Left: Information on a chart, similar to that in this box, will show how to make corrections if the chart's map datum is not WGS84.

Check the notes

There are often notes in the title area relating to special information on a particular chart. Study these carefully, as they will contain important navigational information.

What are chart corrections?

Charts are correct at the time of printing, apart from British Admiralty charts, which are corrected prior to sale (although their leisure charts are correct only to the date of printing). The date of issue and the latest correction incorporated will be shown in the chart's margin. Corrections are published regularly by national authorities and are usually available from their websites; users are responsible for correcting their own charts after buying them.

Chart depths and heights

Standard international charts use very similar color schemes and symbols, but they are not identical. Ideally, you should purchase a chart symbol publication from the same source as your charts.

Leisure charts often use different colors from those used in standard hydrographic office charts, but the symbols are much the same. Some charts have the chart symbols and other data printed on the reverse.

Depths
On all charts the contours of the sea bed are denoted by lines known as depth contours. Charted depths are indicated by numbers in the water areas of the chart. Decimal points are not used; tenths are shown instead as subscripts. On metric charts, the depths are in meters and on others, in feet. Areas permanently underwater are colored blue or white — or a mid-blue where it is relatively shallow and lightening as the water deepens.

Some heights and depths are shown inside brackets, which means that they can't be put on the chart in exactly the correct place, as it would obscure the detail — instead, they are placed as close as possible and enclosed in brackets.

Drying areas
Areas that are sometimes covered by the tide and at other times uncovered are shown in italics, with the depth underlined. Tenths are shown in subscript and not underlined. Drying areas are colored green, dry land is yellow, and heights are shown with decimal points.

Underwater dangers
Rocks, wrecks and obstructions are shown by special symbols, the most common of which need to be committed to memory.

Buoys and other navigation marks
Buoyage is indicated on the chart, and the color of port and starboard buoys differs according to whether the chart is under system IALA A or IALA B. Lit buoys have a teardrop, with the light characteristics printed alongside. Some symbols are much bigger than their physical counterparts — they are out of scale. The actual geographical location of the symbol is shown by a small circle at the base of the symbol.

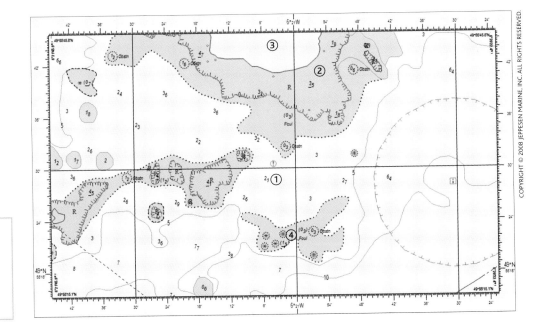

KEY
1. Depths
2. Drying areas
3. Dry land
4. Underwater dangers

Sectored lights

The light from fixed lights, such as lighthouses, isn't always visible from every direction. Sometimes it is obscured by obstructions and this is shown on the chart.

Where it is desirable for boats to keep in a channel or stay clear of a danger, the light is often deliberately "sectored." This means it may have several different colors in tight beams located on particular bearings. These "sectors" are shown on the charts either in black, with the initial letter of the color shown, or in the correct color.

Understanding the chart

The level of the sea is constantly changing as the tide rises and falls, so depths of water and drying heights are measured from chart datum, or from the Lowest Astronomical Tide (LAT) and Mean Lower Low Water in the U.S.

This is the lowest level to which the tide is expected to fall due to any combination of astronomical conditions.

Chart datum

Chart datum is the level below which all charted depths are given and the level above which the height of tide and drying areas are measured. Surprisingly, chart datum is not constant across the whole chart, because, for various reasons, the lowest level of the tide varies from place to place along the coast. When proceeding up a river, there may be dramatic changes in chart datum; charts often show a profile of these changes.

The following two pages show you the terminology you will need to know when undertaking chartwork.

Dangers and obstructions

Certain symbols should be remembered, as you may not have time to look them up before you encounter an unknown danger or obstruction:

If you are approaching a charted symbol you don't recognize, check what it means before you get too close!

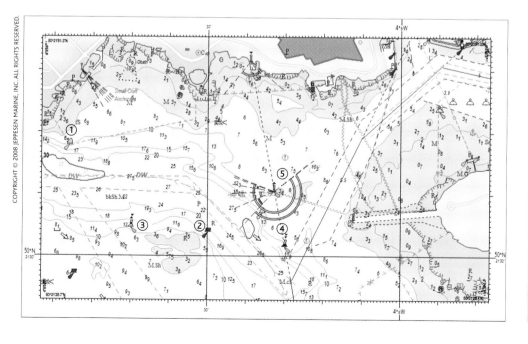

KEY
1. Starboard-hand buoy (IALA A)
2. Port-hand buoy (IALA A)
3. West cardinal buoy
4. South cardinal buoy
5. Sectored light

Chart depths and heights (2)

Tide terminology

The chart datum is the level of water that depths on a chart are measured from. Common chart datums are Lowest Astronomical Tide (LAT) in Europe, Canada and Australia and Mean Lower Low Water (MLLW) in the United States.

Charted depths and drying heights on charts are given relative to chart datum. Some height values, such as vertical clearances under bridges or overhead wires, are measured from Mean High Water (MHW) in the United States.

Cross-section of a chart

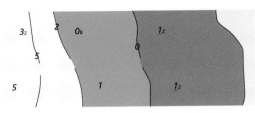

Above: **Here, depths are marked in feet. Underlined numbers show how much they would dry out above chart datum. The depths of water on charts and drying heights are calculated from chart datum.**

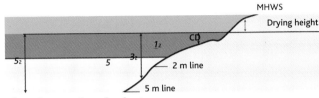

Above: **Cross section of a chart.**

Below: **On British Admiralty charts, depths and drying heights are measured from chart datum, while the heights of objects on land are measured from the level of Mean High Water Springs (MHWS). Some countries measure the height of objects from Mean Sea Level (MSL), halfway between MHWS and MLWS.**

Tidal heights and chart datum

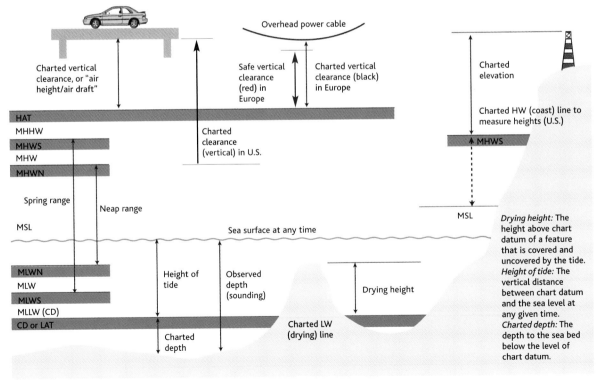

Standard definitions are used but always check they apply to your particular chart.

Definitions

Mean High Water Springs (MHWS):
The average height of high water at spring tides.

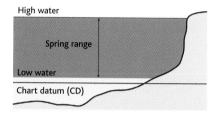

Mean Low Water Springs (MLWS):
The average height of low water at spring tides.
Mean High Water Neaps (MHWN):
The average height of high water

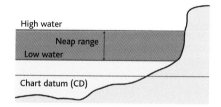

Mean Low Water Neaps (MLWN):
The average height of low water at neap tides.
Highest astronomical tide: (HAT):
The highest water level that can be predicted to occur under any known astronomical conditions.
Mean Higher High Water (MHHW):
Average of higher high tide heights.
Mean High Water (MHW):
Average of high water heights.
Mean Sea Level (MSL):
Average of sea leve heights.
Mean Low Water (MLW):
Average of low water heights.
Mean Lower Low Water (MLLW):
Average of lower low water heights.

Chart datum and height of tide

Studying the chart provides information on whether a rock is covered at the lowest tide you are ever likely to meet (chart datum).

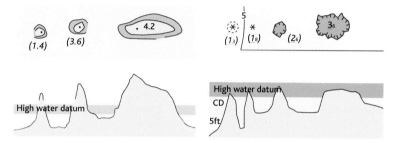

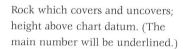

Rock which does not cover; height above height datum.

Rock which covers and uncovers; height above chart datum. (The main number will be underlined.)

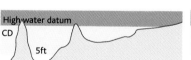

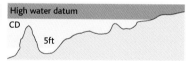

Rock awash at chart datum.

The depth is unknown over a permanently submerged rock but is considered dangerous to navigation.

Using tide tables

Tide tables give the height of the tide above chart datum. This makes it possible to calculate the depth of water at a given point and a given time by adding the charted depth to the height of the tide.

To calculate how deeply an area that dries is underwater, subtract the drying height from the height of the tide to give you the depth of water. This will be covered more fully on pages 274–75.

The international buoyage system

The international system of buoyage was introduced in the 1970s by the International Association of Lighthouse Authorities (IALA). Before this there had been around 30 different systems, but now there are just two: IALA A and IALA B.

The systems comprise several different groups of buoy, used for different purposes.

What are cardinal buoys?

Cardinal buoys are used to indicate in what direction it is safe to pass a hidden danger. As the name denotes, there are four cardinal points — north, east, south and west — with a buoy denoting each. A north cardinal buoy indicates that a ship may pass safely to the north of the buoy, as the danger lies to the south. The same principle applies to the other three.

In order to use the cardinal buoys, you need a compass to work out the cardinal directions. Cardinal buoys are the same throughout both IALA systems.

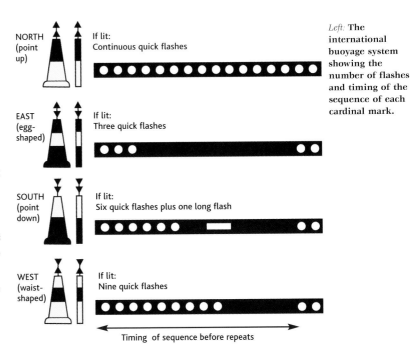

NORTH (point up)
If lit: Continuous quick flashes

EAST (egg-shaped)
If lit: Three quick flashes

SOUTH (point down)
If lit: Six quick flashes plus one long flash

WEST (waist-shaped)
If lit: Nine quick flashes

Timing of sequence before repeats

Left: **The international buoyage system showing the number of flashes and timing of the sequence of each cardinal mark.**

What are lateral buoys?

Lateral buoys mark a narrow channel. No knowledge of compass direction is needed, but you do need to know the general direction of buoyage. In rivers, estuaries and when approaching harbours, the direction of buoyage is upstream or towards the harbour. The general direction of buoyage is shown by a special symbol on the chart.

There are two systems of lateral buoyage: IALA A and IALA B. Charts will show which system is applicable in that area.

IALA A lateral buoys

When moving in the general direction of buoyage, the starboard buoys are colored green and have a conical shape. You leave these on your starboard side when going "inbound." This is the system used in much of the world.

IALA B lateral buoys

When moving in the general direction of buoyage, the starboard buoys are colored red, but still have a conical shape; leave the red buoys to starboard when proceeding "inbound." A good method of remembering this is "red right returning." This system is used in the U.S. and a few other countries.

Bifurcation marks

Where a channel splits into two, red or green bands are added to the buoy to indicate the preferred channel. These are bifurcation marks or modified lateral marks.

Safe-water buoys

These buoys are often used at the start of a narrow channel and may be passed on any side.

Isolated danger buoys

These buoys are placed directly on or above an isolated danger. The danger may be large enough to require keeping well clear. A large-scale chart should indicate the extent of the danger.

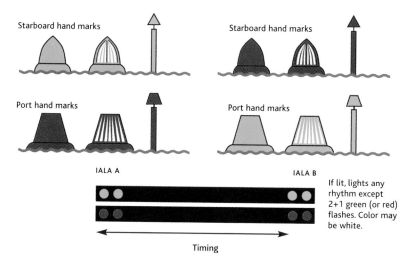

IALA A

IALA B

If lit, lights any rhythm except 2+1 green (or red) flashes. Color may be white.

Timing

Above: **IALA A buoyage:** The lateral buoys refer to the side of the channel when going upstream.

Above: **IALA B buoyage:** The lateral buoys refer to the side of the channel when going upstream.

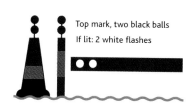

Top mark, two black balls
If lit: 2 white flashes

Above: **Isolated danger mark** used to indicate a limited or isolated area of danger and which has navigable water around it.

Top mark, if fitted, red ball

If lit: a long flash every 10 seconds (isophase or occulting, morse letter A).

White light

Above: **Safe water marks** are used at the center of a channel, indicating deep navigable water.

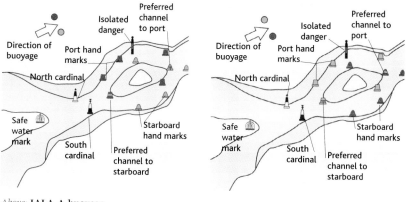

Above: **IALA A buoyage.**

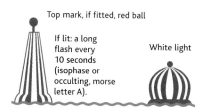

Emergency wreck-marking buoy
If lit: blue and yellow flashes

Above: **A temporary buoy** to indicate an area where a wreck as been located.

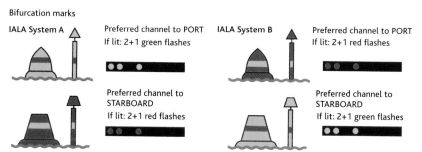

Bifurcation marks

IALA System A — Preferred channel to PORT — If lit: 2+1 green flashes

Preferred channel to STARBOARD — If lit: 2+1 red flashes

IALA System B — Preferred channel to PORT — If lit: 2+1 red flashes

Preferred channel to STARBOARD — If lit: 2+1 green flashes

Above: **Bifurcation marks** are modified lateral marks, used to mark the point where the channel divides or to indicate the main or preferred channel.

What are special buoys?

Special buoys may be used to mark such things as gunnery ranges, prohibited areas or traffic separation schemes. Some, such as racing buoys, have no navigational significance.

At the moment, buoys marking wrecks are not part of the IALA system, but they are being used to mark a new wreck prior to the establishment of an IALA buoy.

What are tides?

Tides are caused by the gravitational pull of the moon, and to a lesser extent the sun, on the earth's oceans. This pull creates a bulge in the surface of the oceans in the direction of the moon, increased or decreased according to the relative position of the sun.

Because the earth spins on its axis this bulge in the ocean surface appears to rotate around the earth, and as it approaches and recedes we experience a rise and fall in sea level. This rise and fall is greater between narrowing shorelines than in the open ocean.

Although the gravitational pull of the moon creates only one bulge (imagine a giant egg), the solid earth beneath the ocean (the yolk) is influenced by the same pull and moves sideways inside the "egg." This decreases the thickness of the main bulge, while at the same time causes a thickening of the water (or increased depth) on the opposite side of the globe.

Because the earth revolves around the sun as well as spinning on its own axis, it takes about 24 hours and 40 minutes to make a complete revolution in relation to the moon, and for the bulge to rotate around the earth. This is why high tide occurs about 40 minutes later each day.

What are spring and neap tides?

The position of the moon relative to the sun changes throughout the lunar month (28 days), resulting in the cyclical "phases" of the moon. When sun and moon are in line (new moon) or directly opposite

Above: **The gravitational pull of the moon on the world's oceans creates a bulge in the direction of the moon.**

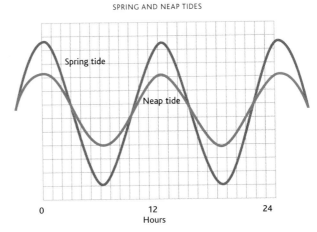

SPRING AND NEAP TIDES

Spring tide

Neap tide

0   12   24
          Hours

Left: **The difference between spring and neap tides: spring tides have high "high water" and low "low water"; neap tides have low "high water" and high "low water."**

Above: **The solid earth beneath the ocean also reacts to the moon's gravity, shifting sideways within the "envelope" of the ocean.**

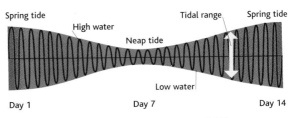

Spring tide   High water   Tidal range   Spring tide
                          Neap tide

                          Low water

Day 1   Day 7   Day 14

VARIATION FROM SPRING TIDE TO NEAP TIDE

Left: **The difference between the height of high water and the height of the preceding or following low water is called the tidal range.**

each other (full moon), their gravitational pulls combine to create the largest bulge or "spring" tides. When they are pulling at right angles to each other (half moon) the forces are decreased, producing a smaller bulge or "neap" tides. The bulge lags about two days behind the actual phase of the moon.

Spring tides have a high "high tide" and a low "low tide," whereas neap tides have a low "high tide" and a high "low tide." Spring and neap tides are not the same each month. They vary cyclically, with the largest spring tides occurring near the equinoxes and the smallest spring tides occurring near the solstices.

What is a tidal curve?

A tidal curve is produced by a number of authorities to indicate how the height varies throughout the tidal cycle. Each curve is based on long-term statistical analyses.

Where do I find tidal data?

Tide tables are predictions of the times and heights of both high and low tide throughout the year for selected places around the coasts. Tidal data can be found in almanacs, on websites, or from harbor authorities. Computer software is available that not only details high and low tides, but also allows the height of tide at hundreds of named places to be calculated for any given moment throughout the year.

Why do tidal heights differ in different places?

Tidal range — the difference between succeeding high and low, or low and high, tides — is less than 3 feet (1 m) in the open ocean. However, where the bulge is "squeezed" between narrowing shorelines it banks up to 49 feet (15 m) in the Bristol Channel, U.K., and to a massive 56 feet (17 m) in Nova Scotia's Bay of Fundy.

MEAN HIGH AND LOW WATER LEVELS

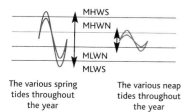

The various spring tides throughout the year

The various neap tides throughout the year

Above: **Average tidal data is given for ports in the form of "mean" levels for high and low water, both at spring and neap tides.**

What other factors affect the height of tide?

Atmospheric conditions can significantly affect the height of tide. Low atmospheric pressure will cause higher tides while high pressure has the reverse effect.

A strong wind blowing for some days, either with or against the direction of the tidal flow, can cause changes in height by a few feet or more. This is particularly the case where the tidal flow is funneled into a narrowing gap, where very high tidal surges can occur.

Tidal curves

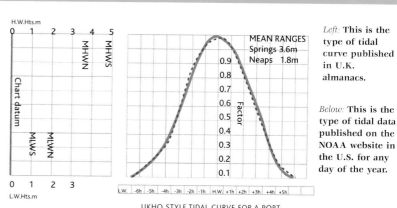

H.W.Hts.m

MEAN RANGES
Springs 3.6m
Neaps 1.8m

UKHO STYLE TIDAL CURVE FOR A PORT

Left: **This is the type of tidal curve published in U.K. almanacs.**

Below: **This is the type of tidal data published on the NOAA website in the U.S. for any day of the year.**

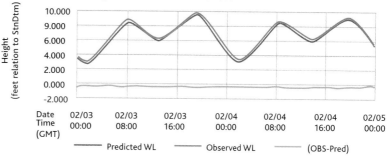

Tide Data – NOAA/NOS/CO-OPS
Point Reyes, CA, 2007/02/03–2007/02/04

| | Predicted WL | Observed WL | (OBS-Pred) |

TIDAL CURVE, PROJECTION AND ACTUAL LEVELS

What causes tidal flow?

Water wants to flow to the lowest possible level. This means there will be a tendency for tidal flow to move "downhill" from the crest of the tidal bulge toward the trough.

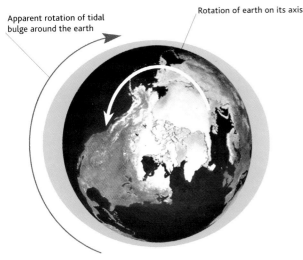

ROTATION OF THE TIDAL BULGE AROUND THE EARTH

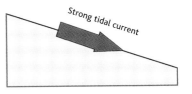

Right: **Tidal current flow from high water to low water The rate of flow depends on the slope's gradient.**

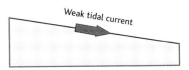

Tidal flow is negligible in wide areas of water such as the open ocean, where the distance between the tidal bulge's crest and trough could be 6,000 miles (10,000 km) and its difference in height less than a few feet. However, when the distance between crest and trough is only a few hundred miles, the height difference may be as much as 50 feet (15 m), and tidal flow can reach speeds approaching 10 knots.

How does tidal flow vary?
Tidal flow varies in strength and direction during the tidal cycle. Because the rate of flow depends on the "downhill" effect, it is at a minimum at high and low water (known as slack water) and at a maximum at "half tide." The direction of the flow depends on which way is "downhill."

Because the slope is greatest at spring tides, the tidal speeds are greatest then. At neap tides, when the slope is at its least, tidal speeds are slowest.

How do I find out what the tidal flow is?
There are two methods of finding the speed and direction of the tidal flow: tidal diamonds and tidal atlases.

Tidal diamonds
Many marine charts have tidal flow data printed on them. Because the flow varies from hour to hour, the speed can't be printed on the chart. Instead, symbols consisting of diamonds with a letter of the alphabet are placed at various positions. A table then gives values of the tidal flow for high water and

each of the six hours either side of high water for each of the tidal diamonds (or areas) for both spring and neap tides. These can be used to calculate the flow at any time.

Direction is given in degrees true, and tide flows "toward," so that a direction of 270 degrees means the tide is flowing in a westerly direction. Tidal diamonds are useful if you want to know the flow at a particular place, but tidal atlases have more detail.

Tidal atlases
Tidal atlas chartlets have arrows representing the tidal flow printed on them. Alongside the arrows are two numbers giving the speed for spring and neap tides respectively. There is one chartlet for the time of high water and others for each of the six hours before and after high water. Tidal atlases are much easier to use than tidal diamonds for passage planning and normal navigation.

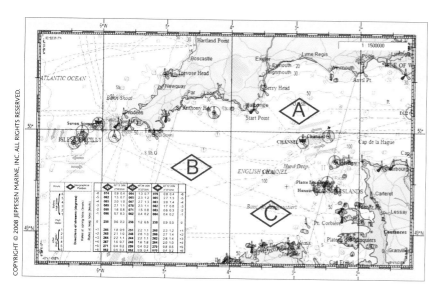

Left: **Many charts have "tidal diamonds," which give the tidal flows at specific points for the six hours either side of high water.**

Below: **Tidal flows may be shown in real time on some chart plotters and computer chart plotting.**

Electronic chart plotters and chart-plotting software sometimes incorporate a "real time" tidal atlas. This allows you to see what the tide is actually doing "now," and you can also scroll backward and forward in time — useful for planning a trip.

What time of high tide do I use?

For both tidal diamonds and tidal atlases, the tidal reference port is stated. This is not necessarily the nearest port, nor even a port on the chart or atlas. It is the port that gives the most accurate tidal information for that area. Unlike calculating tidal heights, you will not need to interpolate any data depending on where you are.

Strong wind can modify the surface current, as can high or low atmospheric pressure.

Above: **Tidal curve and height and time data is available on some chart plotters and computer software.**

Left: **Tidal atlases show the tidal flows for the six hours either side of high water.**

Tidal height calculations

Sailors need to be able to calculate heights of tide at any time in order to check that there is enough water for safe navigation. They also need to be able to check if there is enough room to pass safely under overhead obstructions.

Calculating the height of tide

To do this you need the time and heights of high and low water. This is obtained from the tide table, adjusting for Daylight Saving Time if necessary.

Normally the "rule of twelfths" can be used. This states that the tide will fall 1/12 of the range in the first hour after high water, 2/12 of the range in the second hour and 3/12 in the third, at which time it is half tide. In the fourth hour it will fall a further 3/12, in the fifth another 2/12 and in the sixth hour a final 1/12 to low water. In areas where coastal features such as offlying islands distort the tidal flow, the tidal curve for each harbor must be used instead.

Tidal curves

Tidal curves can be used to calculate the time at which a required water depth can be expected or the water's depth at a particular time. A tidal curve is a graph showing a complete cycle of tide, with slightly different curves shown for springs and neaps. Normally the tidal curves are based on the time of high water, but where low water can be predicted more accurately, this can be used instead.

Right: **The "rule of twelfths" assumes that the tide rises and falls in a symmetrical way and the duration of the rise or fall is six hours. It should be used with caution if high accuracy is required.**

RULE OF TWELFTHS

Multiply the range by the number of twelfths to get the fall from high water

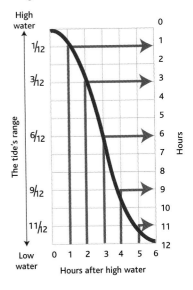

Using a tidal curve

1. Enter the local time of the day's nearest high tide in the HW box and hours before and after HW.

2. Enter the height of high water on the upper scale and low water on the lower scale. Join the two marks together.

3. To find the height of tide at a selected time, enter the required time on the timescale grid. Draw a line up to the curve. If the tide is close to springs, join this to the spring curve. If it is close to neaps, join it to the neaps curve. If it is in between, interpolate by eye.

4. From the intersection of the curve and the vertical line, draw a horizontal line across to meet the angled line drawn previously.

5. Draw a line up to meet the top scale. This number is the height of tide above chart datum at the time you require. To obtain the depth of water, add this number to the depth (at chart datum) shown on your chart.

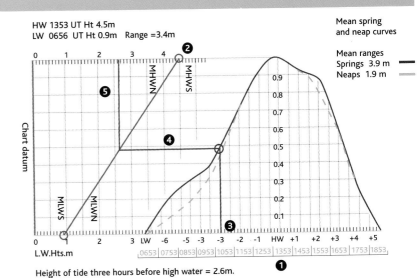

Height of tide three hours before high water = 2.6m.

Note that where Daylight Saving Time is practiced, you will need to adjust the UT calculations accordingly.

Calculations

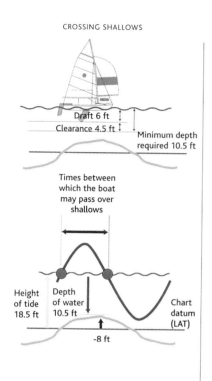

CROSSING SHALLOWS

Draft 6 ft
Clearance 4.5 ft
Minimum depth required 10.5 ft

Times between which the boat may pass over shallows

Height of tide 18.5 ft
Depth of water 10.5 ft
Chart datum (LAT)
-8 ft

MINIMUM DEPTH REQUIRED		10.5
DEPTH OF WATER = HEIGHT OF TIDE		18.5 FT
– DRYING HEIGHT 8 FT		= 10.5 FT

Above: **How to check if there's enough depth of water to cross a particular shallow area.**

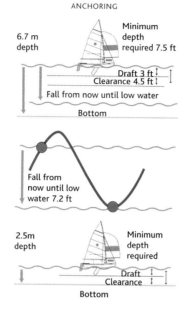

ANCHORING

6.7 m depth
Minimum depth required 7.5 ft
Draft 3 ft
Clearance 4.5 ft
Fall from now until low water
Bottom

Fall from now until low water 7.2 ft

2.5m depth
Minimum depth required
Draft
Clearance
Bottom

FALL		= 7
PLUS MINIMUM DEPTH		7 + 4.5
DEPTH TO ANCHOR		= 11.7 FT

Above: **If you are going to stay in the same anchorage over several tides, use the lowest "low tide" for the period you're going to be at anchor.**

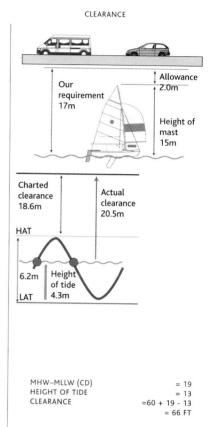

CLEARANCE

Allowance 2.0m
Our requirement 17m
Height of mast 15m

Charted clearance 18.6m
Actual clearance 20.5m
HAT

6.2m
Height of tide 4.3m
LAT

MHW–MLLW (CD)		= 19
HEIGHT OF TIDE		= 13
CLEARANCE		=60 + 19 - 13
		= 66 FT

Above: **The clearance marked on the chart, plus the difference between current height of tide and that of highest astronomical tide (HAT), gives the total clearance if the chart uses HAT.**

Calculating the depth of water

To calculate the depth you need the charted depth or the drying height for the place you wish to go. Then apply the actual height of tide for the time concerned to get the depth of water. For navigation purposes, it is preferable for the depth sounder to show depth below the waterline, as this makes the calculations much simpler.

Anchoring

When anchoring, you don't actually need a charted depth. By subtracting the fall of tide level until low water from the indicated depth now, you can calculate how much water will remain below the keel.

Clearance under cables

On modern British Admiralty charts, which measure clearance from highest astronomical tide (HAT), there will never be less clearance than the chart shows — see page 266. However, some countries' charts calculate clearance from a lower level, so that at high-water springs there may be less clearance than shown.

A position line

A position line is a line on which you are known to lie, drawn on the chart. In other words, if you take a bearing on a landmark and plot that bearing on your chart, your position must be somewhere on that line. If you plot another position line from another object, where they cross is where you are.

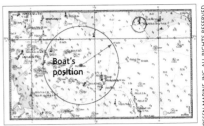

Above: There are plenty of buoys on the chart, but few will be visible or identifiable from your boat's position. Only the ones within the 2-mile circle will be visible during daylight, though the choice may be greater at night.

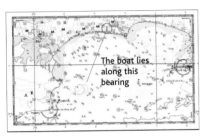

Above: An easily identifiable landmark provides a good position line.

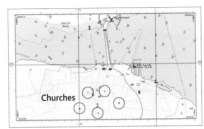

Above: It will be difficult to identify which church you are looking at if you take a bearing on one of five! It will not provide a successful position line.

What is a visual position line?

Visual position lines are normally obtained using a hand-bearing compass. This bearing must be converted to a true bearing by applying the appropriate variation, obtained from the chart (see page 261), in order to plot it. Taken from a boat, the bearing will swing about, so ensure that you stand with your legs well apart to get the steadiest possible bearing. Generally speaking, the accuracy is unlikely to be better than five degrees.

How should I choose a bearing?

The first priority is to choose an object that can be readily identified both visually and on the chart. Don't choose a church tower if there are several in close proximity!

Buoys should not be used as a source of bearings unless there is no alternative, because their position will move under the influence of the tide. If a bearing must be taken on a buoy, the further away it is the better. Fixed seamarks are fine.

How far away can you see a seamark?

Two factors affect the range at which seamarks can be seen. The size of most buoys means they are visible only within a range of 2 miles. The curvature of the earth will give a distance to the horizon of a little over 3 miles for an eye height of 2m.

What is a transit?

A transit is the most accurate position line. If two objects marked on your chart are in alignment, you must be somewhere on the projection of that line drawn on the chart. Unless the transit is familiar to you, take its magnetic bearing to ensure you have identified it correctly.

Depth as a position line

If there is a distinctive depth contour, or depth feature, this can be used as a position line, but you'll need to know the height of tide to use it properly.

A position line using radar range

Radar is very effective in obtaining the range (or distance) from an object. It can be used for measuring the distance from a distinctive land feature, but exercise care where the land slopes gently, as the feature will be difficult to identify. Seamarks are often unsatisfactory because it can be hard to identify them on the radar screen.

The distance — or range — to the horizon from a radar mounted 4m above the waterline is only about 5 miles, so if the coast is further away, you'll be seeing the hills, not the shoreline.

A position line using a radar bearing

Radar bearings are not as accurate as radar ranges (distances). They are affected by compass deviation, magnetic variation, misalignment of the radar scanner and the width of the radar beam. Each of these can be allowed for, but they make the process slow and prone to error. If it's all you have, however, by all means use it.

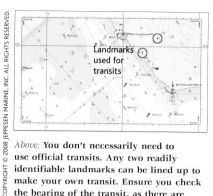

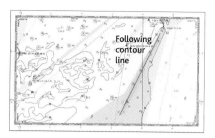

Above: **You don't necessarily need to use official transits. Any two readily identifiable landmarks can be lined up to make your own transit. Ensure you check the bearing of the transit, as there are several monuments on the chart and you could easily use the wrong one.**

Above: **Readily identified depth features make good position lines. A contour can also be used, provided the area isn't generally flat or is only gently sloping.**

Above: **The depth feature makes an excellent position line.**

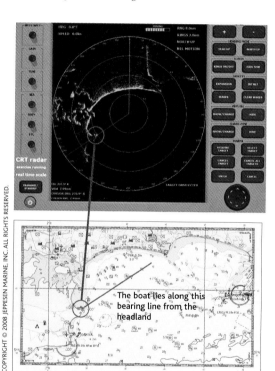

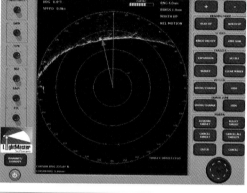

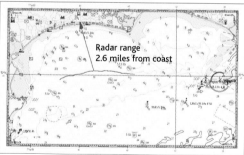

Above: **A radar bearing can be used as a position line, but it isn't as accurate as one using radar range (distance).**

Above right: **Radar range (or distance) from a landmark can produce an excellent position line, provided you understand that the radar's range to the horizon is little more 5 miles. Here we can't identify any feature on the shoreline, but that presents no problem. We are 2.6 miles from anywhere along it, so the position line is not straight, but a wiggly line parallel to the shore.**

Drawing bearings

The ideal tool is the Portland-type plotter, which allows the magnetic variation to be set without calculation. With the direction measured using the hand-bearing compass set on the plotter, ensure that the plotter's big arrow points toward the targeted object.

Fixing a position

Although most sailors have GPS, there may be times when you need to resort to traditional methods to fix your position. On open-water passages, you need to regularly plot your position on a chart. Traditional fixing relies on visual fixes and the use of position lines, which can be drawn on the chart and used in combination.

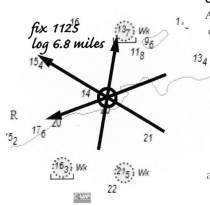

Using position lines

Although in theory the intersection of two position lines will fix your position, it's much better to use three, since this will immediately show if there's any error.

Ideally, the three position lines should make equal angles; that is, they should cross at 60 degrees. This isn't always practical, but you should aim for as close to this as possible.

What is a cocked hat?

It's rare to get a perfect fix when using three position lines. They will form a triangle, known as a cocked hat. It is usual to assume that your position is in the center of the cocked hat. The position lines do not have to be of the same type. Often you can't take sights on three readily identifiable objects so you may need to compromise and use radar range or depth as well.

Using the standardized system of marking a fix ensures that anyone looking at your chart will automatically understand what you are doing. This makes for safer operation. The position of a fix is shown by a circle centered on the position. Alongside this should be the time the fix was taken and the distance log reading.

Visual fixes

The easiest way to fix your position visually is by passing close to a navigation mark, noting its name or identifying it in some way, and then marking the position on the chart. If it's a buoy, circle it on the chart. This also helps to keep track of where you are if the buoys aren't named.

Above left: **It's important that you use the standard method for drawing a fix on your chart.**

Right: **As you pass an identified buoy, put a circle around it on the chart. This is particularly important in a marked channel, especially in poor visibility and at night. This fix signifies you passed a buoy at 14.45 when the log reading was 21.7 miles.**

Right: **You don't need to draw the position lines all the way to their origin, as shown by the red lines. Just mark the fix, as shown in black. The time of the fix was 0935 when the log read 12.7 miles.**

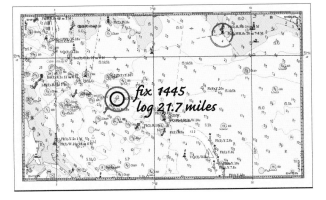

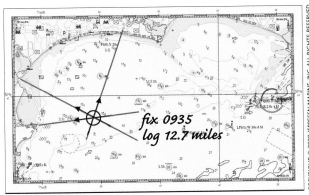

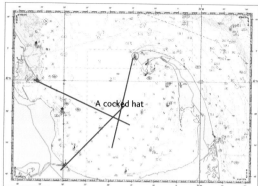

A cocked hat

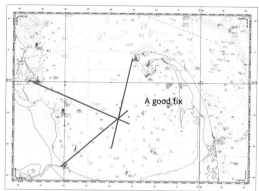

A good fix

The order in which you take the bearings is important, especially at higher speeds. Let us suppose it takes two minutes to take three bearings from the cockpit of your boat and you are traveling at 5 knots. In that time you will have traveled about 1,000 feet (300 m), which means that at least one line will have an error of 1,000 feet. If the time of your fix is to be the time of your last bearing, take the bearing that is changing least first. That is the one closest to ahead or astern. Take the bearing that is changing quickest last.

What if I don't have a chart table?

You can clip your chart to a suitably sized piece of plywood. If you place a sheet of transparent plastic over the chart, you can use a wax pencil to do your plotting. This is ideal if you are on a small sailing boat as it can be used in the cockpit and the chart won't blow away or be spoiled by water. Even a dinghy can be navigated in this way.

Above: **If you get a big cocked hat, check your data, but don't force it to fit. The probability is that you are somewhere within the triangle.**

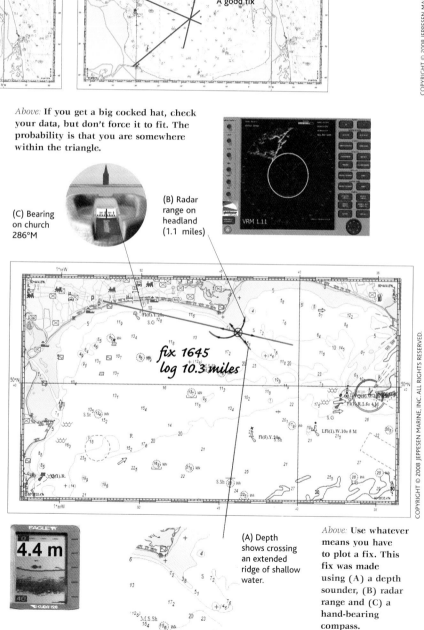

(C) Bearing on church 286°M

(B) Radar range on headland (1.1 miles)

VRM 1.11

fix 1645 log 10.3 miles

4.4 m

(A) Depth shows crossing an extended ridge of shallow water.

Above: **Use whatever means you have to plot a fix. This fix was made using (A) a depth sounder, (B) radar range and (C) a hand-bearing compass.**

What is GPS?

GPS is the Global Positioning System. It is a satellite-based navigation system owned and operated by the U.S. military. However, it is used everyday by people all over the world.

Left: **The GPS receiver computes its distance from the satellite. The receiver will be somewhere on this circular position line.**

Below: **If the distance from three suitably positioned satellites is computed, three intersecting circular position lines are obtained. The receiver must be where they intersect.**

Position of receiver

How does GPS work?

There are over two dozen satellites in 12-hour orbits 11,000 miles (18,000 km) above the earth. There should be between five and eight of them in view at any one time. Each satellite has a very accurate time clock on board.

It transmits this time, together with the satellite's current position, at frequent intervals.

The GPS receiver computes the time it takes the satellite signal to reach it, and knowing the speed of the transmitted signal (the speed of light) it can compute the distance from the satellite at any time. Because, for reasons of cost, the receiver has a much less accurate clock than the satellite, processes are used to synchronize the clocks and calculate the time delay.

Above: **A constellation of GPS satellites circle the earth, transmitting their data freely to all who wish to use it.**

The receiver must lie on a circular position line on the earth's surface where all positions are equidistant from the satellite. With signals received from two more satellites, three position lines will produce a position fix. Because of variations in the atmosphere, there will be errors in the actual distance traveled by the signals due to the time delay, so extra position lines are desirable.

Where are the satellites?

When you switch your GPS on, it takes a little while to download the data and compute its first fix. It will indicate how many satellites it expects to see, those it can actually see, and the signal strength of the received data from each satellite. This display allows you to make a judgment of the accuracy of the resulting fix.

Do all receivers give the same position?

Each manufacturer uses different methods of calculating the fixes and reducing errors. Therefore there's no guarantee that the position displayed on different sets will be the same. However, it's unlikely that the differences will be significant.

What are the possible errors in the displayed position?

The accuracy of a displayed GPS position is 50 feet (15 m) for 95 percent of the time. For the remaining 5 percent, much larger errors are statistically possible, with intermittent short-term errors of 330 feet (100 m) not uncommon. Occasional errors of greater than 1 mile (1.6 km) can occur.

If a satellite transmits erroneous information it will be used by the receiver to compute its fix. No indication of the error will be available to the user, who will be unaware of the inaccuracy in position. It generally takes the U.S. military a couple of hours to recognize and deal with the problem.

What is selective availability?

The U.S. military is able to induce random errors in the signals available to civilian users and they can do this without warning in times of emergency. Accuracy with selective availability turned on is 330 feet (100 m) for 95 percent of the time.

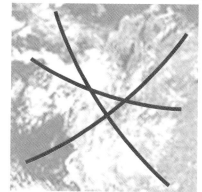
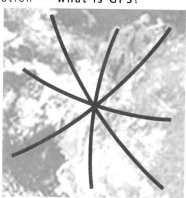

Above: **Initially, the computed data will give a cocked hat position. The receiver carries out a number of complicated calculations, uses data from extra satellites and then produces a good position fix.**

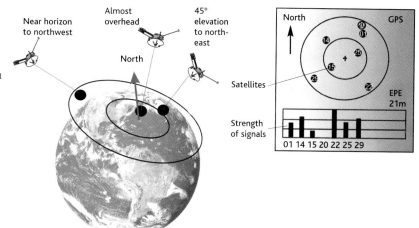

Above and right: **On startup, the receiver displays the position of the satellites and the signal strength of the received data. The center of the circle is directly above the receiver, the inner circle is at an elevation of 45 degrees and the outer one is the horizon.**

Can the GPS system fail?

GPS signals are extremely weak. Solar flares can cause complete disruption of the signals, as can deliberate jamming, which is occasionally generated by the military for test purposes. In some places, local microwave transmissions will completely swamp the GPS signals, and no GPS position will be available.

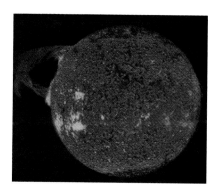

Left: **Solar flares can cause significant errors in the GPS displayed position.**

What is GPS? (2)

If a fixed GPS receiver compares its known position to its computed position, it can calculate the GPS error and supply a correction to other GPS receivers. This is known as differential GPS (DGPS). DGPS requires an additional receiver and is restricted to about 200 miles (320 km) from the base station. DGPS has been overtaken by satellite DGPS.

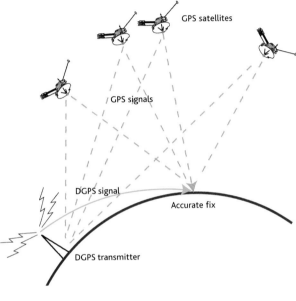

GPS satellites

GPS signals

DGPS signal

Accurate fix

DGPS transmitter

Left: **Terrestrial DGPS: the ground station transmits the GPS error to DGPS receivers within range.**

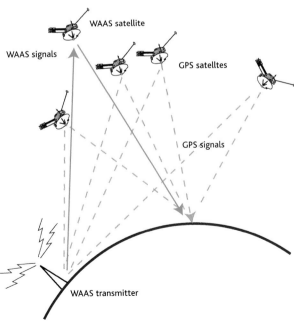

WAAS satellite

WAAS signals

GPS satelltes

GPS signals

WAAS transmitter

Left: **Satellite DGPS (WAAS): the ground station transmits the GPS error to satellites, for the use of GPS receivers within the area of coverage.**

What is satellite DGPS?

Satellite DGPS transmits the error correction information via satellite. The system over the United States is called WAAS (Wide Area Augmentation System). Any WAAS-enabled GPS can also handle the European system. Satellite failure is indicated and erroneous information discarded.

The 95 percent accuracy when using WAAS is 16 feet (5 m). Large intermittent errors (greater than 50 feet (15 m) are unlikely. WAAS-equipped GPS receivers are therefore very accurate, provided they are in the coverage area of a satellite DGPS system; your receiver will be able to tell you if you are getting a usable WAAS signal. However, even with WAAS, GPS is not accurate enough for pilotage in confined waters without other means of fixing your position.

How does GPS measure ground speed?

Ground speed or Speed Over Ground (SOG) is not automatically available but has to be calculated by the receiver. Once position has been calculated by the GPS, it knows where it is. If the receiver is moved, it once again knows where it is. It also knows the time interval between the two positions and because it knows the shape of the earth, it can calculate the distance the receiver has moved. Knowing the time taken to move a specific distance allows the calculation of SOG.

For a boat, SOG is the speed through the water modified by the effect of wind and tide. It is used to calculate how long a trip will take.

The accuracy of SOG depends on the accuracy of position, which is dependent on the accuracy of the contiguous fixes, i.e. position. The default interval between position updates on a GPS receiver is around 4 seconds but this may be increased or decreased by the user (if there are random errors in the fixes, increasing the time interval will increase the accuracy of SOG).

How does GPS measure Course Over Ground?

In the same way that your GPS receiver measures SOG, it can calculate the direction in which the receiver has moved between fixes. This is the Course Over Ground (COG).

Course Over Ground allows for the effect of tide and wind. It indicates where the boat is going, not where it's pointing. Because COG is measured in the same manner as SOG, its accuracy will depend on any transient errors in GPS position. Update rates can be adjusted by the user. Rapid updates give instant response to changes in COG but less stability.

Can a GPS act as a compass?

When stationary, the GPS receiver has no idea where north is. Once it is moving, however, because it knows the COG, it also knows the direction of true north.

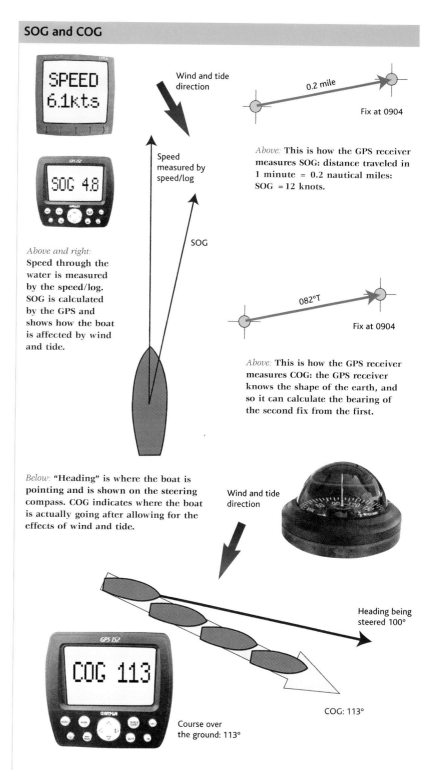

SOG and COG

Wind and tide direction

Speed measured by speed/log

SOG

Above and right:
Speed through the water is measured by the speed/log. SOG is calculated by the GPS and shows how the boat is affected by wind and tide.

0.2 mile

Fix at 0904

Above: **This is how the GPS receiver measures SOG: distance traveled in 1 minute = 0.2 nautical miles: SOG = 12 knots.**

082°T

Fix at 0904

Above: **This is how the GPS receiver measures COG: the GPS receiver knows the shape of the earth, and so it can calculate the bearing of the second fix from the first.**

Below: **"Heading" is where the boat is pointing and is shown on the steering compass. COG indicates where the boat is actually going after allowing for the effects of wind and tide.**

Wind and tide direction

Heading being steered 100°

COG: 113°

COG 113

Course over the ground: 113°

Using GPS for position

Your GPS display gives you your latitude and longitude, but in order to use this for navigation it needs to be plotted on your chart.

Plotting the latitude and longitude on your chart

You can plot latitude and longitude on the chart using your plotter or dividers; a parallel ruler or long straightedge may be used as well. Take care to identify the latitude and longitude accurately on their respective scales or the grid.

Plotting position using a cross-track error grid

A route set up in your GPS displays the distance to the point you have designated as your destination. On a GPS this is called a waypoint. The GPS also indicates the cross-track error (the distance you are off a course on either side). Once you are under way this information can be used from the GPS for quick and easy plotting on the paper chart.

On your chart, draw a series of lines — spaced 1 mile apart — parallel to your direct track; five such lines either side should do. Now draw a series of lines at right angles to the cross-track error, each 5 or 10 miles further from the destination waypoint. You now have a grid of cross-track error and distance to go.

When underway, you can plot by eye the cross-track error and distance to go. This is as accurate as you will need, very quick and can be done even in rough weather.

Plotting position using bearing and distance to a waypoint

You can use data from a waypoint in the GPS to plot your position on your chart. Draw a series of lines radiating from the waypoint. These should be spaced at angles of 10 degrees and labeled with their directions toward the waypoint. Now draw a series of arcs, centered on the waypoint so that each is 5 or 10 miles farther away. Once under way, you can plot your position using bearing and distance to the waypoint by eye.

Below: **A much faster method of plotting can be achieved using a prepared grid of cross-track error and distance to a waypoint. Plotting is done by eye, which is easier in a waterway.**

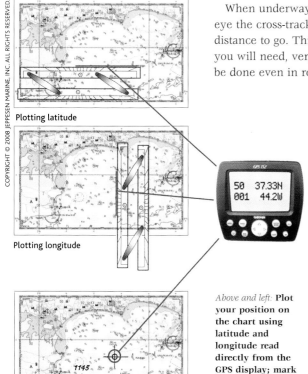

Plotting latitude

Plotting longitude

Above and left: **Plot your position on the chart using latitude and longitude read directly from the GPS display; mark on the chart the time and log reading.**

1145
log 66.6 miles

50 37.33N
001 44.2W

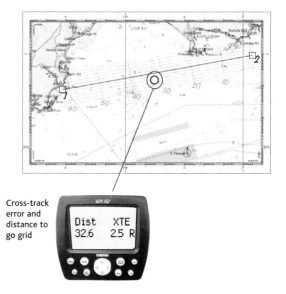

Cross-track error and distance to go grid

Dist   XTE
32.6   2.5 R

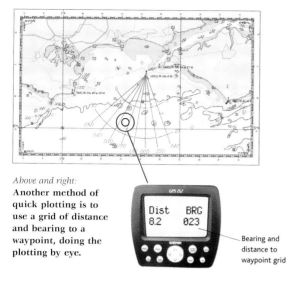

Above and right: **Another method of quick plotting is to use a grid of distance and bearing to a waypoint, doing the plotting by eye.**

Bearing and distance to waypoint grid

Above: **A distance and bearing grid is also very useful if you are tacking toward a waypoint.**

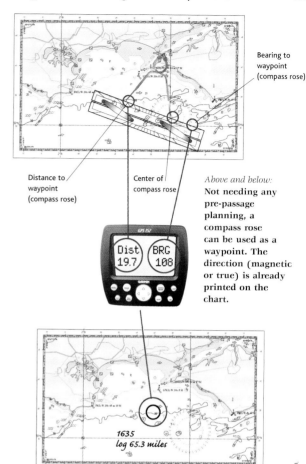

Bearing to waypoint (compass rose)

Distance to waypoint (compass rose)

Center of compass rose

Above and below: **Not needing any pre-passage planning, a compass rose can be used as a waypoint. The direction (magnetic or true) is already printed on the chart.**

1635
log 65.3 miles

Plotting position using a compass rose as a waypoint

You don't necessarily have to go to a waypoint. If you enter the latitude and longitude of the compass rose (printed on the chart) into the GPS as a waypoint, a distance and bearing to the compass rose can be displayed.

This is all the chart preparation you need. Once underway, a straightedge can be used on the compass rose to plot the bearing, and dividers then measure your distance from it. Although you still need to use plotting tools, there's far less chance of error than when plotting latitude and longitude.

Plotting position using a danger as a waypoint

You don't necessarily need to do any actual plotting on the chart to use this method. If the position of the danger is loaded into the GPS it will give a continuous bearing and distance to the danger so that you can keep well clear.

Right: **By placing a waypoint at an unmarked danger and using the GPS in its compass mode, you have a really good indication of where the danger is and can keep well clear of it.**

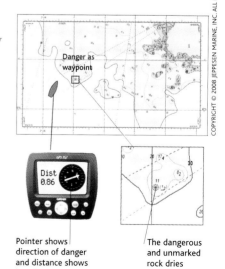

Danger as waypoint

Pointer shows direction of danger and distance shows how far away it is

The dangerous and unmarked rock dries at 1.2m

Traditional chartwork

Traditional chartwork allows the navigator to plot a boat's position and to work out how to get from "A" to "B" without using electronic aids.

Why do you need traditional chartwork?

Loss of electrical power or a satellite system fault can cause your GPS to fail, so it's important to know how to use traditional chartwork. Use the standard symbols on your chartwork, so that anyone else can understand what you have plotted.

What is leeway?

Leeway is the lateral movement of a boat off its course (i.e., sideways drift), caused by the wind. The angle of leeway depends on the strength of the wind, the angle you are sailing to the wind, how well your sails are trimmed and how efficient your keel is; leeway is greater when close-hauled than when the wind is on the beam. It's usual to assume leeway is 0, 5 or 10 degrees.

How do you make a deduced reckoning plot?

Deduced reckoning, or DR (also called "dead reckoning"), is plotting the position of your boat using only the heading steered and the distance traveled through the water. It makes no allowance for tide. However, where there is no tide, it will give you a very good idea of where the boat is.

Make the DR plot from your last known position, e.g., when passing a buoy. On the chart, draw the true course steered. Adjust this by applying leeway — the amount that the wind is blowing you sideways. Sight your boat's wake with a hand-bearing compass and compare it with your boat's heading to give some idea of the amount of leeway. Always draw the wind direction and strength on your chart, too.

Using dividers, mark along this line the distance traveled since the last fix, obtained from the distance log. This is your DR position. It is worth keeping this position plotted at hourly intervals throughout the passage so you have some idea of where you are at all times.

Right: **First plot the average course steered by the helm. Always plot in degrees true. You will then need to apply leeway downwind and plot this on the chart.**

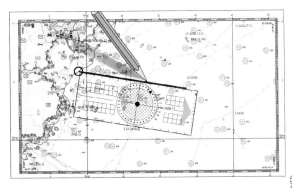

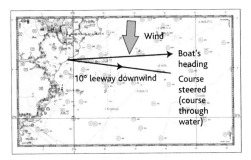

Above: **All boats will be moved sideways through the water by the wind. You will develop your own judgment about how your boat reacts to different conditions.**

Right: **Mark the distance traveled on the course line. (Subtract the log distance at the last position from the log distance to get this.)**

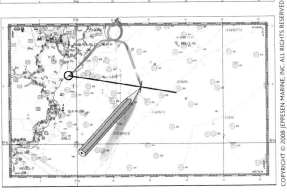

How do you plot your estimated position?

An estimated position (EP) is one that takes into account the course, distance traveled, leeway and the speed and direction (known as the "set") of the tidal stream. EP therefore applies the tidal effect to your DR position to find your most likely position at a given time.

A tidal stream flowing directly against you will reduce your speed by the rate of its own flow. You will be going just as fast through the water, but more slowly over the ground. Conversely, if the stream is traveling in your direction you will move faster, adding its speed to yours.

Note the time and height of high water and the range of the tide at the reference port from the almanac (see page 272). Find the tidal atlas chartlet for the time before or after high water that covers the time of your plot — e.g., the time of your passage may be five hours before high water — and also check if it is a spring or neap tide. Using the appropriate tidal atlas page, use the plotter to transfer the tide's direction to your chart.

Above: **Draw the tidal direction on the chart.**

Above: **Mark off the tidal distance on the direction line. If you've been on this course for only half an hour, you need only half the distance.**

Plot the direction of the tidal vector from your DR position. Mark the distance the tide will have carried the boat during the period of the plot. That's your EP.

How accurate is an EP?

If you draw a circle of error — with a radius of 10 percent of the distance run since the last good fix —

Plotting symbols

This is a universal form of shorthand when plotting a course. Symbols vary slightly in the U.S. from other parts of the world.

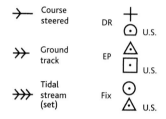

The standard method of drawing and labeling an EP diagram:

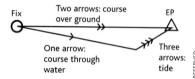

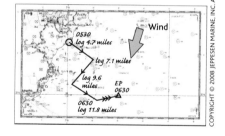

around your EP, you should be somewhere within this circle. In practice you should be closer to the center than the edge of it, but assume that your position within the circle is at the point nearest to any danger, and act accordingly.

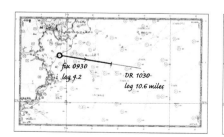

Above: **This position is the DR position at the time the log distance was taken.**

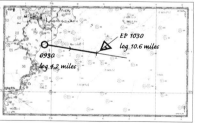

Above: **This gives your EP. This should be pretty close to your GPS fix. If it's not, check that you've plotted both correctly. A large unresolved error may be resolved by taking a new GPS fix.**

Above: **Although you can make an adjustment for the tide at the end of each leg, it's usually better to do so at the time you plot your DR position, as above.**

Planning your destination

In tidal water, you can't just point the boat toward your destination. You must work out the course you need to steer to allow for the tide. This involves doing some chartwork known as "shaping a course." The resulting plot will also allow you to work out how long the trip will take.

How can you find the course to steer?

Draw a line from your position to your destination and beyond. This is your ground track, so mark it with two arrows.

Measure the distance from your position so that you know how long it will take to get to your destination and thus for how long the tide will be affecting you. If your boat sails at 5 knots and the distance is 4.5 miles, then the time taken will be a little less than an hour.

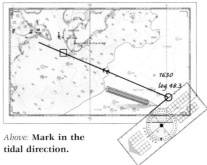

Above: **Mark in the tidal direction.**

Transfer the tidal direction to your position fix. Ensure the direction arrow is in the direction of the tide.

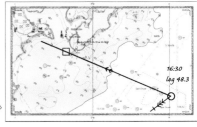

Above: **The ground track and the tide are now in place on the chart.**

Open up your dividers to the water speed of the boat (using the latitude scale on the side of the chart) to get the distance traveled in one hour. Place one leg on the end of the tidal vector and make a mark where the other leg touches the ground track or extended ground track.

Above: **The desired ground track.**

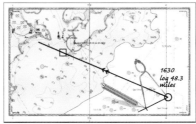

Above: **Mark in the speed of the tide.**

Mark off the distance the tide will move the boat; in this case it's 0.8 miles in the full hour. If the vector triangle was for half an hour, you would use only half the tide (0.4 miles).

You now have the ground track and the tide marked on your chart.

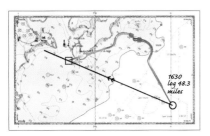

Above: **Measure the distance to the destination.**

If the time you are sailing is one hour before high water at the reference port, use this tidal atlas chartlet. Check if it's a spring or neap tide. Line up your plotter with the tidal arrow.

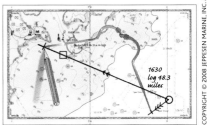

Above: **Draw in the water speed from the end of the tidal vector to where it cuts the extended ground track.**

Don't join the end of the tidal vector to your destination, as this will produce a triangle where each side represents a different time interval.

In this case, the water speed in one hour takes us beyond our destination. This means you will get there in less than one hour.

Lay your plotter along the course to steer line. Align the inner circle with north, and you can then read off the course to steer — either the true course directly against the zero line, or the magnetic course to steer from the error scale: with a magnetic variation of 5 degrees west you read the magnetic course against the west error scale. Add together any compass deviation and the variation, and apply the error at one go, so 5 degrees west (variation) and 3 degrees east (compass deviation) equals 2 degrees west total.

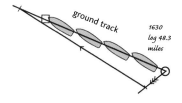

Above: **The boat "crabs" along the ground track while steering the calculated course.**

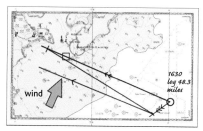

Above: **Apply leeway into wind to get the actual course to steer.**

When will you get to your destination?

Measure the length of the ground speed line in the vector triangle. Here, it's 5.3 knots. The tide is helping you along the way, so your actual speed is more than the boat's water speed of 5 knots.

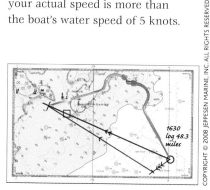

Above: **Measure the ground speed.**

Above: **Course to be steered to destination.**

5° west variation

True course

Magnetic course = 305°M

True course = 300°T

This can then be applied to the true heading of 300 degrees on the plotter to get a compass course to steer of 302 degrees.

The boat departs the fix at 1630, steering the course to steer, but the tide pushes the boat sideways so that it "crabs" along the ground track line.

If you think there's going to be any leeway, you can apply this as well. Remember you need to steer into the wind. If the magnetic course to steer was 305 degrees, the wind was from a south westerly direction, and the leeway was 10 degrees, then you would need to steer 295 degrees (i.e., into the wind).

At the start, you measured the distance to your destination: 4.5 miles. The ground speed is 5.3 knots. A good "guesstimate" is that the journey will take about 50 minutes.

How accurate is this working?

It all depends on the tide being as predicted and the water speed remaining constant. When you're sailing, the boat speed will be dependent on the wind speed and direction.

But accuracy will be surprisingly good, and it's much better using this method than sailing on with no allowance for tide. You just need to fix your position and make adjustments as necessary.

A route for your GPS

Although the GPS always gives your position, it doesn't tell you how to navigate to a position unless you tell it where you want to go. This requires you to load the latitude and longitude of each position (waypoint) on your route into the GPS set. You first need to draw the route on your chart and then transfer the coordinates to the GPS.

What is a waypoint?

A waypoint is a geographical position that you want to go to, defined by its latitude and longitude. There's no standard symbol for a waypoint, but many people use a square with a cross in the middle. A route consists of a series of waypoints to which you wish to navigate in a specific order.

Putting the route on your chart

If possible, use a chart of a scale that allows you to plot the whole route on it. Place your first waypoint close to your departure point, the second at a point where you will have to change direction, and subsequent waypoints all the way to your destination to give a series of straight tracks.

If the forecast conditions are good, you can keep close in, but in stronger tides and winds you may need to position the waypoints clear of overfalls and eddies shown on the chart. If it's a long trip, look at the waypoint positions on a larger scale chart to avoid potential dangers.

Measure the waypoints' latitude and longitude, and the distance and bearing between them.

Loading the waypoints into your GPS

Most GPS sets don't have an alphanumeric keyboard. You have to scroll though the numbers and it's easy to make mistakes, so double-check everything.

Right: **Look at the waypoint positions on a larger scale chart to ensure they're safely positioned. Note their latitude and longitude. Continue checking along the route, all the way to the final waypoint. If necessary, revise the waypoint positions on the small-scale chart.**

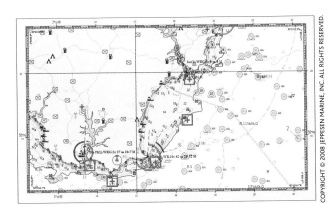

Right: **Join up the waypoints by a series of straight track lines and name the waypoints.**

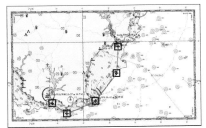

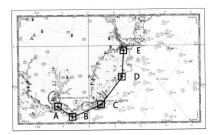

Once the waypoints have been loaded into your GPS as a route, go to the page that allows you to view the distances and tracks between each waypoint. Compare these with the distances and bearings on your chart. Ensure you allow for variation if you have elected that the GPS shows magnetic tracks.

Check that the tracks between waypoints do not pass too close to any hazards. Name the waypoints. If the GPS has no alphanumeric keyboard, just use numbers; it will be easier to enter them.

TIP

Don't put a waypoint too close to a buoy or other seamark: you might hit it! Also, if everyone uses that buoy, you may get too close to other boats.

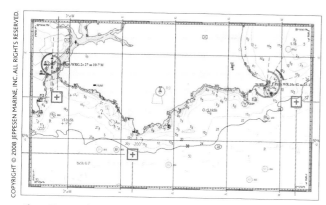

Above: **Ensure the waypoints are positioned safely and measure their latitude and longitude.**

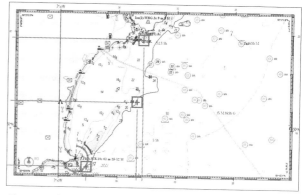

Above: **Continue checking the safe positioning of the waypoints.**

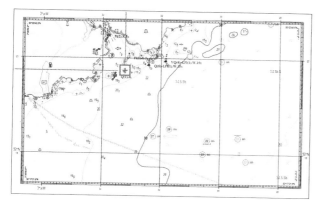

Above: **Check the positioning of the final waypoint.**

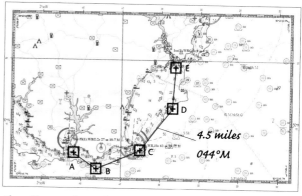

Above: **Measure the tracks and distances.**

Right: Note the latitude and longitude of each waypoint. Measure the tracks and distances of each leg of the route. Apply the magnetic variation to each track to get the magnetic courses.

WAYPOINT			DISTANCE	TRACK (T)	VARIATION	TRACK (M)
A	50° 12.96	003° 45.8		126		
			2.2		+4	130
B	50° 13.62	003° 43.48		069		
			3.9		+4	73
C	50° 13.00	003° 36.54		040		
			4.5		+4	44
D	50° 15.67	003° 34.45		004		
			3.3		+4	008
E	50° 19.72	003° 33.22				

Left: Once you have entered the waypoints into the GPS and constructed the route using them, check the tracks and distances shown for the route to ensure you've made no mistakes. Note that Garmin GPS sets show the running (cumulative) distance for each leg rather than the actual leg distance, which makes extra work for the user, with mistakes more likely.

TIP

Do not string together a series of waypoints directly into your GPS without first checking them against your chart: there may be dangers between them.

Interpreting GPS displays

Your GPS screen will have a number of different pages, which can be displayed as required. You can also set up the GPS to show information in the form you wish. Because there's no standardization, you'll need to read the instruction book to get the most out of your set.

When you switch on the GPS, the first thing you'll probably see is a warning that you should not rely on GPS as your sole aid to navigation. Then it will show a "sky view" while obtaining its first fix. Once it has done this, it will display your present position in latitude and longitude.

The GPS can also show your course over ground (COG) and speed over ground (SOG). While the boat is stationary, these will default to preset values and have no meaning. Depending on the make, tidal heights may be available, together with sun and moon data.

How can you make a route or waypoint active?

There are a number of ways:
- ❂ you can select "GO TO," pick a point to go to, and then press enter;
- ❂ you can choose a waypoint from a list and press enter;
- ❂ you can pick a route from a list and press enter.

Any of these will make the first point or waypoint "active."

What do you see once you have an active waypoint?

Once you have an active waypoint, the GPS can give you the following navigational information:

- ❂ the distance and bearing to the waypoint;
- ❂ the cross-track error from the position when you made the waypoint active, and the waypoint itself;
- ❂ the time it will take from your present position to reach the waypoint at your current SOG.

Some sets will also give the estimated time of arrival (ETA) at the end of the route. It's worth noting that this is only an estimate, as it makes no allowance for future changes of tidal stream or boat speed.

Above: **The initial sky view, showing position and signal strength of the satellites.**

Above: **Once the GPS has fixed its position, the display will show latitude and longitude.**

Left: **Sets will often be able to display astronomical data, such as sunrise and sunset times.**

Above: **Until there's an active waypoint, the only dynamic information is COG and SOG.**

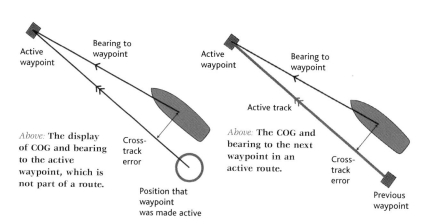

Above: **The display of COG and bearing to the active waypoint, which is not part of a route.**

Above: **The COG and bearing to the next waypoint in an active route.**

Above: **In normal navigation, the highway display gives a very good guide to the next active waypoint.**

What is the compass display?

This pointer shows the bearing of the waypoint. As you turn the boat, the arrow keeps pointing at the waypoint, allowing easy navigation. A line on the rim of the compass and another on the compass rose indicates the COG. Keeping these aligned allows you to make an allowance for the tide.

What is a highway display?

The highway display shows how you lie on the "road" toward the waypoint. This is probably the easiest way to navigate to a waypoint.

How do you get back to a man overboard (MOB) position?

The first thing you need to do is press the MOB key. This puts a waypoint at that position.

You can then use any of the methods indicated for an active waypoint to get back to the MOB position. The easiest under these circumstances is the compass page, as the pointer indicates the direction to go. It will also slow the distance to run.

Be aware that wind and tide may carry the casualty away from the MOB position, as strong winds have a bigger effect than the tide.

Above: **A good way to display the position of an MOB is by using the compass page.**

Above: **A typical receiver displaying the compass page.**

Electronic chart plotters

An electronic chart plotter is a GPS receiver that incorporates electronic charting and gives a graphic display of the chart and your position on it. There is a great temptation to rely on this as your only means of navigation, but you need to be aware of the possible pitfalls.

Above: **Continue entering all the waypoints to the end of your route.**

Chart plotters

These come in different sizes, the screen being measured diagonally. For ease of use, bigger is definitely better, but you need to find room for it. Traditionally, plotters have been fitted at the chart table, but for most efficient use they need to be in the cockpit.

There are a number of providers of electronic charts in different parts of the world. Your chart plotter may use a single make, or occasionally two. The charts (called vector charts) are loaded onto data cards, which are then inserted into the chart plotter.

The charts comprise a number of different layers, and the closer you zoom in, the more detail you see. When you zoom out, the detail is reduced to prevent the chart being cluttered.

These vector charts often contain additional data, such as photographs and marina details.

How can you enter a route?

Entering a route is much easier than on a basic GPS, and is far less prone to error. However, because the screen is far smaller than a paper chart, you need to keep zooming in and out and scrolling the chart. This is why bigger is better.

✪ Using the menu, go to the route page, select "NEW" and give the route a name. As models vary, you'll need to study exactly how to do this on your chart plotter.

✪ Zoom in to your departure point on the chart, move the cursor to the position of the first waypoint and enter it as described in your user manual.

Above: **Check the whole route for safety, zooming in and out as required.**

Above: **A standard electronic chart plotter.**

Above: **Select and name your route.**

✪ Zoom out if necessary, move the cursor to where you want to place the next waypoint and enter once more.

✪ Continue to the end of your route.

✪ Backtrack your route with the cursor, zooming in and out as necessary, to check that the tracks joining the waypoints do not get too close to any hazards. This action is vital.

✪ Save the route as shown in the handbook.

Above: **Move the cursor to the position of your first waypoint and enter.**

Above: **Continue to the second waypoint and enter again.**

Above: **You can also follow the route by using the compass pointer.**

Above: **Once you are ready, make your route active, usually by selecting "GO TO." Once this is done, your screen will indicate course, bearing and distance to the first waypoint, and the time it will take to get there. You can follow the route by steering the boat icon toward the next indicated waypoint.**

If you stop at this point, then — should your chart plotter fail — you'll have no idea where you are or how to get to your destination. Write down the latitude and longitude of each waypoint and the tracks and distances between them. Write these in your logbook so that you can pick up the navigation should the electronics fail.

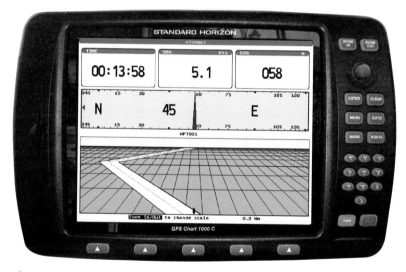

Above: **You can use the highway display and follow the road.**

How do you make the route active?

Using the menu or the "GO TO" facility, put the cursor on the first waypoint and enter. This will normally make the route active, though check your handbook.

How do you follow the route?

Once you are underway, the boat symbol on your chart will follow the boat's current position as it moves across the chart. The screen will also indicate the COG, SOG, distance and bearing to the next waypoint, and probably the time to the waypoint as well. A line from

the front of the boat symbol will indicate your COG. Steer the boat so that the boat symbol travels in the correct direction. Just keep the COG line pointing at the next waypoint. You will also have a compass and a highway display, so you can use these if you prefer.

The accuracy of electronic charts

Electronic charts are based on paper charts produced by national hydrographic offices. As electronic charts are vector charts and not direct scans, it's possible for transcription errors to occur. Additionally, some of the survey data is very old. For these reasons, significant errors can occur on electronic charts.

How old are your electronic charts?

By using the menu on your chart plotter you will be able to access the chart information. This will tell you which "paper" chart it's based on and the date the electronic chart was updated. However, it doesn't tell you the date of the actual survey.

Is there a source diagram?

Some chart authorities show a chart source diagram on their paper charts giving the date and type of survey that various parts of it are based on. Beware: some ostensibly up-to-date paper charts are based on 19th-century surveys! See page 262 for more.

Is the same chart datum used as for paper charts?

All electronic charts are drawn with WGS84 as their datum. This is the default datum of your GPS receiver, unless you have set something else. The paper chart may easily have been drawn to a different, local, datum, such as USGB36. In the course of digitizing the electronic chart, the datum will have been converted to WGS84. The conversion is different for every portion of the chart and could have errors.

Is it accurate enough?

The modern electronic chart plotter is an excellent tool, but it is only one aid to navigation. It is too easy to come to rely on your chart plotter and forget about all the other navigation tools at your disposal.

Accuracy can be checked using the following:

- checking your position as you pass buoys or other markers;
- comparing your radar and chart plotter;
- looking at the land and asking the question: "Does it look right?"

Can your electronic charts be updated?

Chart corrections are issued for paper charts as required. They are incorporated into electronic charts, but the collective corrections are issued only infrequently. Users cannot correct electronic charts themselves but have to buy updated electronic charts when available. Options vary according to the make, but usually a discount is offered for the updated chart cartridge. Updates

Above: **Using the menu, you can find the source data.**

Above: **This tells us that the data is based on UKHO chart 2450 and that this electronic version was updated on November 2, 2006.**

Chart error

A electronic chart route was constructed to avoid the island in the entrance of this bay on the coast of Spain. These three charts have the same latitude and longitude grid.

A is an older electronic chart showing the track followed by a yacht approaching the anchorage.

B is a modern electronic chart of a different make showing the track of this yacht running over the island and and where the yacht is anchored.

C shows another electronic chart. The position of the yacht is shown.

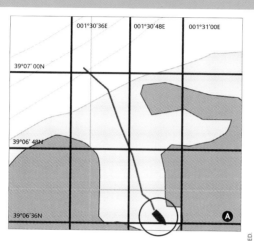

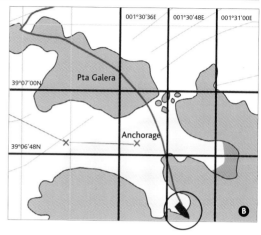

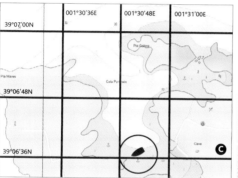

It is evident that the accuracy of electronic charts varies and that complete reliance on electronic charts may be entirely misplaced.

The green areas show the radar picture overlaid on top of the electronic chart. The radar "echo" of this coast should line up with the coast on the chart, but here it doesn't, showing that either the radar or the chart is in error.

Below: If you have radar overlay on your chart plotter, the radar return shows the true position of land. In this case the error was caused not by the charting, but by the radar having been incorrectly set up and compass deviation not being rectified.

normally incorporate changes only for areas used extensively by merchant vessels, such as harbors and their approaches.

Some rivers and entrances change over short periods. Harbor authorities make amendments to buoyage as necessary but these seldom find their way into any chart corrections. There's often a note to this effect on the chart or in the pilot guide.

Radar

Radar is an electronic device that transmits pulses of microwave energy from a rotating scanner. If any of these pulses bounce off a solid object, they are depicted on the radar's display, showing the object's position. Radar can thus help you avoid collisions and pilot the boat.

How does radar measure distance and bearing?

The transmitted pulse travels at the speed of light, and the time it takes for the pulse to travel to the target and back to the scanner is used to measure the distance, or "range."

The radar set knows which way the scanner is pointing when the returning pulse arrives. This gives the direction relative to the bows of the boat. If the radar set receives the boat's heading from other instruments, direction can be presented in degrees true or magnetic if desired.

How far can radar see?

Radar can't see round corners or "over the horizon." The radar horizon for a scanner mounted on the mast 18 feet (4 m) up is only 4.5 miles (7.2 km). This means that a small object on the surface can be seen at a maximum range of 4.5 miles, though the radar beam can travel much further and "see" objects, such as large ships and cliffs, visible above the horizon.

The strength of the returning pulses (echoes) depends on the size of the object (target), the target's reflective properties and the distance to it. A more powerful radar can see smaller targets as well as those further away. A cliff will give a better return than a gently sloping shore.

Radar is also affected by the heel of the boat. The radar beam will lift clear of the sea's surface at about 12 to 15 degrees, so a sailing boat may have to be depowered from time to time when beating to windward to give accurate information.

Above: **The screen of a radar set. Radar sets are available for all sizes of vessel from small boats to the largest ships. Their main function is to detect land or other vessels. However, it is up to you to make the correct action to avoid collisions.**

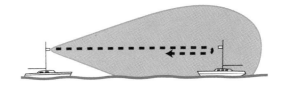

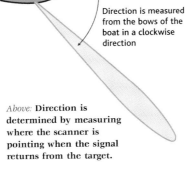

Direction is measured from the bows of the boat in a clockwise direction

Above: **Direction is determined by measuring where the scanner is pointing when the signal returns from the target.**

Left: **Radar range is measured by timing the pulse on its journey to a target and back again. The radar converts this into range (distance).**

Below: **The radar beam curves just slightly around the earth's surface, so that its horizon is just a little beyond yours. Objects projecting above the horizon can be seen (as they can by eye) up to 24 or 36 miles (38 or 58 km) away depending on the radar's power and the height of the object above sea level.**

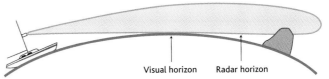

Visual horizon   Radar horizon

Target projects upward into radar beam beyond horizon

How do you use radar?

Radar needs practice and training to use properly. It's a legal requirement that if radar is fitted and serviceable, the user must have the knowledge to use it for the purposes of collision avoidance. It is highly recommended that you attend a proper course run by organizations with radar expertise.

Collision avoidance using radar

If a target on the radar screen is on a constant bearing and getting closer, action to avoid a collision is required. In order to be fully aware of what is happening and to determine the action required, you will need to carry out a plot on a radar plotting sheet, which requires skill and practice.

More expensive radar sets have a Mini Automatic Radar Plotting Aid (MARPA), which can give the target's speed, course and closest point of approach (CPA) on the screen and alerts the user to potential conflicts. However, this still needs skill and practice to interpret.

Radar in fog

If a vessel is detected only by radar, the normal collision regulations are superseded by Rule 19 of the *Regulations for the Prevention of Collisions at Sea* (Colregs), i.e., there is no "stand-on vessel" and *all* vessels must be prepared to give way.

Navigation and pilotage using radar

Radar sees the land exactly where it is, rather than where the chart says it should be. For this reason, it is an excellent aid to navigation and pilotage, especially when the visibility is poor or at night, when it would be unsafe to use GPS on its own.

Radar target on a constant bearing

Above: **A target on a constant bearing and getting closer is on a collision course.**

Below: **You will get a better reading against steep cliffs than an open shore.**

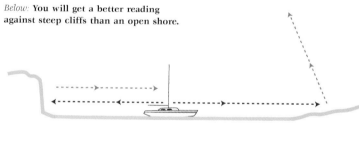

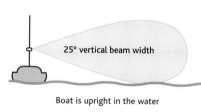

25° vertical beam width

Boat is upright in the water

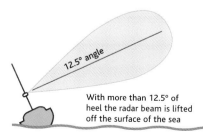

12.5° angle

With more than 12.5° of heel the radar beam is lifted off the surface of the sea

Left: **The effect of heel on a radar beam is to lift it well over the surface of the sea at about 12 to 15 degrees, so a sailing boat may have to be depowered when beating to windward.**

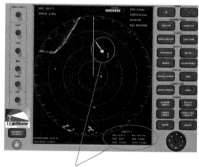

MARPA   Target 1, bearing 061 T, Range 0.87nm. Its course is 000, speed 5.0 knots, CPA is 0.5 miles and time to CPA 11.0 minute

Above: **Some radar sets have MARPA, where targets can be selected and information on their course, speed and how close they will approach is calculated by the radar. This information is sometimes incorrect due to inaccuracies, in heading data especially, so common sense is needed.**

Pilotage

Pilotage is the method of visually positioning the boat using landmarks and seamarks. It's normally associated with leaving and entering harbor, but in fact any navigation relying on visual cues rather than plotting your position is pilotage.

Following a buoyed channel

Probably the easiest form of pilotage is to follow a narrow channel that has frequent and regularly placed buoys. You need to stay on the starboard side of the channel, keeping the starboard buoys on your starboard side when traveling in the direction of buoyage. In a curving channel, take curving tracks between buoys; proceeding in a straight line between them could cause you to run aground. Sometimes the channel markers are right on the edge of the channel and there may be insufficient depth if you approach them too closely at low water.

Keeping on a transit

If there's an official marked transit, then keeping on that transit will ensure you keep clear of hazards, provided there's sufficient depth of water. If the transit is unfamiliar to you, make sure you check its bearing once you are on it, so that you know you have picked up the correct marks. Confirm from the chart or pilot book that the transit is still viable.

You can often choose a couple of objects from the chart, which if you keep visually aligned, will allow safe passage.

Going to a buoy

Take care in tidal water when proceeding directly to a buoy or other seamark/landmark. If you just keep the bows pointing at the buoy, you can be swept sideways by the tide and end up approaching the buoy directly into the tide, and you may end up in shallow water if you are pushed further downtide. Make an allowance for the tide, either by estimation or working out a course to steer. If there's a feature in the background, keep it aligned and you'll go straight to the buoy.

Using clearing bearings

If there's no seamark to keep you clear of a hazard, but there's some other feature you can take a bearing on, you can use a clearing bearing (bearings beyond which would take you into danger). Mark the clearing bearing on the chart, and then by frequently checking your bearing from the chosen object using a hand-bearing compass you can ensure that you stay within the safe range of bearings. This is easier than trying to stay exactly on one bearing and particularly useful if you are tacking.

Using depth

Allowing for the tide, depth from a calibrated depth sounder can help establish your position during pilotage. For instance you could stay on a transit until you reach the required depth, prior to altering course.

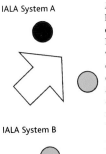

IALA System A

IALA System B

Left: **Ensure you know the direction of buoyage by looking for the "general direction of buoyage" arrow on the chart you are using. By convention, this is into a harbor or upriver. So, in IALA A, when entering you keep green buoys to starboard and when leaving you keep red buoys to starboard. The reverse is true for IALA B.**

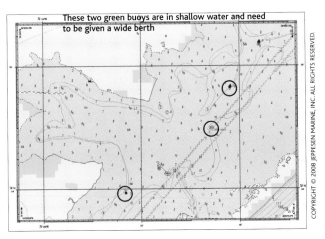

These two green buoys are in shallow water and need to be given a wide berth

Left: **Note that channel markers may sometimes be in shallow water, the channel may not be marked equally on each side, and red and green buoys may not be opposite each other.**

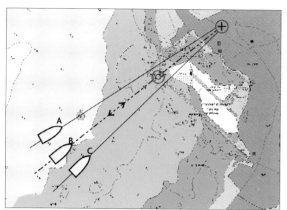

Transit to be followed

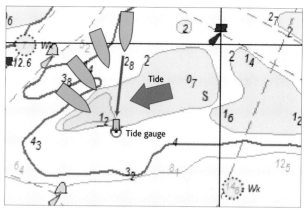

Above: If you keep pointing the boat at an object, such as a buoy that indicates danger when there's a cross-tide, you stand a good chance of hitting the hazard. As the tide pushes you sideways, with the bows pointing at the buoy, you'll end up approaching the buoy from down-tide, which in this case puts you aground!

A Right of transit – turn to port

Above and left: There may be transits marked on your chart. If not, you can often make up your own. In both cases, the principle of use is the same — keep the marks in line and you'll be in safe water.

B On the transit

C Left of transit – turn to starboard

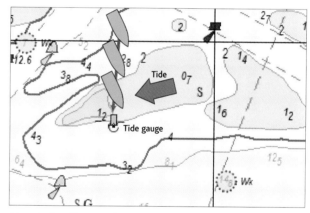

Above: Make allowance for the tide. This ensures you will approach the buoy on your desired course. You can calculate the course to steer, make an estimate, or maintain the correct COG on your GPS.

Initial transit alignment

Left and below: By sighting a feature in the background and keeping it aligned with the buoy as you approach it, you will ensure that you don't drift downtide. Remember to alter course as you near the buoy or you will hit it.

The buoy has moved to starboard – turn to starboard

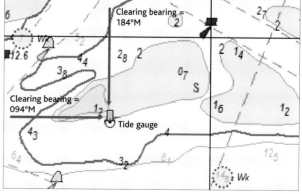

Above: To avoid running aground on the sand bank, use clearing bearings.

The buoy has moved to port – turn to port

A pilotage plan

Pilotage can be demanding in some places. Merchant vessels are required to use specialized pilots in many areas and they have to make a plan for each trip. Pilotage can be very much simplified if you have a good plan but it needs to be carefully prepared to avoid mistakes.

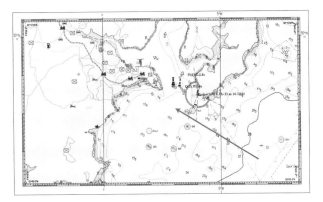

Above: **The small-scale chart is fine for the approach, but you will need a larger scale chart for the actual pilotage.**

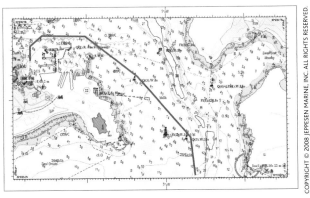

A pilotage plan

Unless you are familiar with a particular area, you need to prepare a pilotage plan. This may consist of a sketch plan, notes or a combination of both.

Here is a pilotage plan into a yacht haven, to show how a pilotage plan could be constructed. You'll need to consider the draft of your boat, and if you're short of crew, you'll need to choose the easiest route. Here are some items to note:

⊙ You will need to check your almanac, harbor masters' notices or some other source to find out if there are any special rules to follow. You may have to keep to a "small craft channel," or there may be speed limits.

Above: **Choose your route passing close to things you'll recognize. If your draft allows, you don't have to keep to the main channel, and that helps keep clear of the bigger ships.**

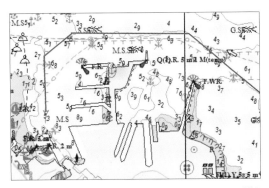

Above: **Have a good look and see if depth contours will be helpful. By watching the depth sounder, you can see that as soon as you cross the 5 m contour (ensuring that you've crossed the deeper water first) you can turn west. The next turn onto south-west is signalled as you cross the 5 m contour again with the water getting deeper. Turn south when you once more cross the 5 m contour into shallower water.**

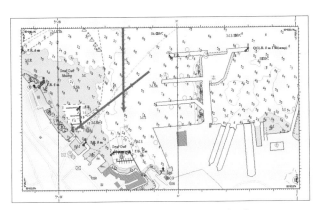

Above: **The final approach is made on a transit that keeps you in the dredged channel. You will need to identify this before you get to it. The pilot book often shows photographs of the transit marks that can help you identify them. Check the bearing of the transit with your hand-bearing compass to ensure you have identified it correctly.**

✪ You may find there's a signal station, which shows "traffic lights." The almanac explains what the signals mean, though sometimes small craft don't have to comply with them. When the emergency lights are showing, all movements are banned.

✪ Mostly leisure yachts don't need to call harbor authorities, but it's always good practice to listen on their channel so that you know what big ships are doing.

Who does the piloting?

Ideally the pilot should have no other job, so let someone else steer the boat. Make sure you let the helmsman know what you want them to do, that they know what course to steer and that they have identified any mark you want them to steer toward.

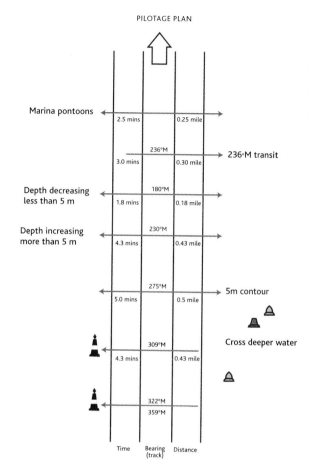

PILOTAGE PLAN

Marina pontoons — 2.5 mins | 0.25 mile

236°M — 3.0 mins | 0.30 mile → 236°M transit

Depth decreasing less than 5 m — 180°M — 1.8 mins | 0.18 mile

Depth increasing more than 5 m — 230°M — 4.3 mins | 0.43 mile

275°M — 5.0 mins | 0.5 mile → 5m contour

309°M — 4.3 mins | 0.43 mile → Cross deeper water

322°M
359°M

Time | Bearing (track) | Distance

Left: **You may prefer to use a strip map for your pilotage plan, which breaks up the passage into sections outlining its main features. Tick off each mark as you pass it.**

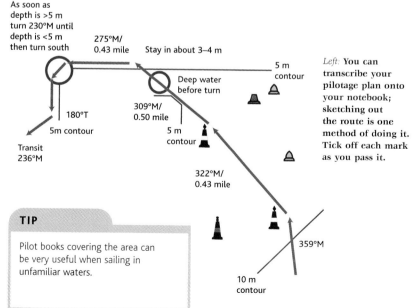

As soon as depth is >5 m turn 230°M until depth is <5 m then turn south

275°M/ 0.43 mile — Stay in about 3–4 m

Deep water before turn

309°M/ 0.50 mile

180°T

5m contour

Transit 236°M

5 m contour

5 m contour

322°M/ 0.43 mile

359°M

10 m contour

Left: **You can transcribe your pilotage plan onto your notebook; sketching out the route is one method of doing it. Tick off each mark as you pass it.**

TIP

Pilot books covering the area can be very useful when sailing in unfamiliar waters.

What tools do you need?

A hand-bearing compass, the boat's steering compass, depth sounder, and log (to assess distance run) are essential. Also useful are:

✪ Stopwatch — an excellent back up for the distance run.

✪ Binoculars — very useful for identifying marks and transits.

✪ GPS COG — exceptionally useful when allowing for the tide, as it helps you to maintain the desired track if the tide is setting you sideways.

Passage planning

Passage planning is the process of deciding when and how to sail to your destination. It includes tidal planning, consideration of the weather, the capabilities of your crew and provisioning of the boat.

The route

Look at the entire passage on a small-scale chart and draw up your planned route (see page 290).

Consider the following:

✪ Are there any tidal constraints at departure, destination or en route?

✪ Which route makes best use of tidal streams and available navigation aids?

✪ Are there any shipping lanes and Traffic Separation Schemes that you will need to cross at right angles?

✪ What are the times of sunrise and sunset? (This could influence departure or arrival times because of difficulty of pilotage and recognising lights at long range.)

✪ What soundings might give you a progress check?

Make a draft outline plan, noting distance and likely passage time. You are now in a position to consider things in more detail.

Tides and tidal streams

Note the times and heights of high and low water at your departure and destination points. Note also the time of high water and range at the reference point for the tidal atlas and tidal diamonds if used. Identify limiting depths and fast streams causing tidal gates, amending your plan as necessary. Identify any lights, land and seamarks that will be useful for navigation. It may be beneficial to alter your route slightly to make better use of any aids.

Your detailed plan

Now you need to make your detailed plan. Work out timings that best allow for tidal gates, depth of water at critical points, availability of daylight or moonlight and so forth. Using the estimated passage time, work out your estimated time of arrival and the time at which you will reach any critical points along the way. You may have to rework your departure time to make the plan work, or you may need to anchor on the way if you can't make critical points on time.

Left: **Choose your route and identify ports of refuge and any other useful details.**

Below: **Examine your tidal atlas to obtain the times of favorable tidal flow.**

Tide starts Eastwards HW Dover +3½
Tide starts Westwards HW Dover -2½

On 21st June HW Dover is 0116, 1344 and 0204 on 22nd
Eastgoing tide 0445 until 1115 and 1645 until 2230

Entry into Yealm not between 1310 and 1530 for 0.5m clearance
or   1200 and 1610 for 1.0m clearance

Average tide is 0.6 knots favorable or 0.6 knots against
Trip time 6.30 with tide or 7.40 against tide

Two of the possible choices:
Depart Falmouth 0445 Arrive Yealm 1115 on falling tide (with tide)
or
Depart Falmouth 0830 Arrive Yealm 1610 on rising tide (against tide)

DEPARTURE DATE 21ST JUNE

PLYMOUTH			YEALM ENTRANCE			DOVER	
HW	0815	4.9m	HW	0804	4.7m	HW	0116
LW	1415	1.4m	LW	1420	1.3m	HW	1344
HW	2023	5.1m	HW	2029	5.0m	HW	0204
Range		3.6					
Sp range		4.7					
Np range		2.2					
Tide halfway between springs and neaps							

Left: **Look at your tide tables and note all the relevant tidal times and heights for the day of intended departure.**

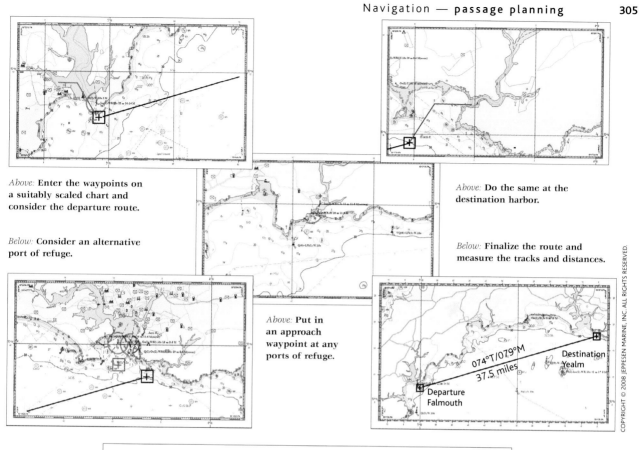

Above: **Enter the waypoints on a suitably scaled chart and consider the departure route.**

Below: **Consider an alternative port of refuge.**

Above: **Do the same at the destination harbor.**

Below: **Finalize the route and measure the tracks and distances.**

Above: **Put in an approach waypoint at any ports of refuge.**

Left: **Prepare a table of waypoints, tracks and distances ready for entry into your GPS.**

PASSAGE PLAN FALMOUTH — YEALM							
WAYPOINT	LONGITUDE	LATITUDE	TRACK True	TRACK Magnetic	DISTANCE	SPEED Knots	TIME (no tide)
WP1	50° 01.20W	005° 01.20W					
			74	79	37.5	6	0615
WP2	004° 06.3W	004° 6.3W					

How will the weather affect the route?
You will need to consider how wind direction and strength on the day, especially if there's a strong "wind over tide," will affect the route, and you may need to consider under what conditions the trip might be unwise. You also need to consider the availability of suitable ports of refuge should conditions deteriorate once you are on your way.

Mark on your chart areas of Coastguard coverage and note any VHF radio channels you may need to use. List all your waypoints, tracks and distances, ready to load into your GPS.

Make your pilotage plans
Make pilotage plans for your departure, destination and any ports you may need to use on the way (see page 300).

You will need to plan the food required, when and how it will be prepared (especially if rough conditions are forecast) and when mealtimes are to be scheduled.

On the planned day of departure, check the weather forecast for the whole period of the trip and decide if the weather is suitable to go ahead.

Navigation on passage

Once you set off, you will need to navigate the boat. That means working out courses to steer, monitoring your position and making tactical decisions to get to your destination most efficiently. The skipper will need to keep an eye on the weather and ensure the well-being of the crew.

If you know the time you are setting out the first three steps can be done before you set out or you can do them at the first waypoint.

First use the atlas to establish the time of high water at the reference port for the day of the passage. Put the times applicable to each diagram on the atlas. Mark up your track on your passage chart.

Prepare your passage by drawing in the tidal vectors and planning your course to steer (see pages 288–89). Using the tidal offset for each hour, sketch in the expected ground track. If you are sure of the arrival time at the first waypoint this can be done before you go.

You now have the chart ready to plot your passage.

Using the chart

As well as your planned route, you should plot your boat's actual position at regular intervals. Estimated positions can also be plotted to check your position fixes — or used in their place if there's an equipment failure. In tidal waters you will use the chart for working out courses to steer.

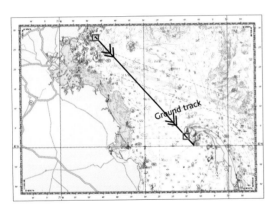

Above: **Mark up your track on your passage chart.**

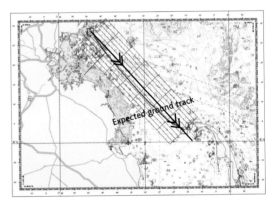

Above: **Using the tidal offset for each hour, sketch in the expected ground track. If you are sure of your arrival time at the first waypoint, this can be done before departure.**

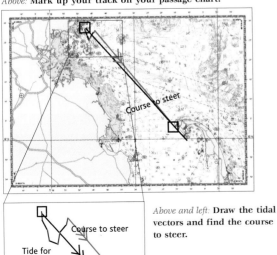

Above and left: **Draw the tidal vectors and find the course to steer.**

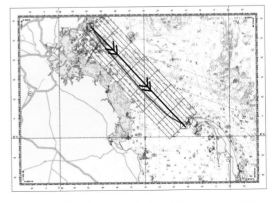

Above: **The chart is now ready for plotting your passage.**

How often should you plot your position?

Never leave too long an interval between plotting fixes. Regular plotting means that, in the event of equipment failure, you won't be too far from your last known position when you start your traditional plotting. On a sailing boat, hourly position fixes are appropriate.

People often plot their position every hour on the hour. This is not necessarily the best policy, as the change of the tidal vector rarely occurs on the hour. So if HW is at 10:35, it would be better to plot every hour at 35 minutes past the hour. You then use the tidal vector for the next full hour.

What course should you steer in a cross-tide?

If there's a cross-tide, it's much more efficient at sailing boat speeds to steer a course allowing for the total tide on that leg. This means you will always be making best use of the tide. If you try to keep exactly on track, you'll always be fighting the tide, and on a 60-mile open-water trip that means taking well over an hour longer.

If you are tacking, make a note of the time and your log reading every time you tack. Plot your position every hour. If you have to start working out your estimated position, put in the DR tracks each time you tack, but you need to put the tide in only every hour to work out your position (EP).

When thinking about altering course, provided there's no large error building up, leave things alone until you're halfway, then alter course to get to your destination. Do the same at the next halfway

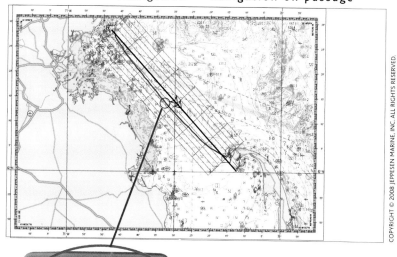

Above: **Plotting your position using the GPS and the quick plotting grid.**

Right: **In this case, the GPS fix would seem to be in error in comparison with the EP. However, it would be worthwhile checking the compass — and the helm — to ensure the correct course has been steered.**
This can be done against the hand-bearing compass while still on course. The accuracy of the helmsman's steering can also be checked.

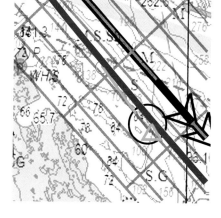

point (three-quarters of the total) and so on. For a long cross-tide leg, estimate your ground track as you start. Provided you stay close to this, don't alter course.

The logbook

The logbook (ship's log) is the document you use to record the planned route, weather forecasts and observations, navigational information and position fixes. From the information documented there, it will be possible to reconstruct

all details of the actual passage. In larger vessels it's a legal requirement to keep an accurate log.

TIP

If you are estimating your position, don't let yourself be swept downtide. Aim uptide and it will be easier to get to your destination. Mark up your track on your passage chart.

Navigation at night

The lights on buoys and lighthouses only show for short, intermittent periods which means you need to plan your night sailing carefully in advance.

What's the best way to carry out pilotage at night?

First, you need to make a clear plan that can be easily read in dim light. The plan needs to detail the tracks, distances and times of each leg and, importantly, the characteristics of the lights.

✪ Use the GPS to give the bearing to the next waypoint and, most useful of all, the COG, which can then be compared with the track required.

✪ Use your autopilot, if you have one, as this will help you hold an accurate course.

✪ Identify the lights of seamarks, using your hand-bearing compass to establish where you need to look for them.

✪ When you ask the helm to steer for a light, ensure he is looking at the correct mark. Identify it yourself, then point at it over the helm's shoulder and, as it flashes, call out each flash.

✪ Once you are established on a leg, start looking for the next light. If it's a buoy it's unlikely you'll be able to see it from more than 2 miles (that's 20 minutes at 6 knots), so you've plenty of time.

✪ Remember to mark each light off on your plan as you pass it, and to restart your stopwatch as well.

Left: As it gets dark, lights may be all you can see at night. Your pilotage plan must be easy to read at night and include the characteristics of the lights you intend to use.

Right: **This pilotage plan breaks up the passage into sections outlining its main features. Lights are the most important features so note down how often they flash. Tick off each mark as you pass it.**

Below: **The GPS COG is an important aid for night pilotage.**

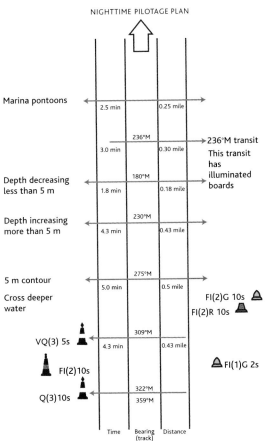

NIGHTTIME PILOTAGE PLAN

	Time	Bearing (track)	Distance	
Marina pontoons	2.5 min		0.25 mile	
		236°M		→ 236°M transit
	3.0 min		0.30 mile	This transit has illuminated boards
		180°M		
Depth decreasing less than 5 m	1.8 min		0.18 mile	
		230°M		
Depth increasing more than 5 m	4.3 min		0.43 mile	
		275°M		
5 m contour	5.0 min		0.5 mile	Fl(2)G 10s
Cross deeper water				Fl(2)R 10s
		309°M		
VQ(3) 5s	4.3 min		0.43 mile	
				Fl(1)G 2s
Fl(2)10s				
Q(3)10s		322°M		
		359°M		

Right: **Against a well-lit shoreline, your light may be difficult to pick out. Prepare for this by measuring the direction in which you will look for your light from a position prior to the turning point.**

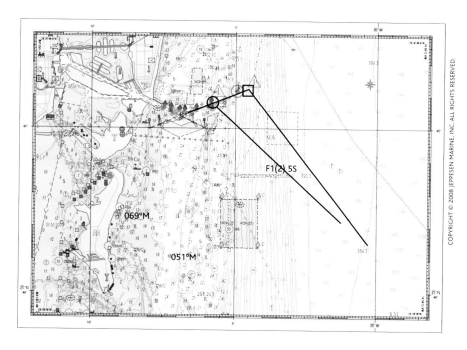

✪ If you don't see a light around the time you expect to, look either side for it, as after 20 minutes you would be 60 m "off track" for each degree of heading error. Don't get fixated with looking dead ahead.

How do you find a light among all the shore lights?

Where the background for the light is a shoreline with lots of lights, it can be very difficult to pick out marine lights, which may be flashing at only 15-second intervals. Mark up your chart with a position from which you expect to be looking for the light and measure the light's bearing. From this position, align your hand-bearing compass on the bearing and your light will probably be obvious. Pick something in the background close to your light and you'll know where to look as you approach your turning point.

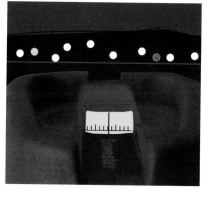

Left: **Look on the bearing you have measured and it will be easier to identify your light.**

Remember to look out

It is very easy to concentrate so much on your pilotage that you forget about other boats around you. Keep a good 360-degree lookout, especially for the relatively dim lights found on small craft.

TIP

Night vision takes about 30 minutes to become fully established, but after 10 minutes it will be quite good. Vision can be instantly ruined by any bright light. Keep cabin and cockpit lighting to the absolute minimum. Traditionally, red light is used to maintain your night vision, but dim green light is better.

Weather

6

The effect of weather

Weather affects the sailor in a number of different ways, but probably the most significant of these occur with wind and visibility. Temperature contributes to our enjoyment, as does the lack of rain.

What causes weather?

The weather itself is caused by solar heating of the earth's surface. Because the earth is a sphere, the amount of solar energy falling on its surface varies from not a lot at the poles to a great deal more at the equator. This means the equatorial regions are much warmer than the poles. The heated regions cause air in contact with the surface to heat up, reducing its density so that it tends to rise, leading to reduced surface pressure. At the poles, the heavier cold air tends to sink, causing raised surface pressure.

What causes clouds?

When air rises, it cools. As it cools, its ability to hold moisture decreases so that its "relative humidity" rises. When it reaches 100 percent and the air can hold no more "invisible" moisture, cloud forms.

Air may rise because it's heated, but also because it's forced to rise by hills, mountains and weather fronts.

Why do we have seasons?

The system is complicated by the tilt of the earth's axis of rotation, which moves the region of maximum solar heating between the tropics of Cancer and Capricorn. This means that the region of low equatorial pressure moves seasonally between the two tropics, giving us the summer and winter seasons.

What causes wind?

Wind is caused by air moving from high pressure to low pressure. The air rising in the low pressure area needs to be replaced, and this comes from the sinking air in the region of high pressure. The spin of the earth causes wind to flow in a spiral pattern due to a phenomenon called geostrophic force. Without this, air would flow directly from the poles to the equator, evening out the pressure so that there would be no wind. The earth's rotation causes wind to be deflected to the right in the northern hemisphere and to the left in the southern as it tries to flow from high to low pressure.

The global wind pattern

The global pattern is more complex than the simple equatorial and polar

Below: **Cells of sinking and rising air cause air to want to flow from high pressure to low pressure. The earth's spin causes the moving air (wind) to be deflected to the right in the northern hemisphere and to the left in the southern.**

Above: **Over a coastline, warm air from the land can react with cooler air over the sea. This cools down the warm air and brings it toward the dew point, where it condenses, creating fog.**

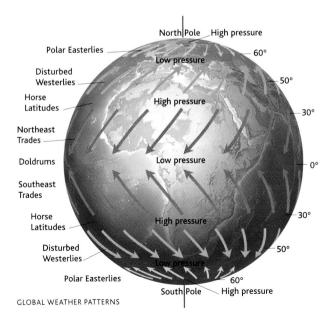

North Pole — High pressure
60°
Polar Easterlies
Low pressure
50°
Disturbed Westerlies
30°
Horse Latitudes
High pressure
Northeast Trades
Doldrums
Low pressure
0°
Southeast Trades
Horse Latitudes
High pressure
30°
Disturbed Westerlies
50°
Low pressure
Polar Easterlies
60°
South Pole — High pressure

GLOBAL WEATHER PATTERNS

system, since there is another circulation between the two. This gives a band of high pressure at around 40 degrees north and south and a band of low pressure at around 60 degrees north and south.

As the sun moves from the southern hemisphere to the north, the bands get compressed in the northern hemisphere and stretched in the southern. The reverse happens as the sun moves southward. This gives seasonal variation in the pressure system and in the prevailing winds.

What causes poor visibility?

Visibility is reduced by water droplets or dust in the atmosphere. At the surface of the earth, if the air has been cooled sufficiently by contact with the sea to give a relative humidity of 100 percent, we have fog (cloud touching the surface) or rain. If the wind is blowing from a dusty surface such as a region of desert, visibility can be reduced significantly.

Right: **The difference in surface temperature causes regions of rising air at the equator and sinking air at the poles. There is also another cell of circulation between the two.**

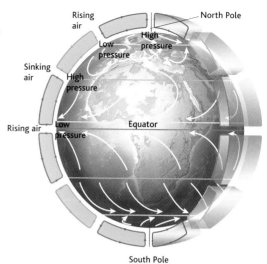

Right: **The tilt of the earth's axis causes seasonal variations, so that in the northern summer the circulation cells are squashed up toward the poles. The opposite happens in the northern winter (southern summer).**

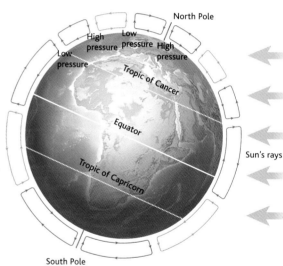

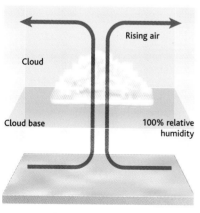

Left: **If the air is moist enough, rising air will cause clouds to form.**

SURFACE OF SEA OR LAND

Right: **Much more heat per square foot of surface reaches the equatorial regions than the polar regions, hence the difference in surface temperature.**

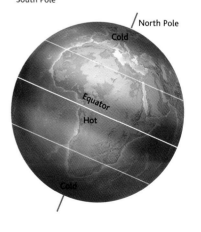

Where does weather come from?

The body of air sitting over a continent or an ocean takes on the characteristics of that area, being either wet or dry, hot or cold, and is known as air mass. As it moves away from its source area, it maintains its original characteristics and is the catalyst of our changing weather.

Heating of the air

A hot surface will heat the lower layers of the air and this heat will be carried upward to higher altitudes. The longer the air is in contact with the hot surface, the hotter it will get. Similarly, air in contact with a cold surface will be cooled.

The effect of moisture

There is a large amount of evaporation from the sea, and this moisture is transferred to the air. The higher the temperature, the higher the rate of evaporation. Unless the air is saturated (relative humidity of 100 percent) this moisture will be invisible.

If the air mass is in contact with warm sea for a long time, it will hold a lot of moisture. Conversely, where the surface is very dry, the air mass will become very dry too.

The effect of a moving air mass

As an air mass moves, its surface characteristics will be modified by the changing character of the surface. It will be cooled if the surface is cooler; it will become drier if the surface is dry.

What are the different types of air mass?

Let's look at one particular geographic area as an example. Northwest Europe encompasses all types of air mass.

Tropical maritime: Air in contact with the warm sea becomes warmed and very moist.

Polar maritime: Air in contact with the cool sea is cooled and evaporation is reduced, as is the air's ability to hold moisture. The air is cool and damp.

Arctic maritime: The air is very cold with much reduced ability to pick up and hold water.

Polar continental: The air is very cold from contact with the bitterly cold land and it is also very dry.

Tropical continental: The hot land heats the air, which also becomes hot. There is no water to evaporate, so the air is very dry.

Seasonal changes

The land mass of Eastern Europe and Russia is the source of polar continental air in the winter and tropical continental air in the summer. The same is true of the northern U.S. and Canada.

The passage of the sun northward moves the area of maximum heating northward also, with both the land and sea being heated. The rise in temperature lags behind the position of the sun by a couple of weeks over land, but much longer over the sea.

Outside the tropics, the sea will still be cool in early summer and won't reach its maximum

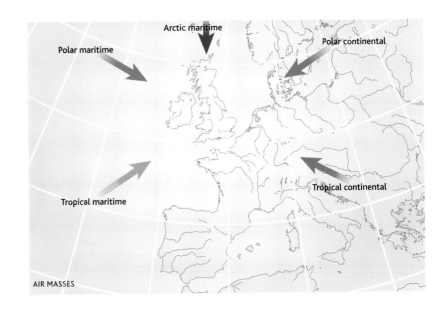

Right: **Air masses take on the characteristics of the "source" area, which determines the initial temperature and water content of the air mass.**

Polar maritime

Arctic maritime

Polar continental

Tropical maritime

Tropical continental

AIR MASSES

temperature until the end of summer, but the land heats up and cools down much more rapidly. The differential between land and sea temperatures has a major effect on weather. The characteristics of the air, either side of the boundary between two adjacent air masses, are different. This sudden change creates much of the weather in temperate latitudes.

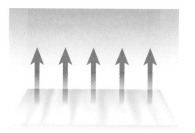

Above: **Evaporation of water from the warm sea into warm air results in a high moisture content of the air.**

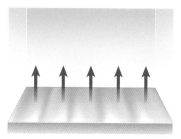

Above: **Evaporation from a cold sea into cold air is much less, so the water content of the air will be less.**

Below: **Coastal sailors feel the effect of the difference between land and sea temperatures. When a cold airstream travels over warmer sea or land it picks up heat and may form clouds and produce gusty weather. When a warm airstream travels over colder land or sea it quickly cools and stops rising. This creates layer cloud and steadier winds.**

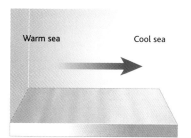

Above: **The air mass is not static. If it moves toward a cooler area, the surface temperature reduces, increasing the relative humidity.**

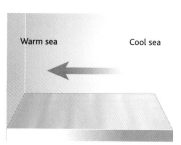

Above: **If the air mass moves to a warmer area, the air temperature rises. If no more evaporation takes place, the relative humidity falls.**

TIP

You need to look at a weather chart to find the source of the air mass, as the wind direction may have curved around, giving a false impression of where the air has come from.

Weather systems

Weather systems are the result of the interaction between areas of high and low pressure. Wind is the resulting airflow around the systems and the weather is caused by vertical movement of air within the systems.

What is an isobar?

Lines joining places of equal pressure are called isobars. They are just like contours on a map and represent the "hilliness" of the pressure pattern. A low pressure area is like a valley and a high pressure area like a mountain.

What is low pressure?

The average atmospheric pressure is 1013.2 millibars (Mb) — now known as hectopascals — of mercury, but not all pressure below this is low pressure. In reality, a low-pressure area is one that is low compared with its neighbor; so 1020 is low compared with 1030Mb, but high relative to 1010Mb.

How does the air flow round a pressure system?

Air would like to flow "downhill" from an area of high pressure to an area of low pressure, but because of the rotation of the earth the airflow is deflected — to the right in the northern hemisphere, and to the left in the southern hemisphere. Thus the airflow is around the system parallel to the direction of the isobars. The wind flows along the isobars, either clockwise or counterclockwise.

What determines wind speed?

Just as the closeness of the contours of a hill show how steep it is, the closeness of the isobars show how steep the pressure gradient is. The steeper the gradient, the stronger the wind. The wind speed and direction can be measured directly from the isobars using scales on a weather chart, and is called the geostrophic or gradient wind.

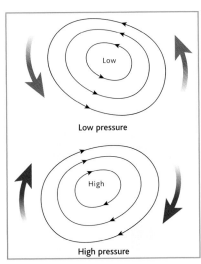

Above: **In the northern hemisphere the circulation of air around a low pressure system is counterclockwise. Around a high pressure system, it is clockwise.**

What is a depression?

A depression is an area of low pressure. Because air flows into the depression at the surface, air rises within it. Depending on the "stability" of the air and its moisture content, clouds will form, often producing rain.

Below: **Each of these lines is an isobar. The outer one joins all points that have a pressure of 1000Mb. The inner one joins all points having a pressure of 1012Mb.**

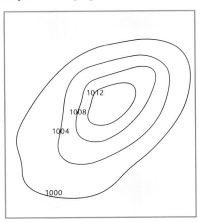

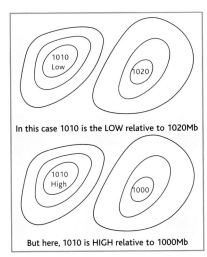

In this case 1010 is the LOW relative to 1020Mb

But here, 1010 is HIGH relative to 1000Mb

Left: **Whether a given pressure is considered high or low depends on what the pressure is adjacent to it.**

TIP

Buys Ballot's Law
In the northern hemisphere, with your back to the wind, hold out your left arm. The low pressure is on your left. In the southern hemisphere, your right arm points at the low pressure.

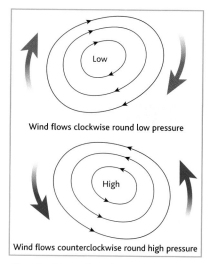

Wind flows clockwise round low pressure

Wind flows counterclockwise round high pressure

Above: In the southern hemisphere, the circulation is reversed.

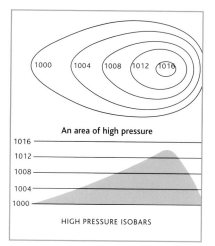

Above: The pressure pattern resembles contours on a land map. Closely spaced isobars indicate a steep slope, the "contours" representing a hill in the case of high pressure.

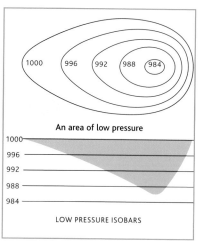

Above: Around a low pressure, the contours represent a valley, with closely spaced isobars indicating a steep slope.

Air stability

As moving air rises in the atmosphere, its temperature drops by about 4°F (2°C) for every 1,000 feet (300 m). The static atmosphere also gets cooler higher up. On average, it, too, cools at 4°F (2°C) for every 1,000 feet (300 m).

✪ If the rising air cools faster than the atmosphere cools, the air is stable and will be stopped from rising very far. The atmosphere in this case is stable.

✪ If the rising air cools more slowly than the atmosphere, it remains buoyant and will rise much higher quite rapidly. The atmosphere is said to be unstable. The cloud base will be where the relative humidity reaches 100 percent. The cloud top will be where the air stops rising, which is dependent on the atmosphere's stability in that area.

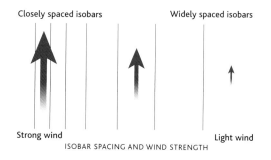

Left: Closely spaced isobars indicate a "steep slope" producing a strong wind. Widely spaced isobars indicate light winds, as there's not much gradient to drive them.

Right: The atmosphere's stability determines the vertical development of any clouds that form.

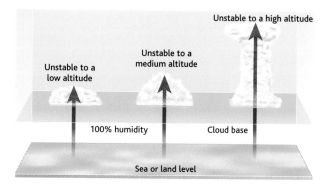

Will it rain?

If the air has a relative humidity of 100 percent, water droplets will form, producing cloud. Water droplets can coalesce into larger ones that become too heavy to remain in the cloud, and eventually they fall to earth as rain.

The boundary of an air mass

Two adjacent air masses will differ; they will have different moisture contents, different temperatures and different stabilities. Even if the differences are small, the two air masses will react with one another.

What is a weather front?

The boundary between two different air masses is called a weather front and normally the air masses will be moving at different speeds and in different directions. Because one of the air masses will be colder than the other, the cold air on one side of the front will be more dense than the warm air on the other side. The warm air will ride up over the cold air, and it is this riding up of the warm air that produces frontal weather.

A warm front

When the faster moving air is warmer than the slower colder air, you get a warm front. The warm air pushes up and over the cold air. The resultant slope of the front is at a very shallow angle, rising from the surface to an altitude of around 30,000 feet (9,000 m) — depending on season and latitude — over a distance of up to 600 miles (950 km). The uplift of the air

causes its temperature to fall and, depending on moisture content and stability, cloud will form.

Because the approaching frontal system will start at high altitude, with thin wispy cloud, you get plenty of warning of a warm front. The cloud base will steadily lower and the cloud will thicken. With sufficient moisture in the air, drizzle will start to fall, eventually turning to continuous rain, which may be heavy, bringing reduced visibility.

The sailor should expect a gradual decrease in visibility (possibly fog), with increasing rainfall as the front approaches. As the front passes, the wind is likely to veer (change in a clockwise direction).

Below: **With the relative stability of the warm air overriding the cold, cloud formation is nonturbulent and layered. Water droplets are small and initial rainfall is in the form of drizzle. Rain gets heavier and continuous. Fog forms where the front is very close to the surface.**

A cold front

Where the faster moving air is colder than the slower moving air, it will push downward, undercutting the warm air and causing it to rise. This is a much more vigorous process than in a warm front, with the surface distance being only about 200 miles (300 km).

Any cloud forming on a cold front will rise rapidly to great altitudes if the air is unstable, and can produce violent and heavy showers. Because the first thing that approaches you is

Below: **A cold front is much more active than a warm one. The steep frontal surface produces large vertical air currents and cumulonimbus cloud. Raindrops can be large and hail is common, as are thunder and lightning. Squally downdrafts of cold air burst from the bottom of the cloud in all directions, with high wind speeds.**

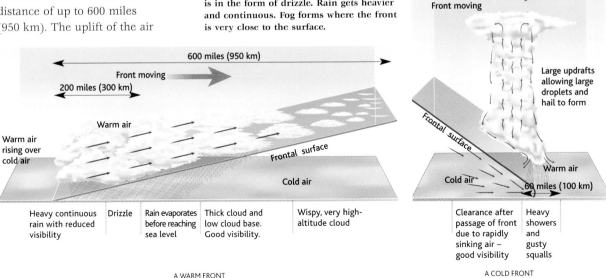

A WARM FRONT

A COLD FRONT

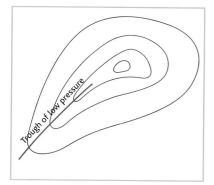

Above: Where the isobars of a depression are elongated, and turn sharply, cold front-like weather can occur along the trough of low pressure.

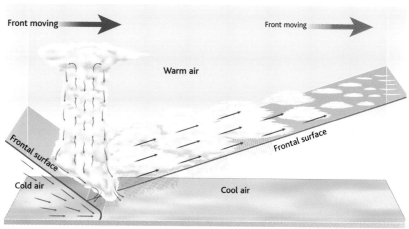

COLD OCCLUDED FRONT

the surface position of the cold front, you get little warning of its arrival. After the cold front passes, you often get clear skies, with no cloud at all for several hours.

Expect locally squally winds and heavy showers, so reef down early if you have inexperienced crew or are short-handed. Cooking may be difficult in squally conditions, so prepare some food in advance.

What is an occluded front?
When a cold front catches up with a warm front, the front becomes "occluded." If the cold air behind the cold front is warmer than the cold air of the warm front you get a warm occlusion, where the weather on the front is more like a warm front. The continuous rain of the warm front will have areas of very heavy rain and hail; these are due to the cumulonimbus clouds of the lifted cold front that have become embedded within the warm front.

Right: Where the air of a cold front is warmer than the cold air under a warm front, the cold front rides up over the warm front. This gives weather characteristic of a warm front.

If the cold air behind the cold front is colder than the cold air of the warm front, the weather is much more like that associated with a cold front. The typical line of thunderstorms of the cold front will be preceded by the ever-lowering cloud of the warm front bringing increasing rainfall prior to the heavy showers.

In both cold and warm occlusions, the significance to the sailor is that there may be little visual warning of the gusty squalls which may occur, unlike the clear warning of those associated with a cold front.

Above: When the air of a cold front is colder than the cold air under the warm front, it pushes under the warm front. Although the initial weather is that of a warm front, it then becomes much more like a cold front, with heavy, squally showers followed by clear skies behind the front.

What is a frontal trough?
Where there's a rapid change of direction of the isobars in a depression, the air feeding into this trough causes air to rise and, though there's no actual front (there's no change in air mass), weather similar to a cold front can form.

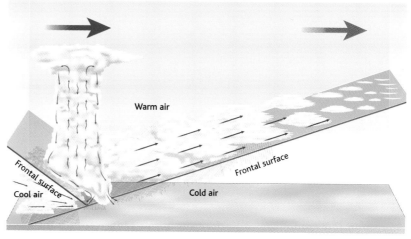

A WARM OCCLUSION

High-pressure systems

High-pressure systems are relatively benign, because air is descending, and they often give long periods of quiet conditions. Any moving air in contact with the surface is subject to friction, which changes the speed and direction of the wind.

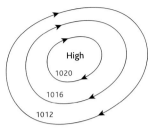

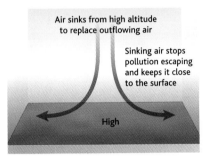

ANTICYCLONIC GLOOM

Above: **The longer the anticyclone persists, the more likely that visibility will worsen.**

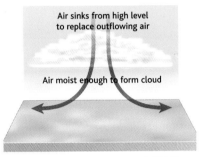

STRATIFORM CLOUD IN AN ANTICYCLONE

Above: **With moist air circulating round the anticyclone, cloud can form but will be of stratus type due to the descending air. With sufficient moisture, rain is possible.**

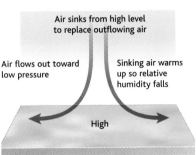

ANTICYCLONE (HIGH PRESSURE)

Above: **The anticyclone is an area of descending air, replacing the air flowing out. The descending air warms in descent, becoming drier as it does so.**

What is an anticyclone?

An anticyclone is an area of high pressure. It is often an area of settled weather, especially when the pressure is very high, above 1030Mb. At the surface, air is flowing outward and therefore upper air is sinking into it. This sinking air warms as it descends, so frequently there's no cloud at all, giving good clear weather.

If the air is moist enough, cloud can form in a continuous layer (stratiform). Given enough moisture, it can produce light rain or drizzle.

Anticyclones tend to be slow-moving and slow to dissipate, so can be a dominant feature for many days. It is common to associate high pressure with calm conditions. Sailors should be aware that you can still get closely packed isobars, and thus strong winds, even in areas of high pressure. Have a look at the isobars on a proper weather chart.

What is anticyclonic gloom?

When air pollution is present, the sinking air in an anticyclone prevents it from rising and being dispersed. Pollution is then trapped in a thin layer at the surface, and its density builds up as the quiet days pass. In areas of heavy pollution, the resulting "smog" will last until there's a change of air mass from the moving weather system.

What is the effect of friction?

Friction between the earth's surface and the moving air slows down the air, and in slowing it also changes direction so that it flows slightly into the area of low pressure. Over the sea, the deflection is about 15 degrees and the reduction of speed about 20 percent, depending on the atmospheric and surface conditions. Over land it's about 30 degrees and 40 percent. The wind at the surface is simply called the "surface wind."

How deep is the friction layer?

The effect of friction is greatest at the surface, its effect reducing with an increase in altitude. In stable conditions, it ceases to have an effect at about 2,000 feet (600 m). The isobars indicate the wind direction at 2,000 feet (600 m), but you'll need to take friction into account when calculating the direction of the surface wind.

The effect of turbulence

Over terrain that is rough and hilly, the turbulence caused by stronger winds blowing over the surface can result in the "2,000-foot" wind being brought right down to the surface, causing gusty conditions.

At night, over land, the turbulence reduces as the land cools, and the friction effect can reduce the wind considerably. It may even become calm, only to rise again once the land begins to warm up.

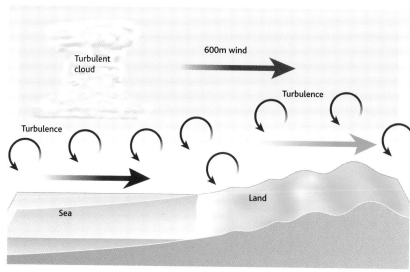

Turbulent
cloud

600m wind

Turbulence

Turbulence

Turbulence

Land

Sea

THE EFFECT OF TURBULENCE

Above: **When low-level turbulence is present, it will bring down the 2,000-foot (600 m) wind to the surface, giving gusty conditions.**

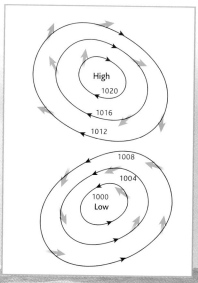

Surface
wind

Surface
wind

2,000-foot
(600 m)
wind

2,000-foot
(600 m)
wind

SURFACE WIND
OVER LAND

SURFACE WIND
OVER SEA

Above: **Friction causes the wind at the surface to reduce in speed and turn in toward the low pressure. The effect is greater over land than sea.**

When the air is unstable and there are cumulus-type clouds about, the turbulence within them can bring the 2,000-foot (600 m) wind right down to the surface, giving gusty winds, variable in both speed and direction. This is of particular relevance to sailors, who will experience continually changing wind conditions.

Turbulence due to cumulus clouds over the sea is not reduced at night, so there will be no night calm and gusty conditions will continue.

What is backing and veering?

If the wind changes direction you may need to know how it has changed.

✪ Backing is when the wind changes in an a counterclockwise direction.
✪ Veering is when the wind changes in a clockwise direction.

High
1020

1016

1012

1008

1004

1000
Low

Above: **When looking at a weather map — or synoptic chart — with isobars, the 2,000-foot (600 m) wind will follow the isobars, but the surface wind will turn in towards the low pressure.**

The movement of weather systems

A weather system's speed and direction is normally forecast. If, however, you have access only to a weather chart, it is helpful if you can make your own judgments, based on what you can see.

Forecasting the movement of a weather system over a day or so is reasonably accurate, but the further you look ahead the less confidence you can place in any forecast.

Despite this, sailors can use their own knowledge to make a decent stab at short-term forecasting. Long-range forecasts are based on

The frontal depression

Although the front starts off just as the boundary between two air masses, it soon starts to take up the classic V-shape of a cold front following a warm front. The cold front moves faster than the warm front, catches it up and then forms an occluded front. The speed of the

Which way does a depression move?

If you look at the direction of the isobars in the warm sector, the arrows indicate the direction of the advance. You'll need to look to the east of the low, to see if there is any high pressure area, as these areas are pretty stubborn and won't move

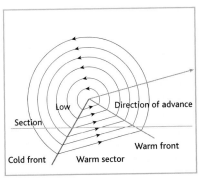

STRUCTURE OF A FRONTAL SYSTEM

Left and below: **A section through a warm and cold front.**

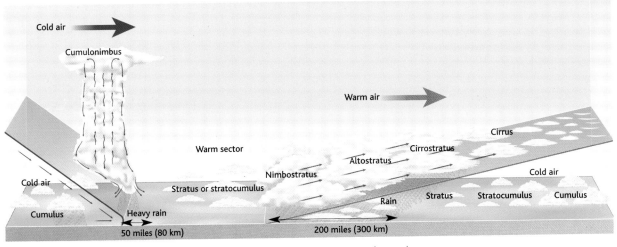

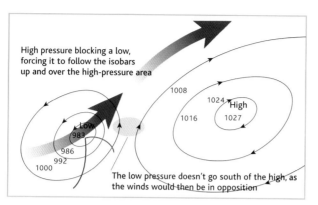

Right: **High pressure blocking a low in the northern hemisphere. In the southern hemisphere the low pressure would follow the isobars south of the blocking high.**

High pressure blocking a low, forcing it to follow the isobars up and over the high-pressure area

The low pressure doesn't go south of the high, as the winds would then be in opposition

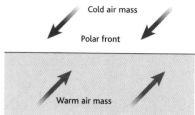

Cold air mass

Polar front

Warm air mass

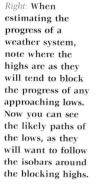

Right: **When estimating the progress of a weather system, note where the highs are as they will tend to block the progress of any approaching lows. Now you can see the likely paths of the lows, as they will want to follow the isobars around the blocking highs.**

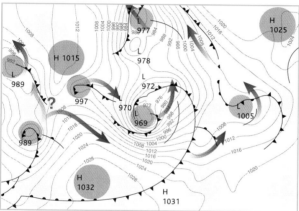

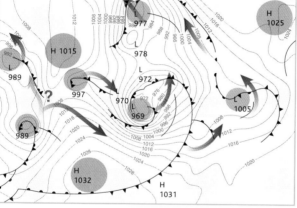

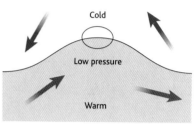

Cold

Low pressure

Warm

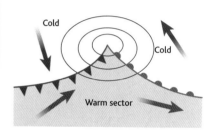

Cold

Cold

Warm sector

The geostrophic wind scale

This wind scale allows measurement of wind speed by measuring the distance apart of the isobars. They are calibrated for either 2 or 4Mb spacing. The scale is valid only for a specific latitude and scale of the met chart. For charts covering a large area, the geostrophic wind scale takes both these parameters into account.

How fast do the fronts move?

Warm fronts move at approximately 90 degrees to the direction in which the front is depicted on the weather chart, at a speed of about 90 percent of the wind speed. Cold and occluded fronts move at about 130 percent of the wind speed, again at 90 degrees to their alignment on the weather chart. They both get more curved as they advance. Some weather charts have special geostrophic scales for measuring wind and frontal speeds.

Above: **A frontal depression occurs when a pocket of warm air encroaches into a neighboring band of cold air along the polar front.**

How does high pressure move?

High-pressure systems are sluggish in their movement, but tend to drift slowly eastward. In some land areas, the high is a semipermanent feature. This is also true over some sea areas, such as near the Azores, where a semipermanent high pressure area exists for long periods, with little movement. These high-pressure systems will block the eastward movement of any approaching lows and deflect them toward the nearest pole.

Local winds

With local winds, the strength and direction are different from the gradient winds you would expect from examining the isobars. They are temporary, and may be due to topographical features, heating or cooling. In some places they may be so common and pronounced that they have special names, such as the Mistral and the Bora in the Mediterranean.

What is a topographical wind?
Wind is lazy and doesn't like climbing hills, so if a hill gets in the way, the wind will want to flow around it. Because there will be less room for the wind to flow, it will accelerate.

Between islands, there are acceleration zones where the wind may double in strength when it's blowing from certain directions, for example around the Canary Islands. Steep-sided valleys also accelerate the wind in certain wind directions; the Mistral in the South of France is a good example.

Localized heating of the land
In good, sunny conditions during the summer, the surface of the land heats up rapidly. Air in contact with the land is heated and so rises, causing the pressure to fall, giving a localized low-pressure area. Air rising in these conditions can be quite vigorous. As the heating diminishes, the land cools and the pressure returns to normal.

What is a sea breeze?
If the coastal area is heated during the day, the air rising over it is replaced by air flowing off the sea, the temperature of which has not risen. This is the sea breeze. The air can rise to a considerable height and require a lot of air to replace it, so the process can be powerful.

A clear, calm, sunny morning may well be followed by winds of force 4 or more in the afternoon as the sea breeze sets in. Keep in mind if you are going to sail into this strong wind that it can extend out to 5 miles (8 km) from the coast in good conditions. By about 1600 hours the wind will be dropping off, so plan your day accordingly.

Localized cooling of the land
At night, in clear conditions, the land cools, cooling air in contact with it. The cooled air sinks, giving a localized high-pressure area,

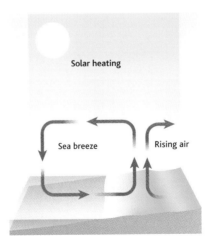

Above: **Where solar heating occurs along the coast, a sea breeze can arise.**

which returns to normal once the land is heated again. This is a very gentle process.

What is a land breeze?
If the coastal area is cooled during the night, the sinking air will flow out to sea. This is a weak process, so the cooled, sinking air will only flow a short distance, and the resulting wind will be light.

What is a katabatic wind?
A katabatic wind is due to the land cooling, but occurs where the land slopes. The air in contact with the

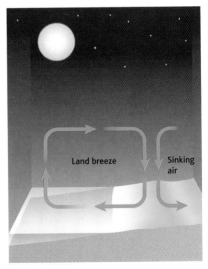

Above: **A land breeze generated by cooling will be weak, unless the land slopes, in which case it is known as a katabatic wind.**

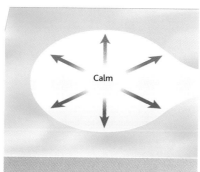

Far left: **A katabatic wind can be quite fierce and the resulting wind flowing offshore can be strong and gusty.**

Left: **A circular sea breeze can be generated over an enclosed body of water.**

cooled land is heavier and wants to sink. This time it can roll downhill, gaining momentum. The steeper the slope, the stronger the wind.

On the coast, this fast-moving air can blow out to sea for quite a distance and gale force winds can result where there are coastal mountains. Not only can a katabatic wind be quite strong, it may also be squally. Where a katabatic wind occurs close to a steeply sloping shore, it can literally knock a yacht flat, as heeling will not have the usual effect of spilling wind out of the sails.

Local winds on lakes

A sea breeze over a lake or almost land-locked bay can cause a "circular" wind, where the wind blows onto the shore at right angles all the way around. The wind will be calm in the middle.

Below: **Sailing on a fine summer's day. Heated land has caused rising air, which has created cumulus clouds over the coastal area.**

Stormy weather

Storms are often short in duration, but can cause strong and variable winds and poor visibility. They often occur during weather that otherwise produces good sailing. Sometimes they are not forecast when the sailor sets sail, because the system develops very rapidly.

Thunderstorms

These occur when the instability of the air allows moist air to rise to high altitudes. A trigger is needed to make the air rise in the first place.

- Air flowing toward rapidly rising terrain is pushed upward. This can affect the sailor if the mountains are on the coast, as the effects spill out over the coastal water.
- Air warmed by solar heating is a frequent trigger. In this case, the morning starts clear, with thunderstorms developing during the day and dying out in the evening.
- Air in a warm sector is pushed upward by a cold front. The thunderstorms are located along the cold front itself.

- Air in a frontal trough or depression is pushed upward by air entering the low pressure area. In a trough, the thunderstorms can be found along its axis, while in a "thundery low" they can occur anywhere.
- Air rising rapidly in a cumulonimbus cloud is able to carry large droplets of water. The resulting rain and hail showers can be very heavy and bring with them "downbursts" of rapidly moving cold air, which spread out in all directions from the cloud base. Gusts can be very strong.
- Where the gust blows against the gradient wind, wind will fall very lightly, but when it blows in the same direction, gale force gusts may occur. Large buildups of static electricity occur within the cloud, and lightning will reach the surface.

Line squalls

A line squall occurs where several thunderstorm cells combine, forming a long line of squally conditions, rather than a more isolated storm. A common source of line squalls is a cold front, with the squall line ahead of it. The sailor will see a long band of dark cloud, probably with rain falling from it. Strong gusts will jet forward from the line, reinforcing the existing wind. Behind, there will be lulls as the gusts oppose the wind. Reef down early when a line squall approaches.

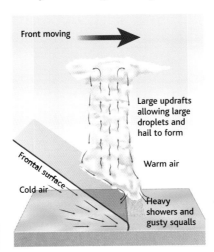

A THUNDERSTORM

Above: **The strong updrafts and downdrafts in a thundercloud (cumulonimbus) produce heavy showers of rain and hail and strong gusts in all directions beneath it.**

A THUNDERSTORM ON A COLD FRONT

Above: **Thunderstorms may be triggered by unstable air being forced to rise up a cold front.**

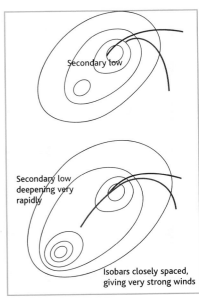

DEVELOPMENT OF SECONDARY LOW

Above: **A secondary low may deepen very rapidly and unexpectedly.**

A secondary low

A secondary area of low pressure can develop in a frontal depression. Usually this is not a terribly significant feature, but occasionally it can deepen very rapidly, causing very strong winds.

Often this rapid deepening is not forecast, or is picked up only at the last minute. It's quite possible for the sailor to set off with a reasonable forecast, only to be caught out by this secondary low.

Below: **When squall gusts combine with the existing wind ahead of the squall, wind speeds will increase. After the squall passes, the squall gusts will oppose the existing wind, which will fall flat.**

Monitor the forecasts as often as possible in order not to be caught out in changing conditions.

Storm force winds

Wind speeds greater than 48 knots are storm force. They can be detected on a weather chart by inspecting the closeness of the isobars. The passage of these storm force winds is normally fairly rapid, generally lasting no more than 12 hours.

Below: **Line squalls can occur on a cold front when cumulonimbus clouds merge together along the line of the front.**

Above: **A good strong breeze disguises the power of the sun, making some of this crew likely to suffer from sunburn.**

Hurricanes

Called hurricanes in the Atlantic and tropical cyclones elsewhere, these are a phenomenon of tropical seas, driven by high sea temperature and high moisture content. They occur in certain areas of the Atlantic, Indian and Pacific oceans and are seasonal. They should be avoided at all costs.

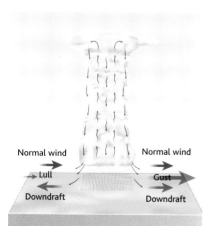

THE EFFECT OF DOWNDRAFTS AND THE WIND

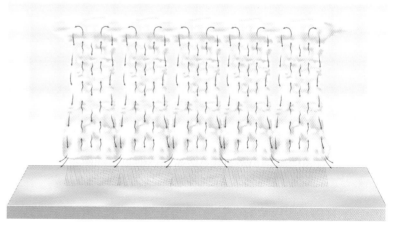

A LINE SQUALL

What is fog?

Fog is cloud in contact with the surface. Fog reduces visibility due to water droplets suspended in the air — the denser the concentration of droplets, the worse the visibility. The definition of fog is a visibility less than 0.6 miles (1 km). Visibility of 0.6–1.2 miles (1–2 km) is termed mist.

Reduced visibility in rain

Rain can reduce visibility to such an extent that the effect is the same as fog. Heavy rain can occur on the approach of a warm front, from cumulonimbus clouds or from a line squall.

What is frontal fog?

Close to the surface position of a warm front, the thickness of the nimbostratus cloud above produces very heavy rain. Low stratus cloud forms below the frontal surface and comes right down to ground or sea level. Because the frontal surface has only a gentle slope, the area of frontal fog can be large, and if the frontal system is slow moving, it will persist, remaining until the front has passed.

What is sea fog?

Sea fog (advection fog) is seasonal and needs a cool sea surface and moist air above it.

Sea fog requires a warm, moist air mass to move over a sea surface that is getting progressively cooler. If the air in contact with the cool sea surface is cooled sufficiently to increase the relative humidity to 100 per cent, fog will form. Sea fog in the spring and early summer is caused by a tropical maritime air mass moving over cold seas, not yet heated by the summer sun.

Where there are areas of cold water that have risen to the surface from below, fog may form as the air close to the surface is cooled by

Above: **The low stratus cloud close to the surface position of a warm front can reach sea or ground level and, together with the heavy continuous rainfall, can severely reduce visibility.**

Frontal fog   Warm frontal stance

80%   90%   100%

Fog forms

Above: **Warm, moist air cooled by a cold sea can produce sea fog as the relative humidity of the surface layer of air is increased to 100 percent.**

contact with the cold water. This causes "fog patches." To a much greater extent, this occurs over the Grand Banks of Nova Scotia.

Some coasts experience sea fog where polar maritime air moves over a warmer sea. Evaporation into the cold, dry, air is sufficient to raise its humidity and cause fog to form.

With sufficient wind strength, sea fog may rise off the surface and sit about 6–13 feet (2–4 m) above it. Sea fog needs a change of air mass, such as the passage of a front, to clear it.

What is radiation (or ground) fog?

Radiation fog occurs where moist air is cooled by contact with land that has cooled by radiation at night. This, too, is seasonal fog.

On a clear night, the lack of a cloud blanket allows the surface of the land to cool rapidly. This cools the air and if the cooling

and moisture are sufficient, 100 percent relative humidity is reached in a shallow layer in contact with the ground.

The conditions required for the formation of radiation fog are limited. If the wind speed is less than about 2 knots, there is not enough turbulence to keep the water droplets airborne and all you will get is dew. If the wind is greater than 4 to 5 knots, the turbulence will lift the fog off the ground resulting in "low stratus" cloud.

TIP

If patchy fog is forecast, you may well experience continuously good visibility, but you may equally run into lots of fog. Sailors should not undertake a passage lightly when patchy fog is forecast, particularly if the yacht does not have radar.

Right: **Radiation of heat from the ground on a clear night can cool the air sufficiently to produce fog, which can roll downhill and flow over an estuary or bay. There will be good visibility out to sea and this localized fog will clear during the morning with solar heating.**

Radiation at night with a clear sky

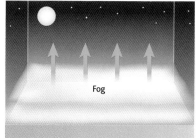

Fog forms if there's a very light wind

Only with wind speeds between 2 and 4 knots will ground fog form.

Radiation fog is cleared by solar heating during the day. If you are in an estuary in the morning and it's foggy, don't assume it's foggy out at sea. It may be radiation fog that's drained into the valley, in which case there's good sailing to be had if you can find your way out to sea.

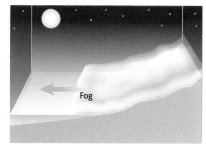

Dense cold air (fog) rolls down hill

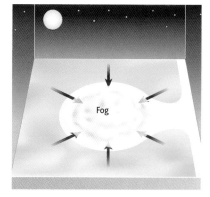

Fog drifts over bays and inlets and will clear with solar heating

Below: **Poor visibility can quickly deteriorate to fog if there's an upwelling of cold water. Over the sea, wind doesn't "blow the fog away."**

Air temperature

Air is heated and cooled by the surface it is in contact with, but rising and descending air currents on a global scale transport heat around the world. In any particular area, the air temperature is that of the air mass flowing over it, and this temperature is affected by local conditions.

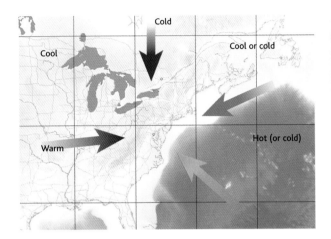

Above: **The source of the air mass will give a good idea of the air temperature, but you'll need to consider the season.**

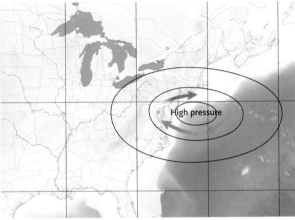

Above: **In this high pressure situation, the wind over New York is from the southwest, indicating that it is dry continental. But the air mass originates from the Atlantic so it will be cool, rather than hot in the summer and cold in the winter. It will also be moist.**

For the sailor, short-term local variations are most likely to determine enjoyment and well-being.

What is wind chill factor?

The body experiences a greater loss of body heat if a wind is blowing. The wind chill factor is said to be half the wind speed in knots. In other words, in a 16 knot wind (force 4) it will feel $14\,^{\circ}F$ ($8\,^{\circ}C$) cooler than the air temperature. This is no problem if the temperature is $77\,^{\circ}F$ ($25\,^{\circ}C$), but critical if it's only $50\,^{\circ}F$ ($10\,^{\circ}C$).

Weather charts don't normally give air temperatures. Nor do shipping forecasts, but for the sailor they can be an important factor in decision making. A local forecast will usually provide you with expected air temperatures.

The temperature of the air mass

Given enough time, the temperature of the air in contact with a tropical sea at a temperature of, say, $82\,^{\circ}F$ ($28\,^{\circ}C$), will attain the same temperature. Any air mass will have an underlying surface temperature according to its source.

The temperature of an air mass will rise or fall as it passes over a warmer or cooler surface and will vary with the seasons.

Where has the air come from?

The wind direction will give some idea of the source of an air mass. However, it's best to consult a weather chart to see if the wind (following the isobars) has curved around and is really coming from somewhere else. This, and the season, will give you a good idea of the underlying air temperature.

The passage of a warm front

The definition of a warm front is that the air on the "far side" is warmer. This difference can vary. In the cool air and with the cooling effect of the rain, the sailor should dress accordingly. On passage of the warm front, you should feel more comfortable.

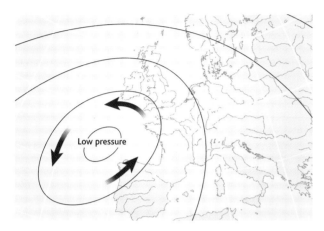

Left: **In this case the southeasterly wind belies its source from over the Atlantic ocean.**

TIP

It's easy to be fooled that you won't get sunburned at sea because it's too cold. If you're sailing, especially if you are going to windward, you'll feel cool because of the wind chill factor. You can still get severely burned, so cover up or use plenty of sunscreen.

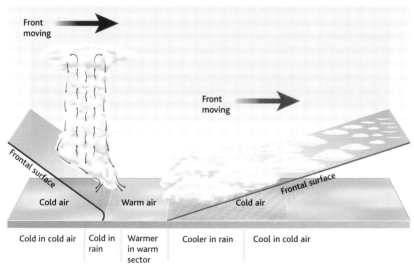

Left: **Temperature changes that might be expected on the passage of a series of fronts. The actual temperatures will depend on your location and the season.**

The passage of a cold front

The fall in temperature during the passage of a cold front can be much more dramatic. The sailor will be traveling from warmer air into colder air and if the difference is large a change of clothes may be required. Often, too, the wind strength increases and the heavy showers on the front will be cold.

The temperature in fog

In fog, the relative humidity is 100 percent and water can take much more heat from the body than dry air. Even if there's no change in air temperature as you enter fog, your body will start to lose much more heat and you will start to feel significantly colder.

What do clouds mean?

Some knowledge of the different types of clouds will help you forecast what might happen with the weather.

The stability of the atmosphere, and how its temperature varies with height, controls what happens to rising air. The air temperature of the atmosphere falls with increasing height, but the exact rate of this fall depends on many factors. Moving air rising in the atmosphere cools at a rate of 3.5°F (2°C) every 1,000 feet (300 m). Where the fall in temperature with height is less than the fall in temperature of rising air, the atmosphere is said to be stable and the air will stop rising. Where the fall is more, the atmosphere is unstable and the air will continue rising until stability is once again reached. This determines the vertical extent of clouds.

Stratus and cumulus-type clouds
Stratus clouds are "layered" clouds. They form in stable air and need a sloping surface, be it terrain or a frontal surface, to force the air to rise, or they occur when only a very shallow depth of the atmosphere is unstable. Cumulus clouds have a greater vertical extent and need an unstable atmosphere to allow them to push themselves upwards.

The height of the cloud
The prefixes attached to stratus and cumulus clouds designate their height.
- High level: Cirrostratus and cirrocumulus
- Mid-level: Altostratus and altocumulus
- Low level: Nimbostratus and statocumulus

Types of clouds

✿ *Rain from a nimbostratus cloud.* The rain drags stratus cloud down with it. Because this section of the warm front is 150–200 miles (240–320 km) in extent, you could experience about six hours of continuous rain.

✿ *Stratus and stratocumulus.* Possibly due to the presence of mountains; beware of embedded cumulonimbus with associated strong gusts and heavy showers.

✿ *Stratus cloud* with a good breeze, typical of a warm sector (after a warm front and preceding a cold front). There may be occasional drizzle. Any change in the wind strength is likely to be only gradual.

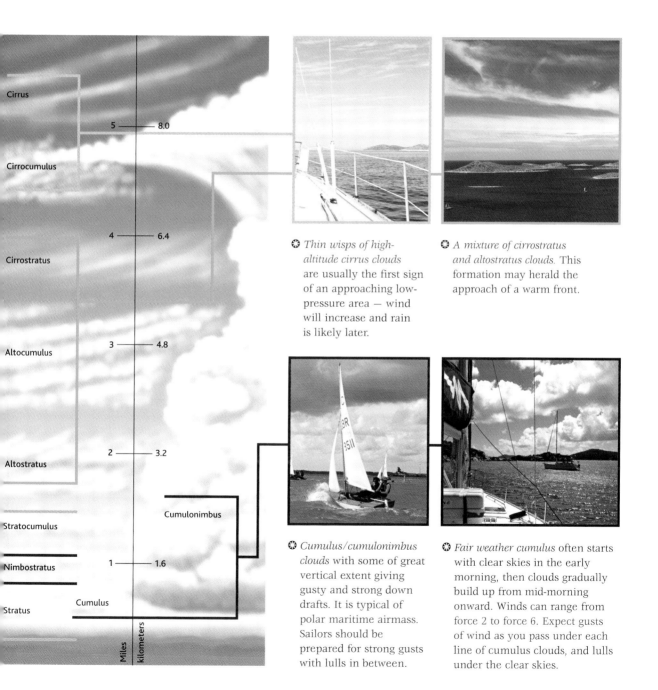

Cirrus

5 ——— 8.0

Cirrocumulus

4 ——— 6.4

Cirrostratus

3 ——— 4.8

Altocumulus

2 ——— 3.2

Altostratus

Cumulonimbus

Stratocumulus

Nimbostratus

1 ——— 1.6

Stratus

Cumulus

Miles kilometers

☼ *Thin wisps of high-altitude cirrus clouds* are usually the first sign of an approaching low-pressure area — wind will increase and rain is likely later.

☼ *A mixture of cirrostratus and altostratus clouds.* This formation may herald the approach of a warm front.

☼ *Cumulus/cumulonimbus clouds* with some of great vertical extent giving gusty and strong down drafts. It is typical of polar maritime airmass. Sailors should be prepared for strong gusts with lulls in between.

☼ *Fair weather cumulus* often starts with clear skies in the early morning, then clouds gradually build up from mid-morning onward. Winds can range from force 2 to force 6. Expect gusts of wind as you pass under each line of cumulus clouds, and lulls under the clear skies.

Weather forecasts

There are several sources of weather forecasts, but many are not very suited to the requirements of a sailor because they give insufficient indication of the wind strength and direction. Some forecasts you can access from shore, and some from your boat.

Gather your weather forecast information before you set sail, but have some means of getting updates while you are afloat if you are going to be on the water for some time. The more you know about weather, the easier it is to judge the likely accuracy of any forecast.

National and local radio
Coastal and shipping forecasts are available from both national and local radio, depending on your location. They are broadcast at specific times, but beware: broadcast times are subject to change.

Other media
Television is a good source of general forecasts, but these are usually tailored to a general audience. Local TV sometimes has a sailing forecast. Newspapers

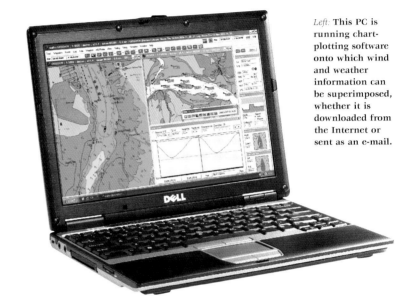

Left: **This PC is running chart-plotting software onto which wind and weather information can be superimposed, whether it is downloaded from the Internet or sent as an e-mail.**

often have weather charts, which can be useful before you sail. Watch what is happening for several days prior to departure to get a feel of how the weather is developing.

Marina or harbormaster
If you have access to a marina or harbormaster's office, they will have forecasts and will often supply you with copies, including the weather charts. Beware: some receive forecasts only for the weekend but leave them on display during the following week, so check the dates!

Left: **A weatherfax receiver, which plots the weather chart from a number of different sources.**

Internet
The Internet is an excellent source of weather information. If you belong to a club or association, its website will have links to weather information. Otherwise, do a search for marine weather using an Internet search engine.

Marine VHF radio
The coastguard or other authorities broadcast weather reports and forecasts on a regular schedule. Their websites or sailing almanacs will give details of the schedules and the channels to select to listen to them. In some areas in Canada and the United States, weather broadcasts are made continuously, so you can listen in at any time.

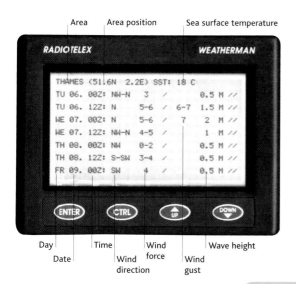

Area   Area position   Sea surface temperature

RADIOTELEX   WEATHERMAN

THAMES (51.6N 2.2E) SST: 18 C
TU 06. 00Z: NW-N   3   /   0.5 M //
TU 06. 12Z: N   5-6 / 6-7   1.5 M //
WE 07. 00Z: N   5-6 / 7   2 M //
WE 07. 12Z: NW-N   4-5 /   1 M //
TH 08. 00Z: NW   0-2 /   0.5 M //
TH 08. 12Z: S-SW   3-4 /   0.5 M //
FR 09. 00Z: SW   4   /   0.5 M //

ENTER   CTRL   UP   DOWN

Day   Time   Wind   Wave height
Date   Wind   force   Wind
         direction   gust

Left: A weatherfax decoder, which displays the weather data in a quickly read form.

Navtex

Navtex is an international system whereby weather and safety information is transmitted in English on a regular schedule. A special receiver is required, which is left on standby continuously, so you can look at the forecast when you need to. Transmissions have a range of 200–300 miles (300–480 km) from the broadcasting stations, but their coverage is not worldwide.

TIP

Listen to what local fishermen or boaters have to say. Their knowledge and experience of the conditions to be expected is invaluable – their livelihood depends on it.

Below: A Navtex receiver capable of receiving marine weather and safety information.

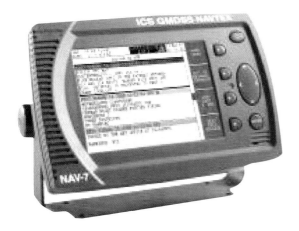

Radiotelex

Weather forecasts and reports, as well as other data, are transmitted by radio telex, for which special receiving equipment is required. There are several leisure sets available, which decode the information and present it on an LCD screen.

Cellular or satellite phone

Forecasts can be sent as text messages to your phone, but you need to subscribe to a service. Some packages will compress all the data, which can then be decoded by the supplied software, so the call charges are not prohibitive.

Alternatively, you can connect your computer to the Internet with your phone if it will handle data. You can then get all the Internet forecasts. These data calls can be expensive, although there are some good deals now available.

Left: Sophisticated "smart phones" can display weather charts as well as forecasts.

Beaufort scale

This scale, which gives the sailor a good idea of how strong the wind is, was popularized by Admiral Sir Francis Beaufort in 1805.

Beaufort scale

Beaufort number	Description	Wind speed, in knots	Signs on land	Water state
0	Calm	Less than 1	Smoke rises vertically	Mirror smooth
1	Light air	1–3	Smoke drifts	Ripples with appearance of scales
2	Light breeze	4–6	Leaves rustle	Small wavelets, crests of glassy appearance, not breaking
3	Gentle breeze	7–10	Flags not extended	Large wavelets, crests begin to break, scattered white caps
4	Moderate breeze	11–16	Light flags extended	Wave height 1–4 feet (0.3–1.2 m); small waves becoming longer, numerous white caps
5	Fresh breeze	17–21	All flags extended; trees in motion	Wave height 4–8 feet (1.2–2.4 m); moderate, longer waves, many white caps, some spray
6	Strong breeze	22–27	Tree branches in motion	Wave height 8–13 feet (2.4–4 m); larger waves forming, white caps everywhere, more spray
7	Moderate gale	28–33	Walking into wind difficult	Wave height 13–20 feet (4–6 m); sea heaps up, white foam from breaking waves begins to be blowing streaks in direction of wind
8	Fresh gale	34–40	Twigs break from trees	Wave height 13–20 feet (4–6 m); moderately high waves of greater length, edges of crests begin to break into spindrift, foam is blown in well-marked streaks
9	Strong gale	41–47	Roof and fence damage	Wave height 20 feet (6 m); high waves, sea begins to roll, dense streaks of foam along wind direction, spray may reduce visibility
10	Storm	48–55	Trees uprooted; structural damage	Wave height 20–30 feet (6–9 m); very high waves with overhanging crests, sea looks white, as foam is blown in very dense streaks, rolling is heavy and shock-like, visibility is reduced
11	Violent storm	56–63		Wave height 30–45 feet (9–14 m); exceptionally high waves, sea covered with white foam patches, visibility still more reduced
12 plus	Hurricane	64 and upward		Wave height over 45 feet (14 m).

Barometric tendency

In forecasts, the term "tendency" means how the pressure is going to change and is often given for the next three hours.

Steady	Less than 0.1Mb
Rising slowly or falling slowly	0.1–1.5Mb
Rising or falling	1.6–3.5Mb
Rising quickly or falling quickly	3.6–6.0Mb

❂ If you observe on your barometer a rise or fall of 1Mb per hour a wind of force 6 is likely.

❂ If you observe on your barometer a rise or fall of 2Mb per hour a wind of force 7 to 8 is likely.

❂ If you observe a rise or fall of 3Mb per hour a wind of force 8 or more is likely.

When will it happen?

Imminent	In the next 6 hours
Soon	Between 6 and 12 hours
Later	Between 12 and 24 hours

Wave length

Wave length — the distance between crests — is nearly as important as height. Six-foot (2 m) hight swells in the ocean are of little concern to sailors. However, in a narrow channel, where the distance between waves is not as great, they can create tough sailing conditions, especially in shallow water.

See also pages 34–35.

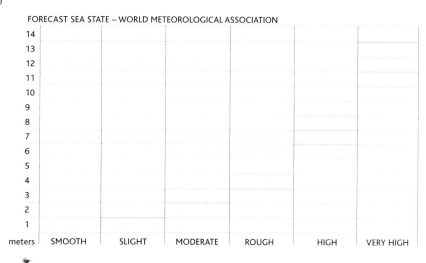

FORECAST SEA STATE – WORLD METEOROLOGICAL ASSOCIATION

meters	SMOOTH	SLIGHT	MODERATE	ROUGH	HIGH	VERY HIGH
14						
13						
12						
11						
10						
9						
8						
7						
6						
5						
4						
3						
2						
1						

Left: **A barometer, installed in the boat, will give an idea of wind force to be expected, by observing the rate of change of pressure.**

Below: **Light winds will provide a comfortable if unexciting sail.**

Maintenance

Refitting

Most routine annual boat maintenance is carried out during the refit winter period. With proper maintenance comes reliability and peace of mind. Ongoing maintenance is preferable to expensive repairs that might easily have been prevented.

At the end of the sailing season comes the time to take your boat out of the water so that you can carry out the annual maintenance program. Some boats may stay in the water for the refit period, but at some stage they will have to come out for an inspection and a coat of antifouling paint on the hull (to prevent marine growth).

Health and safety
Protecting yourself
During the refit period:
- Physically protect yourself from dirt, grime and paint splashes by wearing overalls large enough to move around in comfort.
- Use work gloves when handling rough materials such as sawed wood or when painting, especially when using antifouling paint. Fine rubber gloves are handy for delicate operations such as servicing the engine or toilet.
- Safety glasses should be worn if there is a possibility of something getting in your eyes. They are essential for jobs such as grinding metalwork, power sanding woodwork, painting in general, and working with caustic liquids.
- If you stand on the rung of a ladder for any length of time, you will appreciate wearing a pair of boots or shoes with thick soles.
- Wearing a hat will keep your head warm and protected against dust and paint splashes.
- Use a face mask to protect against dust and smells. Cutting up MDF or plywood generates a lot of dust. Try not to inhale the smell of strong glue. Always apply in a well-ventilated area.
- Keep a first-aid kit on board for minor scratches and abrasions.
- Check the policy of the boatyard concerning liability insurance, which may be required.

Protecting others
- After laying out and connecting out water pipes or temporary electric cables, ensure they do not obstruct others or form a tripping hazard.
- If you intend to carry out grinding, sanding or painting operations, and there is a likelihood of annoying neighbors, put up a screen or cover up near other people's property. Modify your schedule so that you don't damage their paintwork, and they don't damage yours.
- Dispose of hazardous substances in a way that does not damage the environment or others.
- Keep your space tidy and clean up at the end of a day.

Using electrics
- All non-battery power tools should be connected to a circuit breaker and any extension cords should be fully unwound.

Below: **Well protected, this refitter is wearing overalls, hat, goggles and face mask. He is preparing the hull for antifouling paint using a belt sander with an extractor bag to collect the dust.**

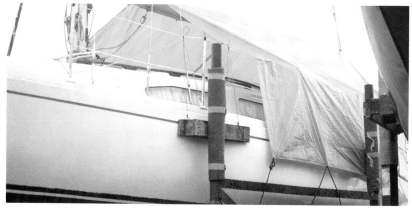

Left: **The reinforced blue plastic sheeting protects the cockpit area from the elements and forms a temporary workshop area for refitting.**

Below: **Ensure the ladder is secured to a stanchion and extends above the top guardrail at the correct angle.**

⚙ It is not advisable to work with power tools in the rain, or in/over water.

⚙ If possible, try to use battery-operated tools; they are low voltage and do not have cords that can hinder your work. A second charged-up battery pack will avoid wasted time.

⚙ Try to work in company with others, either on your own boat or with the owner of the boat next door, in case you need help.

⚙ If you are carrying out maintenance when the boat is in the water, put your tender alongside and be sure to have the boat's ladder over the side.

⚙ If possible, attach a lanyard to the tool you will use and secure the other end to the boat, to prevent dropping tools in the water.

⚙ All electrical equipment should be in good condition and have the correct fuses.

Using equipment

⚙ Most accidents occur through tripping or equipment slipping.

⚙ Place all ladders at the correct angle (1:3) and extend them above the guardrail. The top of the ladder should be tied to the guardrail or a similar solid structure. If the ladder footing is on sloping ground, wedge the bottom by securing pieces of plywood to form a level foundation. Tie in the bottom of the ladder to the boat. Hang identification markers, like fenders, over any low-level lines that you use to do this.

⚙ All platforms should be erected on level ground and be at least 18 inches (45 cm) wide, with little or no deflection in the middle. The boards should preferably be tied to the platform framework and none should be cantilevered. For longer, deep-keeled yachts, use a scaffold or a ladder.

⚙ When stripping paint, use a hot air gun rather than a gas blowtorch. A blowtorch can be surprisingly strong in inexperienced hands.

⚙ A fire extinguisher should be accessible when using an open flame; for example, if using a blowtorch.

Care of equipment

Before leaving the boat at the end of the day, remove all ladders and equipment and lock them up. Do not tempt unwanted guests to steal from your boat while you are away.

Refitting (2)

Left: **Pulling a boat up a boat slip onto dry land. In the boatyard the hull will be hosed down, ready for the yearly refit.**

Preparing to come out of the water

Clean and prepare your cradle/boat space by removing tenders, equipment, ladders and other obstructions. Arrange for a tractor, crane or travel hoist to take your boat out of the water. You may also need to organize other help to assist you at the lift-out.

✪ Do you intend to take the mast down this year? If so, book the mast crane and arrange any help you will need.

✪ Carry out a thorough inspection of the boat trailer/cradle. Are the wheels and tires in good condition and at the correct pressure? Is there any rust that will affect the structural stability?

When out of the water

Wash the hull and deck with a pressure washer to remove the season's marine growth, barnacles and other unwanted hull attachments.

Once the travel hoist or tractor has put you in your designated compound space, you should carry out the following:

Externally:

✪ Inspect the outside of your boat for wear and tear: look for worn lines/halyards, dents and scratches, loose and missing connections. Note them in the refit maintenance list.

✪ To reduce frapping (rubbing), secure all lines away from masts.

Remove items such as sails, "doggers" and the spray hood; if left in place they will cause windage problems.

✪ Remove the anchor chain from the chain locker by rolling it out over the bow roller, and flake it out on a wooden pallet at ground level. Pressure-wash the anchor chain to remove any salt and marine sediment, and then vacuum the chain locker clean.

✪ Take off warps, sheets, lines and halyards and wash them in a washing machine. Put lines into a tied bag to prevent tangling and replace halyards with temporaty thin lines.

Internally:

✪ Work your way around the interior. Operate all electrical and mechanical systems to ensure that they work and have not been affected by moisture.

✪ Carry out an internal inspection for wear and tear. Are there missing galley items? Is the toilet working properly? Are the seacocks stiff? Add any items to be repaired or replaced to the refit maintenance list.

✪ Before starting routine maintenance, take out every movable item that could hold moisture. Remove food and drinks, paper charts and books, bunk cushions and galley equipment, and carry out a general clean.

When at home

As well as carrying out repairs, washing and cleaning boat items, you should also carry out any paper chart corrections.

Check your boat papers, including:
- ⚙ ship's registration documents
- ⚙ bill of sale
- ⚙ safety identification program
- ⚙ partnership agreement
- ⚙ insurance documents
- ⚙ ship's radio licence
- ⚙ liferaft service certificate
- ⚙ fire extinguishers service certificate
- ⚙ flares (list the expiry dates).

Keeping a maintenance log

Boat maintenance should be broken down into elements: hull, deck, engine, sails, and so on. By keeping such a log, you can look back to when you bought particular items.

Above: **Removing marine growth using a pressure washer. This should be done as soon as the boat is taken out of the water.**

Above: **Flaking out the anchor chain ready for power washing to remove salt deposits.**

The lists of repairs that you compiled during the sailing season should now be incorporated into the maintenance program.

And finally, most yacht and sailing clubs organize a "refit party," so be sure to sign up and enjoy the social event!

Left: **One section of a maintenance log.**

Maintenance Log
Refit

Hull and deck	Date	Comments
Wash the hull and deck with a pressure washer		
Check for damage to hull and deck		
Carry out repairs to hull and deck		
Check rudder/rudder stock and steering gear		
Clean, adjust and oil steering cables or quadrants, etc.		
Confirm emergency steering is still operational		
Visually check for keelbolt movement		
Check drainage holes are free and that water can drain freely away from the boat		
Check bilge pumps are working and pump the hull dry		
Clean boat speed impeller		
Paint topsides, following the paint manufacturer's recommendations		
Prepare hull and deck for polishing by using compound to clean the hull		
Polish hull and deck		
Prepare and apply antifoul and boot topping		

Hull and deck

Whatever material your boat is made of, when it comes out of the water it will need to be cleaned and possibly repaired. Inspect the hull and deck for damage, check the security of the keel and assess the condition of the rudder and bearings.

Below: **Put the silicone or wax polish on by hand and polish off the hull using a mains-powered polisher.**

Above: **A small mechanical grinder can be used to remove an osmosis blister from the hull of a boat prior to repair by filling with gel coat.**

Left inset: **Repair a pitted hull with epoxy resin primer before filling with resin and applying gel coat.**

Hull maintenance
Fiberglass

If your hull and deck are made of fiberglass, clean them by using a proprietary compound (by hand or with a slow-speed mechanical polisher). Over time, using an abrasive compound will reduce the thickness of the gel coat (the smooth outer covering of the boat); at some point you will have to think about painting the hull and deck. However, on a new boat, first clean with a non-abrasive cleaning compound before polishing.

Inspect the hull for "osmosis." This manifests itself in a blistering gel coat, indicating moisture trapped between the gel coat and the underlying laminate. Older boats are most likely to suffer from osmosis.

To repair isolated areas of osmosis or damage, grind out the affected areas, leave them to dry out fully, fill with an epoxy-resin proprietary marine filler, and finish with a matching gel coat. Seek professional advice if the areas are widespread.

Check the underside of the keel for wear, especially if you have run aground during the sailing season.

After cleaning and carrying out any repairs, polish the hull and deck using a marine polish applied by hand or with a slow-speed mechanical polisher. At least two coats of polish are advisable.

Wood, ferro-cement, steel and aluminum

If your boat is made of wood, ferro-cement, steel or aluminum, it will normally be covered with a paint system, varnish or other form of protection. Hulls and decks made of wood will probably need to be repainted every other year using a single-pack polyurethane paint or varnish (a single-pack system is more flexible than a two-pack one).

To repair small isolated areas of a painted wooden boat, cut out damaged areas back to solid wood and then fill with a proprietary marine filler. Fair off and apply the paint system. If the damage is larger or the wood is to be varnished, cut out the damaged area, then cut and glue in what is termed a "graving" piece (a piece of wood similar in size, shape, grain and color to that being removed).

Hulls and decks made of ferro-cement or steel must be painted every four years or so with a two-pack polyurethane paint system. Leave aluminum hulls to the elements, to oxidize and form their own protection. If aluminum is to be painted, use a two-pack polyurethane paint system.

Follow the manufacturer's recommendations and instructions when painting or varnishing.

Left: **A small electric palm sander can be used to prepare small surfaces, odd corners and fiddly angles.**

TIP

Think seriously about your capabilities. If you are unsure get someone competent to undertake work rather than attempt it yourself.

Normally, two coats of marine polish should be applied to the painted surfaces by hand or with a slow-speed mechanical polisher. Once painted, it will only require polishing until a new layer of paint is needed.

Below: **Preparing the gunwale using carborundum abrasive paper, ready for varnishing on an extensively refurbished wooden boat.**

Decks

All decks can be protected by laid teak strips, canvas sheeting or non-slip surfacing. If you have deck protection, check that it still performs its original function, is still attached to the deck and does not form a tripping hazard. If the protection is getting thin or worn out, now is the time to replace it.

You should seek advice from a professional boatyard on more extensive hull and deck damage, no matter what material has been used in the construction.

Deck fittings

Inspect the security and operation of your deck fittings; stanchions, guardrails, chain plates, cleats, fairleads, winches, tracks, hatches, windows and so on.

Deck fittings are potential sources of water ingress, so where these are held down with bolts or screws, check the tightness. If loose, remove, clean and reseal them with marine sealant before retightening. Marine sealant has a limited lifespan and over time will harden and crack. Even if the fitting is tight it may still leak. If so, it will have to be removed, resealed and refitted.

Steel and aluminum boats generally have all their deck fittings welded to the deck, so check the welding for possible stress fractures and splits.

Above: **Sealing a loose hatch rubber gasket using a general-purpose glue to keep the hatch watertight.**

Hatches and windows

Check the hinges, catches and rubber seals on your opening hatches and windows for wear and water tightness; this can be checked when you power-wash the decks.

Fixed windows have a neoprene gasket (a plastic edging to hold the window in place) in an aluminum or similar frame. Neoprene deteriorates, and as it loses its flexibility, it should be removed and replaced. Some windows are made of toughened glass but most are polycarbonate, which tends to degrade and craze after a time. When this happens, windows should be replaced.

Through-hull fittings

Most boats have a number of through-hull fittings (skin fittings): engine intake and exhaust, heads in and out, galley sink out, self-draining cockpit, to name but a few. Check all your through-hull fittings for tightness, corrosion and leaks, and check the operation and movement of all the seacocks. Metal seacocks should be taken apart, greased, reassembled and adjusted, especially if the operation of the fitting is stiff.

If you have a nylon seacock that does not operate as it should, remove it, take it apart, clean, check rubber seals and reassemble. Do not oil or grease nylon, as this will make the material expand.

Right: **The main sheet track can be removed and resealed by putting marine mastic between the track and the deck** *(top).* **The track is then replaced in position** *(bottom).*

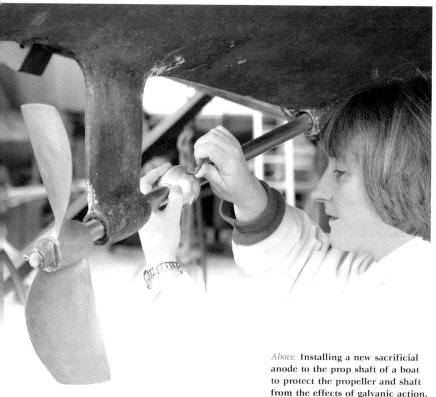

Above: **An anode that has been used for a season and suffered the effects of galvanic action. It is not completely worn out but, if left in position, may not last the next season.**

Above: **Installing a new sacrificial anode to the prop shaft of a boat to protect the propeller and shaft from the effects of galvanic action. The anode should be replaced every year.**

Metal through-hull fittings are susceptible to corrosion caused by galvanic action. Installing a sacrificial zinc anode should overcome any potential problems. Install a new one every year and check on its state of erosion. A zinc anode should protect your stainless steel prop shaft and bronze propeller.

The fitting of zinc anodes on wooden or metal boats is especially important: the anode should erode before the metal hull or metal fastenings can corrode. Zinc anodes should never be painted. If you see signs of corrosion on a metal skin fitting, withdraw it for inspection and possible replacement.

All seacocks should operate smoothly, as there may come a time when you need to close them quickly.

Keelbolts

Keelbolts are another through-hull fitting; regularly check these are watertight and sufficiently tightened. Look for rust stains and movement between the keel and hull. If you suspect a problem, seek advice from a marine surveyor.

Rudder and prop shaft bearings

Check your rudder bearings by trying to move the rudder from side to side and back and forth. If any appreciable wear is indicated, the bearings should be replaced. This will involve removing the rudder from your boat.

While your boat is out of the water, check the prop shaft by moving it from side to side and up and down. Again, have the bearings replaced if there is significant wear.

Above: **Replacing the bottom space washer of the rudder pinion tightens up the rudder and helps it to operate smoothly.** *Inset:* **Tightening the rudder pinion.**

Mast, spars, rigging and sails

At the end of the sailing season carry out an inspection of the mast, spars and rigging, either with the mast up or unstepped (temporarily removed with the assistance of a crane) and laid on trestles on the ground. It is far easier to inspect the mast at ground level rather than having to be hoisted up it. Sails should be taken to a sailmaker for laundering and repairs.

Masts and spars

By far the most common material used for masts and spars is aluminum, but wood and carbon fiber are also used. Whatever the material, your visual inspection should look for similar signs of deterioration. Wash the mast, spars and rigging to remove any buildup of salt deposits prior to inspection.

Once the rig is clean, inspect each component for stress cracks and wear. Inspect, too, for corrosion, especially where different materials come together — e.g., aluminum and stainless steel.

Carefully inspect the spreaders, shroud and stay fixing points, and the mast step, as these are vulnerable areas. Also inspect the gooseneck fitting and bolt for wear, where the boom joins the mast. If you do find corrosion, it is advisable to seek professional advice on how to carry out any remedial treatment.

Finally, polish all the aluminum surfaces with a recommended proprietary polish, or prepare and apply at least two coats of varnish, oil or stain to wooden masts and spars. Stainless steel should be buffed to provide a smooth surface.

Carbon fiber masts and spars can be painted using a two-pack polyurethane paint system according to the manufacturer's recommendations.

Standing rigging

The standing rigging, shrouds, fore and backstays are usually made of galvanized or stainless steel wire and require little maintenance. But check for any broken wires or suspect fittings, and replace as required. One end of a standing rigging wire is attached to the hull or deck via a chain plate, a toggle fitting and an adjustable bottlescrew. The other end is attached to the mast by a special mast fitting. Bottlescrew threads should be greased, and bottlescrews should be "moused" with seizing wire or clips to prevent them coming undone.

Inspect all the split pins, split rings, nuts, bolts and clevis pins for wear; replace if worn or missing. If in doubt, have a professional rigger check the rigging. Read the small print on your insurance policy; it may be a condition that you replace the standing rigging every 10 years.

Below: **Working on a mast is easier when it is placed on trestles on the ground. You can replace wiring in the mast and check for wear on shrouds and rigging.**

Taking a winch apart

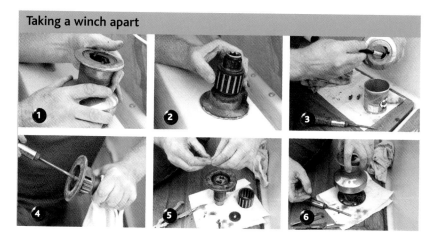

Left to right: **1. Remove the retaining clip and winch drum. 2. Remove the roller bearing for cleaning. 3. Wash away old grease from the drum with paraffin liquid. 4. Remove the retaining screw from the gears. 5. Remove the springs and pawls from the gears. 6. Temporarily reassemble to confirm smooth operation. Different makes and sizes of winch may need slightly different techniques, but this is typical.**

Below: **Carrying out a sail repair using a sailmaker's palm (similar to a dressmaker's thimble).**

Running rigging

Your running rigging will comprise halyards, sheets, reefing lines, uphauls and downhauls. Inspect all lines for chafing and replace them if worn. Wear near the end of a line can be overcome by cutting off the damaged end and rewhipping it.

When removing in-mast lines, rove a temporary drawcord, or "mouse" through in place of the halyard. End-for-end the running rigging after a few years so any possible wear is via a different point.

Fittings

Check that pulley blocks and sheaves (wheel blocks) are running free, are in good condition and not worn — especially at the mast head. A seized pulley or sheave will make hoisting a mainsail difficult and will wear the main halyard. Lubricate pulleys and sheaves by applying a silicone spray.

Clutches require little maintenance other than checking for serviceability and lubricating the spring with silicone spray.

Winches are robust pieces of equipment but will still require servicing periodically. Before carrying out a winch service, obtain the manufacturer's diagram of the associated parts. Follow service instructions — and place a see-through plastic bag over the winch to prevent springs and pawls jumping out and getting lost. Lay out the parts in order of removal; clean, oil or grease as per recommendations, before reassembling.

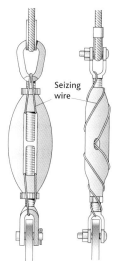

Left: **The use of seizing wire to mouse two different types of rigging screws. This prevents the threads from coming unscrewed while sailing.**

Seizing wire

TURNBUCKLE SCREW

BOTTLESCREW

Sails

It is advisable to take your sails to a sailmaker at the end of the season for valeting. The sailmaker will launder and check them, remove salt, and repair any damage.

To reduce the amount of wear on your sails, inspect them regularly throughout the sailing season. Check the sails when hoisting and before putting them away, looking for holes, rips and loose stitching — the most vulnerable part of a sail. Carry out any temporary repairs, either by using a proprietary sticky patch, stitching them, or by patching with a spare piece of sailcloth. When sailing try not to let your sails flog or flap. This weakens the fabric, causing it to stretch and lose shape.

The engine

Although your boat will have sails as the main form of propulsion, it will undoubtedly also have an engine, be it an inboard or outboard.

In today's modern marina you will need an engine to maneuver into and out of a tight berth. The engine will also be used for motoring in calm periods and charging the boat's batteries that power the navigation lights and instruments, so looking after your engine is as important as looking after your sails.

Inboard engine service

The following assumes your boat is fitted with a diesel engine, but if you happen to have a gas engine, the service follows almost exactly the same format.

At least once a year or every 100 hours of engine running time (see manufacturer's recommendations) you should carry out an engine service as per the service manual. The full annual engine service is often carried out during the refit.

For a diesel engine service:
* change the engine oil
* change the engine oil filter
* top up or change the gearbox oil
* change the fine fuel filter
* change the agglomerator filter (also known as the water separation filter)
* check and adjust the drive belt
* remove the diesel injectors for cleaning, and check for spray pattern. Pour a little oil into the cylinders to lubricate the piston rings and the bores; when putting back the fuel injectors, a light smear of non-seizure grease

Above: **Use a torque wrench to tighten the cylinder head nuts prior to adjusting a valve tappet. Ensure the cylinder head nuts are all tightened according to with the manufacturer's recommendations.**

Above: **Adjust a valve tappet using two spanners and a feeler gauge (*see* center) set to the manufacturer's recommendations. One spanner is used on the locking nut; the other adjusts the tappet.**

Above: **Remove the old fuel injectors to be refurbished and recalibrated by a qualified mechanic. Put back the refurbished injectors using non-seizure grease around the injector to assist future removal.**

Above: **Remove old oil using a sump pump to suck it out through the dipstick hole into a plastic bottle, which should be taken to a disposal depot.**

around the injectors will assist future removal
* check the tightness of the cylinder head bolts, then adjust the tappets for valve clearance

* remove and inspect the water impeller. Replace if worn; remove the impeller during the refit period to allow the rubber to return to its original shape.

Above: **Put a thin smear of new engine oil on the seal of a new oil filter prior to fixing it in position. Oil filters are changed every season or approximately every 100 hours.**

Above: **Use paraffin to wash out the air filter to remove dust and grime from the metal filter. Manually agitate the air filter to get the paraffin to thoroughly clean it out.**

Above: **Pour new engine oil into the engine through the rocker box filler hole. Do not fill completely with the recommended quantity of oil until it has settled in the sump, to avoid overfilling.**

The main difference between a diesel and a gasoline engine (a 2-stroke or 4-stroke) is the method of igniting the fuel. Gas engines will have spark plugs for the fuel ignition. Change the spark plugs on a gas engine every year.

With gas engines, the gas supply to the engine should be shut off during the refit so as to reduce any fuel seepage. If installed, the extractor fan (non-sparking) under the gas engine should be operated at frequent intervals to extract any gas vapor that may have accumulated. Prior to the end of the season, try to use up as much gas in the main fuel tank as you can and drain off the rest. Gas will degrade over time and can cause ignition problems.

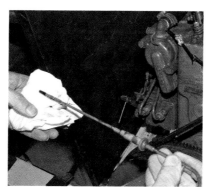

Above: **Use the dipstick to check the level of oil in the sump. Adjust the quantity of new oil until it is between minimum and maximum levels on the dipstick.**

Above: **Check the fan belt tension to within the tolerance specified by the engine manufacturer.**

TIP

Use a plastic bottle with a larger capacity than the oil being removed from the sump. This allows you to remove all the oil in one go and avoids changing bottles and potential oil spills.

The engine (2)

Inboard engine service

- ⚙ Fill or top up the fuel tank or tanks to prevent condensation and stop any bugs contaminating the fuel.
- ⚙ If the engine has a freshwater cooling system with a heat exchanger, drain off the cooling water from the internal cooling system and refill with a mixture of antifreeze as recommended by the engine manufacturer.
- ⚙ Flush out the raw-water side of the engine by connecting a hose from a barrel of water hanging off the stern and fed to the engine intake. Keep the water level in the barrel at the same level as the sea water level when the boat is afloat, to prevent any siphoning. Fit a pipe from the exhaust outlet back into the barrel, to form a water loop. Run the engine with the barrel filled with fresh water, changing the contaminated water frequently to remove salt deposits. Finally, fill the barrel with a 50/50 mixture of antifreeze and fresh water, and run the engine once to allow the mixture to circulate around the system. Turn off the feed from the water barrel when not in use.
- ⚙ Remove rust on the engine by wire brushing and paint affected areas with engine paint. Then spray it with de-moisturizer.
- ⚙ Thoroughly clean out the engine tray; an absorbent pad such as a disposable diaper is ideal for this.
- ⚙ Finally, crank over the engine by hand at least every two weeks. This will keep the oil moving around the engine.

Stern gear

Your shaft seal or stern gland (the seal between the propeller shaft and the hull of the boat) will require little maintenance, but check for corrosion of the stainless steel jubilee clips around the seal and the seal itself. Some seals may require the stuffing around the shaft to be replaced after a time, and the stuffing box repacked with grease.

The outer shaft bearing or cutlass bearing needs to be checked for wear by trying to move the shaft up and down and from side to side. If worn (that is, showing signs of movement) it should be replaced.

When out of the water, the shaft anode should be replaced, even if the existing worn anode is still in place. If it is left in place it may vibrate on the propeller shaft before falling off naturally. Also check that the propeller is firmly attached to

Left: **Running up the engine using a water drum connected to the engine water intake. The engine pumps water back into the drum via the exhaust pipe. Some marinas don't permit engines to run in yachts ashore, so check local rules.** *Inset:* **Detail of a typical water drum.**

Left: **The propeller is fixed on the prop shaft and secured by a nut. The nut is kept in place by a split pin and a locking tab washer. This propeller is in good condition and shows no sign of wear from galvanic action.**

Right: **Flushing fresh water through the running outboard engine, placed in a freshwater tank. The flowing water confirms it is being flushed through.**

the shaft and that the nut and split pin are still in place. Polish or antifoul the propeller and check for de-zincification (the appearance of copper spots on the bronze propeller). The zinc anode should protect the propeller against de-zincification. If spots are found, seek professional advice from a yacht surveyor or the boatyard.

Outboard engine service

You should carry out an outboard engine service at least once a year, as per the engine-maker's service manual. Most outboard engines are either 2-stroke (a mixture of gas and oil) or 4-stroke gas engines. For an outboard engine service:
- drain off the gas
- change the gearbox oil
- change the engine oil and filters of a 4-stroke engine
- clean the carburetor and fuel filters
- change the spark plugs and rota arm if fitted
- flush out the cooling water system by running the engine in a tank of fresh water to remove any salt deposits.

At the end of the season, use up the gas stored in the spare fuel can. Keep pure gas rather than premixed gas and oil in the spare can, since pure gas, uncontaminated by oil, can be used for cleaning and various other purposes. Add the recommended mix of oil and gas directly to the outboard tank when needed.

Above **Change the spark plug every season on the outboard engine using a box spanner; keep the old one as a spare.**

Electrical

The most vulnerable part of your boat is the electrical. Moisture, verdigris (a sort of green rust that forms on copper), salt deposits or the wrong size of wire can all form a resistance in the wiring circuits. Incorrect voltage, amperage and short circuits can cause instruments to give spurious information and light filaments to dim or to flicker.

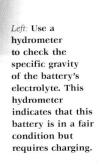

Left: Use a hydrometer to check the specific gravity of the battery's electrolyte. This hydrometer indicates that this battery is in a fair condition but requires charging.

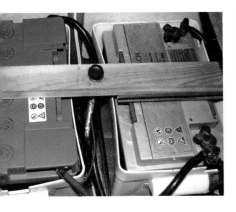

Left: This battery area contains two batteries secured with a locking bar to prevent them from moving around. Batteries are in their own spillage containers in case of battery acid spillage.

Right: Batteries being charged using a battery charger attached to the power supply.

The refit period is a good time to check all the electrical connections and the state of the wiring.

Batteries

There are normally two or three batteries on board a boat: one for starting the engine and the others for domestic appliances (lights, instruments, and so on). They should be recharged at the end of the season, and periodically tested and recharged throughout the refit.

If possible, take your batteries home for charging. Check the distilled water level and the specific gravity of the electrolyte by using a hydrometer. Top up as required.

If any cell fails to hold a charge, take the battery to a battery supplier for a test. Should you need to replace one or both batteries, purchase a good quality marine "deep cycle" battery rather than an automobile battery.

Below: A boat circuit. Battery number 1 is the engine starting battery and number 2 is the domestic battery on a two-battery system that feeds the lighting system of the boat.

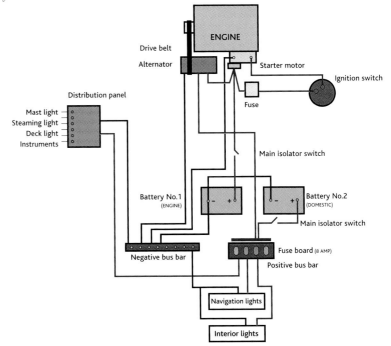

When servicing the engine, it is vital to ensure that the drive belt is correctly tensioned. A slipping belt will not allow the alternator (the charging device) to charge the batteries correctly, while a belt that is too tight will wear out the alternator bearings.

Circuits

Obtain a wiring diagram of your boat to assist you in tracing any particular circuit. Update the diagram after an alteration is made.

✪ Test any suspect wiring and check all navigation and domestic lights, pumps and instruments.

✪ Check and clean the contact ends of replaceable-type fuses and consider replacing them with ones that can be reset easily with the flick of a switch.

Rewiring

When rewiring existing circuits or putting in new ones, use marine grade "tinned" cable (that is, each strand is coated with solder). Within the outer plastic insulation, the strands of an un-tinned cable will go dull and attract verdigris, which insulates each strand from its neighbor. These strands then set up their own resistance rather than working as part of a whole. To save on the cost of tinned cable, you can

Left: **Wiring behind the instrument panel. This shows neat wiring where a possible fault can easily be traced.**

purchase red (positive) and black or blue (negative), and then attach colored end sleeves about 1 inch (2.5 cm) long to both ends of the cable before making the connection. The color of the end sleeves should correspond with the wiring diagram.

✪ "Tin" the ends of cables

(especially un-tinned cables) using a soldering iron and solder before making any connection. This makes sure each strand is attached to its neighbor.

✪ Spray the connections with demoisturizer.

Right: **Spray the connections with demoisturizer to make a waterproof connection.**
Inset: **Comparing new yellow wire with existing old yellow wire. Old wire has hard, cracked, brittle casing and the copper strands do not make contact with one another.**

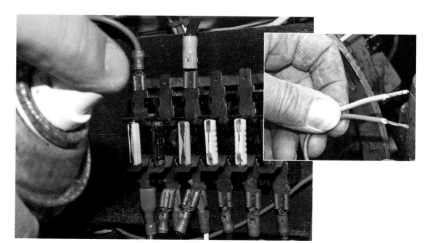

Plumbing

Thorough cleaning and maintenance of your plumbing systems is essential. You will rely on the boat's pumps to get fresh water, pump the bilge and operate the toilet, so they must operate effectively. Fresh water and wastewater systems must be clean to avoid bacteria.

Through-hull fittings

The boat's skin fittings (through-hull vents that attach to an interior pipe for waste) will be made of either marine-grade metal or plastic and will require little maintenance, other than periodical inspection for cracks or corrosion. When checking a skin fitting make sure that any soft material pipes attached to it are fitted with two marine-grade stainless steel jubilee clips so that if one corrodes or becomes loose you still have another securing the pipe to the fitting.

Also make sure that the correct size of tapered wooden plug is attached by a cord to the fitting for emergencies. Instruments that use a skin fitting, such as the speed/log, should be withdrawn, cleaned and put back with a little vegetable cooking oil or water pump grease.

While checking the skin fitting and the seacock for the sea water intake to the cooling system of your engine, remove the stainless steel water strainer basket. Remove debris, clean it and put it back.

Plastic seacocks

The modern plastic seacock is lever operated and the body of the valve is generally made of fiberglass. Being made of plastic it is non-corrosive and requires little maintenance. However, regular inspection, operation and lubrication are required. The seals can be lubricated with vegetable cooking oil or water pump grease.

Metal seacocks

Most metal seacocks are lever operated and made of a marine-grade metal (gun metal or phosphor bronze). The valve plug fits into the main body of the valve with a tapered friction fit. It is adjustable, rather like the glass stopper in a decanter. The valve body will also have a grease nipple fitted so that the valve can be lubricated when the boat is in the water.

When your boat is out of the water, take the valve apart, clean the valve and plug, grease all parts, reassemble and adjust the friction. Check for any wear, cracks or corrosion and do any remedial work that may be required.

The other form of metal seacock is similar to the domestic plumbing gate-valve. If you have these types of valves fitted consider changing them. They are wheel operated and it is hard to see if the valve is open or closed. They could also be made of brass and therefore easily corrode in a marine environment or get jammed with debris and therefore not open or close fully, which will restrict the flow of water.

Below: **Withdrawing the speed/ log unit from the skin fitting for cleaning.**

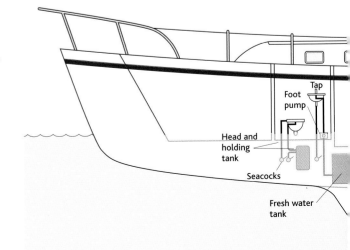

Right: **Section through a boat showing a simple diagrammatic plumbing layout.**

Tap

Foot pump

Head and holding tank

Seacocks

Fresh water tank

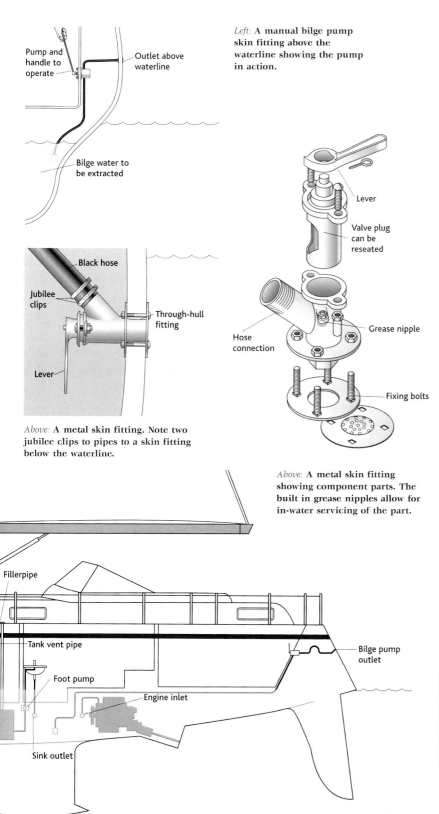

Pump and handle to operate

Outlet above waterline

Bilge water to be extracted

Left: **A manual bilge pump skin fitting above the waterline showing the pump in action.**

Black hose

Jubilee clips

Through-hull fitting

Lever

Above: **A metal skin fitting. Note two jubilee clips to pipes to a skin fitting below the waterline.**

Lever

Valve plug can be reseated

Grease nipple

Hose connection

Fixing bolts

Above: **A metal skin fitting showing component parts. The built in grease nipples allow for in-water servicing of the part.**

Fillerpipe

Tank vent pipe

Foot pump

Engine inlet

Sink outlet

Bilge pump outlet

Pumps

Check all your pumps — whether manually or electrically operated — for effective operation. If a pump is not operating effectively, it may just be down to a loose pipe letting in air rather than a defect in the pump itself. If the pump still fails to operate as it should, remove it for servicing. Most pump manufacturers supply a service kit including fitting instructions.

A manually operated bilge pump should have a "strum box" (a coarse strainer) fitted to the end of the pipe in the bilge. Remove the strum box from the end of the pipe, dismantle and clean it to remove all debris. Reassemble and refix it to the end of the bilge pipe. Test the pump after the service.

An electrically operated (automatic or manual) bilge pump has a fine filter fitted in the base to protect the rubber impeller from damage. Unclip the main body of the pump from the hull fixing, remove the fine gauze filter from the pump body, clean, reassemble, and connect to the hull fixing.

Check the tightness of all stainless steel jubilee clips securing pipes to their respective pumps.

TIP

A thin smear of petroleum jelly around the rubber ring will assist in the removal and replacement of the speed/log unit.

Plumbing (2)

Above: **Checking the operation of a gas tap after fixing a new armored hose to the stove.**

Your butane or propane gas system's efficiency and safety should be checked annually by a registered installer who is authorized to issue a compliance certificate.

Gas cylinders

If you can't easily determine the level of gas in the cylinder, compare your cylinder's weight against that of a full one to decide if you need a refill. Check the retaining straps securing the cylinder to your boat.

Hoses and pipes

High-pressure rubber hoses, copper distribution pipes and the regulator valve should be inspected for corrosion and security. Check the tightness of the jubilee clips on the high-pressure rubber hoses and for any wear where the distribution pipes pass through the plastic protection sleeves of a bulkhead. Check there is a loop in the copper distribution pipework to allow for expansion and contraction.

Gas locker

Confirm that the gas vents to the top and bottom of the gas locker are free from debris and open to the atmosphere. A registered installer should check that the gas leak detector (bubbler device) functions correctly by deliberately slackening the outlet side of the detector and running off a small quantity of gas in the gas locker, which can then escape via the gas locker drain. After confirming the operation of the gas leak detector, the slackened nut should be retightened and the system checked for leaks. Check the operation of the cabin-switched shut-off gas valve in the gas locker if fitted. Many people prefer a manually operated shut-off.

Stoves

Check that all the flame-failure devices on the stove are working correctly and that they shut off the gas supply. Also check the operation of the manual tap near the stove and inspect the armored hose for wear and corrosion.

Gas alarms and portable sniffers

Your registered installer will test the operation of the electronic gas leak detector that you have in the bilge. Some electronic gas leak detectors are fitted with a motorized valve that will automatically shut off the gas supply if any gas is detected. Test the battery in your portable carbon monoxide detector to ensure it is working efficiently.

Head (onboard toilet)

Servicing the toilet is not as messy as it sounds. Most manufacturers supply a service kit including fitting instructions. To remove calcium buildup from the pan and the hoses, use a proprietary descaling solution. On reassembly, check the tightness of all the hoses and the operation of the anti-siphon loops on the inlet and outlet pipes. Pour a little vegetable oil into the pan and flush the system to lubricate the rubber valves. Do not, under any circumstances, use bleach in the toilet pan; it will rot the rubber valves.

Below: **Using a spring balance, check the weight of a used gas cylinder and compare it with the weight of a new cylinder to gauge how much gas there is left in the old one.**

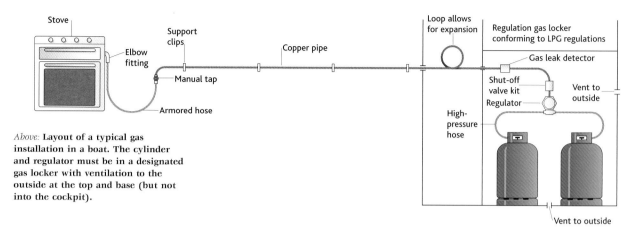

Above: **Layout of a typical gas installation in a boat. The cylinder and regulator must be in a designated gas locker with ventilation to the outside at the top and base (but not into the cockpit).**

Holding tank

If you have a holding tank, flush the contents out at sea (at least 3 miles from shore, or more, depending upon the country's regulations) or empty it at a pump-out station. Flush the system through with fresh water and a proprietary treatment solution.

Heaters

Ducted warm-air cabin heaters can be either gas or diesel operated. Both types should be serviced by a qualified installer and meet regulation standards.

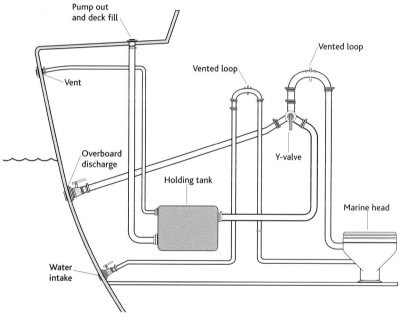

Above: **A pump circulates water from outside into the head and flushes the waste overboard or into a holding tank.**

Above: **Put chlorine tablets into a full tank of water and flush the system out once a year.**

Fresh water

Flush out your fresh water tank and pipes by putting the recommended amount of chlorine tablets into the full water tank and pumping through all the supply pipes and pumps. Fill the water tank with fresh water and flush though the system again. Repeat until you are satisfied the water is fresh. If an inline filter is fitted on the hose to the galley tap, check whether the filter cartridge needs replacing.

Personal and boat safety

You can service most, if not all, of your personal safety items at home, but some boat safety items have to be inspected and serviced on board or sent away for servicing.

Below: **Inspect lanyards by checking the stitching is tight. Lightly oil the springs and moving parts.**

Personal safety items
Lifejackets

The main personal safety items on any boat are the lifejackets: look after them. At the end of the sailing season, wash them to remove any salt deposits, and inspect them for wear. When dry, carry out an inflation test by orally inflating them and leaving them for 24 hours. A little air loss over 24 hours is acceptable, but if a jacket has deflated, investigate where it is leaking by inflating the jacket and holding it under water in the bathtub. If it leaks through the oral inflation stopper, some manufacturers will supply a new stopper. If it leaks elsewhere, invest in a new jacket. Your life is worth it!

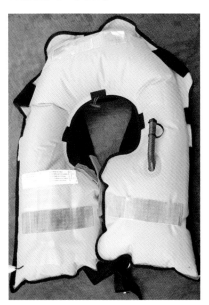

Above: **Inflate your lifejacket and leave for 24 hours to check for any air leaks. Check the battery light is working and that the automatic inflation device and cylinder is secure and within its expiry date.**

Having confirmed that all the jackets are serviceable, deflate them by removing the oral inflation stoppers and depressing the valve. Next, check the automatic or manual gas inflation units by unscrewing and removing the gas cylinders and inspecting the threads for corrosion. Replace any corroded cylinders. If a cylinder has been used to inflate a lifejacket, the manufacturer will supply a re-arming kit.

Harnesses, crutch straps and lanyards

Inspect all the boat's safety harnesses and lifejacket straps for wear. Most modern lifejackets have an integral harness and crutch straps. If any of your jackets do not have crutch straps, these can be purchased separately. Check the lanyards for wear, especially the stitching, and oil the spring attachment hooks. Replace any that don't work.

Lights, whistles, markers, spray masks

Lifejacket lights can be manual, automatic or water activated, and can be attached to your lifejacket or arm. Whatever type you have, it will have a manual test switch or override switch. Test the unit by activating this. Some lights have a facility to change the battery; others are sealed units.

A plastic whistle should be attached to the lifejacket by a length of cord. Check the cord and the operation of the whistle.

Spray masks and small personal dye markers are now officially recommended as lifejacket attachments; consider purchasing them if yours do not have them.

Above: **Check the expiry dates on your flares so that they will all be in date during the next season. If any are out of date, take them to a licensed organization for disposal.**

Radio beacons

Your boat's EPIRB (Emergency Position Indicating Radio Beacon) and your PLBs (personal locator beacons) should be cleaned and inspected and will have a manual test switch for testing the unit. Carefully follow the manufacturer's instructions.

Boat safety items
Liferaft

Your boat's largest safety item is the liferaft, whether it is a canister or valise type. Wash off any salt and inspect the retaining straps or clips for wear, but also take the liferaft to

an authorized depot for regular servicing (normally required every three years, but this varies according to the manufacturer).

Grab bags, flares and fog horn

Check the contents of the grab bag, making sure that the flares are in date for the next season and any batteries are replaced, and check that the boat's flares are in date, too. Physically test your oral and gas-operated fog horns. and put the marine mobile radio on charge.

MOB system, lifebelts and heaving line

Your MOB system will likely comprise a horseshoe lifebelt, a danbuoy pole with flag, a drogue, a dye marker, a whistle and an automatic floating light, all tied together with a floating line. The horseshoe lifebelt should be marked with your boat's name and have reflective tape attached. There may be an automatic light at the top of the danbuoy, activated when deployed. Check and inspect the batteries in both the automatic floating light and the danbuoy for corrosion, and ensure they are fully charged.

Your heaving line is a floating line, one end attached to the boat and the other to a rubber rescue life

Above: **Test your foghorns work at the start of the season.**

preserver. Repack the line in its bag so that when the life preserver is thrown, the line is free to run out.

Your other lifebelt should also be marked with your boat's name and have reflective tape. It should have an automatic floating light, whistle, drogue and dye marker attached.

Guard wires, jackstays and lanyard attachments

The guard wires around the boat and the stanchions should be checked for corrosion and security. Jackstays (the safety line onto which harness lanyards are clipped) should be checked for wear, and also check the security of the cockpit lanyard attachments.

Fire extinguishers and fire blanket

Your fire extinguishers will be either a serviceable type, and have a date for the next service, or will be a non-serviceable type, having an expiry date stamped on the casing. Service or replace them, as necessary.

Left: **If necessary, replace the batteries of the lifebuoy lights. Check the bulbs and test the unit to see if it works.**

Pre-season preparation

The final stage is preparation for the sailing season. Put on board the items you stored ashore, inspecting them as you do so. Also put on board your corrected charts, pilot books, the new almanac, the boat's documents (the "ship's papers") and the manuals for equipment operation.

Prior to launch

- Run the engine and confirm that it is working correctly, including the cooling system. Make sure the engine is in neutral so the propeller won't turn. Check and top up the fuel in the main fuel tank and in any portable containers.
- Bend on the mainsail and headsail, and half-hoist the reefing and furling gear when there is no wind.
- Put on board all warps, lines and fenders ready for the launch.
- Fill up with fuel and run the outboard.
- Check that all the radios work, both receiving and transmitting.
- As the last item of refit, apply the antifouling paint to the hull.

After the launch

Check for leaks around seacocks, stern gland and skin fittings. Go around the boat and check the standing rigging for equal tension and ensure the adjustable bottlescrews are secured with special clips or mousing wire to stop the screws from unwinding.

Above: **A short "shake down" sail at the start of the season is a good way of finding out whether everything still works.**

Left: **Apply antifouling paint with a brush or roller. For best results, do this just before the boat goes back in the water. Normally, antifouling needs to be applied every year.**

Contents of the toolbox

Now go for a "shake down" sail (a short sail to test equipment), checking that the wind, log, speed and depth instruments/alarms are functioning, the engine operates correctly, and the sails/reefing lines are not twisted when hoisted.

Replenish spares

Replenish the spares you used during the refit and last season.

- First-aid box and medical box: e.g., bandages, pain relievers, seasickness tablets.
- Engine: lubricating oil, oil and fuel filters, fan belt, water pump impeller, grease, outboard spares, bilge cleaner.
- Electrical: navigation and cabin light bulbs and fuses, spare dry cell batteries, distilled water for the main batteries.
- Plumbing: bilge and galley pump spares and toilet service kit.
- General: screws, nuts and bolts, tape, air horns.

Engine tools
- Spanners
- Adjustable wrenches
- Torque wrench
- Straps to remove filters
- Feeler gauge for spark plug gaps and valve clearances
- Hammer
- Hammer with one soft end
- Screwdrivers — a selection of both slot and star ends
- Socket set

Electrical tools
- Drill and drill bits
- Crimping tool
- Cable stripper
- Soldering irons (boat battery voltage and regular voltage)
- Spare cable — size as on board
- Spare connectors — size as on board
- Solder
- Multimeter
- Torch

General tools
- Carpenter's saw
- Portable vice
- Bolt croppers
- Multitool or pliers
- Hand brace
- Mole grips
- Circlip pliers
- 10 lb axe

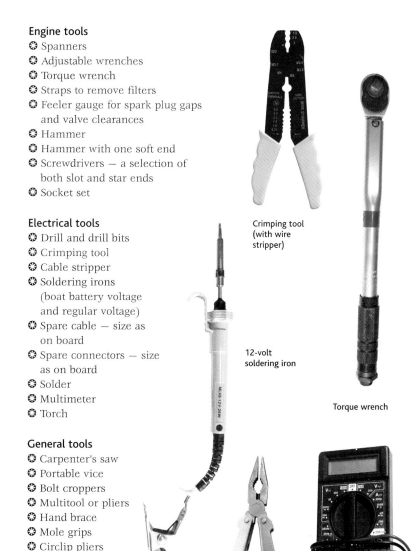

Crimping tool (with wire stripper)

12-volt soldering iron

Torque wrench

Multimeter

TIP

Always remember that maintenance is preferable to expensive repairs or worse — dangerous failures.

Safety at Sea

8

Planning for safety

While most sea passages will be uneventful, the crew of a yacht must be prepared to deal with any unexpected eventualities and skippers must plan for such occurrences. Before a voyage, skippers need to brief their crew so they fully understand safety equipment and procedures.

Safety at sea is based upon knowledge and practice. Any hypothetical situation may need to turn into an emergency plan of action. Being aware of how to use your boat's equipment, interpreting what you see and acting appropriately may save lives in an emergency.

Practicing procedures will give you a better chance of doing something instinctively. Practice a man overboard drill each time you go out for a sail. Practicing sailing without a rudder or maneuvering without an engine in controlled conditions will allow you to gain the skills and confidence for dealing with a real situation.

Safety planning: skipper's briefings

Make sure the crew is prepared for the voyage. Introduce them to each other, and informally ask each crew member to give you a description of their experiences, qualifications and if they have any special dietary requests. Assess the strengths and weaknesses of your crew and plan any special stores. Ask about any medical conditions they have (certain conditions could restrict a planned passage) and confirm they have their medication with them.

Remember that as skipper you are responsible for the safety of both boat and crew. You take the decision to put to sea based upon the information gained from your crew.

If you are sailing to other countries, ensure all crew members

Above: **Read all the information you can about the port you are visiting. The tide, weather conditions and estimated length of the passage will influence when you arrive.**

Below: **When passage planning, always start with a chart that covers both departure and destination ports, to find total distance and the most suitable passage to get there.**

Left: **The skipper's briefing should cover all aspects of safety before a voyage, including MOB, fire, flooding, distress signals, restricted visibility and first aid.**

have their passports with them, as these are likely to be requested and inspected by foreign authorities.

Safety briefings

Familiarise your crew with the yacht, its sails, the engine, the average speed under sail and/or engine, the distance and duration under engine, and the sea motion to be expected during the passage. Explain where to find the boat's equipment and where to stow personal gear.

List the safety equipment carried on board and where it is stowed (liferaft, lifejackets, safety lines, fog horn, fire extinguishers, grab bag, etc.). Show them how to operate the main radio and the procedure to speak to the coastguard or send out a "mayday." A laminated card next to the radio will act as a memory aid.

Make sure all crew members have brought a sun hat, sunglasses, shorts and sun-block, or waterproofs, boots and warm clothes, etc, depending upon the weather.

Show the crew how and when to use the boat's safety equipment. Outline emergency procedures and demonstrate how to put on a lifejacket. All crew should check their lifejackets fit correctly.

Passage plan

The skipper should discuss the passage plan with the crew. The written plan will list ports of call, anticipated weather conditions, sea state, the duration of passage, night orders, navigational strategy, contingency plans, tides and GPS waypoints.

Form your crew into watches (a small group of crew members) with

a watch leader in charge of each group. A watch will have the responsibility of running the boat for a specified length of time. A watch system will allow you to delegate responsibility and will give all crew members a sense of purpose and recognition. A watch system on long passages is essential so that the skipper and crew get plenty of rest and sleep.

In the event of seasickness, the sufferer should go to their bunk to rest, keep warm and acclimatize to the boat's motion. Drink plenty of water. Any crew member wishing to stay on deck or in the cockpit should wear a lifejacket, dress warmly and keep active, to avoid suffering from cold.

Safety equipment

It is essential to know how to use safety equipment on board. Organizations, manufacturers and sailing clubs run plenty of courses aimed at teaching you about safety.

Personal safety at sea

A buoyancy aid or flotation aid will only assist in keeping you afloat, whereas a lifejacket or personal flotation device (PFD) is designed to turn you over if inverted so that your nose and mouth are clear of the water. When purchasing equipment, read the inside label of a lifejacket or PFD for restrictions, size and weight.

for offshore and rough weather use and is designed to turn you over so that your nose and mouth are clear of the water.

⦿ *Level 275* is a lifejacket for offshore use when carrying extra weight (jackets, trousers and thermal gear) that requires extra buoyancy. It is designed to turn you over so that your nose and mouth are clear of the water.

harness or an integral harness in your sailing jacket.

⦿ *Lanyard:* A lanyard or safety line is approximately 6 feet (1.8 m) long with double-action hooks at either end. One end of the lanyard is attached to the D-ring of your harness, the other to a safety point on the boat.

⦿ *Spray hood:* This is a hood with a see-through face panel that fits over the head to stop water or spray hindering your breathing.

⦿ *Crotch straps:* These are designed to stop the lifejacket from riding up if you are in the water.

Above: **This lifejacket would be suitable for use offshore in extreme conditions.**

Above: **This PFD is designed for extended survival in rough, open water, and should turn an unconscious person face up.**

Above: **An inflated lifejacket with spray hood, designed to keep water away from the face if you fall overboard. The spray hood can be kept folded, attached to a lifejacket.**

In Europe (including the U.K.), buoyancy aids and lifejackets are available in four main levels of buoyancy, measured in Newtons.

⦿ *Level 50* is a buoyancy aid intended for use only if you are a swimmer close to shore.

⦿ *Level 100* is a buoyancy aid for sheltered waters.

⦿ *Level 150* is a lifejacket intended

Lifejacket added extras

Carry your personal lifejacket with as many of the following attachments as possible:

⦿ *Harness:* Lifejackets can be purchased with an integral harness and D-ring to attach to a lanyard. If you do not have lifejackets with integral harnesses then you should have a separate

❂ *Light:* A light can be attached to your lifejacket or sailing jacket, which can be activated manually or automatically when in contact with the water.

❂ *Whistle:* This should be attached to the lifejacket via a thin line.

❂ *Reflective strips:* Your lifejacket should have some retro-reflective tape attached for extra visibility.

❂ *Dye marker:* A marine dye marker is for daytime visibility.

❂ *PLB:* A personal locator beacon transmitting on 121.5 MHz, used as a homing device for search and rescue services mainly in the U.K.

Above: **There should be safety points in the cockpit of the boat, to which you can attach your lanyard.**

❂ There are also lifejackets designed for children and animals.

In most of the world, including the United States, there are numerous types fof PFDs:

❂ *Type I offshore lifejacket* has the highest flotation (22 pounds/ 10 kg) of the PFDs — enough to keep most adults turned face up, even if unconscious.

❂ *Type I hybrid lifejacket* provides both foam and an inflatable system in one jacket.

❂ *Type II near-shore buoyant vest* comes in several sizes and is not suitable for offshore use. Some models have a crotch strap and collar handle. It is a good choice for inshore sailing and for children and provides a minimum of 15.5 pounds (7 kg) of buoyancy; many will turn an unconscious person face up in the water.

❂ *Type III flotation aids* are vests or full-sleeved lifejackets that provide a minimum of 15.5 pounds (7 kg) of buoyancy, and may be inflatable or made from foam. They are versatile and comfortable, but will not normally turn an unconscious person face-up in the water.

❂ *Type IV throwable special-use device* is a seat cushion or ring buoy designed to be thrown to a person in the water to hold. It cannot be worn or used for children, unconscious people or anyone who cannot swim.

❂ *Type V wearable special-use device* must be worn for the activity stated on the label. Hybrids include some inflatable lifejackets, wetsuits and survival suits.

❂ All recreational boats must carry one wearable Type I, II, III or Type V PFD for each person aboard. A Type V PFD provides a similar performance to a Type I, II, or III PFD. Any sailing boat of 16 feet (5 m) or longer must also carry one throwable Type IV PFD.

Using your lifejacket or PFD

❂ To work best, a lifejacket or PFD must be worn with all straps, zippers and ties fastened.

❂ Make sure the lifejacket or PFD is maintained in good condition and kept in an easily accessible place, as you may need to find it quickly.

❂ Extend the life of your lifejacket or PFD through proper maintenance. Never use it for any other purpose other than for personal safety.

❂ To prevent mildew, dry lifejackets or PFDs completely before storing. Store in a well-ventilated space — not on a boat that is not in use.

Standards, regulations and approved equipment vary from state to state in the U.S., and from country to country.

Right: **This type of EPIRB is an unregistered homing device. Despite being slowly phased out in the U.S., they are still widely used in Europe.**

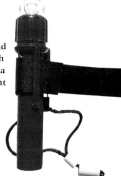

Right: **A flashing light can easily be attached to a lifejacket and makes it much easier to find a person at night or in poor visibility.**

Safety equipment (2)

Boat equipment

✪ *Deck gear:* On either side of the deck, there will be guardrails and jackstays that run from the bow to the stern on the deck. Hook onto the jackstays with your harness lanyard so that you can move around and still be attached to the boat. Guardrails prevent you from falling overboard. There should be safety eyes to hook your lanyard onto when in the cockpit, too.

✪ *Pumps:* Your boat should have an automatic bilge pump, a manual bilge pump in the cockpit, and a portable emergency bilge pump.

✪ *Communication equipment:* For communicating with others, most boats will have a main VHF radio, a standby emergency VHF aerial, a handheld VHF radio, a boat's mobile phone, possibly an EPIRB (Emergency Position Indicating Radio Beacon), a SART (Search and Rescue Transponder), a fog horn, a radar reflector, flares, a large powerful flashlight and maybe a set of signal flags. An anchor ball displayed during the day and an all-around white light at night will indicate that you are at anchor. Displaying your triangular motor cone will indicate to others that you are using your engine for propulsion even though you have your sails up.

✪ *Alarms:* Gas and carbon monoxide alarms should be installed.

Essential safety items

❶ Navigation lights	⓴ Hand-held compasses
❷ Anchor and chain	㉑ Fire extinguisher
❸ Anchor warp	㉒ Fire blanket
❹ Winch for anchor	㉓ Tool kit
❺ Bucket with lanyard	㉔ Seacock
❻ MOB equipment	㉕ Emergency steering
❼ MOB recovery ladder	㉖ Flares and orange smoke
❽ Fuel	㉗ First-aid kit
❾ Gas tank (and spare)	㉘ Life jackets
❿ Dinghy, oars and repair kit	㉙ Flashlights
⓫ Radar reflector	㉚ Kedge anchor
⓬ Bilge pumps	㉛ Hand-held radio/mobile
⓭ Life raft	㉜ Grab-bag
⓮ Heaving line	㉝ Radio equipment
⓯ Foghorn	㉞ Signal flags
⓰ Drinking water	㉟ Lead line
⓱ Detection devices	㊱ Jackstay
⓲ Anchor ball	㊲ Warps
⓳ Navigation display	㊳ Winch handle

✪ *Instruments:* Your depth sounder, speed log, radar, GPS and other instruments will all help to determine your position and the depth of water.

✪ *Man overboard (MOB) gear:* Your MOB marker system will consist of a danbuoy with automatic light and a day-glo flag connected to a horseshoe lifebuoy with an automatic light, drogue, dye marker and whistle. Your horseshoe lifebuoys should be marked with the boat's name and have retro-reflective tape attached. There are many ways to retrieve a casualty from the water once they are attached and alongside. You can use the boat's boarding ladder, a retrieval sling or strop, a sail or net, or a proprietary retrieval system. A buoyant heaving line should also be carried and attached to the stern. There is a good chance that you will be able to throw the line and make contact with the MOB very quickly after stopping your boat.

✪ *Liferaft:* The size and type of liferaft you choose will depend upon the size of your crew and your cruising area — inshore, offshore or ocean. As well as your liferaft and its contents, always carry an emergency grab-bag with SART (Search and Rescue Transponder), TPAs (Thermal Protection Aids), mobile VHF radio, boat documents, flares and the EPIRB.

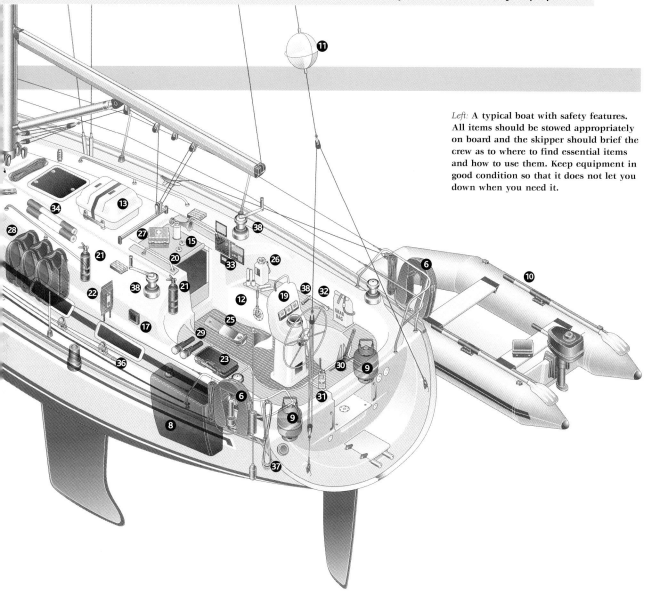

Left: **A typical boat with safety features. All items should be stowed appropriately on board and the skipper should brief the crew as to where to find essential items and how to use them. Keep equipment in good condition so that it does not let you down when you need it.**

❂ *Fire-fighting equipment:* The number and size of fire extinguishers on board will depend upon your boat's size. They should be accessible from the forecabin hatch, the main companionway hatch, and any other boat entrance. Install an automatic fire extinguisher in the engine compartment, with a fire blanket near the stove.

❂ *Medical:* A recommended minimum contents list for your cruising area can be obtained from various first-aid organizations. Include tablets for pain relief, seasickness and stomach upsets, etc.

❂ *Other safety items:* You should have emergency tools such as cable cutters and hacksaws, storm sails

(a storm jib and trysail if you do not have roller reefing), a main anchor and chain, a kedge anchor and warp. Carry a sea anchor/ drogue and a lead-line (a lead weight attached to a thin line) as a standby depth sounder. A rubber or rigid tender with an outboard engine. Paddles can tow your boat if there is little wind and the main engine fails (see page 378).

Collision avoidance

Avoiding collisions requires caution and common sense. Always keep a good lookout and be prepared to slow down, change course or stop the boat. Make your intentions clear by changing course through a big angle. Never assume the other skipper understands the rules of the road or is keeping a good lookout.

Rules of the road under sail

- Power gives way to sail. But sail may have to give way to power if the boat under power cannot maneuver or is constrained by its draft or is a commercial vessel.
- Overtaking boat must keep clear. This also applies to a boat under sail overtaking a boat under power.
- Port tack gives way to starboard tack. However, the port-tack boat may have to give way if the starboard-tack boat calls "Water!" when sailing away from a very shallow area.
- When boats are on the same tack, the leeward boat has right of way. This means that the boat sailing closest to the wind must give way. For instance, a boat that is beating on port tack has right of way over a boat that is reaching on port tack.

Rules of the road under power

- Keep to the starboard side of a narrow channel. Always remember to drive on the right, both on the way out and on the way in.
- If two boats are converging head-on, both should change course to starboard. Signal your intentions clearly by making an obvious turn to starboard in plenty of time.
- If two boats are converging, the boat that is on the other boat's starboard bow has right of way. This means that if you can see the other boat's port side, which would be illuminated by a red navigation light in poor visibility, you must give way. It's simple — green for go; red for give way.

Right of way

A: The vessel under engine keeps clear of the vessel under sail.
B: The overtaking vessel keeps out of the way of the vessel that has right of way.
C: The vessel on port tack keeps clear of the vessel on starboard tack.
D: The windward vessel must keep clear.

Yachts under power:
E. The vessel to port must give way and not attempt to cross ahead unless well clear.
F. Both vessels must turn to starboard in a channel or when meeting head on and keep to the starboard side.

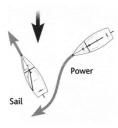

A. Engine power gives way to sail power

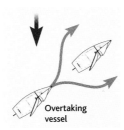

B. Overtaking vessel gives way

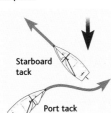

C. Port tack keeps clear

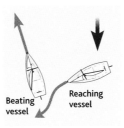

D. Windward boat keeps clear

E. Vessel to port gives way

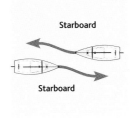

F. Both vessels turn to starboard when meeting head on

> **TIP**
>
> It is worth remembering Rule 7 of the Collision Regulations, which states that every vessel shall use all available means to determine if the risk of a collision exists. If there is any doubt, assume that it does exist, and be ready to take action if necessary.

Rules of the road: common sense

- It is your responsibility to avoid a collision. Keep a good lookout at all times and make sure you understand the rules of the road.
- Adjust your speed for the conditions. For instance, slow right down when passing through an anchorage.
- If you need to give way, take immediate action and make your intentions clear with a definite change of course. Be prepared to stop or slow right down.
- If you have right of way, hold a steady course. But you must take avoiding action if the other boat fails to respond early.
- If two boats are converging and the bearing between them does not change, they will eventually collide. Use a hand-bearing compass to check the bearing and change course if required.

Above: **Risk of collision exists if the compass bearing from your vessel to another does not change, or if they do not appear to be moving against the shore or other fixed object.**

Left: **Keep a lookout for ships. If you are in a shipping channel, a ship in the distance can approach much faster than expected.**

Below: **Lower the sprayhood if your view is obstructed. Beware of other craft that may be hidden by the headsail. Keep a good lookout at all times.**

Collision avoidance (2)

Shapes and signs

Black signals are day marks that provide specific information about a vessel.

✿ A triangular cone is hoisted forward of the mast with its pointed end down to indicate that a yacht is motorsailing.

✿ A ball is hoisted forward of the mast to indicate that a yacht or motor vessel is at anchor.

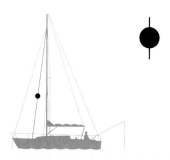

✿ Two cones hoisted point to point indicate that a boat is fishing. If an additional cone points upward, it indicates fishing gear extends for more than 490 feet (150 m).

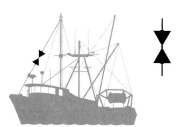

✿ A cylinder indicates that a vessel is constrained by its draft.

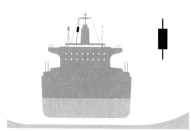

✿ Ball, diamond, ball shows lack of manoeuvrability. If two diamonds and balls are also displayed, the vessel is likely to be a dredger.

✿ Two balls indicate lack of command.

✿ Three balls in a line indicate the vessel is aground. Three balls in a triangle indicate minesweeping.

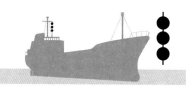

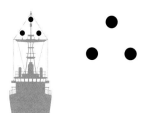

✿ One triangle at the back of the tow indicates a tug with a towing length under 650 feet (200 m). Triangles on both tug and tow indicate a towing length more than 650 feet (200 m).

Beware divers!

✿ The blue and white "A flag" indicates that divers are down.

Sound signals

Sound signals made by a foghorn, bell or gong are vital in poor visibility.

▬▬ ■ ■ One long blast followed by two short blasts, sounded every two minutes, indicates a boat under sail. It may be used by any craft that cannot maneuver quickly.

▬▬ One long blast, sounded every two minutes, indicates a craft under power or motorsailing.

🔔 Rapid ringing of a bell for five seconds, sounded every minute, indicates a craft at anchor.

🔔 🔔 🔔 Three bells, followed by rapid ringing for five seconds, followed by three bells, indicates a craft that has run aground. This signal should also be given every minute.

Sound signals are also used to make intentions clear in good visibility. Large vessels, which cannot stop or change direction quickly, frequently use this method to signal to small craft.

■ One blast indicates turning to starboard.

■ ■ Two blasts indicates turning to port.

■ ■ ■ Three blasts indicates engines in reverse.

■ ■ ■ ■ ■ Four blasts followed by one blast indicates turning all the way around to starboard.

■ ■ ■ ■ ■ ■ Four blasts followed by two blasts indicates turning all the way around to port.

▬ ▬ ■ Two long blasts followed by one short blast indicates overtaking to starboard.

▬ ▬ ■ ■ Two long blasts followed by two short blasts indicates overtaking to port.

■ ■ ■ ■ ■ Five blasts is a warning signal telling craft to get out of the way.

▬ One long blast indicates a vessel approaching a blind bend.

International code of signals

A:	I am involved in diving operations. ALPHA		**O:**	Man overboard. OSCAR	
B:	I am involved in carrying dangerous goods. BRAVO		**P:**	Blue Peter. All persons report to the vessel. PAPA	
C:	Yes. CHARLIE		**Q:**	My vessel is healthy and I require free pratique (licence to enter port). QUEBEC	
D:	I am disabled. DELTA		**R:**	You are dragging your anchor. ROMEO	
E:	I am altering course to starboard. ECHO		**S:**	My engines are going astern. SIERRA	
F:	I am disabled, communicate with me. FOXTROT		**T:**	Keep clear, I am engaged in pair trawling. TANGO	
G:	I require a pilot. GOLF		**U:**	You are running into danger. UNIFORM	
H:	I have a pilot on board. HOTEL		**V:**	I require assistance. VICTOR	
I:	I am altering course to port. INDIA		**W:**	I require medical assistance. WHISKEY	
J:	I am on fire, have dangerous cargo, keep clear. JULIET		**X:**	Watch for my signals. X-RAY	
K:	I wish to communicate with you. KILO		**Y:**	I am dragging my anchor. YANKEE	
L:	You should stop your vessel immediately. LIMA		**Z:**	I require a tug. ZULU	
M:	I have stopped. MIKE		**N/C:**	I am in distress and require immediate assistance.	
N:	No. NOVEMBER				

Keep clear of ships

- Make your intentions obvious when changing course; for instance, change course by 90 degrees even though it may not be necessary.
- When possible, stay out of the deep water area of busy shipping channels and keep to shallower water at the sides.
- If you need to cross a traffic separation area, take the shortest possible route straight across the channels while going at full speed. In a busy shipping lane, aim to pass close astern of ships, not across their bows!

- If you appear to be on a collision course, turn away from the approaching ship and sail in a parallel direction until it has passed. Do not turn toward the ship, in case it has changed direction to cross your stern.
- Ships rely on radar to spot small craft, so a suitable radar reflector must be hoisted at night or in poor visibility, if not permanently mounted above the spreaders.
- Navigation lights may not be conspicuous on a small yacht. Flashing a powerful flashlight on white sails helps make a yacht easier to spot in the dark.

What you see at night

Varous combinations of lights are used for different types of craft. They display basic navigation lights, which indicate the aspect, and also one or more steaming lights that display what a vessel is doing and the direction in which it is travelling. These are some of the lights you may see at night, viewed from the port side.

Lights

- A small boat up to 23 feet (7 m) in length must show an all-around white light at night or in poor visibility. At over 7 knots, sidelights should also be displayed.

- A yacht of 23–65 feet (7–20 m) in length must show port (red), starboard (green) and stern (white) lights when sailing. These lights may be combined in a masthead tricolor light or separate lights at the stern (white) and bows (red and green). When motoring, separate sidelights and stern light plus a steaming light approximately two-thirds of the way up the mast are used.

- A powercraft must show port (red) and starboard (green) lights, with a white masthead light, which is clearly seen to be at a higher level. The latter can double as a stern light.

AT ANCHOR

MOTORSAILING

FISHING

TRAWLING

PILOT VESSEL

HOVERCRAFT

TOWING

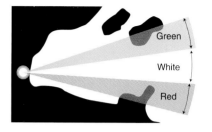

Lighthouse sectors

A sectored light is split into three areas. White indicates the safe area, usually on the approach to land. Red indicates your course is too far to port; green indicates your course is too far to starboard.

VESSEL RESTRICTED IN ABILITY TO MANEUVER

UNDERWATER WORK, E.G., DREDGER

Cardinal marks

North cardinal: Cones point upward. Continuous short flashes. Pass to the north to clear the hazard.

East cardinal: Cones back to back — it is egg-shaped. Three short flashes. Pass to the east to clear the hazard.

South cardinal: Cones point downward. Six short flashes and one long flash. Pass to the south to clear the hazard.

West cardinal: Cones point to point — it has a "waist." Nine short flashes. Pass to the west to clear the hazard.

LARGE SAILING VESSEL (RARE)

MINESWEEPING

VESSEL CONSTRAINED BY ITS DRAFT

SHIP OVER 165 FEET (50 M)

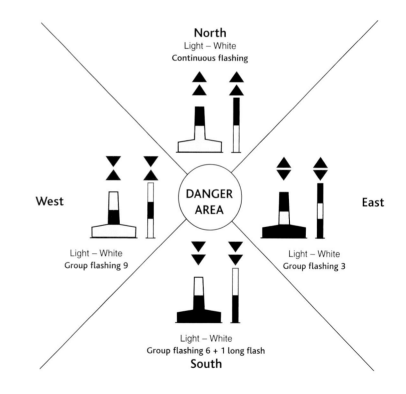

North
Light – White
Continuous flashing

DANGER AREA

West
Light – White
Group flashing 9

East
Light – White
Group flashing 3

South
Light – White
Group flashing 6 + 1 long flash

Other navigational buoys

1. Isolated danger marks.
2. Safe water marks (safe deep water).
3. Special marks (meaning varies). See also pages 268–9.

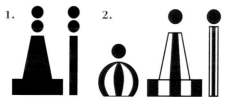
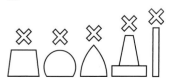

Emergency procedures

Practice emergency procedures whenever you can, particularly "man overboard" drills. Also, try sailing without a rudder and maneuvering in confined spaces without an engine. Involve all your crew in every aspect of the procedure, including being in charge of an emergency situation.

TIP

When the steering fails or the propeller is fouled, try returning to port using your tender. Lash it alongside and steer, using the tender's outboard engine.

Man overboard

The first thing to do is to stop your boat by putting the bow into wind and "heaving to." The aim is to retrieve the person in the water as soon as possible. Each member of the crew should be able to start the engine, drop the sails and motor back to the man overboard. Practice your procedure in various weather and water conditions using a fender and a bucket.

Grounding

If you have run aground, lean the boat over by having the crew stand on one side and then try to motor out the way you came in. Use the tender and outboard to lay the

Below: **If grounded, put weight on the boom to heel over, then try to motor out.**

kedge anchor and warp, and attempt to winch yourself out of the situation. If you still cannot get off, there is no choice but to wait for the tide to rise. Deploy the main anchor to stop further grounding. If the tide is falling, make sure the boat dries out leaning up any slope, propped up if necessary with bunk cushions and sail bags, or it may fill up as the tide rises.

Lines around the propeller

Never let any lines fall over the side while the propeller is turning. Unfortunately, the propeller may still snag a discarded fishing net or line, in which case the engine will stop as the propeller shaft jams. If it proves difficult to free the line from the back of the yacht, you will need to go over the side. Only attempt

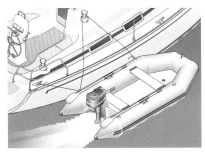

Above: **If the engine fails, one option is to use the tender, powered by the outboard, to move your boat.**

Below: **Once the boat is maneuvered alongside the person in the water, the crew will need to help him or her get back onboard the boat.**

this in flat calm water, with the engine ignition off. If possible, wear a wetsuit and use a snorkel and mask. Secure yourself to the yacht with a safety line, and cut away the tangled line using a sharp knife.

Loss of steerage

Whether your boat has a wheel or tiller, keep an emergency tiller on board in case the tiller breaks or the steering cables fail. If your rudder is disabled you will need to create a makeshift steering system.

Make a steering oar using the spinnaker pole with a makeshift blade such as a locker board. Lash the pole to the stern pulpit or lash it across the stern pulpit with a bucket and lanyard attached to each end. The bucket will act as a drogue and pull the boat to one side or the other.

You can also steer by adjusting the sails. Reducing or releasing the pressure on the headsail will turn the boat up into wind; doing the same on the mainsail will turn it away from the wind.

Holes in hull or deck

Find out if water coming into your boat is from a broken skin fitting, a hole in the hull or a broken or loose hose. If it is a small hole in the hull or a broken skin fitting, then a tapered wooden plug can be rammed into the hole, or use duct tape.

If the hole is bigger and below the waterline you will have to move quickly. Place a bunk cushion over the hole, then cover with stiff material (a floorboard or metal tray) and prop this with a pole. Pump out the water using the automatic bilge pump and the manual cockpit pump. This should help the boat stay afloat long enough to get to a safe haven, but if water is coming in faster than it can be pumped out, abandon the vessel. Wrapping a spare sail around the outside of the hull reduces the water pressure.

Below: **If a hole in the hull is taking in water, it is best to try to block it, in addition to using a bilge pump or a bucket. However, it is better to abandon ship if the water intake cannot be controlled.**

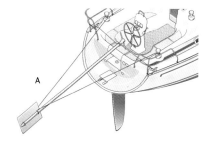

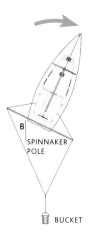

Above and right:
(A) Use a washboard as a rudder.

(B) Clip a spinnaker pole to the back of the vessel in order to create a steering system. You can turn the boat using a bucket dragged from one side of the boat to the other.

(C) Adjusting the sails will also steer the boat if the rudder isn't jammed.

Left: **If in need of a tow, try to keep the tow line as long and elastic as possible, and be as gentle as you can.**

Dismasting

If you are unlucky enough to be dismasted at sea, the main priority is to get the sail and rigging out of the water and onto the boat as quickly as possible, to reduce drag and avoid further damage. Disconnect the bottlescrews between the shroud wires and chain plates by removing the split pins or cutting the wires with cable cutters or hacksaw. Salvage as much of the rigging and sails as possible for a jury rig if you have no engine. Only start the engine when all rigging and lines are safely on board.

Towing

If you accept a tow from another vessel then you could be classed as salvage. Think carefully before accepting a tow. Towing can put a huge strain on a yacht or the craft that is towing it. Securely attach the tow line to the strongest deck fittings. If unsure, back it up with additional lines led aft. You may need to release the line in a hurry, so make sure you can let it go when the tow craft provides slack. Beware of chafe: protect the line.

Fire on board

If you have a fire on board, do not panic. Turn off the gas supply from the gas tank and use your fire extinguishers to put out the fire; if the stove has caught alight, use the fire blanket. If you cannot put the fire out, prepare to abandon the boat. Call for assistance on the mobile VHF radio.

Fog or bad weather

Instruct all crew members to put on lifejackets when in fog, poor visibility, rough weather, at night, or on any other occasions you deem jackets necessary. If a crew member is on deck in rough weather or a dangerous situation, they must clip onto a jackstay. When in the cockpit, they should clip onto the cockpit securing eye.

Shipping lanes

If you are in a shipping lane and the wind dies, you are obliged to proceed through the lane as quickly as possible. Start the engine and motor through quickly. If your main engine fails, use your outboard engine attached to your tender lashed alongside. You may not get far but you might get out of trouble.

If you cannot get out of the situation, inform the coastguard. They will advise you on what to do and will also notify ships in your vicinity that you are a hazard to shipping. Prepare your liferaft ready for launching and put on your lifejacket. If you see a large ship approaching, call them on your VHF radio — bridge to bridge (channel 13) or channel 16 (distress, safety and calling).

Attracting attention for assistance

❂ *Flares*: Use a gloved hand when using flares. The skipper or first mate should release the flares, but if they are incapacitated the crew must do so. Instructions

Below: **If the mast comes down, move with caution on the deck, as the motion of the boat changes and crew may fall.**

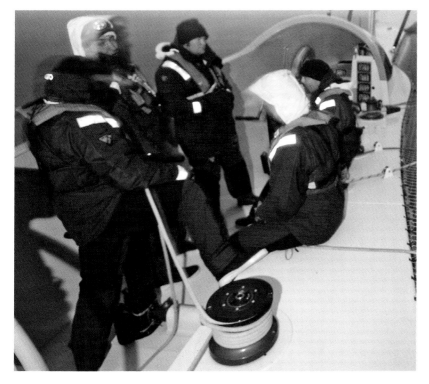

Left: **Safety is paramount at all times so be prepared with warm clothes, harnesses and lifejackets.**

for use are normally printed on the side of each flare. The skipper's briefing should have demonstrated how to use flares.

⊙ *Visual:* Wave your arms up and down, hoist flag F (I am disabled; communicate with me) or other distress flags (N over C, V and W), or flash the Morse code signal SOS at night.

⊙ *Sound:* Make a continuous blast on the fog horn or send the Morse code signal SOS.

⊙ *Radio:* Send out a distress call on the VHF radio, either a "mayday" or "pan pan," giving your position, nature of emergency, the number of people on board and any assistance required.

Above: **Always use a gloved hand for flares and ensure you have an adequate stock on the boat.**

Above: **Only get into a liferaft if the boat is about to sink or is on fire. Grab warm clothes, wet weather gear and grab-bag with safety equipment.**

For a liferaft launch

Attach the liferaft's umbilical cord to your boat and put the raft overboard. Tug the cord and the raft will automatically inflate. Only get into the life raft when the yacht is going under the water, and let the strongest get in first to stabilize the raft and help others in. Take with you the grab-bag, with extra safety equipment. Cut the cord with the knife carried in the liferaft and stream the raft's sea anchor. Activate your EPIRB and SART. Make sure the crew take seasickness pills.

First aid

Most illness or injuries on board a yacht will be little more than a mild dose of seasickness or minor cuts and bruises. In some situations, however, the use of first aid and ship-to-shore assistance may be required.

Contents of the first-aid kit

All yachts should carry a first-aid kit. When items are used, be sure to replace them. Prestocked first-aid kits are also available. The following are typical contents:

- 4 triangular bandages
- 8 standard dressings (medium and large)
- 2 sterile dressings (extra-large)
- 6 medium-size safety pins
- 20 adhesive dressing strips (assorted sizes)
- 2 sterile pads
- 2 packages of sterile cotton
- 5 pairs of disposable gloves
- 50 pain relief tablets
- 50 seasickness tablets
- 20 adhesive butterfly skin closures
- A pair of scissors
- A pair of forceps
- A clinical thermometer
- Antiseptic wipes
- Ice and heat gel packs
- A first-aid manual.

Call for help

Don't delay in calling for assistance. Contact the emergency services by VHF radio or cell phone. In serious situations, it may be necessary to connect to a hospital doctor. Be prepared to provide the following information:

In cases of injury

- Age and sex of patient
- Time and nature of accident
- Any loss of consciousness
- Previous illness or injuries
- Medication taken by the patient
- Recent alcohol intake
- Patient's current state
- Pulse and breathing
- Blood loss
- Description of injuries
- First aid already given
- Advice that you require.

In cases of illness

- Age and sex of patient
- How long the patient has been ill
- Whether the illness came on suddenly or gradually
- Complaints or symptoms
- Previous illness or operations
- Medication taken by the patient
- Recent alcohol intake
- Any loss of consciousness
- Patient's current state
- Pulse and breathing
- Obvious symptoms, such as swelling
- First aid already given
- Advice that you require.

Take a first-aid course

First-aid courses are highly recommended. A number of organizations run short courses that provide a sound working knowledge of first aid, sufficient to save lives in an emergency.

Feeling sick

- Seasickness is the most common complaint on a yacht. The sufferer may feel terrible while the yacht is underway, but will recover quickly on dry land!
- Medication can prevent seasickness, but needs to be taken before you head to sea.

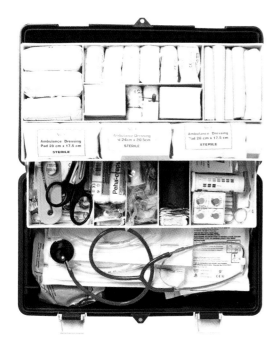

Left: **A well-stocked first-aid kit for a yacht.**

Side effects can include drowsiness, so best to try them out beforehand.

☀ The combination of feeling cold, sitting in the cockpit with nothing to do, and watching the horizon bobbing up and down, helps to induce seasickness. So if it's a chilly day, keep the crew warm and busy. Make sure they dress appropriately before you start sailing and give everyone a turn steering the boat.

☀ The best treatment before you start to feel really sick is to go below and lie down in a berth, with a sleeping bag for warmth.

☀ If anyone needs to vomit, give them a bucket and tip it over the leeward side: don't let them lean over the side. They will generally feel a lot better afterward. Dry crackers and water will all go down well.

Below: **To help prevent seasickness, take a turn at the helm and stay busy. Wrap up warmly if you are inactive.**

Feeling cold

Getting very cold — particularly when wet — is progressive. In the worst case it leads to hypothermia, meaning that the body's temperature has dropped below 95°F (35°C). The patient will shiver and may have difficulty talking. If the heat loss continues, the victim will become physically and mentally unable to cope, leading to unconsciousness and, eventually, death. They must be sheltered from the wind and gradually warmed up by being wrapped in sleeping bags and given warm drinks.

Feeling hot

☀ Sailing in hot sunshine can cause sunburn and dehydration. Both are not only unpleasant but also dangerous. Wear sunblock and protect yourself when sailing in a hot climate. Wear a hat, or cover the entire cockpit with a bimini. Keep drinking plenty of water — at least 8–12 glasses on a hot day.

☀ Never allow anyone on board to get sunburned. Tell them to cover up or send them below. If they get too hot and don't drink, heat exhaustion will creep up by the end of the day with symptoms such as headache, cramps, moist skin and a weak racing pulse. The obvious treatment is to get out of the sun and cool down, drink water and replace lost salt.

☀ Full-blown heatstroke will lead to dangerously raised body temperature. It is vital to cool the victim down, e.g., by covering them in wet towels or sheets.

First aid (2)

Burns

- If you are careless, the galley can be a dangerous place. Beware of burns from boiling hot liquids while the yacht is rolling around.
- Immersion in cold water for 15 minutes is the straightforward way to cool down a burn. If it is severe, the burn should be lightly protected with a non-adhesive dressing held in place by a bandage. Seek advice from the safety services and treat for shock if required.
- Do not pull away clothing that has stuck to the skin, or attempt to remove loose skin or prick blisters. Do not apply ointment or cream.

Above: **Cool down the burn by immersing it in cold water for at least 15 minutes.**

Above: **Protect the burn with a non-fluffy sterile dressing and a paraffin gauze.**

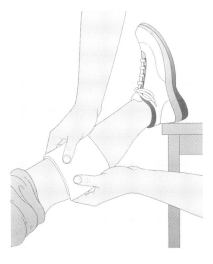

Cuts

Protect cuts from infection by cleaning the area with fresh water and applying adhesive or sterile dressings. For severe injuries, pressure must be applied to stem blood loss, and the injured area elevated above the heart.

Shock

Shock is caused by a sudden fall in blood pressure. This is normally a result of bleeding, burns or broken bones. Internal bleeding may be caused by damage to an internal organ and may be indicated by a swelling and symptoms of shock.

Symptoms of shock include a pale and gray appearance, cold and moist skin, weakness or giddiness, weak and rapid pulse, shallow and fast breathing, restlessness, feeling sick and, possibly, unconsciousness. The patient should lie down with legs raised and clothing loosened, protected from extremes of heat

Above: **Once the bandage is secure, elevate the limb.**

Left: **For deeper cuts or wounds that are bleeding profusely, apply continuous direct pressure with a bandage.**

and cold. No drinks should be given, although lips may be moistened with water. If breathing becomes difficult, place the victim in the recovery position.

When dealing with shock you should give reassurance and keep positive and calm. Cover the patient with a coat or blanket to keep them warm if necessary.

Head injury

Any blow to the head that is heavy enough to cause a bruise can result in concussion. This is a short period of impaired consciousness. The patient may be dazed and confused and may not remember the events that led up to the incident. It is important to ensure that the patient has a complete recovery, as there may be a delayed reaction. If the patient is unconscious, place them in the recovery position, check their breathing and call for medical assistance as quickly as possible.

Mouth-to-mouth

○ Dinghy sailors are vulnerable to getting water in the lungs by getting trapped under a boat when it turns upside-down.

○ If the patient is unconscious, their airway must be cleared so that they can breathe — it may be obstructed by the tongue. Once breathing, put them into the standard recovery position.

○ If the patient has stopped breathing, commence mouth-to-mouth resuscitation. This entails blowing into the victim's mouth with their nostrils held closed in order to inflate their lungs, and then removing your lips to allow their lungs to deflate. Continue the sequence at the rate of one inflation per second.

○ If the victim vomits, turn them onto their side and clear the airway before recommencing resuscitation.

○ Hypothermia may be a related problem. Once breathing is established, put the victim in the standard recovery position, remove wet clothing and protect them from the cold.

Left: If the patient is in the water and is not breathing, do not waste time trying to move them. Give mouth-to-mouth where they are.

Right: For hypothermia, once the patient is breathing, put them in the recovery position, remove their wet clothes and get them insulated.

Below: The standard recovery, or coma, position can be used for hypothermia or shock.

Checklist for examining a patient

○ **Breathing** — rate, depth, difficulty.
○ **Heartbeat** — fast or slow pulse.
○ **Mouth** — pale lips, coherent speech, feeling thirsty.
○ **Forehead** — high temperature, sweating.
○ **Eyes** — pupil size, visible injury, bloodshot.
○ **Chest** — pain, tenderness, swelling, bruising.

○ **Conscious state** — memory, level of responsiveness, dizziness.
○ **Wounds** — bleeding, diarrhea, constipation, vomiting, urine.
○ **Limbs** — pain, swelling, tenderness, bruising, deformity, loss of movement, loss of sensation.
○ **Abdomen** — pain, tenderness, bruising, swelling, feeling sick.
○ **Nails** — color.

TIP

Keep several hot water bottles on board. They are useful for anyone who has become very cold on deck and cannot get warm. Anyone suffering from extreme cold should not be warmed up too quickly.

Glossary

A

abeam At a right angle to the length of the boat.

aft Toward the rear (or stern) of the boat.

agglomerator filter The filter that separates water (caused by condensation) from the diesel in the engine.

aground When the hull or keel touches bottom in shallow water.

ahead Forward movement, or in front of the boat.

aid to navigation Any fixed object that a navigator may use to find his or her position, such as a buoy or lighthouse.

aloft In the rigging above the yacht.

anchor A heavy metal object designed in such a way that, when lowered to the lake or sea bed, its weight and shape will help to hold a boat in its position.

anchor chain A chain attached to the anchor. It acts as a weight to keep the anchor lying on the sea bed so that it can hold better.

anchor light A white light, used when at anchor, which can be seen from all around.

anchorage A place where a yacht anchors. It is usually a designated area marked on a chart.

antifouling Special paint for the underside of the yacht, to deter sea growth from attaching to it.

apparent wind The direction of the wind as it appears when the boat is moving.

astern Backward movement, or behind the boat.

auxiliary An engine used as a secondary means of propulsion.

B

backing A counterclockwise shift in the wind direction. The opposite of "veering."

backstay A wire that leads from the top of the mast to the stern of a boat and prevents the mast from falling forward.

backwinded When the wind pushes on the wrong side of the sail, either directly or reflected off another sail.

bail To remove water from a boat, normally using a pump, scoop or bucket.

balance When the boat is in perfect balance and there is no pull on the tiller.

barometer An instrument used to measure atmospheric pressure, usually measured in millibars.

battens Battens are attached to a sail to stiffen the leech to make a better sail shape.

beam The width of a boat.

beam reach On a point of sail where the apparent wind is coming from the beam (side) of the yacht.

bear away Alter course by swinging the boat's bow away from the wind.

bearing The direction, usually measured in degrees, of a fixed point or another vessel.

beating Pointing as close to the wind as the boat will sail.

Beaufort wind scale A method of measuring the force of wind, named after Admiral Beaufort who created the system.

bend on To attach a sail and get it ready for use.

berth A place where a yacht can be secured.

bifurcation marks Buoys that indicate the place where a channel divides in two.

bilge The lowest part of a yacht, just above the keel, where water can collect.

bilge pump A pump used to remove water from the bilge.

bimini A canvas cover used to shelter the cockpit from the sun.

binnacle The housing for a compass, usually found on the wheel's pedestal.

blanketing Blocking the wind from getting to another boat's sail. The leeward boat is said to have been blanketed.

block One or more wheels free to spin between parallel "cheeks." Used to change the direction of a line's travel and often to increase mechanical advantage.

boat hook A pole with a hook attached at the end, used for picking up objects or fending off other boats.

boom The spar to which the foot, or bottom, of the sail is attached.

boom vang A method used to hold down the boom, to help it maintain a good sail shape, especially when on a run or a broad reach.

bow The front, or forward end, of the boat.

bow line A mooring line at the bow.

bow roller A fitting with a small wheel for anchor and chain roll-over when dropping or raising the anchor.

bowline A knot used to make a loop at the end of a line.

bowsprit A spar extending from the bow of a boat to which the jib stay is attached.

breast line A line attached from a boat to a pontoon, preventing the boat moving away from the pontoon.

broaching When a boat turns up into the wind and, partly due to the wind and partly to centrifugal force, heels violently the other way. Most common under spinnaker.

broad reach Sailing with the apparent wind coming across the aft quarter of the boat.

bulkhead An interior partition in a yacht, running side-to-side.

buoy A floating device used as a navigational aid.

burgee A distinctive pennant, often used to identify a vessel as belonging to a particular yacht club.

C

cam cleat A cleat (fitting) used to hold a line. It uses two spring-loaded cams that come together to clamp firmly on the line.

capsize When a boat turns over in the water and lies on its side.

cast off To remove mooring lines when leaving a pontoon.

catamaran A twin-hulled boat.

centerboard A retractable keel that slots into the hull of a dinghy, and hinges backward.

channel A safe route on a waterway, usually marked by buoys.

channel marker A buoy or other mark used to indicate the edge of a channel.

chart datum The water level used to record data on a chart. It is defined as the depth of water at the lowest astronomical tide.

cleat A fitting to which lines can be easily attached.

clew The aft corner of a triangular sail, to which the sheet(s) are normally attached.

close hauled To sail as close to the direction of the wind as possible.

close reach Sailing with the wind coming from forward of the beam.

close winded A boat that is able to sail close to the direction from which the wind is blowing.

clove hitch A knot formed either at the end or in the middle of a rope, best used when strain will be equal on both sides — centering a tiller.

cockpit Usually the place from which the boat is steered and where the crew sit on deck.

cold front A mass of cold air moving toward a mass of warm air. Normally associated with strong winds and rain.

come about To tack. To change a boat's direction, bringing the bow through the wind.

companionway A stairway leading from deck to cabin.

compass rose A circle on a chart indicating the direction of true and magnetic north.

course The direction in which the boat is sailing.

cringle A large eyelet, typically in a sail, through which a line can be passed.

cunningham A line used to control the tension along a sail's luff in order to maintain proper sail shape.

currents The flowing of the sea in one direction; they can be periodic, seasonal or permanent.

D

Dacron A synthetic polyester material.

daggerboard Similar to a centerboard, except that it is raised vertically. It prevents a dinghy being pushed sideways by the wind.

danbuoy A floating safety device thrown off a boat to mark the man overboard position.

deduced reckoning (DR or dead reckoning) Calculation of the vessel's position based on course and distance run (speed x elapsed time).

depth sounder An instrument that uses sound waves to measure the distance to the water bottom.

distress signal Any signal used to indicate that a vessel is in distress.

downhaul A line used to pull down on a spar or sail.

downwind In the direction the wind is blowing.

draft The depth of a boat, normally measured from the lowest point to the waterline.

drag Resistance to movement, e.g., of a propeller.

E

echo sounder See "depth sounder."

emergency tiller A tiller that is designed to be used if wheel steering fails.

EPIRB Emergency Position Indicating Radio Beacon. An emergency device that uses a radio signal to indicate a vessel's position.

estimated position (EP) A boat's DR position, with further allowance for tidal currents and leeway.

F

fair-lead A fitting, typically on or through the yacht's toe-rail, through which a mooring line is led. Its main purpose is to reduce chafe.

feathering prop A propeller that can have the pitch of its blade changed to reduce drag when it is not being used.

fend off To push a boat away from another boat or from a pontoon.

fender A device hung from the side of a boat to protect it from rubbing against a pontoon or another vessel.

figure-eight A knot used at the end of a sheet as a stopper.

fix See "visual fix."

foot The bottom of a sail.

footstrap A strap attached to the cockpit to put feet under when hiking, if sailing a dinghy.

foredeck The front of a boat, ahead of the mast.

forward Toward, or near, the front of the boat.

furl To roll a sail in.

G

galley The kitchen area on a boat.

gel coat A protective layer of resin on a fiberglass hull.

genoa A large jib that overlaps the mast. Also known as a jenny.

gimbals Hinges that allow objects (such as the stove) to remain upright as the boat rolls.

Global Positioning System (GPS) A system of satellites that allows a boat's position to be calculated with great accuracy using an electronic receiver.

go about To tack.

goosewinging Sailing with the wind behind and the jib held out to the opposite side of the mainsail.

gybe See jibe.

H

half hitch A simple knot usually used with another knot or half hitch.

halyard A line used to hoist a sail, spar, burgee, etc.

hank Sprung metal fitting that attaches a non-furling sail to a stay.

head-to-wind When the bow of the boat is in the direction that the wind is coming from.

head up To turn the bow more directly into the wind.

heading The direction you are sailing at any given time.

headsail Any sail forward of the mast, such as a jib.

heave-to Back the headsail in order to limit or halt forward progress.

heeling When a boat leans sideways, caused by pressure of wind against the sails.

helm The wheel or tiller of a boat.

helmsman (or helm) The person who is on the helm and steering the boat.

high tide The point when the tide is at its highest.

hiking Sitting out over the side to counteract the heeling of a boat.

hitch A knot used to attach a line to any fixture, or back to itself.

hoist To raise a sail.

holding tank A storage tank in a boat where sewage is stored until it can be removed and treated properly.

hull The main structural body of the boat.

I

impeller A device that pumps water around the engine to keep it cool.

isobars Lines drawn on a weather map (synoptic chart) indicating regions of equal pressure.

J

jackstay A strong line along the side decks of a boat to which a safety harness can be attached.

jib A triangular sail attached to the forestay. A jib that overlaps the mast is known as a genoa.

jib sheets Lines used to control the position of the jib. There are two sheets: the working sheet, and the lazy sheet.

jibe To go about with the wind behind the boat.

jury rig A temporary rig and sail plan using whatever materials are available, often created after dismasting.

K

keel A projection from the underside of a boat. It provides resistance to minimize leeway, and is weighted to counteract heeling caused by wind on the sails.

kicking strap A control line from the mast to the underside of the boom, used to hold the boom down.

knot The nautical measurement of speed. A speed of 1 knot is 1 nautical mile per hour.

L

land breeze A wind moving from land to water caused by temperature changes in the evening.

lanyard A safety line with a clip that can be attached to a strongpoint.

launch To put a boat in the water.

lazy jacks Lines running from either side of the mainsail to the boom to help keep the sail flaked and off the deck when it is lowered.

lead line A marked line that has a weight on the end, used to measure depth.

lee helm The tendency for a sailboat to swing away from the direction of the wind.

lee shore The shore that the wind is blowing toward and from which you need to keep a safe distance.

leech The rear edge of the sail.

leech line A line used to tighten the leech of a sail, helping to create good sail shape.

leeward The direction away from the wind and the opposite of windward.

leeway The sideways movement of a boat away from the wind.

life jacket A device used to keep a person afloat. Also called a PFD (personal flotation device).

lifeline A rope or wire stretched fore and aft along the deck of a boat in adverse weather.

life raft A small, self-inflating, covered raft, carried aboard most yachts as a refuge of last resort for the crew, should the yacht sink or catch fire.

lighthouse A navigational light placed on a structure on land.

log (1) A device used to measure the distance traveled through the water, normally using an electronic or a paddle wheel. (2) A boat's written record.

low tide The point when the tide is at its lowest.

luff The leading edge of a sail toward the bow of a boat.

luffing The flapping motion along the luff of a sail.

M

magnetic course A yacht's course measured in degrees from the earth's magnetic pole.

magnetic deviation The error in a vessel's compass caused by magnetic fittings and other items aboard the boat itself.

magnetic north The direction to which a magnetic compass points.

magnetic variation The difference between magnetic north and true north, measured as an angle.

mainsail The principal sail of a sailing vessel on the main mast.

mainsheet The line used to control the mainsail.

making way Moving through the water.

marina A place where boats can moor, find fuel, water and other services.

masthead The top of a mast. Wind direction indicators and radio antennas are normally positioned on the masthead.

masthead light An all-around white light positioned at the top of the mast, frequently used as a combined steaming and stern light in motorboats of under 39 feet (12 m), or as an anchor light in any vessel under 165 feet (50 m).

MAYDAY An internationally recognized distress signal used on a radio to indicate a life-threatening situation.

minute One minute is 1/60 of 1 degree; a minute of latitude equals 1 nautical mile.

mizzen The sail on the aft mast of a ketch or yawl-rigged sailboat.

mizzen mast A smaller aft mast on a ketch or yawl-rigged sailboat.

monohull A boat with one hull.

multihull Any boat with more than one hull, such as a catamaran or trimaran.

N

nautical mile Measurement of distance at sea. A nautical mile is equivalent to about 1.15 statute miles (6067.12 feet) or 1,852 meters. A minute of latitude is equal to 1 nautical mile.

navigation aid Any fixed object that a navigator may use to find his or her position, such as permanent land or sea marks, buoys and lighthouses.

navigation lights Lights on a boat that help other boats determine its course and position.

neap tide The tide with the least variation in water level. The lowest high tide and the highest low tide occur at neap tide.

O

occulting lights A light on a navigation aid that is lit for longer periods than it is unlit.

offshore wind Wind that is blowing away from the land, toward the water.

onshore wind Wind that is blowing toward the land, away from the water.

osmosis The blistering found on many fiberglass boat hulls caused by water getting into the laminate.

outboard engine An engine used to power a small boat. Outboard engines are normally mounted on a bracket on the stern.

outhaul A line used to tension the foot of a sail and so maintain proper sail shape.

outrigger A flotation device attached to one or both sides of the hull to help prevent a capsize.

P

painter A line attached to the bow of a dinghy and used to tie it up or tow it.

palm A tool worn on the hand, with a thimble-shaped structure — used to help a needle go through a sail.

passage A journey from one place to another.

pinching Steering too close to the wind, causing the sails to luff.

pintle A pin used to attach a stern-mounted rudder.

pitchpoled When a boat's stern is thrown over its bow.

planing A boat rising slightly out of the water so that it is gliding over the water rather than through it.

plot To find a boat's actual or intended course or mark a fix on a chart.

point of sail The angle of a yacht or dinghy in relation to the wind.

port The left side of the boat from the perspective of a person standing at the stern of the boat and looking toward the bow.

port tack Sailing with the wind coming over the port side and the boom on the starboard side of the boat.

prevailing winds The typical winds for the time of year.

preventer A line run forward from the boom to a secure fitting to prevent the boom from jibing accidentally when going downwind.

pulpit The railing around the deck on the bow.

R

radar An electronic instrument that uses radio waves to find the distance and location of other objects.

radar reflector An object designed to increase the radio reflectivity of a boat so that it is more visible on radar.

radio beacon A navigational aid that emits radio waves for navigational purposes. Its position and direction can be found by using a radio direction–finding instrument.

reaching Any point of sail with the wind coming from the side of the boat.

reef To partially lower and furl a sail so that it is smaller.

reefing lines Lines used to pull the reef in the sail. The reef line passes through reef cringles, which become the new tack and clew of the reefed sail.

refit To prepare a boat for winter.

relative bearing A bearing relative to the boat's bow or another object, rather than a compass direction.

rigging Both the permanent wires that support a boat's mast(s) and to which the sails are attached

(standing rigging), and the wires and/or lines used to hoist and control the sails (running rigging).

roach A curve out from the aft edge (leech) of a sail. Battens help support and stiffen the roach.

roller reefing A system of reefing a sail by partially furling it.

rudder A flat surface attached behind or underneath the stern used to control the direction in which the boat is traveling.

run aground To make contact between the boat's hull or keel and the water bottom.

running A point of sail where the boat has the wind coming from behind the vessel.

running backstays Adjustable stays used to support and control the shape of the mast.

S

safety harness A webbing harness worn around the upper body to decrease the risk of falling overboard and keep the casualty in contact with the yacht should it happen.

sail trim The position of the sails relative to the wind and desired point of sail.

satellite navigation Navigation using information transmitted from satellites.

scope The length of the anchor chain or line relative to the depth of the water.

seacock A valve used to prevent water from entering the hull.

sector light A navigational light that is visible only from a specific sector or arc of a circle.

shackle A U-shaped metal connector that is attached to other fittings by a pin that is inserted through the arms of the U.

shake out To remove a reef from a sail.

shakedown An initial trip with a boat to make sure everything is operating properly.

sheet A line attached to the clew of a sail, used to control its trim.

shroud Part of the standing rigging that helps to support the mast by running from the top of the mast to the side of the boat.

skiff A small boat.

slack water A period of almost no water movement between flood and ebb tides.

sling Lines used to hoist heavy or difficult-to-move objects.

sloop A style of sailboat with a

single mast, one mainsail and one foresail.

sounding The depth of the water as marked on a chart.

spar Any metal or wooden pole used to help set a sail. Often the boom and spinnaker pole, but may include the mast.

spinnaker A large lightweight sail used at the bow when running or on a broad reach.

spinnaker pole A pole used to extend the foot of the spinnaker beyond the edge of the boat, and to secure the corner of the sail.

splice The place where two lines are bound together end to end.

spreaders Small spars extending toward the sides of the boat from one or more places along the mast. The shrouds attach to the end of the spreaders, so that the shrouds can support the mast.

spring lines Mooring lines that help keep the boat from moving fore and aft while alongside.

spring tide The tide with the most variation in water level, e.g., the highest high tide and the lowest low tide.

squall A sudden intense wind storm, usually with rain showers; often associated with a cold front.

square-rigged A sailboat having square sails hung across the mast.

stanchions Upright posts around the edge of a yacht's deck, used to support the guardrails or wires.

starboard The right side of a boat, from the stern of the boat looking forward.

starboard tack Sailing with the wind coming over the starboard side and the boom on the port side.

stays Lines running fore and aft from the top of the mast (backstay and forestay) to keep the mast upright and carry sails.

stern The back, or aft end, of a boat.

stern light A white light at the stern of the boat. It should be visible through an arc of 135°.

stern line A mooring line at the stern.

stern pulpit A railing around the deck at the stern.

strum box A strainer in the bilge that stops the bilge pump from getting clogged.

swing a compass The act of checking compass readings against known headings in order to determine the compass error.

T

tack (1) The direction a boat is sailing with respect to the wind. (2) To change a boat's direction by bringing the bow through the wind. (3) The lower forward corner of a triangular sail.

tackle Lines used with blocks in order to move heavy objects.

telltale A short length of light line, cloth or plastic attached near the luff of a sail, to indicate air flow and thus aid correct sail trim.

tender A small boat used to take people and supplies between a larger boat and the shore.

through-hull Fittings attached through the hull to which a seacock, or other device, is attached.

thwart A seat running across the width of a small boat.

tidal atlas Small charts showing directions and rate of tidal flow, over a period of hours.

tidal range The difference between a tide's high and low water levels.

tidal stream The movement of water caused by the rise and fall of tidal waters.

tide The regular rising and lowering of water in parts of the world due to the pull of the sun and the moon.

tide tables Tables containing information about the time of the high and low tides and the water level to be expected at that time.

tiller An arm attached to the top of the rudder to steer a boat.

tiller extension An extension to the tiller allowing the helmsman to steer while hiking. Also known as a hiking stick.

topping lift A line running from the end of the boom to the top of the mast used to keep the boom from falling when the sail is not set.

track The path that a vessel is taking.

trailing edge The aft edge of a sail, commonly called the leech.

transit Two navigation aids or other fixed points that can be lined up one behind the other, so creating a line along which the boat must lie.

transom The aft side of the hull.

traveler A track with an attached block, allowing controlled adjustment of a sail's sheet.

trim To haul in on a sheet to adjust the sail angle.

trimaran A yacht with a central hull and two smaller outer hulls.

trip line A line attached to the crown of an anchor to help free it from the ground.

true course The course of a boat after being corrected for magnetic deviation and magnetic variation.

true wind The speed and direction of the wind, in relation to a static object.

turning circle The distance required for a boat to turn in a complete circle.

U

underway A vessel in motion.

upwind To windward, in the direction from which the wind is blowing.

V

vang *See* boom vang *and* kicking strap.

vector A line drawn to show both the direction and magnitude of a force, such as leeway or a current.

veering A clockwise shift in wind direction; opposite of "backing."

VHF Very High Frequency radio waves. VHF radios are the most common ones carried on boats.

visual bearing A bearing taken by visually observing the location of a known landmark.

visual fix A plotted position based on two or more visual bearings.

VMG Velocity Made Good. Actual boat speed after adjusting for such factors as current and leeway.

W

wake Waves generated astern of a moving vessel.

watch A crew division into shifts.

weather helm The tendency of a boat to head up toward the wind.

winch A geared spindle operated by removable handles or electricity, around which a jib sheet or other rope is wound when hauling it in.

windage The amount of a boat, sail or other object that the wind can push on.

windlass A mechanical device used to pull in the anchor chain.

windward The direction from which the wind is blowing.

Index

Acknowledgements

The publisher would like to thank the following for their kind permission to reproduce photographs in this book. (Abbreviations key: t = top, b = bottom, c = center, r = right, l = left)

Australian Severe Weather 332 (t). **Corbis** 2–3, 4–5, 6–7, 10–11, 44 (l), 183, 245, 312 (l), 327 (t), 329, 338-339. **Sarah Doughty** 16, 44, 45, 47 (t), 135 2nd (tr), 206 (all exc. bl), 208 (tl), 219 (br), 254 (bl), 256, 257 (r), 273 (b), 340-54, 355 (b, br), 356 (bl), 358-61, 362 (b), 363, 368 (r), 368 (l), 369 (r), 373 (tr, cl). **Jeremy Evans** 8, 9 (t), 12, 13 (t), 14, 15, 17 (t), 18, 19, 20, 21, 23 (r), 24, 26-7, 29, 31, 32, 33, 34, 35, 36, 37 (t), 38 (b), 39 (b), 40, 41, 42, 43, 48, 51 (b), 52–3, 54, 55, 56, 57, 58, 59, 60, 61, 62, 63, 64, 66, 67 (l), 68, 69, 70, 71 (t, bl), 72–133, 134, 135 (br), 136, 137, 138, 139, 140–67, 168–9, 170, 171, 172, 173, 176–205, 206 (bl), 207, 208 (br), 209, 210, 211–18, 219 (tr), 220, 221, 223–40, 241 (b), 246 (t, tr), 247 (2nd, 3rd and 4th tr), 248 (1st and 2nd, tl), 249 (2nd, tr), 315, 332 (bl, br), 333 (tr, bl, br), 362 (t), 366, 373 (b), 383. **Getty Images** 242, 382. **istock** 46, 47 (b), 246 (bl), 247 (tl), 248 (3rd and 4th, t), 249 (1st, 3rd and 4th, t), 310–11, 321, 325, 333 (tl), 337, 364–65. **Jupiter Images** 50 (br).

Steve Knowlden 47 (br), 250–51, 252 (l) and 253 (background). **Kos Picture Source** 222, 243, 244, 308 (t). **Pat Manley** 252, 253, 273 (r), 277, 279, 281 (b), 283, 284, 285, 291, 292, 293 (tr, r), 282, 283, 294, 295, 296, 297, 299, 307, 308 (b), 309, 334 (tr). **Patrick Roach Picture Agency** 355 (t), 367, 378, 379, 381 (bc, tr). **Rick Tomlinson** 380, 381 (t). **Topfoto** 241 (t).

Photography/illustration courtesy of the following organizations: **Furuno** 298, 334 (l). **Garmin** 293 (bl). **Jepphesen Marine Inc.** for C-Map base charts in navigation section. **Mailspeed Marine** 51 (t), 368 (l), 369 (c). **Musto Performance** 48 (r), 49, 50 (all exc. br), 65 (all), 135 (t), 182. **McMurdo** 335 (b). **Nasamarine** 355 (t). **Nautor's Swan** 9 (b), 13 (b), 23 (l), 28, 37 (b), 386–99. **Raymarine** 254 (r), 255 (tr). **Simrad Yachting** 255 (bl, br). **Standard Horizon** 294 (tl). **Steiner Binoculars** 257 (l, bl). **Suunto** 67 (2nd and 3rd top, r). **Swift Mobile** 335 (b). **Tick Tack** 255 (tl, tc). **UKHO** 262. **Yachtsnet Ltd.** 174, 175.

Ropes supplied by www.ropelocker.co.uk. Compasses supplied by SMR chandlery at Brighton Marina, (www.smrmarine.co.uk).

All illustrations by John Woodcock, Peter Bull, Ivan Hissey and John Fowler with additional artwork by John Mitchell, Les Hunt and Allan Robinson.

Original references for the Weather and Navigation sections supplied by Pat Manley.

Thanks to Jeremy Evans for use of his photographs, including the specially shot pictures used in the book. The following organizations provided assistance at photoshoots: **Minorca Sailing Holidays** (www.minorcasailing. co.uk) for providing facilities for dinghy sequences at their wonderful center on Fornells Bay. **Cobnor Activities Centre** (www.cobonor.com) for providing additional facilities for dinghy photos. **Sunsail** (www.sunsail. com) for their help with yacht photography in suitable sunny locations.

Also thanks to the following magazines: *Yachts and Yachting* magazine (www.yachtsand yachting.com) who helped provide access to many of the dinghies featured in the dinghy section. *Yachting Monthly* magazine (www.yachtingmonthly. com) who helped provide access to many of the yachts featured in the cruiser section.

Thanks to Anne Hammick for her advisory help and assistance with text and pictures.

For editorial assistance thanks to Richard Gogarty, Cindy McCollum, Robin Pridy and Claire Saunders and design assistance from Caroline Marlew and Ginny Zeal.